Benjamin, Barthes and the Singularity of Photography

Benjamin, Barthes and the Singularity of Photography

Kathrin Yacavone

BLOOMSBURY
NEW YORK • LONDON • NEW DELHI • SYDNEY

Bloomsbury Academic
An imprint of Bloomsbury Publishing Inc

1385 Broadway
New York
NY 10018
USA

50 Bedford Square
London
WC1B 3DP
UK

www.bloomsbury.com

Bloomsbury is a registered trade mark of Bloomsbury Publishing Plc

First published 2012 by Continuum
First published in paperback 2013

Library of Congress Cataloging-in-Publication Data
A catalog record for this book is available from the Library of Congress

ISBN: HB: 978-1-4411-1808-0
PB: 978-1-6235-6669-2
ePDF: 978-1-4411-8233-3
ePub: 978-1-4411-0437-3

Typeset by Deanta Global Publishing Services, Chennai, India
Printed and bound in the United States of America

In Memory of Wolfgang

Contents

Acknowledgements viii

List of Abbreviations x

List of Illustrations xii

Introduction 1

Benjamin and Barthes: The Question of Influence 13

Part I: The Birth of the Viewer 29

Chapter 1 Benjamin's History of Photography 33

Chapter 2 Alter Ego: The Childhood Portrait of Franz Kafka 70

Chapter 3 Photography, Memory and Redemption 95

Part II: Photography and Subjectivity 121

Chapter 4 From Semiology to Phenomenology 125

Chapter 5 Lost and Found: The Winter Garden Photograph 161

Chapter 6 Photography and Memory: Barthes's Proustian Quest 187

Postscript: Singularity and Photography in the Age of Digitization 217

Bibliography 227

Index 241

Acknowledgements

I would like to acknowledge a number of institutions and individuals in relation to this book. The Institute for Advanced Studies in the Humanities of the University of Edinburgh provided an ideal environment for its conception and I am grateful to the Institute for its support of my research. The original doctoral research from which this book derives was generously funded by the Arts and Humanities Research Council and the College of Humanities and Social Science of the University of Edinburgh. I am thankful to the École Normale Supérieure in Paris for accommodating a year-long research stay and to the Institute of Germanic and Romance Studies of the University of London for supporting research at the Walter Benjamin Archiv of the Akademie der Künste in Berlin.

I wish to thank Peter Dayan for his careful readings and constructive criticism. I owe much to his close scrutiny and advice. Carolin Duttlinger and Marion Schmid have both provided invaluable suggestions and I am grateful for their input; Peter Davies offered helpful assistance at the early stages of this project and Jon Usher, in particular, was always generous with his time and advice. I have hugely benefited from discussions with other colleagues and friends who provided guidance, encouragement and practical help in different ways and I wish to thank them all for their time and generosity: Martine Beugnet, Mary Breatnach, Patrick Ffrench, Duncan Forbes, Iain Galbraith, Martin Hammer, Steffen Haug, Katja Haustein, Emmanuelle Lacore-Martin, Marielle Macé, Éric Marty, Ursula Marx, Magali Nachtergael, Lucy O'Meara, Guillaume Perrier, Mirjam Schaub and Detlev Schöttker. Jean Duffy, Eddie Hughes, Ann Jefferson, Laura Marcus and Paddy O'Donovan have considerably encouraged me in my academic endeavours and I thank them as well. Mary Breatnach, Peter Dayan and Patrick Ffrench have kindly read and commented on parts of earlier versions of the manuscript and Ela Kotkowska offered valuable advice and help in preparing it. Haaris Naqvi at Continuum has been hugely supportive and I thank him for the enthusiasm he showed for this project from the very beginning. I am also grateful to all the individuals and institutions who kindly gave permission to reproduce the images featured in this book.

Finally, I wish to thank my families on both sides of the Atlantic for their support and forbearance, and especially my mother for her trust and understanding. My deepest gratitude belongs to Daniel Yacavone. Without his love and support this book could not have been.

List of Abbreviations

Due to the notorious difficulty of translating the specific nuances of Benjamin's and Barthes's thought into English, the German and French texts provide the basis for the argument of this book. English translations, which have on occasion been silently modified, appear immediately after the original quotations. References to Benjamin and Barthes are inserted into the text in parentheses using the abbreviations listed below, followed by volume and page number (in Roman and Arabic numerals, respectively). Translations without references are my own. All italics in quotations are the authors' emphases unless indicated otherwise.

Walter Benjamin

AP *The Arcades Project*, trans. Howard Eiland and Kevin McLaughlin (Cambridge, MA and London: Belknap/Harvard University Press, 1999).

GB *Gesammelte Briefe*, 6 vols., eds. Christoph Gödde and Henri Lonitz (Frankfurt a.M.: Suhrkamp, 1997).

GS *Gesammelte Schriften*, 7 vols., eds. Rolf Tiedemann and Hermann Schweppenhäuser, with the collaboration of Theodor W. Adorno and Gershom Scholem (Frankfurt a.M.: Suhrkamp, 1972–1989).

GSS *Gesammelte Schriften. Supplemente*, 3 vols., eds. Rolf Tiedemann and Hella Tiedemann-Bartels (Frankfurt a.M.: Suhrkamp, 1999).

OG *Origin of German Tragic Drama*, trans. John Osborne (London: Verso, 2003).

SW *Selected Writings*, 4 vols., eds. Michael Jennings et al. (Cambridge, MA and London: Belknap/Harvard University Press, 1996–2003).

Roland Barthes

CC *La Chambre claire. Note sur la photographie* (Paris: Cahiers du cinéma/Gallimard/Seuil, 1980).

CL *Camera Lucida. Reflections on Photography*, trans. Richard Howard (London: Vintage, 2000).

ES *Empire of Signs*, trans. Richard Howard (London: Jonathan Cape, 1983).

ET *The Eiffel Tower and Other Mythologies*, trans. Richard Howard (Berkeley and Los Angeles: University of California Press, 1997).

GV *The Grain of the Voice. Interviews 1962–1980*, trans. Linda Coverdale (London: Jonathan Cape, 1985).

IMT *Image, Music, Text*, selected and trans. Stephen Heath (London: Fontana Press, 1977).

JD *Journal de deuil* (Paris: Seuil/IMEC, 2009).

LA *Le Lexique de l'auteur. Séminaire à l'École pratique des hautes études 1973–1974, suivi de fragments inédits du Roland Barthes par Roland Barthes*, ed. Anne Herschberg Pierrot (Paris: Seuil, 2010).

M *Mythologies*, selected and trans. Annette Lavers (New York: Hill and Wang, 1994).

MD *Mourning Diary*, trans. Richard Howard (New York: Hill and Wang, 2010).

N *Le Neutre. Cours au Collège de France (1977–1978)*, ed. Thomas Clerc (Paris: Seuil/IMEC, 2002).

OC *Œuvres complètes*, 5 vols., ed. Éric Marty (Paris: Seuil, 2002).

PN *The Preparation of the Novel. Lecture Courses and Seminars at the Collège de France (1978–1979 and 1979–1980)*, trans. Kate Briggs (New York: Columbia University Press, 2011).

PR *La Préparation du roman I et II. Cours et séminaires au Collège de France (1978–1979 et 1979–1980)*, ed. Nathalie Léger (Paris: Seuil/IMEC, 2003).

RB *Roland Barthes by Roland Barthes*, trans. Richard Howard (Basingstoke: Macmillan, 1977).

List of Illustrations

1. *Le Nouvel Observateur*, *Spécial Photo*, 2 (1977), 7 (courtesy of Robert Delpire). 21
2. *Le Nouvel Observateur*, *Spécial Photo*, 2 (1977), 10–11 (courtesy of Robert Delpire). 22
3. Roland Barthes, *La Chambre claire. Note sur la photographie* (Paris: Cahiers du Cinéma/Gallimard/Seuil, 1980), 148–149. 23
4. *Die Literarische Welt*, 38 (1931), 3 (© Hamburger Stiftung zur Förderung von Wissenschaft und Kultur/Suhrkamp Verlag; collection of the Deutsches Literaturarchiv Marbach). 37
5. David Octavius Hill and Robert Adamson, Elizabeth Johnstone Hall, Newhaven fishwife, 1843–47 (collection of the Centre for Research Collections of the Edinburgh University Library). 48
6. Karl Dauthendey, Self-portrait with Miss Friedrich, 1857 (Helmuth Bossert and Heinrich Guttmann, *Aus der Frühzeit der Photographie 1840–70. Ein Bildbuch nach 200 Originalen* (Frankfurt a.M.: Societäts–Verlag, 1930), fig. 128). 53
7. Walter and Georg Benjamin, Schreiberhau, 1902 (courtesy of Gerhard Oberschlick; collection of the Österreichisches Literaturarchiv der Österreichischen Nationalbibliothek Wien, Nachlass Günther Anders (ÖLA 237/04)). 63
8. Walter, Georg and Dora Benjamin, around 1904 (collection of the Walter Benjamin Archiv in the Akademie der Künste, Berlin). 65
9. Franz Kafka, 1888/89 (collection of the Walter Benjamin Archiv in the Akademie der Künste, Berlin). 73
10. Alexander Gardner, Lewis Payne, 1865 (collection of the Library of Congress, Washington D.C.). 157
11. Daniel Faunières, Roland Barthes, 1979 (rights reserved). 165
12. François Lagarde, Roland Barthes, 1979 (© François Lagarde). 166
13. Philippe and Henriette Binger with their grandfather, 1895/96 (Roland Barthes, *La Chambre claire. Note sur la photographie* (Paris: Cahiers du Cinéma/Gallimard/Seuil, 1980), 163). 168

14. Henriette Barthes, Biscarosse, around 1932 (Roland Barthes, *Roland Barthes par Roland Barthes* (Paris: Seuil, 1975), fig.1). 196
15. Daniel Boudinet, *Polaroïd*, 1979 (© Ministère de la culture – Médiathèque du Patrimoine / Daniel Boudinet / dist. RMN). 205
16. James van der Zee, Family portrait, 1926 (Roland Barthes, *La Chambre claire. Note sur la photographie* (Paris: Cahiers du Cinéma/Gallimard/Seuil, 1980), 75) (rights reserved). 210
17. Léon and Berthe Barthes with their daughter Alice (Roland Barthes, *Roland Barthes par Roland Barthes* (Paris: Seuil, 1975), 17, fig. 11). 211

Introduction

In January 1839, the French physicist and politician François Arago announced the invention of the daguerreotype to the Parisian Académie des Sciences. Shortly afterwards he asked the Commission of the Chamber of Deputies to remunerate Louis Daguerre and Nicéphore Niépce's heir for the patent for this groundbreaking process, which enabled light images obtained with the aid of the *camera obscura* to be fixed. During the same month, William Henry Fox Talbot's invention of the calotype was presented to the London Royal Institution, and he was subsequently granted a patent for this paper-based photographic process. These two parallel events constitute the official birth of photography after many decades of experimentation with new image-production devices. Since then, and since the myriad developments in image-making technology that have followed, numerous practitioners, critics, writers and philosophers have grappled with the vexed question as to what photography's specificity and unique 'genius' may be.

From a twenty-first-century perspective, looking back over more than 170 years of photographic history and theory, we are faced with an extensive but by no means homogenous corpus of writing that testifies to a rich and multifaceted tradition of critical, aesthetic, polemical and satirical reflection on the photographic medium. Walter Benjamin and Roland Barthes are widely considered to be two seminal figures in this eclectic discourse on photography: reputations based on a relatively small number of highly influential writings, including Benjamin's 'Kleine Geschichte der Photographie' ['Little History of Photography'] and 'Das Kunstwerk im Zeitalter seiner technischen Reproduzierbarkeit' ['The Work of Art in the Age of Mechanical Reproducibility'] and Barthes's *La Chambre claire. Note sur la photographie* [*Camera Lucida. Reflections on Photography*]. Although these writings now sit alongside one another in anthologies of photographic theory and on university reading lists in cultural and media studies, and although their insights and approaches have been compared and contrasted, to date there exists no published book entirely devoted to Benjamin's and Barthes's theories of photography.[1] This study attempts to fill this gap, offering new perspectives on

1 There is, of course, a vast library of scholarship on Benjamin and Barthes, with photography being typically the most frequent subject of comparison between them. See, for example, Gabriele Röttger-Denker's study on Barthes, *Roland Barthes zur Einführung* (Hamburg: Junius, 1989), 107–12. Rolf

their writings, both in relation to each other and against the backdrop of photographic history as well as twentieth-century intellectual, philosophical and critical discourses more generally.

Benjamin and Barthes entered the historical and critical debate on photography at pivotal moments: Benjamin's burgeoning interest in the medium coincided with the artistic pinnacle of the European avant-garde movements of the 1920s and the ensuing stimulus to photographic practice and theory they provided, whereas Barthes's first engagement with photography overlapped with the rise of Marxist-ideological critique and semiotic analysis as a critical response to mass-media culture during the 1950s and 1960s, at a time when photographic images were already a ubiquitous part of the visual and mental landscape of the twentieth century. Even after the first emergence of digital image technologies in the late 1980s and their rapid expansion throughout the next two decades until the present, which represented a departure from optical-chemical picture production on which Benjamin's and Barthes's writings are based, their reflections on the photographic medium and on individual photographs continue to be major points of scholarly and critical reference.

However, the authoritative position that Benjamin and Barthes occupy in the theoretical discourse on photography and the apparent necessity of continuing to refer to their writings in any theoretical consideration of the medium have contributed, in some cases, to an assumption that each of

---

H. Krauss's book on Benjamin discusses Barthes's *La Chambre claire* as an important example of the post-1963 reception of Benjamin's essay on photography (*Walter Benjamin und der neue Blick auf die Photographie* (Ostfildern: Cantz, 1998), 107–13). Ronald Berg juxtaposes Benjamin and Barthes in a more comprehensive fashion, aligning their understanding of photography with that of Talbot (*Die Ikone des Realen. Zur Bestimmung der Photographie im Werk von Talbot, Benjamin und Barthes* (Munich: Fink, 2001)). In a more recent study on Benjamin by Jessica Nitsche, Barthes's concept of the *punctum* is related to Benjamin's discussion of the portrait of the Newhaven fishwife (*Walter Benjamins Gebrauch der Fotografie* (Berlin: Kulturverlag Kadmos, 2010), 163–70). Additionally, there is at least one doctoral thesis on Benjamin, Barthes and photography (Jeanine Ferguson, *Developing Clichés: Walter Benjamin and Roland Barthes at the Limits of Photographic Theory*, PhD University of Minnesota, 1997). While offering some valuable insights on the subject, this study is now out of date in a number of significant respects given the relevant primary and secondary material published or discovered since 1997 with respect to both authors. By and large, critical studies that make some reference to the similarities between the two writers' views since the publication of *La Chambre claire* in 1980 are too numerous to list here.

their conceptions of photography is consistent, unequivocal, clear-cut and easily summarized. In reality, they are marked by a complexity, ambiguity, idiosyncrasy and multivalence from which much of their richness and continual interest derives.[2] Regarding the canonical writings noted above as mainly providing ready-made, generally applicable, theoretical concepts often neglects the fact that these writings perform and enact specific text-and-image dynamics, sometimes supporting and sometimes opposing their discursive arguments. Together with close analysis of this complex word-image interplay, a principal aim of this study is to highlight the at times contradictory, emphatically subjective and impressionistic nature of the engagement of both theorists with the photographic medium in general, and their evaluations of specific images and photographers in particular, while nonetheless reaffirming their seminal contributions to any general theory or philosophy of photography.

Benjamin's and Barthes's understanding of photography cannot be fully appreciated in isolation from their lives and wider intellectual projects. In this larger context, we are met with a number of fundamental differences. These involve the well-known conceptual trajectories of their respective careers, which not only reflected major movements in twentieth-century intellectual history but also helped to shape them: namely, in Benjamin's work, a general shift from metaphysical and theological concerns to Marxist and sociological ones, and, in Barthes's, a transition from linguistic and semiotic preoccupations to what would become codified as poststructuralist thought.

Further differences between Benjamin and Barthes that have a potential bearing on their views of photography are found on the surface of the two writers' biographies. In certain respects, Benjamin's life – as an itinerant intellectual who fled Nazi-Germany in the early 1930s and lived, like many of his Jewish compatriots, in exile in Paris in precarious circumstances – is radically different from that of Barthes. For Benjamin, the loss of his fountain pen was a traumatic blow; in contrast, towards the end of his career as an established professor of semiology at the prestigious Parisian Collège de France and speaking to crowded lecture theatres, Barthes informed his audience of his recent purchase of 16 bottles of ink pigment (see N, 80–1).

Yet, for some time, Barthes shared Benjamin's status as an outsider in relation to the established academic world, and he, like Benjamin, often

2 For these reasons, when I refer to Benjamin's and Barthes's 'theories' of photography, it is for convenience but not to discount the potential problems of labelling their views on the medium 'theories' in a sense that stresses a high degree of formal systematization and logical coherence.

contributed to non-academic journals and newspapers.[3] Together, their output consists of relatively short books, essayistic texts, journalistic articles and fragmentary and aphoristic pieces, which makes it difficult to contain the writings of Benjamin and Barthes either within a particular school and theory or even within a specific discipline or discourse, such as philosophy, literary theory or art and cultural criticism. In their entirety, their œuvres can be characterized as anti-academic and, by some standards, certainly unsystematic. Apart from biographical considerations, however, there is also a deeper methodological explanation for these traits.

Both authors share a general approach to cultural phenomena, including photography, which Benjamin's friends and contemporaries Siegfried Kracauer and Theodor W. Adorno called, with respect to Benjamin's work, a 'monadological' method.[4] This is characterized by approaching a given cultural object or phenomenon as a concrete reality in itself – hence the allusion to Leibniz's metaphysical theory of self-enclosed and self-defining 'monads' making up the universe – before abstracting any larger theoretical or philosophical significance from it. For both Benjamin and Barthes, the monadological approach translates into a relative lack of retrospective systematization that assimilates the object of investigation into a larger deductive system of thought (with Barthes's structuralist work, however, being a notable exception). It is in relation to this fundamentally open-ended approach to cultural artefacts that photography emerges as one of the major historico-cultural phenomena through which Benjamin's and Barthes's interests in history, modernity and society are channelled and overlap through distinct concepts, including 'aura' and *punctum*, which shed light not only on the nature of the medium per se but

3 Barthes's chronic pulmonary illness during adolescence prevented him from preparing for entry to the École Normale Supérieure and also from obtaining a postgraduate degree. This led to a rather circuitous academic career. Although Benjamin completed a PhD, his plans for an academic career as an orderly professor at a German university were thwarted in 1925 with the rejection of his *Habilitation* on German tragic drama. Despite this similarity, however, the last decade of their lives, before their tragic and untimely deaths, could not offer a more pronounced contrast. (As is well known, Benjamin committed suicide at the Franco-Spanish border in 1940, after attempting to escape the French Nazi collaborators, and Barthes died of the consequences of a car accident while crossing the Rue des Écoles in Paris in 1980.)

4 See Siegfried Kracauer, *Das Ornament der Masse. Essays* (Frankfurt a.M.: Suhrkamp, 1963), 249 and Theodor W. Adorno, *Über Walter Benjamin* (Frankfurt a.M.: Suhrkamp, 1970), 20.

also on fundamentally existential, psychological and cultural-historical experiences of photographic images.

Despite the different historical, philosophical, cultural and linguistic contexts of their work, this study seeks to demonstrate that Benjamin and Barthes engage with similar themes and constellations of questions posed by photography and, in some cases, that they offer similar 'answers' arrived at through similar conceptual strategies and philosophical orientations. Rather than beginning with an external, a priori conceptual framework which the texts and their arguments are forced into accommodating, bringing together Benjamin's and Barthes's writing on photography in a comparative fashion rooted in detailed analysis of key texts and then proceeding to more general and theoretical issues helps to reveal a number of significant connections and affinities that have gone unnoticed. These include, for example, the pronounced ethical dimensions of their discussions of portrait photography as centred on the relation of the viewing self to the sitter. At the same time, however, in the texts in question, the personal, fictional, theoretical and historical are interwoven in a complex fabric that, to some degree, must be acknowledged and examined as a whole before one can single out and focus exclusively on any one particular strand. The productive tension between theoretical reflection and autobiographical anecdote that characterizes each author's approach to the medium will be highlighted in order to draw out their pronounced dialectics between the general and the particular, the universal and the local. These dialectics are central to the content of their insights on photography as well as their form and expression.

Benjamin's and Barthes's accounts of photography are thus directly rooted in personal, and highly poignant, experiences of particular photographs. This sharply differentiates them from much of their respective contemporaries' photographic theory and criticism, which, generally speaking, are more comprehensively and objectively concerned with the technological, aesthetic and socio-cultural development of photography (in the early twentieth century), or the ideological and sociological implications of photographic representation (in the second half of the twentieth century), and also lack the strong emphasis of both Benjamin and Barthes on the perceptual, imaginative and affective activity of the viewer. Although this focus on the viewing subject has a clear and explicit autobiographical dimension in each case, it cannot be reduced to it. Rather, the necessary presence of the photograph's beholder as a key component of any consideration of photography on Benjamin's and Barthes's views also resonates with the general phenomenological orientation they each adopted at certain stages in their careers.

Together with well-known photographic theorists of Weimar Germany, including Siegfried Kracauer and László Moholy-Nagy, Benjamin is part of the first generation of writers who approached photography as an autonomous and sui generis medium as opposed to a scientific and artistic curiosity, as it had mainly been conceived in nineteenth-century discourse. The departure from normative definitions at the beginning of the last century opened up the field to many differently oriented perspectives on photography.[5] Kracauer took an almost exclusively socio-historical line (which also characterized his later film theory), whereas Moholy-Nagy pursued an aesthetic-formalist strategy. In contrast, Benjamin's perspective was strongly autobiographical and subjective from the very beginning. In his first text on photography, the 'Kleine Geschichte der Photographie', which discusses nineteenth-century work as well as later photography, including his own childhood family portraits, Benjamin's response to all of these arresting visual artefacts is often equally profoundly personal. This subjective current parallels and intersects with more philosophical, historical and cultural-critical arguments about photography, rather than precluding them. However, although the two tendencies are often mutually supportive, they are also sometimes in tension with each other, as will be analysed in the first part of this study.

The oscillation between the subjective and the objective, the personal and the collective, the autobiographical and the philosophical-critical as well as their interpenetration, together with an overarching focus on the viewing subject which characterizes Benjamin's treatment of photography, is also notably present in Barthes's studies. During the late 1950s and 1960s, Barthes was a major practitioner of the semiotic theory rooted in Saussurean linguistics that had already begun to influence critical writing on photography and film. Such linguistic and communication-theory based approaches to visual media pay close attention to the recipient of images as a constitutive element of their meaning. In this context, the viewer is introduced into photographic theory in the form of the semiotically defined receiver of the 'photographic message'. As a corollary, the photograph is understood as a visual 'text' that has to be 'read'. However, as will be traced in the second part of this study, although this conceptual framework provides for an abstract viewer-reader of photographic images, as it evolved further, Barthes's conception of photography pushed beyond the boundaries of semiotic theory to accommodate more personal

5 Cf. Wolfgang Kemp's characterization of the first decades of photographic theory as normative, *Theorie der Fotografie*, 3 vols. (Munich: Schirmer/Mosel, 1979–1983), vol. 2, 35–6.

and existential concerns anchored in the subject's complete psychological and emotional engagement with photographic images. Here the Proustian dimension of Barthes's writing on photography comes to the fore and no more so than in *La Chambre claire,* which reprises Benjamin's juxtaposition of Proust's conceptions of voluntary and involuntary memory with certain aspects of photography. (In this connection, one important part of this study will be a photography-centred explication of the significance of *À la recherche du temps perdu* [*In Search of Lost Time*] as a pivotal inter-textual reference point for both Benjamin and Barthes).

In general, as these introductory remarks indicate, an emphasis on the viewing subject, together with the existential and historical contexts in which images are directly encountered – and the ethical implications of such an encounter – represent the most significant commonality between Benjamin's and Barthes's views on photography. For this reason, both writers may aptly be seen as pursuing a general phenomenology of the photographic image. In Barthes's case, especially in his late work, notably *La Chambre claire*, this is explicitly acknowledged. In Benjamin's work, the phenomenological orientation of his early writing on photography is more submerged and embryonic, not least by virtue of the fact that it largely predates the mid-twentieth-century turn towards 'existential phenomenology' in continental thought, as represented, most notably, by the philosophy of Jean-Paul Sartre and Maurice Merleau-Ponty. As Adorno noted, however, Benjamin anticipated this phenomenological revolution in philosophy,[6] and I would argue, no more so than with respect to photography.

Beyond any general phenomenology, rooted in an abstract viewing subject, however, Benjamin's and Barthes's concern with how the individual viewer concretely experiences photographic images is inextricably tied to their respective relationships with photographs in their possession. In a striking coincidence, these are both late nineteenth-century childhood portraits taken against the backdrop of a winter-garden setting: in Benjamin's case, a studio portrait of the Jewish, German-speaking writer Franz Kafka at the age of five or six, and, in Barthes's case, a double portrait of his mother, Henriette Binger, then aged five, and her brother.[7]

6 See Adorno, *Über Walter Benjamin*, 14. In a similar fashion, Sigrid Weigel has suggested that paintings serve Benjamin as material for a phenomenological consideration of cultural history (*Walter Benjamin: Die Kreatur, das Heilige, die Bilder* (Frankfurt a.M.: Fischer, 2008), 287).

7 Although their engagements with these particular photographs have profound psychological dimensions, as we shall see, it is in the context of a

In each instance, the prized image is placed within a complex network of both contradictory and complementary anecdotes and arguments, which serve to situate it in dialogical relation with other photographic images and with the medium. In Benjamin's and Barthes's writings, it is in this perpetual dialectic between the privileged childhood portraits and all other photographs, mirroring the aforementioned tension between the unique and personal versus the general and theoretical, that the overarching theme of the *singularity of photography* comes to the fore.

Conventionally, photography is first regarded as a medium of fast and easy image reproduction and multiplication. This is a starting point for Benjamin's interpretation of the photo-based mechanical reproduction of artworks in his celebrated essay 'Das Kunstwerk im Zeitalter seiner technischen Reproduzierbarkeit' – one that has influenced a great deal of scholarship on Benjamin's conception of photography. As we will see, although reproducibility undermines the photograph's uniqueness, understood in terms of an irreproducible material object, singularity in the sense to be defined is unaffected by any such physical-material considerations. At the same time, another consideration, namely the photograph's indexicality, its causal relation to what it pictures, is closely aligned with the theme of singularity, providing a necessary but ultimately insufficient criterion for its affective-ethical experience.[8]

If singularity is not wholly dependent on the photograph as a material or perceptual object, it must be located elsewhere. The writings of Benjamin and Barthes suggest that the figurative space of singularity is the relation between the photograph, its referent or sitter and the beholder of the image. This relational dynamic is most pertinently exemplified in and through each writer's engagement with the respective winter-garden portrait of Kafka as a child and Barthes's mother. As I will show, in the most profound sense of the term, the singularity of photography, for Benjamin and Barthes, is, in fact, the experiential singularity of a particular photograph. All other technological, ontological and historico-cultural factors of the medium, as also discussed in their wide-ranging texts, ultimately go towards supporting and defending this experiential singularity rather than opposing it. The singularity that emerges with respect to the two

---

general phenomenology rather than psychoanalysis that the similarities and differences between Benjamin and Barthes can be foregrounded in a more holistic way.

8 As this indicates, the digitization of photography during the early 1990s does not directly negate the relevance of this concept, as will be discussed in the Postscript.

exceptional winter-garden photographs is a result of the complex relation between perceiving and remembering, with emphasis on lived history and its narrative transformation into writing. For both Benjamin and Barthes, the childhood portraits represent a potentially life-changing encounter with otherness in the form of the photographic representation of the absent or even dead other – an encounter that is in its turn bound to a felt responsibility towards that other. To anticipate where we will eventually arrive, Benjamin and Barthes seek to do justice to a tripartite singularity – as belonging to the photographic encounter itself, the unique individual represented in a portrait photograph, and the unique relation between the beholder and the photographed person – through a practice of 'redemptive criticism'.[9] This is a practice rooted in the attempted saving of the past, the lost and the dead. In other words, Benjamin and Barthes write on photography in part to redeem that which has to be rescued from the flux of transience and contingency that photography is thought both to picture and arrest. Replete with theological connotations, at the heart of this redemptive mode of criticism is a profound sense of ethical obligation or commitment to the depicted other. While these are all also central themes in the works of Jacques Derrida, Derek Attridge and Giorgio Agamben, it is in Benjamin's and Barthes's writings that they are most notably prompted, almost necessarily, by the powerfully felt ontological, phenomenological and psychological effects of the photographic image.

The notion of singularity explored throughout this study in relation to the theoretical and historical dialectic of photography as treated by Benjamin and Barthes is indebted to the three aforementioned theorists: specifically to Attridge's concept of the 'singularity of literature', Agamben's Benjaminian interpretation of photography's 'exigency' and Derrida's reflections on photography as a medium that entails a mournful presence/absence of the other. As suggested above, singularity describes a phenomenon that is, in itself, fundamentally relational. Attridge rightly argues that singularity is an 'event' that occurs in the process of engaging with an

9 This concept is modelled on, yet also distinct from, the German expression 'rettende Kritik', which has, in the wake of Jürgen Habermas's seminal essay, become a central concept in critical literature on Benjamin ('Bewußtmachende oder rettende Kritik – die Aktualität Walter Benjamins', in Siegfried Unseld (ed.), *Zur Aktualität Walter Benjamins. Aus Anlaß des 80. Geburtstags von Walter Benjamin* (Frankfurt a.M.: Suhrkamp, 1972), 173–223). Yet, it was Kracauer who, as early as 1928, drew attention to the redemptive aspect of Benjamin's cultural criticism which he saw closely related to his own critical projects (*Das Ornament der Masse*, 252).

aesthetic object or artefact.[10] He further claims that this engagement with the singularity of a work takes the form of a demand made upon the viewer, reader or audience. But it is Agamben's more photographically oriented notion of 'demand' that provides an even more fitting model for photographic singularity and one which I will trace in the writings of Benjamin and Barthes.

In a short aphoristic text titled 'Judgement Day', Agamben reflects on the 'exigency' of portrait photographs, a concept he develops in dialogue with Benjamin's description of a mid-nineteenth-century portrait of a Newhaven fishwife.[11] For Agamben, the demand that the photograph makes on the viewer is inseparable from the past presence of the subject in front of the camera and his or her unique existence, or, in Derrida's terms, the 'singularité absolue de l'autre' ['absolute singularity of the other'].[12] This singularity of the other, understood as a specific human being,[13] imbues the photograph's demand with an unavoidable existential confrontation between the self and the other, wherein the viewer necessarily meets his or her own 'being in the world', to borrow Martin Heidegger's concept of *Dasein*. Derrida links the appearance or emergence of this singularity of the other (with which the self is in constant dialogue) with, quoting Barthes, the 'photographic referent', understood as that person or object in the world that has been captured and preserved in a two-dimensional form.[14] In sum, while the commonplace notion of photography's immortalization

10 Derek Attridge, *The Singularity of Literature* (New York and London: Routledge, 2004), 67. As this study draws on Attridge's work (as its title indicates), Attridge's concepts of singularity and event, and the work's demand on the reader, in turn, are highly indebted not only to Derrida's philosophy and to Levinas's ethics but also to the hermeneutic aesthetics of Hans-Georg Gadamer and Paul Ricœur.

11 Giorgio Agamben, *Profanations*, trans. Jeff Fort (New York: Zone Books, 2007), 25.

12 Jacques Derrida, 'Les Morts de Roland Barthes', *Poétique*, 47 (1981), 269–92: 272; 'The Deaths of Roland Barthes', in *The Work of Mourning*, ed. Pascale-Anne Brault and Michael Naas (Chicago: University of Chicago Press, 2001), 34–67: 39.

13 My emphasis on the 'other' as a concrete human being (rather than an abstract text or artefact) resonates with Levinas's definition of the Other as 'Autrui', and yet differs from his transcendental concept. See Derek Attridge, 'Innovation, Literature, Ethics: Relating to the Other', *PMLA*, 114 (1999), 20–31: 23–4. To mark this difference as well as to avoid confusion with the Lacanian 'Other', I shall keep the word in lower case throughout this study.

14 Derrida, 'Les Morts de Roland Barthes', 272; 'The Deaths of Roland Barthes', 39.

of a unique moment in time is for these reasons part of the photograph's radical singularity, it also involves larger relations not only between the photograph and the depicted person, but, necessarily, between the photograph and the beholder. It therefore entails the complex dynamics of lived subjectivity that are as much a part of the creation and viewing of photographs as of any other human activity – and even in some ways more – despite the seemingly objective and impersonal nature of the medium.

This focus makes it possible to recognize and avoid certain significant misunderstandings concerning Benjamin's and Barthes's theories of photography. With respect to Benjamin, foregrounding the theme of singularity helps to transcend the predominant and problematic equation of photography with reproducibility, and hence its presumed entirely 'anti-auratic' nature. With respect to Barthes, it ensures that the proper focus is kept on existential and ethical issues, which he clearly prioritizes, rather than on aesthetic ones which he equally clearly de-emphasizes. As may be expected, one of the principal aims of this study will be to reveal the similarities and differences between this theme of photographic singularity and aura and *punctum*, respectively, as Benjamin's and Barthes's best-known and most influential photographic concepts. In addition, a number of related, corollary or supplementary themes, concepts and problematics will also be addressed, including referentiality, subjectivity, temporality, memory and mortality. The vexed question of what the essential nature of photography is, or may be, is, however, largely bracketed in favour of evaluating how each author conceives the medium and how a dialectical relationship between language and photography unfolds within their writings. In meta-theoretical terms, it thus pursues the issues of how the visual nature of the medium impacts on and challenges Benjamin's and Barthes's respective modes of writing about it, and how, in both cases, this leads to the creation of a hybrid discourse that combines theoretical and historical analyses, personal history and memory, and fascinating – in some cases highly self-reflexive – text-and-image interplay.

Taking into consideration the wider critical and photographic discourses that have collected around their writings, this textual, intermedial and comparative analysis will attempt to tackle head-on the complex question of Benjamin's influence on Barthes with respect to the latter's writing on photography and other relevant biographical issues. That said, it is both appropriate and necessary in this context not to think of 'influence' in causal and one-directional terms and as diminishing the 'originality' of the latecomer in favour of the predecessor but as a compounding constellation of themes and ideas that mutually illuminate each other.[15] In strict chronological terms, however, it is true to say that Benjamin either introduced many issues and problems into the Western critical/theoretical and photographic discourse or significantly re-interpreted them, including for instance the experiential dimension of photography in relation to the spatio-temporal aspects of both the image's creation and the resulting object. A number of these issues were later taken up by Barthes in the wake of André Bazin's and Susan Sontag's influential writings on the 'realist' nature of the photographic image, which chronologically fall between Benjamin's last writings on photography and Barthes's *La Chambre claire*. Inversely, reading Benjamin with Barthes sheds new retrospective light on Benjamin's texts and allows for recognition of hitherto unnoticed or underappreciated aspects of both. The similarities between the views of Benjamin and Barthes can therefore be characterized as textual, visual, conceptual and thematic 'correspondences'. Borrowing from Charles Baudelaire's theory of *correspondances*, Benjamin designates an imagistic and imaginary relationship between the past and the present that come together and create a 'Jetzt der Erkennbarkeit' (GS, V, 1038) ['now of recognizability' (AP, 912)], as he writes in his *Passagen-Werk* [*Arcades Project*]. The multifaceted connections between Benjamin's and Barthes's thought indeed manifest such a non-chronological, reciprocally defining relation between past and present, earlier and later. Against this background, although it would be wrong to over-prioritize Benjamin's direct influence on Barthes, any comprehensive comparative study must address this central question, which also takes into account a wider and deeper intellectual and cultural context and thus provides the natural starting point for a comparative analysis of their theories of photography.

---

15 In his famous theory of poetry, Harold Bloom defines influence as a 'matrix of relationships – imagistic, temporal, spiritual, psychological' (*The Anxiety of Influence. A Theory of Poetry* (New York and Oxford: Oxford University Press, 1997), xxiii).

Benjamin and Barthes: The Question of Influence

Despite the wealth of critical commentary on the lives and works of Benjamin and Barthes, reflecting their status as two of the most frequently cited authors of the twentieth century, little research has been carried out to establish the degree to which Benjamin's writings and ideas may have had a direct influence on Barthes, or the nature and extent of Barthes's reading of Benjamin.[1] This is in spite of the fact that at one time or another each wrote on the same authors (Marcel Proust, Charles Baudelaire, Bertolt Brecht and Charles Fourier), historical periods (the mid-to-late nineteenth century and the time of the avant-garde), media and cultural phenomena (photography, cinema and popular culture), and in some respects did so from similar critical and theoretical perspectives.[2] Through the mediation of these subjects some direct or indirect evocation of Benjamin's work may be found in Barthes's writings, and together with certain connections through personal relationships and associations, these provide circumstantial evidence that Barthes was conversant with some of Benjamin's work and his writings on photography in particular.

Benjamin's championing of the work of Brecht, with whom he cultivated an intellectual friendship from their first meeting in 1929 until

1 Even those studies which directly compare their theories of photography, such as, for example, Tim Dant and Graeme Gilloch, 'Pictures of the Past: Benjamin and Barthes on Photography and History', *European Journal of Cultural Studies*, 5 (2002), 5–23, do not address these questions. Some tentative suggestions as to influence can be found in Berg, *Die Ikone des Realen*, 291–2. Although Krauss's study of Benjamin deals with *La Chambre claire* in the context of the reception of Benjamin's writings on photography, the question of Barthes's actual reading of Benjamin is not pursued (*Benjamin und der neue Blick*, 107–13). Catherine Coquio contends that there is simply no reception of Benjamin in Barthes's case ('Walter Benjamin et Roland Barthes', in Klaus Garber and Ludger Rehm (eds.), *Global Benjamin*, 3 vols. (Munich: Fink, 1999), vol. 2, 1147–66: 1147).

2 Catherine Coquio suggests a whole array of other subjects of comparison, 'Roland Barthes et Walter Benjamin: image, tautologie, dialectique', in Catherine Coquio and Régis Salado (eds.), *Barthes après Barthes. Une Actualité en questions* (Pau: Publications de l'Université de Pau, 1993), 195–208). For a discussion of Benjamin's and Barthes's interest in Fourier, see Michael Hollington, 'Benjamin, Fourier, Barthes', *Journal of the Australasian Universities Language and Literature Association*, 81 (1994), 33–53. For an account of their views on language and literature, see John Thobo-Carlsen, 'Barthes Meets Benjamin? A Relating of their Views on the Conjunction between Language and Literature', *Orbis Litterarum*, 53 (1998), 1–41.

the former's death, anticipates Barthes's enthusiasm for Brechtian theatre when it was introduced into France in the 1950s. Having attended the first performance of Brecht's *Mutter Courage und ihre Kinder* [*Mother Courage and her Children*] in Paris in 1954, Barthes became a fervent supporter of epic theatre. This experience also acted as a catalyst for a wider interest in theatre, especially in the renewal of classical French drama, reflected in his journalistic writing for the anti-bourgeois review *Théâtre populaire*. In a commentary from 1960 on a performance by Brecht's Berliner Ensemble, Barthes refers to a French translation of one of Benjamin's texts on epic theatre (see OC, I, 1075) which appeared in *Théâtre populaire* between 1957 and 1958, when Barthes was serving on its editorial board. Around the same time, Barthes may have read other texts by Benjamin on Brecht in the journal *Europe* which, in 1957, published a special issue on Brecht with a translation of Benjamin's comments on his friend's work.[3]

Given that Barthes thus came into contact with Benjamin's writings on Brecht at a relatively early stage in his career, it is surprising that when studying mass culture while employed at the École Pratique des Hautes Études, beginning in 1960, Barthes did not engage with Benjamin's pioneering work on this subject. In 1961, the Centre d'Études des Communications de Masse [Centre for the Study of Mass Communication] was founded under the directorship of Georges Friedmann, an eminent sociologist who attracted the attention of Max Horkheimer.[4] This indicates an acknowledged intellectual affinity between the Frankfurt School of Critical Theory (then based in New York) and the work of the Centre in Paris. Barthes was closely associated with the Centre, and he contributed regularly to its semiotic and structuralist-linguistic review, *Communications*, where he joined the sociologist Edgar Morin and the semiologist Christian Metz, among other important intellectual figures.[5] Issues one and four, from 1961 and 1964 respectively, included two of Barthes's semiotic studies on photography: 'Le Message photographique' ['The Photographic Message'] and 'Rhétorique de l'image' ['Rhetoric of the Image']. He also wrote the editorial article for the

3 The editorial praises Benjamin as 'l'un des plus brillants et des plus profonds essayistes allemands du siècle' ['one of the most brilliant and most profound German essayists of the century'] (*Europe*, 35 (1957), 132).

4 In the early 1950s, Horkheimer expressed a strong interest in Friedmann's contribution to his journal *Sociologica*. See Rolf Wiggershaus, *The Frankfurt School. Its History, Theories and Political Significance*, trans. Michael Robertson (Cambridge: Polity Press, 1994), 470.

5 For a more detailed contextual discussion of the journal's importance, see Patrick Ffrench, *The Time of Theory. A History of Tel Quel (1969–1983)* (Oxford: Clarendon Press, 1995), 32.

inaugural issue, setting out the Centre's agenda and drew attention to the mass media research already underway in other countries. Although Barthes does not mention Benjamin's work in this context, [6] nor makes reference to any other German cultural-critical writings, such as those of Horkheimer and Adorno,[7] he might well have had Benjamin's 'Kunstwerk' essay in mind here, which was first published in French rather than German, in 1936.[8] Although Benjamin's Marxist-dialectical methodology in this essay is certainly not of a piece with Barthes's then predominantly semiotic-linguistic approach to mass cultural phenomena, the latter's support of Marxist ideology during the 1950s might well have rendered him receptive to it. For even if the French intellectual scene at the time was dominated by the Stalinist Communist Party, on the one hand, and Sartrean existentialism, on the other, the *Arguments* group, of which Barthes, together with Morin, was a founding member, acted as a kind of counterweight to these two prevailing political and philosophical influences. Indeed, the *Arguments* journal became a forum for a more flexible and less dogmatic leftism and was always open to new currents in Western-Marxist intellectual debate,[9] including Benjamin's work.

On a more personal level, Georges Bataille and Pierre Klossowski may have helped to expose Barthes to Benjamin's work and its general orientation. Bataille was a founding member of the radical and short-lived Collège de Sociologie, which provided an institutional platform for intellectual debate in the mid-to-late 1930s, and included Michel Leiris and Roger Caillois among its closest allies. Benjamin was among a number of other intellectuals associated with the Collège. Bataille had first met Benjamin in 1933,[10] at the Parisian Bibliothèque Nationale,

---

6 Ottmar Ette suggests that it is difficult to imagine that Barthes did not know Benjamin's work on mass culture and points to some similarities between the two (*Roland Barthes. Eine intellektuelle Biographie* (Frankfurt a.M.: Suhrkamp, 1998), 111–12).

7 The impact of the Frankfurt School's work in France was perhaps delayed owing to lack of translations and the dominance of non-Western Marxism and existentialism in many intellectual circles.

8 For a comprehensive overview of the complicated publication history, see Schöttker's commentary in Walter Benjamin, *Das Kunstwerk im Zeitalter seiner technischen Reproduzierbarkeit und weitere Dokumente*, ed. Detlev Schöttker (Frankfurt a.M.: Suhrkamp, 2007), 120–33.

9 See Mark Poster, *Existential Marxism in Postwar France. From Sartre to Althusser* (Princeton: Princeton University Press, 1975), 210–14 and Ffrench, *The Time of Theory*, 10.

10 See Michel Surya, *Georges Bataille, la mort à l'œuvre* (Paris: Gallimard, 1992), 637.

where Bataille was a librarian and Benjamin a so-called *habitué*.[11] Although Bataille and Benjamin did not engage in any collaborative work, Benjamin was a regular (if taciturn) attendee at the lectures and conferences of the Collège de Sociologie during its two-year existence.[12] Beginning in the 1950s, Barthes contributed to the journal *Critique*, which Bataille had founded in 1946. Although Bataille's intellectual influence on the critical thought of Barthes overshadowed Benjamin's, it is still reasonable to assume that the journal provided Barthes with some access to the German writer's work since *Critique* regularly published articles on Benjamin. The dissemination of Benjamin's work in translation culminated in a special edition in 1969 while Barthes was on the advisory board.[13] Much earlier, during the 1930s and then the 1950s, some of Benjamin's texts and essays also appeared in the existentialist *Les Temps modernes* and *Les Lettres nouvelles*.[14] Barthes was certainly familiar with both literary reviews. In fact, it was for *Les Lettres nouvelles*, a left-wing arts journal (founded by Maurice Nadeau), that Barthes wrote his famous monthly 'mythologies', reprinted in book form in 1957, which is now considered a seminal work in semiotics and cultural theory. In an issue from January 1954 partly devoted to Benjamin, Barthes's 'Jules César au cinéma' ['Julius Caesar in Films'] appeared alongside Benjamin's texts.[15]

11 In 1935 Benjamin mentions Bataille as a referee in a request letter to the director of the Bibliothèque Nationale (see GB, V, 124) and writes to Horkheimer about his frequent encounters with Bataille in a letter from 1938 (see GB, VI, 93).

12 See Denis Hollier (ed.), *Le Collège de Sociologie (1937–1939)* (Paris: Gallimard, 1979), 17. Benjamin was asked to give a lecture at the Collège, which, however, never took place, as Hans Mayer, another German participant, recalls (ibid., 447). For two accounts of Benjamin's potential influence on French intellectual discourses in the 1930s, see Gerhard Rupp, 'Benjamin und Bataille. Deutsch-französische Kreuzungen auf der Suche nach einem anderen Diskurs', in Klaus Garber and Ludger Rehm (eds.), *Global Benjamin*, 3 vols. (Munich: Fink, 1999), vol. 2, 827–38 and Michael Weingrad, 'The College of Sociology and the Institute for Social Research', *New German Critique*, 84 (2001), 129–61.

13 *Critique*, 25 (1969).

14 For a discussion of the publishing context of these and other important reviews of the 1950s to 1970s, see Ffrench, *The Time of Theory*, 38–42.

15 *Les Lettres nouvelles*, 11 (1954), 150–3. Articles on Benjamin came from his personal friends, Adrienne Monnier and Jean Selz, and texts by Benjamin included his essay on the Swiss anthropologist Johann Jakob Bachofen as well as some sections of his autobiographical *Berliner Kindheit um Neunzehnhundert* [*Berlin Childhood Around 1900*].

Before fleeing from Paris in 1940, Benjamin entrusted a number of his manuscripts to Bataille to be hidden in the Bibliothèque Nationale.[16] It was not Bataille, however, but the philosopher, artist and translator Klossowski who potentially secured a 'Barthesian afterlife' for Benjamin's work in the form of an inter-personal link. According to Klossowski's own recollections, he met Benjamin in 1935 during a reunion of the short-lived left-wing *Contre-Attaque* group spearheaded by André Breton and Bataille.[17] Together with Benjamin, Klossowski worked on the French version of the seminal essay on the 'Kunstwerk im Zeitalter seiner technischen Reproduzierbarkeit', a collaboration initiated by Horkheimer (see GB, V, 240). Although both Benjamin and Klossowski remembered the collaborative translation of this essay as a difficult experience,[18] Klossowski also described Benjamin as an 'individu angélique' ['angelic individual'] and contributed a special report on Benjamin in *Le Monde* in 1969.[19] Klossowski's working relationship with Benjamin is of paramount importance in this context because he was later to become a close friend of Barthes. Not only did Klossowski's writings on Friedrich Nietzsche provide Barthes with a new impetus for reading the nineteenth-century German philosopher, but from the late 1940s onwards Klossowski was a neighbour of Barthes in the Saint-Sulpice neighbourhood of Paris, with his wife regularly accompanying Barthes on the piano.[20] In spite of the lack of documented evidence, it is not difficult to imagine Klossowski recounting his time with Benjamin (and the latter's 'puissante originalité' ['potent originality'] as Klossowski wrote in 1952[21]) to Barthes, especially given Barthes's and Benjamin's common interest in mass communication. Even if Benjamin's ideas were a subject of discussion in Klossowski's circle, or indeed among intellectuals close to Benjamin, including Louis Aragon, Maurice Nadeau or Maurice Blanchot,

---

16 These manuscripts were found by Giorgio Agamben in 1981 and are now part of the Walter Benjamin Archiv in Berlin.

17 See Hollier (ed.), *Le Collège de Sociologie*, 586.

18 During 1936 Benjamin reported regularly to Horkheimer and Adorno about the translation process (see GB, V, 243–4; 392; 398–9; 415), and Klossowski recalled the co-operation with Benjamin in an interview with Jean-Maurice Monnoyer (*Le Peintre et son démon. Entretiens avec Pierre Klossowski* (Paris: Flammarion, 1985), 187).

19 See Surya, *Georges Bataille*, 325 and Hollier (ed.), *Le Collège de Sociologie*, 586–7.

20 See Alain Arnaud, *Pierre Klossowski* (Paris: Seuil, 1990), 188.

21 Pierre Klossowski, 'Lettre sur Walter Benjamin', *Mercure de France*, 1067 (1952), 456–7: 457.

these personal encounters and hypothetical conversations are not, however, able to provide us with any conclusive evidence on the question of direct influence. Thus we need to turn to Barthes's writings and interviews for more definitive, textual clues.

Deductive speculation as to the extent of Barthes's reading of Benjamin stems from the fact that, although he mentions Benjamin in his later writings, he rarely cites any specific work; nor does he acknowledge Benjamin as a particularly important intellectual inspiration. Barthes makes only about a dozen or so direct references to Benjamin, with the majority of these found in post-1977 interviews and seminars, yet not in any major text.[22] However, this was not exclusive to Benjamin because Barthes seldom referred to any author in what would be considered a proper academic style, admitting that 'c'est en cela que je suis *léger*, vivant ma culture comme une mémoire incomplète' (PR, 199) ['It is in this sense that I am *a bit cavalier*, living my culture as an incomplete recollection' (PN, 141)].[23] Thus, even if the occasional references to Benjamin scattered in Barthes's teaching and conversations indicate a certain familiarity with Benjamin and some of his texts – suggesting that the latter was indeed part of Barthes's 'incomplete cultural memory' – these again provide no 'smoking gun'.

There is one documented instance that bears exemplary witness to Barthes's peculiar silence with regard to Benjamin's work. On the occasion of a 1977 conference devoted to Barthes at the prestigious cultural centre and renowned colloquium venue Cerisy-la-Salle in Northern France, at which Barthes was present, Hubert Damisch delivered a paper and directly cited Benjamin's text on the reproducibility of artworks. In this he wondered aloud whether Barthes knew the essay, even if Barthes 'ne [le] cite jamais, que peut-être il n'a pas lu' ['never quotes [it], which he

22 Barthes mentioned Benjamin in a 1977 interview on photography and again in a 1978 interview on violence (see OC, V, 932; 551). In Barthes's Collège de France lecture series, *Le Neutre*, there are nine references, mostly to Benjamin's drug experiments as described in his *Haschisch in Marseille* (see N, 41; 62; 69; 76; 111; 127; 137; 189; 202), to which he probably also referred in a previous seminar at the École Pratique des Hautes Études (see LA, 151). In *La Préparation du roman*, there is one allusive paraphrase of Benjamin that cannot, however, be traced to a specific text, as the editor has noted (see PR, 81, n. 2).

23 Antoine Compagnon states that Barthes's bibliography for the Collège de France seminars was almost entirely 'second hand' and that Barthes's rarely ever checked his sources (*Les Antimodernes. De Joseph de Maistre à Roland Barthes* (Paris: Gallimard, 2005), 408).

has perhaps not read']. [24] Damisch goes further, suggesting that Benjamin's 'Kunstwerk' essay may even be 'indispensible' to an understanding of the political dimension of Barthes's work. [25] Although the conference proceedings document that Barthes actively engaged in the ensuing discussion, they also show that he did not respond to this provocative challenge regarding his knowledge of Benjamin's text and its relevance to his writing and concepts.

Traces of Reception

Although the motives for Barthes's silence on Benjamin both in his public appearances, such as at Cerisy-la-Salle, and in his writings remain obscure, there is no doubt that he knew Benjamin's most important text on photography, the 'Kleine Geschichte der Photographie'. Translated by Maurice de Gandillac, the first French version of this essay appeared in 1971 under the title 'Petite histoire de la photographie' in the two-volume collection of Benjamin's *Œuvres*. [26] Although Barthes refers to a different text by Benjamin from the same collection, which he apparently held in the library of his summer house in Urt (see N 26; 34), there is another direct reference to the 'Kleine Geschichte der Photographie'. In 1977, a shorter version of this text's first translation into French was reprinted in a special photography issue of the *Nouvel Observateur*, which Barthes lists in the bibliography of his most important text on photography, *La Chambre claire*. [27] In the *Spécial Photo* of the French weekly magazine, Benjamin's

24 Hubert Damisch, 'La "Prise de langue" et le "faire signe"', in Antoine Compagnon (ed.), *Prétexte Roland Barthes* (Paris: Union Générale d'Éditions, 1978), 394–406: 404–5.

25 Ibid. In an English-speaking context, Peter Collier has made a similar connection, calling for a study on the 'conjunction of Barthes and Benjamin' ('Roland Barthes: The Critical Subject (an Idea for Research)', *Paragraph*, 11 (1988), 175–80: 178).

26 See Benjamin, *Œuvres*, 2 vols., trans. Maurice de Gandillac et al. (Paris: Denoël, 1971), vol. 2, 15–35. This collection is based on a number of earlier translations that were assembled in the *Œuvres choisies*, trans. Maurice de Gandillac (Paris: Julliard, 1959), which, however, do not include the essay on photography.

27 Florence de Mèredieu, Margaret Olin and Daniel Grojnowski all mention this reference without exploring it any further ('La Photographie et la critique photographique: Benjamin, Barthes et la question du référent', in Jean-Marc Lachaud (ed.), *Présence(s) de Walter Benjamin* (Bordeaux: Université Michel de Montaigne, 1994), 11–24: 24; 'Touching Photographs: Roland Barthes's

essay is titled 'Les Analphabètes de l'avenir' ['The Illiterates of the Future'],[28] and the editors praise it as 'un des plus importants [textes] jamais écrits sur la photographie, notamment sur le portrait, qui est ici comme un fil conducteur' ['one of the most important [texts] ever written on photography, especially on portraiture, which here is a kind of leitmotif'].[29] Not only does this introductory note draw particular attention to Benjamin's article, but also, and even more intriguingly, the translation of his text is illustrated with photographs, some of which are reproduced in *La Chambre claire*.[30]

The *Nouvel Observateur* version of Benjamin's essay on photography is, in fact, the first French publication to include illustrations at all. Published in 1977, it coincides with the first German republication that also includes the photographs that accompanied the 'Kleine Geschichte der Photographie' in the original version of 1931.[31] The latest French translation of Benjamin's essay, from 1996, is abundantly illustrated,[32] reflecting the much greater availability of visual material by the late twentieth century. Prior to this and in the absence of huge, digitized image archives, photographic images illustrating books and articles on photography were drawn from the same small pool of images. For instance, the daguerreotype portrait of a collector of butterflies, which accompanies the first page of Benjamin's essay, is also found in a catalogue of nineteenth-century photography edited by Camille Recht.[33] This publication served as an important source for Benjamin's 'Kleine Geschichte der Photographie'.

Out of the 25 photographs that illustrate Barthes's *La Chambre claire*, 6 are taken from the *Nouvel Observateur* special issue. In an interview from

"Mistaken Identification"', *Representations*, 80 (2002), 99–118: 118, n. 43; 'Walter Benjamin, les auras de l'aura', *Critique*, 659 (2002), 287–302: 301, n. 13).

28 The title alludes to Moholy-Nagy's famous prediction that the illiterate of the future will be those who cannot read photography, which Benjamin refers to at the end of the 'Kleine Geschichte der Photographie' (see GS, II, 385).

29 *Le Nouvel Observateur, Spécial Photo*, 2 (1977), 1.

30 Geoffrey Batchen has noted this iconographic link without pursuing it in any detail ('*Camera Lucida*: Another Little History of Photography', in Robin Kelsey and Blake Stimson (eds.), *The Meaning of Photography* (Williamstown, MA: Sterling and Francine Clark Art Institute, 2008), 76–91: 80).

31 See Walter Benjamin, *Aussichten. Illustrierte Aufsätze* (Frankfurt a.M.: Insel-Verlag/Suhrkamp, 1977), 71–106.

32 The illustrations are partly from the original German publication and partly added by André Gunthert, the translator and editor, and also include a reproduction of three pages of the *Literarische Welt* with Benjamin's essay. See Walter Benjamin, 'Petite histoire de la photographie', trans. André Gunthert, *Études photographiques*, 1 (1996), 7–38.

33 See Camille Recht, *Die Alte Photographie* (Paris and Leipzig: Henri Jonquières, 1931), 119.

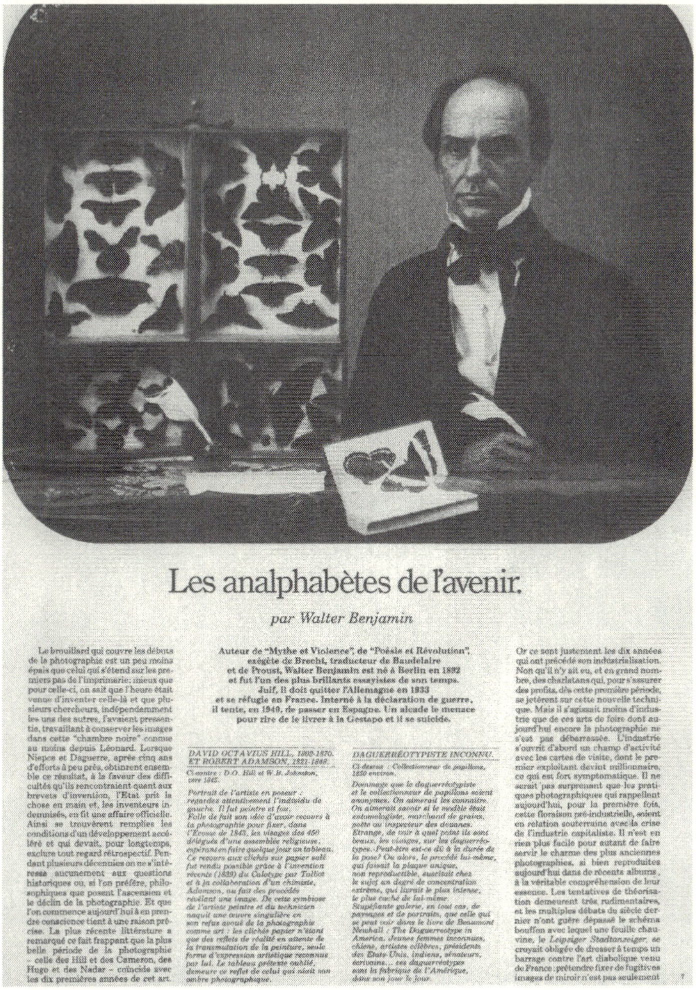

Les analphabètes de l'avenir.

par Walter Benjamin

Auteur de "Mythe et Violence", de "Poésie et Révolution", exégète de Brecht, traducteur de Baudelaire et de Proust, Walter Benjamin est né à Berlin en 1892 et fut l'un des plus brillants essayistes de son temps. Juif, il doit quitter l'Allemagne en 1933 et se réfugie en France. Interné à la déclaration de guerre, il tente, en 1940, de passer en Espagne. Un alcade le menace pour rire de le livrer à la Gestapo et il se suicide.

Le brouillard qui couvre les débuts de la photographie est un peu moins épais que celui qui s'étend sur les premiers pas de l'imprimerie; mieux que pour celle-ci, on sait que l'heure était venue d'inventer celle-là et que plusieurs chercheurs, indépendemment les uns des autres, l'avaient pressentie, travaillant à conserver les images dans cette "chambre noire" connue au moins depuis Léonard. Lorsque Niepce et Daguerre, après cinq ans d'efforts à peu près, obtinrent ensemble ce résultat, à la faveur des difficultés qu'ils rencontraient quant aux brevets d'invention, l'Etat prit la chose en main et, les inventeurs indemnisés, en fit une affaire officielle. Ainsi se trouvèrent remplies les conditions d'un développement accéléré et qui devait, pour longtemps, exclure tout regard rétrospectif. Pendant plusieurs décennies on ne s'intéressa aucunement aux questions historiques ou, si l'on préfère, philosophiques que posent l'ascension et le déclin de la photographie. Et que l'on commence aujourd'hui à en prendre conscience tient à une raison précise. La plus récente littérature a remarqué ce fait frappant que la plus belle période de la photographie – celle des Hill et des Cameron, des Hugo et des Nadar – coïncide avec les dix premières années de cet art.

DAVID OCTAVIUS HILL, 1802-1870, ET ROBERT ADAMSON, 1821-1848.

Ci-contre : D.O. Hill et W.B. Johnston, vers 1845.

Portrait de l'artiste en poseur : regardez attentivement l'individu de gauche. Il fut peintre et fou. Folie de fait son idée d'avoir recours à la photographie pour fixer, dans l'Ecosse de 1843, les visages des 450 délégués d'une assemblée religieuse, espérant en faire quelque jour un tableau. Ce recours aux clichés sur papier salé fut rendu possible grâce à l'invention récente (1839) du Calotype par Talbot et à la collaboration d'un chimiste, Adamson, au fait des procédés révélant une image. De cette symbiose de l'artiste peintre et du technicien naquit une œuvre singulière en son refus avoué de la photographie comme art : les clichés papier n'étant que des reflets de réalité en attente de la transmutation de la peinture, seule forme d'expression artistique reconnue par lui. Le tableau prétexte oublié, demeure ce reflet de celui qui niait son ombre photographique.

DAGUERRÉOTYPISTE INCONNU.

Ci-dessus : Collectionneur de papillons, 1850 environ.

Dommage que le daguerréotypiste et le collectionneur de papillons soient anonymes. On aimerait les connaître. On aimerait savoir si le modèle était entomologiste, marchand de graines, poète ou inspecteur des douanes. Etrange, de voir à quel point ils sont beaux, les visages, sur les daguerréotypes. Peut-être est-ce dû à la durée de la pose? Ou alors, le procédé lui-même, qui faisait la plaque unique, non reproductible, suscitait chez le sujet un degré de concentration extrême, qui livrait le plus intense, le plus caché de lui-même. Stupéfiante galerie, en tout cas, de paysages et de portraits, que celle qui se peut voir dans le livre de Beaumont Newhall : The Daguerreotype in America. Jeunes femmes inconnues, chiens, artistes célèbres, présidents des Etats-Unis, indiens, sénateurs, écrivains... ces daguerréotypes sont la fabrique de l'Amérique, dans son jour le jour.

Or ce sont justement les dix années qui ont précédé son industrialisation. Non qu'il n'y ait eu, et en grand nombre, des charlatans qui, pour s'assurer des profits, dès cette première période, se jetèrent sur cette nouvelle technique. Mais il s'agissait moins d'industrie que de ces arts de foire dont aujourd'hui encore la photographie ne s'est pas débarrassée. L'industrie s'ouvrit d'abord un champ d'activité avec les cartes de visite, dont le premier exploitant devint millionnaire, ce qui est fort symptomatique. Il ne serait pas surprenant que les pratiques photographiques qui rappellent aujourd'hui, pour la première fois, cette floraison pré-industrielle, soient en relation souterraine avec la crise de l'industrie capitaliste. Il n'est en rien plus facile pour autant de faire servir le charme des plus anciennes photographies, si bien reproduites aujourd'hui dans de récents albums, à la véritable compréhension de leur essence. Les tentatives de théorisation demeurent très rudimentaires, et les multiples débats du siècle dernier n'ont guère dépassé le schéma bouffon avec lequel une feuille chauvine, le *Leipziger Stadtanzeiger*, se croyait obligée de dresser à temps un barrage contre l'art diabolique venu de France : prétendre fixer de fugitives images de miroir n'est pas seulement

Plate 1 First page of the French translation of Benjamin's 'Kleine Geschichte der Photographie' in the *Nouvel Observateur*.

late 1979, Barthes admits that in choosing illustrations he limited himself almost exclusively to the *Nouvel Observateur* (see OC, V, 936). Among these images there is a portrait of the Lincoln assassination conspirator Lewis Payne by Alexander Gardner. This image takes centre stage in Barthes's arguments concerning the potential poignancy of portraiture, a poignancy that derives from the temporal nature of photography itself (see Chapter Four).

The Gardner portrait occupies a prominent position in Benjamin's text in the *Nouvel Observateur*. As we can see, it is juxtaposed with George

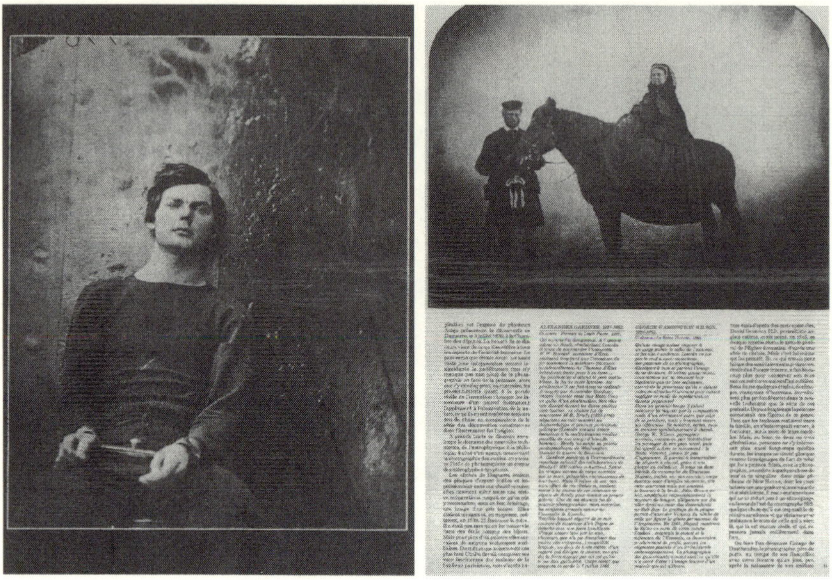

PLATE 2 Double page of the *Nouvel Observateur*: Alexander Gardner, Lewis Payne, 1865, and George Washington Wilson, Queen Victoria, 1863.

Washington Wilson's photograph of Queen Victoria.[34] And this image is also reproduced in Barthes's book. Other photographic images found in both texts of Benjamin and Barthes are the Nadar portrait of Savorgnan de Brazza, posing together with two young black men in sailor suits, the James van der Zee family portrait of an African-American family, the portrait of William Casby by Richard Avedon, and the Lewis Hine photograph of two disabled children in New Jersey. I shall discuss some of these images later (see Chapter Six); their importance for the moment lies in highlighting that Barthes was clearly engaging with Benjamin's 'Kleiner Geschichte der Photographie' while writing *La Chambre claire*. Although Barthes does not quote the essay in his text or refer to it in his bibliography, it can be argued that the playful and knowing nature of Barthes's visual references constitutes an imagistic citation of Benjamin, as opposed to a conventional textual one. Thus, in the context of what he, as well as Benjamin and Sontag, all consider to be the medium of the 'trace',

34 Helmuth Bossert and Heinrich Guttmann's book on early photography, which served Benjamin as another invaluable source for his essay, includes a very similar image of Queen Victoria (*Aus der Frühzeit der Photographie, 1840–70. Ein Bildbuch nach 200 Originalen* (Frankfurt a.M.: Societäts-Verlag, 1930), fig. 172).

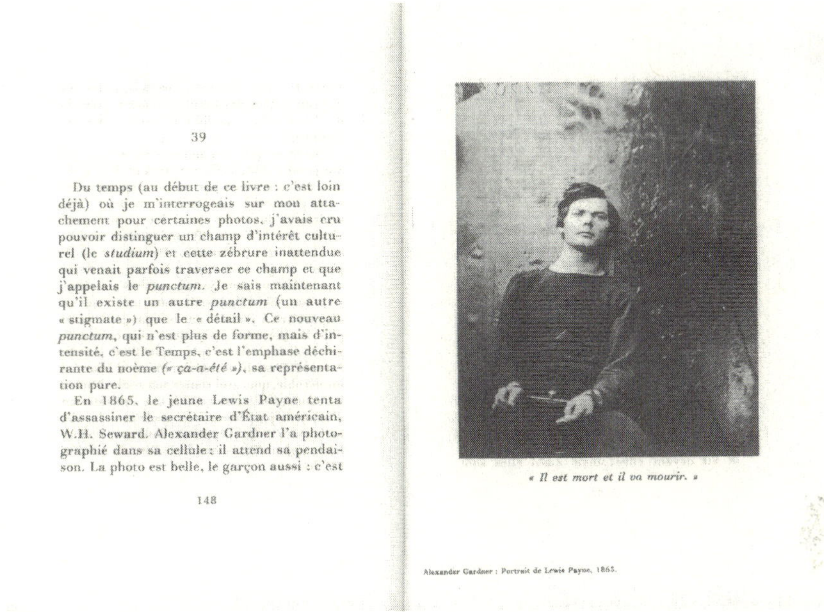

39

Du temps (au début de ce livre : c'est loin déjà) où je m'interrogeais sur mon attachement pour certaines photos, j'avais cru pouvoir distinguer un champ d'intérêt culturel (le *studium*) et cette zébrure inattendue qui venait parfois traverser ce champ et que j'appelais le *punctum*. Je sais maintenant qu'il existe un autre *punctum* (un autre « stigmate ») que le « détail ». Ce nouveau *punctum*, qui n'est plus de forme, mais d'intensité, c'est le Temps, c'est l'emphase déchirante du noème *(« ça-a-été »)*, sa représentation pure.

En 1865, le jeune Lewis Payne tenta d'assassiner le secrétaire d'État américain, W.H. Seward. Alexander Gardner l'a photographié dans sa cellule : il attend sa pendaison. La photo est belle, le garçon aussi : c'est

148

« Il est mort et il va mourir. »

Alexander Gardner : Portrait de Lewis Payne, 1865.

PLATE 3 Double page of *La Chambre claire*: Alexander Gardner, Lewis Payne, 1865.

i.e. photography, Barthes leaves traces of his reception of Benjamin for others to recognize.[35] Although these inter-visual, as opposed to inter-textual, relations between the works of Benjamin and Barthes may be an instance of Barthes's practice of drawing on his 'cultural memory', rather than engaging in bibliographical research and using conventional citations, they also have significant implications for the inter-textual relations between the two authors, which are a key concern of this book.

The only substantial omission from Benjamin's 'Kleine Geschichte der Photographie' in the version published in the *Nouvel Observateur* is his discussion of Eugène Atget, a photographer who played a pivotal role in Benjamin's understanding of the development of photographic history and of visual culture. The subsequent special issue of the *Nouvel Observateur*, however, provides some of the missing argument in the form of an article by Jean-François Chevrier and Jean Thibaudeau,

35 These ideas are developed in more detail in relation to Benjamin's concept of history, in my 'Die Photographien "zu ihrem Rechte kommen lassen". Zu Roland Barthes' Rezeption von Benjamins "Kleiner Geschichte der Photographie"', in Daniel Weidner and Sigrid Weigel (eds.), *Benjamin-Studien 2* (Munich: Fink, 2011), 15–32: 23–4.

in which Benjamin is referred to in a prominent fashion.[36] Barthes lists this article by Chevrier and Thibaudeau in the bibliography of *La Chambre claire*. Two other bibliographical references in Barthes's book deserve particular attention in this Benjaminian context: Gisèle Freund's historical study on nineteenth-century French photography titled *Photographie et société* [*Photography and Society*] and Susan Sontag's well-known essay collection *On Photography*.

Benjamin met the German-born photographer Freund in 1932.[37] Like him, Freund was an exile in Paris, and it is to her that we owe some of the best-known portraits of Benjamin; Freund also wrote compellingly about the medium. By virtue of the friendship between them, and the fact that each had a good knowledge of the other's work, their views on photography evidence a complex symbiosis. In a 1939 review, Benjamin praised Freund's doctoral thesis on *La Photographie en France au XIX*e *siècle* [*Photography in Nineteenth-Century France*]. He had known the work even before its publication in 1937 and indeed refers to it at various points in his essays and correspondence. Benjamin's own reflections on photography during the mid-1930s were published after Freund's doctoral dissertation but prior to *Photographie et société*. Based on her dissertation, this book appeared only in 1974, long after Benjamin's published essays on photography. Since some of his arguments were no doubt inspired by Freund's doctoral study, her quotations from Benjamin's essays on photography and the reproducibility of artworks in *Photographie et société* refer to some extent back to her own work. Given this network of quotation it is at times hard to determine exactly who borrowed from whom. It is, however, fair to say that for these reasons Barthes's later reading of Freund's book on photography was, at least to some extent – and unavoidably – also a reading of Benjamin's.

Barthes acknowledges Sontag's *On Photography* from 1977 as source material for *La Chambre claire*, and it would not have escaped him that the last chapter of Sontag's collection, which assembles diverse quotations on photography, including some by Benjamin, is subtitled 'Homage to W.B.'.[38]

---

36 See Jean-François Chevrier and Jean Thibaudeau, 'Une inquiétante étrangeté', *Le Nouvel Observateur*, *Spécial Photo*, 3 (1978), 5–14: 8; 13.

37 The correspondence between the two testifies to their friendship, which lasted until Benjamin's early death. For a selected publication and commentary of some letters, see Nathalie Raoux, 'Walter Benjamin, Gisèle Freund, Germaine Krull et Hélène Léger. Deutschland-Frankreich; Mann-Weib. Eine Folge von Briefen', *Revue Germanique Internationale*, 5 (1996), 223–53.

38 Susan Sontag, *On Photography* (New York: Dell Publishing, 1977), 181 (the title is included in the French translation as well). Beryl Schlossman has

Barthes's acknowledgement of *On Photography* is the most direct indication of the conceptual tradition within which he situates his own reflections on the medium, namely that of ontological realism with respect to the photographic image and its psychological effects, as defined by the axiomatic notion of the photograph as bearer of a physical trace of the real. Thus Sontag, who was prominent among Barthes's American acquaintances,[39] constitutes another important link between Benjamin and Barthes. However, in a 1977 interview, Barthes suggested that he encountered Benjamin independently of Sontag's essay collection.[40] This reflects the then already established prominence of Benjamin's writings in photography theory: at the time when Barthes returned to photography in a post-semiotic context in the 1970s, Benjamin's views on the aura of nineteenth-century photography and his theses on the photographic reproducibility of artworks had already entered critical discourse on the medium.[41] Accordingly, commenting on Benjamin in the 1977 interview, Barthes echoed the editors of the *Nouvel Observateur*, asserting that Benjamin's text is an important reference point in any serious discussion of photography: 'Il y a peu de grands textes de qualité intellectuelle sur la photographie. J'en connais peu. Il y a le texte de W. Benjamin, qui est bon parce qu'il est prémonitoire' (OC, V, 932) ['There are only a few great texts of intellectual quality on photography. I don't know of very many. There is W. Benjamin's text, which is good because it is premonitory' (GV, 354)]. Although he does not elaborate on the exact ways in which Benjamin's essay on photography is 'prémonitoire', this is Barthes's most direct and emphatic admission of his knowledge of the 'Kleine Geschichte der Photographie'.[42]

In sum, there can be no doubt that Barthes's theories of photography were developed with at least some knowledge of Benjamin's work. The fact

---

commented on this link between Benjamin and Barthes, in 'Looking Back: Luminous Shadows and the Auras of History', *Nottingham French Studies*, 36 (1997), 76–87: 81.

39 See Sontag's commemorative essay from 1980, 'Remembering Barthes', in *Under the Sign of Saturn* (New York: Picador, 2002), 167–77.

40 Indeed, the French translation of *On Photography* was published in 1979, after the interview took place.

41 For instance, in Pierre Bourdieu's study on the social uses of photography from 1965, which Barthes knew, Benjamin is mentioned a number of times (*Un Art moyen. Essai sur les usages sociaux de la photographie* (Paris: Éditions de Minuit, 1965), 111; 178; 230).

42 Jacqueline Guittard has speculated how Benjamin's text might have been premonitory for Barthes ('Jardin d'hiver: formation d'une relique', *Revue des Sciences Humaines*, 278 (2005), 147–61: 160–1).

that a direct reception took place complements our understanding of the inter-textual nature of the existing affinities between their views as well as making the important differences between them more telling and acute. Barthes's references to Benjamin are, however, confined to lectures, seminars and interviews and are hence scattered and unsystematic, suggesting that Barthes's knowledge of Benjamin was clearly limited in both scope and depth, not least because he did not read German. Moreover, the wider reception of Benjamin's works in France began only after Barthes's death in 1980, and is commonly linked to the important conference *Walter Benjamin et Paris* in 1983 and the translation of his *Passagen-Werk* in 1986.[43]

However, the question of why Barthes appeared so reluctant to acknowledge the influence of Benjamin's work on his own remains complex and largely unanswered. This reminds us that scholarly influence, like artistic influence, entails psychological dynamics that are beyond the grasp of any intellectual and cultural historian.[44] In the case of Benjamin and Barthes, the relative absence of consistent academic reference by the latter to the former has not only led to intriguing speculation[45] but is also a likely reason for the predominantly inter-textual approach taken by most comparative studies of Benjamin and Barthes, which largely gloss the issue of conscious influence and intentionality. This focus on the texts rather than authorial knowledge, intention and biography is particularly appropriate, of course, given Barthes's own insistence on the open-ended, allusive and elusive nature of textual interpretation and the emphasis he places on the non-linear and non-chronological nature of artistic and philosophical influence. While the present study both affirms and further pursues this inter-textual approach to the works of Benjamin and Barthes concerning photography, it does not deny the importance of influence, reception and

43 See Heinz Wismann (ed.), *Walter Benjamin et Paris* (Paris: Cerf, 1986). There is also a chronological list of French translations of Benjamin's work (987–92).

44 Cf. Detlev Schöttker's reflections on Benjamin's reception of Wittgenstein, in 'Benjamin liest Wittgenstein. Zur sprachphilosophischen Vorgeschichte des Positivismusstreits', in Daniel Weidner and Sigrid Weigel (eds.), *Benjamin-Studien 1* (Munich: Fink, 2008), 91–105: 105.

45 In 1983, at the Parisian conference on Benjamin, Philippe Ivernel drew attention to the absence of references to Benjamin in Barthes's work and his writing on photography in particular, thereby introducing what would become a perennial issue of debate in comparative scholarship on Benjamin and Barthes ('Paris capital du Front populaire ou la vie posthume du XIXe siècle', in Heinz Wismann (ed.), *Walter Benjamin et Paris* (Paris: Cerf, 1986), 249–72: 255).

biography. As previously noted, given the profoundly autobiographical dimension of their writing on photography, not to do so threatens to cut off the living sources of their theoretical concepts and their roots and prevents a more nuanced understanding of them. Equally, Benjamin's and Barthes's writings on photography cannot be viewed in isolation from larger historical, technological, cultural and critical-theoretical developments as we will trace first with respect to Benjamin.

Part I

The Birth of the Viewer

Written in 1931, Walter Benjamin's 'Kleine Geschichte der Photographie' recasts the discourse of photography's history in a socio-cultural light and also looks forward to future uses of the medium. It is often credited with being among the most influential works of photographic theory,[1] having provided some of its most familiar concepts, including the 'optical unconscious' and 'aura'. The 'Kleine Geschichte der Photographie' is also the first major text to situate the history of photography in relation to the viewing subject. As Benjamin notes in the text, in the early twentieth century, critical and philosophical debates about photography have moved on from aesthetic and technical questions towards the social function of the medium and the actual reception of photographic images in different social and historical contexts (see GS, II, 381). Yet for Benjamin, the viewer is not just a generalized socio-historical subject but an individual who relates to photographs in deeply personal ways through the lens of his or her life experience. This is notably foregrounded in Benjamin's consideration of his family album photographs and a childhood portrait of Kafka he owned as well as the works of acclaimed early photographers. Thus, for Benjamin the formation and formulation of a socio-historical subject for photography coexists with the emergence of a psychological and existential one.

The Benjaminian corpus on photography as a whole, however, is characterized by a pronounced shift from attention to specific photographic images to an examination of the medium's socio-cultural

1 See, for instance, Bernd Stiegler, *Theoriegeschichte der Photographie* (Munich: Fink, 2006), 11. It is noteworthy that there are documents that, as Detlev Schöttker has recently shown, indicate that Benjamin was planning to write another essay on photography in 1934, the early plan of which he discussed with Peter Suhrkamp ('Dolf Sternberger und Walter Benjamin. Ein Photographie-Aufsatz und seine Folgen', *Sinn und Form*, 62 (2010), 437–53). For a comprehensive overview of Benjamin's work on photography, see Nitsche, *Benjamins Gebrauch der Fotografie*.

and psychological reality. This shift needs to be understood against the background of both the changing nature of photography and the larger historical developments in close dialogue with which Benjamin's thought evolved. Pre-twentieth-century photography lends itself to being appreciated as the story of pioneering individual craftsmen and artists testing the potential and limitations of a new representational medium. Benjamin's historical writing in the late 1920s and early 1930s (concerned with mid-to-late nineteenth-century photography) conforms to this tendency in that he reflects on individual bodies of work and specific images and on the contemporary viewer's concrete responses to them. Later, during the mid-to-late 1930s, against the backdrop of social and political upheavals, including the rise of the Soviet Union and the emergence of Nazism, Benjamin became gradually more concerned with the contemporary, ideological and political role of photographic technology as a means of power, control and critique.

This conceptual trajectory in turn reflects Benjamin's view of the history of photography as an expanding cultural practice and a means of communication. As technology changed and photography moved from being the preserve of a few scientifically or artistically minded enthusiasts to a mass medium, it became imperative that the role of the photography critic changed as well. The critic's focus shifted from historical, aesthetic and personal appreciation of past images as realities in themselves to grappling with the fundamental nature of the medium from the present standpoint to better identify its potential ideological uses, whether progressive, as a means of mass liberation, or reactionary, as a means of mass control and exploitation. As a corollary, Benjamin came to believe that the study or criticism of photography could no longer be narrowly confined to its internal history or the nature of the medium: it must now situate photography dialectically in relation to larger psychological, social and economic transformations characterizing modern, post-industrial society.

The theme of the singularity of photography in Benjamin's œuvre emerges primarily in relation to his writing on individual images, especially the Franz Kafka portrait. Yet this must be understood in the context of his wider arguments on photography, which this singular photograph at times affirms and at other times opposes. Such a contextual approach is particularly important due to the fact that even where Benjamin is concerned with photography in its most general manifestations, as a medium of technical reproduction with profound implications for modernity, his arguments are interspersed with observations that cannot conceal the more personal nature of his engagement with photographic images and the insights it provides. Indeed, a comparison of Benjamin's notable reworkings of his autobiographical texts, most notably the *Berliner Kindheit um Neunzehnhundert* [*Berlin Childhood Around 1900*], with the 'Kleine Geschichte der Photographie' and the essay on the 'Kunstwerk' reveals how much this personal experience informed his more objective, critical analysis of the medium, and also indicates an ambivalence as to the extent to which this should be explicitly acknowledged.

Therefore, the dynamic discord within Benjamin's œuvre between a consideration of photography in general socio-historical terms, on the one hand, and the autobiographical and anecdotal writing on the unique childhood photograph of Kafka, on the other, must be examined within the wider context of photographic history and theory. When the multilayered and complex positions adopted by Benjamin with respect to photography are evaluated from a critical-philosophical and historical perspective, it becomes clear how and to what extent the overriding theme of singularity is a result of Benjamin's interpretation of traditional photographic topoi, including referentiality and temporality, combined with his innovative foregrounding of the particularly subjective and affective experiences of photographic images.

With these considerations in mind, the first chapter of the first part of this study, devoted exclusively to Benjamin, begins by mapping his thought on photography from the late 1920s up until the mid-1930s. It pays particular attention to the simultaneous looking forwards and backwards that mark his arguments during this period. On the one hand, he is concerned with the contemporary artistic use of the medium in the context of the European avant-garde and also with its future, potentially political and even revolutionary, function, as tied to his interpretation of Eugène Atget and the documentary nature of his photographs. However, Benjamin looks back at nineteenth-century photography and thematizes the response of the viewer in relation to the portrait photograph's specific demand on the beholder, singling out celebrated portrait photographs by David Octavius Hill/Robert Adamson and Karl Dauthendey in particular. As will be shown, it is what is born from the conflict between attempted objective, historical classifications of photography and sensitivity to the concrete experience of specific images that gives Benjamin's insights their greatest value. This is most evident with regard to his well-known concept of aura, which is simultaneously presented as a historical phenomenon belonging to a particular period of photographic history (the nineteenth century) and a trans-historical one pertaining to a specific experience on the part of the beholder.

Following on from a discussion of the special status of family photographs in Benjamin's writings, Chapter Two will focus more closely on Benjamin's engagement with the winter-garden portrait of Kafka, highlighting the frictional coexistence of his cultural and historical arguments with autobiographical anecdote. Against the background of traditional themes and subjects in photographic theory, such as melancholy, death and magic, Benjamin's preoccupation with the Kafka portrait is shown to be charged with a poignancy rooted in the unique encounter between viewer, photograph and sitter. Intricately linked to his identification with Kafka as a child, Benjamin's superimposition of his own memories and other photographic self-portraits onto the Kafka portrait can be seen as an expression of a singular encounter with the photographic alter ego reconstructed in essayistic form.

Chapter Three will focus on how photography relates to Benjamin's theory of modernity, centred on fundamental changes that human experience and memory undergo as a result of the Industrial Revolution and its aftermath in modern urban life. Bearing out the aforementioned tension between the general and the particular, the collective and the personal, Benjamin's negative assessment of photography as having a detrimental effect on authentic experience and memory will be shown to coexist with a network of references and allusions to a positive, time-defying Proustian memory, which the photograph may allow for (as again centred on the Kafka portrait). Finally, turning to the related theme of photography and redemption, the notable ethical implications of Benjamin's engagement with photography will be considered, as this is rooted in the viewer's encounter with a singular photograph and a way of writing about it, one that extends the photographic encounter with the other in the form of a narrative response to that other.

Chapter 1

Benjamin's History of Photography

Until the late 1920s, when Benjamin brought the photographic image into his wider philosophical and socio-cultural investigations, the theoretical and historical discourses surrounding photography were predominantly preoccupied with the question of whether it was, or could be, a genuine art form. Borrowing heavily from nineteenth-century art history and aesthetics centred on painting, critical writing on photography was mainly concerned with establishing normative justifications either for the medium's artistic significance or, alternatively, its relative insignificance. The for/against positions adopted by Antoine Wiertz and Charles Baudelaire – two writers whom Benjamin juxtaposes in his 'Kleine Geschichte der Photographie' – encapsulate this pronounced divide between advocates of photography as art or non-art. This debate is inseparable from the ways in which the practical and aesthetic uses of photography in the nineteenth century overlapped with, or supplanted, those of painting. For example, photographic portraiture had eclipsed the painted miniature portrait in many contexts by the early 1860s. Similarly, the rise of self-conscious aesthetic movements in photography, principally Pictorialism, which imitated painterly forms and styles, shaped the practice and perception of photography as art from the 1880s onwards. With the decline of Pictorialism and the birth of the European avant-gardes at the beginning of the last century, the terms of the debate changed fundamentally. New ways of using and conceiving photography as an artform emerged, departing from the visual language of painting and fully embracing the technological and scientific dimensions of the medium that had hitherto been seen as detrimental to artistic creativity and imagination owing to the 'impersonal' optical, chemical and mechanical generation of photographic images.

In this context of the pan-European avant-garde movements, photography gained an autonomous artistic status for the first time, where (together with cinema) it was seen as the ideal vehicle for celebrating the power and possibilities of industrialized and mechanized ways of life, which were also being explored in painting and sculpture as part of a new, quintessentially modern aesthetic. In Weimar Germany, theoretical debate about photography developed in response to the practices and theories of New Objectivity (*Neue Sachlichkeit*), together with Constructivism and Surrealism. It took place first in journals and newspapers, such as *Die Form*, *Bauhaus*, *Das neue Frankfurt* and the annual anthology of modern photography *Das Deutsche Lichtbild*.[1] The avant-garde formalism clearly influenced Benjamin's conception of photography in certain respects, but his socio-historical orientation also clearly diverges from it. Moreover, these two poles are reflected in the work of the two writers who exercised the greatest influence on Benjamin with respect to photography: Moholy-Nagy and Kracauer. Within German avant-garde circles, the Hungarian-born photographer, theorist and Bauhaus teacher Moholy-Nagy championed the new artistic calling of photography. He wholly embraced its technology and predicted that, if used creatively, the optics of the camera eye would fundamentally change human perception. Rejecting this utopian vision, and much less concerned with artistic form than with the social impact of photography as a mass medium, Kracauer worried about the alienating effects of this new representational technology.

Given these wider shifts and reorientations of photographic theory and practice in the early twentieth century, and Benjamin's interest in Dadaism and Surrealism in particular, it is not surprising that the earliest written document on photography in his critical output is devoted to the most accomplished surrealist photographer, Man Ray. Dating from 1924, this is a German translation of Tristan Tzara's 'Man Ray, la photographie à l'envers' (1922), a short essay on Man Ray's cameraless photographs (photograms or Rayographs, as he called them), which served as the preface to *Les Champs délicieux* [*The Delightful Fields*], a high-quality artistic publication of Man Ray's early work. Benjamin's translation, 'Die Photographie von der Kehrseite' ['Photography Backwards'] (GSS, I, 8–19), was published in the Dadaist *Zeitschrift für elementare Gestaltung*, the organ of the so-called G-group of artists led by Hans Richter, which counted Moholy-Nagy as one of its members. This group was a major catalyst for Benjamin's interest in the German avant-garde. Even if his translation of Tzara's essay does not provide us with explicit insight into Benjamin's views of the medium at this point in time, its existence, together with where it appeared, nonetheless indicates the larger cultural and artistic context within which Benjamin encountered art photography. Indeed, the extent to which critical and highbrow journalistic discourse on photography was fed by the intellectual euphoria surrounding the medium in the

1 See Herbert Molderings, *Die Moderne der Fotografie* (Hamburg: Philo Fine Arts, 2008), 156.

1920s is reflected in a letter that Benjamin wrote in 1927 to Grete and Alfred Cohn, in which he describes how photography is now a 'hot topic' in intellectual circles, being the subject of articles that filled the pages of respected newspapers, including, for example, the *Frankfurter Allgemeine* (GB, III, 291). In the same letter, Benjamin proudly announces the forthcoming publication of his friend Kracauer's article on photography, simply titled 'Die Photographie' ['Photography']. As we shall see, Benjamin would develop a number of Kracauer's ideas in an original way.

In 1928, some four years after the translation, Benjamin turned to photography anew, in his review of a book by the German photographer Karl Bloßfeldt titled *Urformen der Kunst, Photographische Pflanzenbilder* [*Art Forms in Nature, Examples from the Plant World Photographed Direct from Nature*]. This book publication is an important early example of the rapidly expanding genre of monographs on photography in Weimar Germany aided by its rapidly growing publishing industry,[2] and Benjamin's review highlights the public interest in such art-photography material. In contrast to the Tzara translation, the format of this review left Benjamin more space to begin to develop his ideas about photography and to introduce issues that he expands upon in his 'Kleine Geschichte der Photographie'. In his concise discussion of Bloßfeldt's extreme close-up photographs of sections of plants, depicted in a formal language that can be linked to the aesthetic ideals of New Objectivity, with its interest in abstract and constructed imagery, Benjamin analyses the uniquely photographic features of these images. He draws attention to magnification and other optical techniques that provide them with a formal and aesthetic appeal as powerful as their scientific value. The unusual perspectives of Bloßfeldt's photographs open up, in Benjamin's words, a 'Geysir neuer Bilderwelten' (GS, III, 152) ['geyser of new image-worlds' (SW, II, 156)], implying a new aesthetic rooted in innovative mechanistic and optical developments. Benjamin's later concern with the intersection between the historical emergence of the photographic medium and the 'camera eye', and concomitant changes in perceptual and aesthetic sensibility, is thus here contained in nuce. While the review significantly anticipates the dialectical criticism of Benjamin's later writings (of the mid-to-late 1930s), it is his 1931 essay on the history of photography that proved his most innovative and important contribution to photographic theory.

---

2 Ibid., 191–2.

Historical Classifications and New Photographic Vision

Like the Bloßfeldt review, Benjamin's 'Kleine Geschichte der Photographie' is a direct response to the publication of new anthologies and monographs devoted to the work of specific photographers. Prominent among these were two richly illustrated books on mid-to-late nineteenth-century photography (from 1930 and 1931, respectively), *Aus der Frühzeit der Photographie, 1840–70* [*The Beginnings of Photography, 1840–70*], annotated by Helmuth Bossert and Heinrich Guttmann, and *Die Alte Photographie* [*Old Photography*] by Camille Recht. Benjamin heavily draws on a monograph also from 1931 by Heinrich Schwarz on *David Octavius Hill, Der Meister der Photographie* [*David Octavius Hill, Master of Photography*] and three other publications on the French and German photographers Eugène Atget, August Sander and, once more, Karl Bloßfeldt.[3] And, like the Bloßfeldt review, the 'Kleine Geschichte der Photographie' was published in the highly influential *Die Literarische Welt*.[4] Since its foundation in 1925, this literary journal had become a platform and rallying point for the most prominent intellectuals of Weimar Germany, including Thomas Mann, Alfred Döblin and Robert Musil. Accompanied by a total of eight illustrations, Benjamin's essay was serialized in three parts between 18 September and 2 October 1931, and in this format was itself part of the rapid expansion of photographic technology in print journalism and newspapers, a phenomenon that Benjamin discusses from a historical perspective.

As Herbert Molderings has pointed out, in 1931 there existed no socio-historical study of photography that could have served Benjamin as a model.[5] Although he does not apply a rigorous historical methodology

3 These publications are Camille Recht's *Eugène Atget, Lichtbilder* from 1930, August Sander's *Antlitz der Zeit* from 1929 and Bloßfeldt's *Urformen der Kunst* from 1928. Although the sources for the 'Kleine Geschichte der Photographie' are well known and have been highlighted by Krauss (*Benjamin und der neue Blick*, 14–20) and Berg (*Die Ikone des Realen*, 95), a study on the photographic illustrations and their potential influence on Benjamin's argument, and indeed, the extent to which Benjamin borrowed from these authors, is still lacking. Some suggestions can be found in André Gunthert, 'Archéologie de la "Petite histoire de la photographie"', *Images re-vues*, 2 (2010), paragraphs 5–7.

4 For an account of Benjamin's contributions to the *Literarische Welt*, see Momme Brodersen, *Spinne im eigenen Netz. Walter Benjamin: Leben und Werk* (Bühl-Moos: Elster Verlag, 1990), 174–7.

5 See Molderings, *Die Moderne der Fotografie*, 154. Gunthert makes a similar point, in 'Archéologie de la "Petite histoire de la photographie"', paragraphs 2–3.

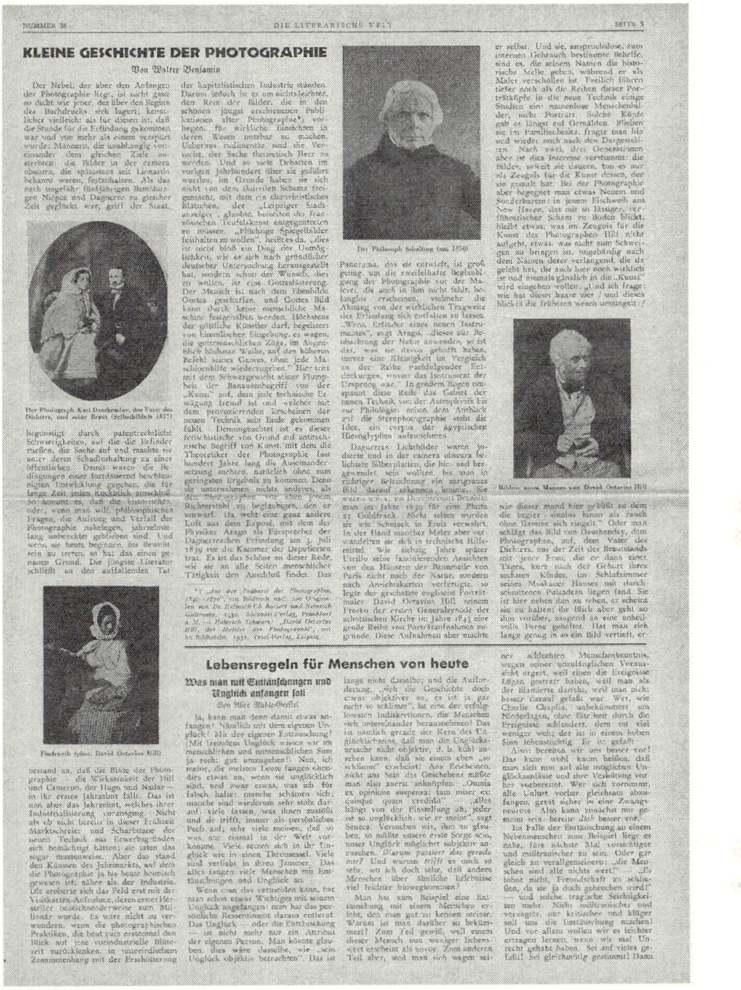

NUMMER 38 DIE LITERARISCHE WELT SEITE 3

KLEINE GESCHICHTE DER PHOTOGRAPHIE

Von Walter Benjamin

Lebensregeln für Menschen von heute

Was man mit Enttäuschungen und Unglück anfangen soll

PLATE 4 First page of Benjamin's 'Kleine Geschichte der Photographie' in the *Literarische Welt*.

to photography, Benjamin divides the history of photography into three distinct periods, implicitly founded on the basis of their effects on the contemporary viewer: these are early or pre-industrial (i.e. nineteenth-century) photography, which is his primary concern, and modern, early twentieth-century imagery with the intermediary period of turn-of-the-century photography evidencing a pronounced transition amounting to a decline in the photograph's artistic qualities. This periodization of photographic history mirrors a stereotypical model of art-historical investigation, introduced in Germany in the mid-eighteenth century by the classicist Johann Joachim Winckelmann. According to this model, an art form's maturity is followed by a decadent period of decline which is, in turn, followed by a revival and so on. Benjamin clearly follows this traditional model, which had been applied to photography by a number of authors whom he draws on, including Recht and Emil Orlik as well as Schwarz, Bossert and Guttmann, who emphasize the high artistic quality of early photography and suggest its subsequent decline.[6]

Yet despite the historical distinction between mid-nineteenth-century, turn-of-the-century and contemporary photographs, Benjamin's evaluative arguments do not always strictly correspond to this chronological classification.[7] It is clear that, although his 'Kleine Geschichte der Photographie' has become one of the canonical texts of photographic history and theory, as noted, its status as such is owing to its conceptual and socio-cultural insights, rather than its historical categorizations.

One such insight is that of the 'optical unconscious', which Benjamin forwards in relation to Bloßfeldt's photographs. Expanding on ideas introduced in his earlier review, Benjamin regards Bloßfeldt's alien, defamiliarizing close-ups as part of a larger development within the history of photography marked by a more radical experimentation with forms and devices that have no analogue in other representational media. His assessment is here in line with the avant-garde ideal of photography as presenting what cannot be seen with the naked human eye, or, depicted in the traditional visual arts. In emphasizing the camera's unique optical capabilities, Benjamin evokes not only Bloßfeldt's microscopic images but also, implicitly and without mentioning his name, Eadweard Muybridge's 'instantaneous photography'.[8] In the

---

6 See Iwan Goll's preface in Recht, *Die Alte Photographie*, 13; Emil Orlik, 'Über Photographie', in *Kleine Aufsätze* (Berlin: Propyläen-Verlag, 1924), 32–42: 37; Heinrich Schwarz, *David Octavius Hill. Der Meister der Photographie* (Leipzig: Insel-Verlag, 1931), 45–9; and Bossert and Guttmann, *Aus der Frühzeit der Photographie* (no pagination).

7 Although Bossert and Guttmann acknowledge that a strict demarcation between the early periods of photographic history is difficult, they nonetheless suggest that there are developments corresponding to three generations of photographers (1839–42, 1842–55 and 1855–70), which for Benjamin are all part of the same generation (*Aus der Frühzeit der Photographie* (no pagination)).

8 At the same time, Benjamin's consideration of slow motion, an inherently filmic technique, in the context of the photo-camera, is an indication that

1870s, Muybridge succeeded in capturing images of movement in a profoundly new and 'realistic' way, challenging established painterly preconceptions of animals or humans in motion. Benjamin had read about Muybridge's pioneering motion studies in Orlik's essay on photography,[9] a work he quotes from elsewhere in the 'Kleine Geschichte der Photographie'.

For Benjamin, the photographic work of both Bloßfeldt and Muybridge served as a paradigmatic example of new ways of seeing. Through the camera eye, hitherto unseen dimensions of objects become visible for the first time, leading Benjamin to propose his famous analogy between photographic technology and psychoanalysis, both tools that systematically uncover previously hidden dimensions of human life: 'Von diesem Optisch-Unbewußten erfährt er [der Mensch] erst durch sie [die Photographie], wie von dem Triebhaft-Unbewußten durch die Psychoanalyse' (GS, II, 371) ['It is through photography that we first discover the existence of this optical unconscious, just as we discover the instinctual unconscious through psychoanalysis' (SW, II, 510–12)]. Just as psychoanalytical insights make it possible to speak about the unconscious in a systematic fashion, exploitation of the camera's technical and optical possibilities provides the beholder with a new visual vocabulary. Unlike Sigmund Freud, however, who argued (one year before the publication of the 'Kleine Geschichte der Photographie') that the photographic camera is a false technical organ of the human 'Prothesengott' ['prosthetic god'],[10] Benjamin does not regard the camera as replacing the human eye. Instead, as Sigrid Weigel has pointed out, Benjamin draws attention to what it provides for the eye, that is to say, a microscopic view of a reality that is otherwise imperceptible.[11]

Benjamin's concept of the optical unconscious is not without difficulties. Rosalind Krauss has argued that it raises the question as to whether

---

cinema is perhaps an implicit reference point for his writings on photography. Accordingly, the passage from his photography essay dealing with the 'optical unconscious' is quoted again in the later 'Kunstwerk' essay, this time in the context of film (see GS, I, 500).

9 See Orlik, 'Über Photographie', 35–6.

10 In his 1930 study 'Das Unbehagen in der Kultur', in Sigmund Freud, *Fragen der Gesellschaft/Ursprünge der Religion* (Studienausgabe, vol. 9) (Frankfurt a.M.: Fischer, 1975), 221–2.

11 See Sigrid Weigel, 'Das Detail in Benjamins Theorie photo- und kinematographischer Bilder. Zur Verschränkung von Kultur- und Mediengeschichte', in *Literatur als Voraussetzung der Kulturgeschichte: Schauplätze von Shakespeare bis Benjamin* (Munich: Fink, 2004), 39–62: 47–8.

the visual field can indeed possess an unconscious in any meaningful sense.[12] Nonetheless, for Benjamin, it provides a convenient shorthand for describing a new photographic vision, which is also promoted by Moholy-Nagy. The Bauhaus teacher and fine-art photographer held that through snapshots, infrared photography and radiography (to name but a few of his categories of new kinds of photographic vision), together with his own photograms and abstract and geometrical compositions taken from unusual angles and distances – all tools for rendering the 'optical unconscious' – the camera provides a 'new instrument of vision'.[13] Like Bloßfeldt's close-ups of flowers and plants, Moholy-Nagy's non-realist photographs of objects, presenting reality in a highly abstract way, make visible what Benjamin, in the 'Kleine Geschichte der Photographie', calls 'Bildwelten, welche im Kleinsten wohnen' (GS, II, 371) ['image worlds, which dwell in the tiniest details' (SW, II, 512)]. The abstract and formalistic image, Benjamin argues, reflects the technological and optical possibilities of the medium to a greater extent than the use of photography for conventional portraiture: 'Strukturbeschaffenheiten, Zellgewebe, mit denen Technik, Medizin zu rechnen pflegen – all dieses ist der Kamera ursprünglich verwandter als die stimmungsvolle Landschaft oder das seelenvolle Porträt' (GS, II, 371) ['Details of structure, cellular tissue, with which technology and medicine are normally concerned – all this is, in its origins, more innate to the camera than the atmospheric landscape or the soulful portrait' (SW, II, 512)]. Along with the introduction of this formalistic and technologically rooted concept of the optical unconscious, Benjamin's 'Kleine Geschichte der Photographie' also begins to lay the ground for his later impassioned defence of the photograph's potential positive political function. This

12 Rosalind E. Krauss, *The Optical Unconscious* (Cambridge, MA and London: MIT Press, 1993), 178–9. Although Krauss's title is based on Benjamin's coinage, she takes the concept in a more art-historical direction to challenge official histories of modernism. Marianne Hirsch has effectively applied the term to the specific genre of family photographs (*Family Frames: Photography, Narrative, and Postmemory* (Cambridge, MA and London: Harvard University Press, 1997), 113–50).

13 László Moholy-Nagy, 'A New Instrument of Vision', in Liz Wells (ed.), *The Photography Reader* (London and New York: Routledge, 2003), 92–5: 93–4. See also his famous book *Painting, Photography, Film*, trans. Janet Seligman (London: Lund Humphries, 1969). Tracing the influence of constructivist aesthetics on Benjamin's argument, Molderings contends that Benjamin's 'optical unconscious' is no more than a paraphrase of Moholy-Nagy's writings on these issues (*Die Moderne der Fotografie*, 160).

function is ultimately rooted in the photograph's capacity for authentic historical documentation as resistance to the over-sentimentalization of the past – of which conventional turn-of-the-century portraiture, with its clichéd and generic iconography, is seen as conspicuously guilty – as well as the excessive aesthetic stylization and distortion of the real found in some of the medium's pre-modern, self-consciously fine-art uses, including the Pictorialist's cultivation of expressive atmospheres in landscapes and portraits. Crucial, in this context, are the related ideas of document, evidence and justice.

The Photograph as Document

For the author of the 'Kleine Geschichte der Photographie', the work of one photographer in particular, which clearly avoids the two tendencies of sentimentalization and stylization, points the way to photography's role in ideological critique: Eugène Atget. Benjamin emphasizes the fact that in Atget's photographs, taken from the 1890s onwards, human beings do not appear.[14] This lack of human presence in Atget's images of Paris depicting cityscapes from which humanity is essentially exiled, as it is in Baudelaire's 'Le Cygne' ['The Swan'],[15] is seen by Benjamin as their main innovation and significance. In his chronicling of the inconspicuous and quotidian in photographs which capture dilapidated houses, deserted side alleys and shop window displays while studiously avoiding iconic Parisian landmarks, Atget is a clear precursor of Surrealism. For Benjamin, Atget's focus on recording the unremarked and forgotten, all that is easily overlooked, is what the surrealists would later associate with chance, coincidence and the *objet trouvé*.[16] Paradoxically, although Atget's depiction of the banal and seemingly insignificant gives his images a suggestive and mysterious power, in historical terms, their subject matter departed so radically from convention in this respect that they were seen to require textual accompaniment to be meaningful. Echoing Freund's labelling Atget the

---

14 For a comprehensive overview of Atget's multi-faceted work, which does include series in which human beings figure prominently, belying Benjamin's claim, see *Atget, une rétrospective* (exhibition catalogue) (Paris: Bibliothèque Nationale de France, 2007).

15 The poem is indeed the poetic equivalent of Atget's images as it also evokes the loss of a pre-Haussmann Paris. Benjamin translated this poem into German (see GS, IV, 27–9) and uses parts of it as an epigraph in both 'Exposés' of his *Passagen-Werk* (see GS, V, 54; 69).

16 André Breton's photo-novel *Nadja* from 1928 abounds in such encounters.

father of documentary photography, Benjamin also sees him as the major figure in archival or reality-based turn-of-the-century photography.[17]

The historical documentary function of the photograph, as based on its power to confirm and authenticate reality, rendered it a vital tool for criminal investigation and state control and surveillance, as Benjamin would later note (see GS, I, 550). In the conclusion of the 'Kleine Geschichte der Photographie', however, he sees a deeper ethical function highlighted by these practical applications.[18] In Benjamin's view, photography at the beginning of the twentieth century was inevitably bound to the issue of historical justice as paralleling the pursuit of criminal justice. Thus, he perceives an analogy between Atget's photographs and images depicting a crime scene or 'Tatort' in the sense that each provides the means to try and reconstruct the truth of a past reality (GS, II, 385). Yet crucially, for the photograph to actually serve this veridical function it must always be coupled with an investigative hypothesis in the form of discursive commentary surrounding the image as rooted in deductive reasoning.[19] In other words, the photograph must be compelled to 'say' as well as to 'show', and only language can help it do this. This is also imperative in any political use of the medium, in which the photograph must speak unequivocally as images seldom do. Thus, it is in anticipation of the programmatic use of photography to persuade and convince that Benjamin draws attention to the necessity of explanatory commentary, including captioning, at the very end of the essay on photography, in the rhetorical question: 'Wird die Beschriftung nicht zum wesentlichsten Bestandteil der Aufnahme werden?' (ibid.) ['Won't inscription become the most important part of the photograph?' (SW, II, 527)].

Given the course of subsequent photographic theory, this premonitory note anticipates the anti-essentialist view of John Tagg and others that the meaning of any photograph is always determined by discourses surrounding it. In Tagg's post-Foucauldian approach, social institutions are regarded as the main generators of a photograph's perceived messages,

17 See Gisèle Freund, *Photographie et société* (Paris: Seuil, 1974), 88.

18 During the 1920s and 1930s, the first-generation members of the North American documentary photography movements, including Jacob Riis and Lewis Hine, were similarly occupied with the ethical implications of their work. For an example of Hine's reflections on these issues, see Alan Trachtenberg (ed.), *Classic Essays on Photography* (New Haven: Leete's Island Books, 1980), 109.

19 Cf. Jean-Marie Schaeffer's semiotic-pragmatic formulation of this problem in *L'Image précaire. Du dispositif photographique* (Paris: Seuil, 1987), 82.

which are seen to predominantly prop up existing social power relations and dominant ideologies.[20] Of course, this is the raison d'être of Barthes's semiotic analysis of photography in the late 1950s onwards, which, in *Mythologies* especially, echoes Benjamin's critique of right-wing ideology, although not (needless to say) with the same urgency that this demanded in the mid-1930s. In the context of the concrete struggle against fascism, Benjamin's argument is not primarily one of ideological critique but instead a prescriptive call to action focused on how to best mobilize the medium as anti-fascist propaganda.

Delivered as a speech at the communist Institut pour l'Étude du Fascisme [Institute for the Study of Fascism] in Paris in April 1934, Benjamin's 'Der Autor als Produzent' ['The Author as Producer'] was written at a time when Hitler's Third Reich was already powerfully entrenched in Germany (four months before he established his position as its dictatorial 'Führer' in August 1934). Influenced by the Soviet aesthetics of the 1920s, Benjamin suggests in this speech that textual commentary accompanying photographic images in a word-image montage may not only be a means of social criticism but also a powerful tool in combating fascist ideology. As an example, Benjamin cites the photographer John Heartfield's left-wing, anti-Nazi photomontages. Heartfield, with whom Benjamin personally discussed photography in the summer of 1935 (see GB, V, 130) and who regularly contributed cover illustrations for the far-left communist journal *Arbeiter Illustrierten Zeitung* of Weimar Germany, provided an ideal model for the coupling of text and photographic image to simultaneously support Marxist revolutionary ends and counter the Nazi's mass media propaganda campaign.[21] Benjamin emphatically demands this creative ability from every politically motivated photographer, that is, 'die Fähigkeit, seiner Aufnahme diejenige Beschriftung zu geben, die . . . ihr den revolutionären Gebrauchswert verleiht' (GS, II, 693) ['the ability to

20 This is the core argument of John Tagg's critical writings from the early 1980s (for instance, 'Evidence, Truth and Order. Photographic Records and the Growth of the State', in Liz Wells (ed.), *The Photography Reader* (London and New York: Routledge, 2003), 257–60) to his most recent work, *The Disciplinary Frame: Photographic Truths and the Capture of Meaning* (Minneapolis: University of Minnesota Press, 2009).

21 However, as Brigitte Werneburg has pointed out, Benjamin sidelines Heartfield's contributions to the journal by mentioning only his now less well-known book cover photomontages for the publisher Malik ('Ernst Jünger, Walter Benjamin und die Photographie. Zur Entwicklung einer Medienästhetik in der Weimarer Republik', in Hans-Harald Müller and Harro Segeberg (eds.), *Ernst Jünger im 20. Jahrhundert* (Munich: Fink, 1995), 39–57: 49).

give his picture a caption that . . . gives it revolutionary use value' (SW, II, 775)], in keeping with the historical moment of political emergency.[22]

Benjamin's speech in 1934, then, represents the full flowering of his position on the simultaneous documentary and political function of photography and its radicalization, which existed only in a relatively muted, embryonic form in the 1931 'Kleine Geschichte der Photographie'. Returning to Atget and pulling these various strands together, in 'Das Kunstwerk im Zeitalter seiner technischen Reproduzierbarkeit', written between 1935 and 1939, Benjamin takes up these subjects again. In this well-known and oft-quoted text, chiefly concerned with the photographic reproduction of artworks, Benjamin includes a résumé of the discussion of Atget's photographs from the 'Kleine Geschichte der Photographie'. Here, the significance of Atget's photographs is most explicitly presented as residing not just in their marking a new and important moment in the history of photography (as a result of what the images are in themselves) but also how their experience as usually accompanied by text reveals photography's role in an ongoing 'process' or 'trial' of history (to render both meanings of the German word 'Prozeß'), in which evidence is produced and justice served. In Benjamin's words:

> Die photographischen Aufnahmen beginnen bei Atget, Beweisstücke im historischen Prozeß zu werden. Das macht ihre verborgene politische Bedeutung aus. Sie fordern schon eine Rezeption in bestimmtem Sinne. . . . Sie beunruhigen den Betrachter; er fühlt: zu ihnen muß er einen bestimmten Weg suchen. Wegweiser beginnen ihm gleichzeitig die illustrierten Zeitungen aufzustellen. Richtige oder falsche – gleichviel. In ihnen ist die Beschriftung zum ersten Mal obligat geworden. (GS, I, 485)
>
> With Atget, photographic records begin to be evidence in the historical trial. This constitutes their hidden political significance. They demand a specific kind of reception. . . . They unsettle the viewer; he feels challenged to find a particular way to approach them. At the same time, illustrated magazines begin to put up signposts for him – whether these are right or wrong is irrelevant. For the first time, captions become obligatory. (SW, IV, 258)

22 In his 'Pariser Brief II' ['Letter from Paris II'], Benjamin critiques Albert Renger-Patzsch's collection of photographs titled *Die Welt ist schön* [*The World Is Beautiful*] (from 1928) and puts similar emphasis on the 'Wichtigkeit der Beschriftung, die als Zündschnur den kritischen Funken an das Bildgemenge heranführt' (GS, III, 505) ['importance of inscription, which serves as fuse for guiding the critical spark to the image mass' (SW, III, 241)]. Werneburg critically contrasts Benjamin and Jünger, arguing that the latter put into practice what the former called for by effectively combining photographs with text in his work ('Ernst Jünger, Walter Benjamin und die Photographie', 47–50).

Although our main focus on portrait photography in Benjamin's writing precludes exploring it in more detail, it is important to note that his conception of photographic images performing an ethical role in public discourse by supporting a call for historical justice as per the metaphor of an ongoing trial has been echoed and re-echoed. Most recently, it has been developed in powerful ways by, among others, the French art historian Georges Didi-Huberman and Susan Sontag (when she returned to photography nearly three decades after her seminal essay collection *On Photography*) in relation to photographs from the Auschwitz death camps and other images of human suffering.[23]

The Fishwife Portrait and the Photograph's Demand

In Benjamin's 'Kleine Geschichte der Photographie', discussions of formalist avant-garde photography and the new vision of reality it provides, on the one hand, and of documentary photography and its political, social and critical function, on the other, are supplemented by reflections on nineteenth-century portrait photographs, dating from the first decades of photographic history. This latter constitutes the chronologically earliest major period of photographic production discussed in the essay. It is in the context of such early portraiture that Benjamin's notion of aura, understood as a perceptual and experiential dynamic between the photographic image and the beholder, comes to the fore. Aura, as belonging to this first pre-modern period, in turn shapes Benjamin's view of subsequent photography, including Atget's images, which are partly defined by lacking the special qualities of these nineteenth-century portraits.[24]

For Benjamin, the auratic quality of early photography is related to their particular aesthetic value, with images produced from the 1840s to 1870s being regarded as constituting a 40-year-long 'golden age' of photography as an art and craft. In his famous Salon review from 1859, Baudelaire harshly criticizes early artistic uses and pretensions of the new medium. At

23 See Gorges Didi-Huberman, *Images malgré tout* (Paris: Éditions de Minuit, 2003) and Susan Sontag, *Regarding the Pain of Others* (London: Penguin, 2003).

24 The reasons for the lack of aura in later photographs are, however, largely bound to the dynamics of the history of photography, and not, as Diarmuid Costello has suggested, related to a 'particular way of depicting persons' ('Aura, Face, Photography: Re-Reading Benjamin Today', in Andrew Benjamin (ed.), *Walter Benjamin and Art* (London and New York: Continuum, 2005), 164–84: 171).

the time of Benjamin's writing, Baudelaire's text was already a canonical critique of nineteenth-century photography. For Baudelaire, photography represented an apposite mechanical tool for the representation of the visible world with a greater exactitude than previously possible. As such, although of great potential significance for science and medicine, it is at best aesthetically negligible and at worst a threat to art. Pierre Taminiaux has argued that Baudelaire's critique of photography is situated in 'the broader context of a general critique of the French spirit of his time',[25] and it certainly reflects the poet's disdain for the aesthetic taste of many of his contemporaries whose idea of art was, in his view, too closely and erroneously focused on the notion of mimetic fidelity, as reflected in nineteenth-century academic Salon painting, as opposed to imaginative transformation. Baudelaire's critique appeared against the background of André Disdéri's patenting of the mass-produced *carte-de-visite* portrait in 1854, allowing for 12 images to be captured on a single photographic plate, reducing the price to one-fifth of a regular portrait.[26] Disdéri's invention was a major contributor to the rapid rise of commercial portraiture and reinforced Baudelaire's contemptuous view of photography as a mere industrial product detrimental to artistic creativity.[27]

Benjamin quotes from Baudelaire's Salon review in the 'Kleine Geschichte der Photographie' but only in support of the photograph's archival value rather than addressing the question of photography's artistic merit. With the benefit of historical hindsight, and in contrast to Baudelaire's contemporary perspective, Benjamin sees the mid-nineteenth century as an epoch that preceded the modern industrialization and the commercialization of the photographic image – to an extent Baudelaire could have never foreseen – and as a period of purity and innocence before the camera and its power were appropriated for largely commercial ends.

25 Pierre Taminiaux, *The Paradox of Photography* (Amsterdam and New York: Rodopi, 2009), 15. Cf. also Nancy Shawcross's discussion of Baudelaire's art criticism in relation to photography and Benjamin and Barthes, in *Roland Barthes on Photography. A Critical Tradition in Perspective* (Gainsville: University Press of Florida, 1997), 46–66.

26 See Freund, *Photographie et société*, 60.

27 See Charles Baudelaire, *Écrits sur l'art*, ed. Francis Moulinat (Paris: Le Livre de poche, 1992), 359–66. In contradistinction to Baudelaire, in the 'Kleine Geschichte der Photographie' Benjamin glosses over the socio-historical and cultural impact of Disdéri's invention, in particular, aspects he addresses in his 1936 'Pariser Brief II', dealing with painting and photography (see GS, III, 502–3). In the *Passagen-Werk*, Disdéri also serves a major reference point for Benjamin (see GS, V, 824–46).

This appropriation and financial exploitation of the medium (beginning in the last decades of the nineteenth century, in Benjamin's view) contributed to an artistic decline that was arrested or counterbalanced only by Atget's deserted street scenes, as we have seen. More generally, Benjamin's preference for early photographs was no doubt informed by his profound and long-lasting interest in cultural phenomena of the nineteenth century, as evidenced by his attempted reconstruction of it in his *Passagen-Werk*. It was also likely influenced by Freund's writings on the same mid-nineteenth-century period of photography, in which it is also seen as an artistic high point of the medium.[28] Finally, Benjamin's celebration of the exceptional character of mid-nineteenth-century photographs was greatly informed by Schwarz's study *David Octavius Hill*, in which Hill is praised as an outstanding 'master' of early photography and by the catalogue on early photography by Bossert and Guttmann, which spans precisely the period from 1840 to 1870 to which Benjamin refers (even if his own attribution of dates to particular images and the periods they belong to is notoriously imprecise).[29]

While thus engaging with, and borrowing from, past and contemporary critics and scholars in the 'Kleine Geschichte der Photographie', to establish the aesthetic value of early photographs, Benjamin departs from these inter-texts in also stressing their profound psychological effects on the contemporary viewer. These cannot be addressed in art-historical, formal or intentional terms alone and instead call for a new experiential and phenomenological description of the viewer's interaction with these images. Benjamin develops his argument by way of two portraits that also serve as the first two illustrations of his text. The first is a now famous and oft-reproduced portrait of a Scottish fishwife, Elizabeth Johnstone Hall, taken by David Octavius Hill and Robert Adamson.[30] This image was part

28 Cf. Berg's discussion of Freund's influence on Benjamin, *Die Ikone des Realen*, 98.

29 For example, Benjamin groups Hill together with Julia Margaret Cameron, Charles Hugo and Nadar as belonging to the first decade of photography's history (see GS, II, 368), even if the latter three took up photography in the 1850s or even 1860s, and therefore well after Hill.

30 Benjamin never mentions Adamson, an omission that is striking given that Adamson brought the vital technical know-how to the productive yet short-lived collaboration with Hill (from 1843 to 1847). But, perhaps, he does not fit Benjamin's characterization of the early generation of photographers as artists. Although Schwarz emphasizes the importance of Adamson in the collaboration, he contends that the artistic (and hence more important) input came from Hill (*David Octavius Hill*, 34–5).

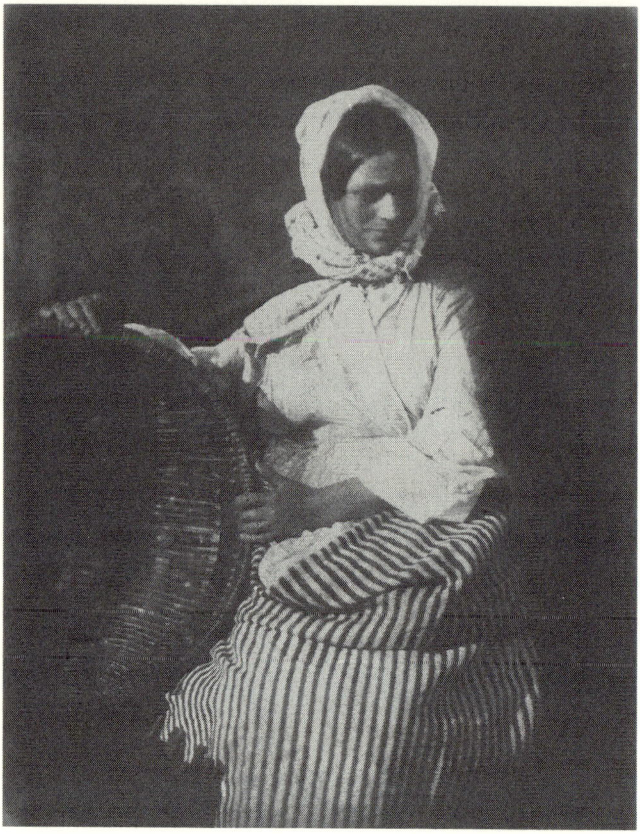

PLATE 5 David Octavius Hill and Robert Adamson, Elizabeth Johnstone Hall, 1843–47.

of a planned publication on *The Fishermen and Women of the Firth of Forth*, documenting life in Newhaven, a fishing village near Edinburgh.[31]

Rather than focusing on traditional aesthetic features rooted in composition, style and iconography, Benjamin draws attention to the powerful psychological effect of this portrait, which by virtue of the medium and its preservation of reality goes well beyond what is achievable in a painted portrait and also surpasses any specific artistic intentions on the part of the photographer. Here we are in the sphere of a confrontation between the viewer and a simultaneously past and present life force that is unique to photography. Benjamin observes:

31 Benjamin would have seen the photograph reproduced in both Schwarz's monograph (*David Octavius Hill*, fig. 26) and Recht's catalogue (*Die Alte Photographie*, 50).

> Bei der Photographie aber begegnet man etwas Neuem und Sonderbarem: in jenem Fischweib aus New Haven, das mit so lässiger, verführerischer Scham zu Boden blickt, bleibt etwas, was im Zeugnis für die Kunst des Photographen Hill nicht aufgeht, etwas, was nicht zum Schweigen zu bringen ist, ungebärdig nach dem Namen derer verlangend, die da gelebt hat, die auch hier noch wirklich ist und niemals gänzlich in die 'Kunst' wird eingehen wollen. (GS, II, 370)
>
> With photography, however, we encounter something new and strange: in Hill's Newhaven fishwife, her eyes cast down in such indolent, seductive modesty, there remains something that goes beyond testimony to the photographer's art, something that cannot be silenced, that fills you with an unruly desire to know what her name was, the woman who was alive there, who even now is still real and will never be wholly absorbed in 'art'. (SW, II, 510)

For Benjamin, the portrait photograph, unlike the painting, testifies to a new phenomenon that has hitherto escaped visual representation: it both preserves and guards something of the life of the represented subject in a way that calls out for that life to be known and understood. The contrast Benjamin draws between photography and portrait painting thus underlines the novelty and strangeness of the psychological dynamic between photograph and viewer as owing to the presence and nature of the sitter which is indexically encoded in the image. Personal identity is thus not contingently associated with an image by virtue of iconic resemblance, as in the case of painting, but is part of the material being and presence of the image itself. Benjamin maintains that, unlike in photography (where it only increases like a physical patina accumulating over time), the viewer's interest in the identity of the person depicted in painting wanes in the course of time. The painting's mimetic function weakens in relation to its aesthetic value and the artist's talent and style, whereas in the case of the portrait photograph it is the inverse.

The French philosopher Jean-Luc Nancy has pointed out that the mimetic or iconic function of a painted portrait is not only a secondary factor in the art of portraiture but often an inessential one.[32] Clearly, this does not apply to photography in the same way, for which iconicity is a norm or standard. Following Benjamin, the viewer's overwhelming curiosity about the sitter is bound to the photograph's particular coalescence of indexicality and iconicity. In consequence, whereas the viewer's interest in a painted portrait often consists largely in an appreciation of the painter's creative artistry, the photographic portrait's fascination and power far exceed the photographer's skills and the purely

32 See Jean-Luc Nancy, *Le Regard du portrait* (Paris: Éditions Galilée, 2000), 39–40.

aesthetic or artistic value of the image. For Benjamin, the photograph's particular presence and resultant demand are, above all, rooted in the nature of photographic representation. The capture and preservation of a past moment in time, to which the image stands in direct causal relation, serves to comparatively sideline questions of aesthetic form and intentionality. Although Benjamin does not use the semiotic terminology of index and icon, which photographic theory has borrowed from the writings of Charles Sanders Peirce, there is no doubt that Benjamin's contrast between photographic and painted portraiture is rooted in the specific photographic relation between the two sign types and their effects.[33]

In sum, what Benjamin emphasizes in relation to the portrait by Hill/Adamson is the singular existence of the woman at a particular moment in time, which, although objectively past, is present and real for the viewer decades later. The fact that he chooses a photograph of an unidentified fishwife,[34] as opposed to one of Hill and Adamson's portraits of a well-known and identifiable historical individual (of which Schwarz's monograph abounds), foregrounds the idea that the sort of presence and identity of a person represented in a photograph, which Benjamin argues opens up a new kind of relation between him or her and the viewer, are not matters of public persona or mere objective identification, but of the full being of the individual and his or her life-world.

---

33 Since the semiotically oriented photographic theories of the 1960s, Peirce's famous differentiation between three types of signs (symbol, index and icon) has become a common reference point. At times problematic and simplistic, the photograph is in this perspective viewed as both index (understood as a sign directly and physically connected to its referent) and icon (through which signification is established by virtue of resemblance between signifier and referent). More recently, indexicality has been forcefully contested by theorists. See James Elkins (ed.), *Photography Theory* (New York and London: Routledge, 2007), 130–203 and Joel Snyder's essay in the same collection, 369–400. In his latest book, Elkins even attempts to find a 'cure' for the idea of the photograph as indexical sign (*What Photography Is* (New York and London: Routlegde, 2011), 24).

34 Although the fishwife was known, Schwarz does not include her name (*David Octavius Hill*, 56, fig. 26). Sara Stevenson comments on how the Newhaven portraits, and especially the one of Elizabeth Johnstone Hall, relate to Walter Scott's novel *The Antiquary*, which influenced Hill's choice of motifs and grouping of sitters (*Hill and Adamson's The Fishermen and Women of the Firth of Forth* (Edinburgh: National Galleries of Scotland, 1991), 35–6).

With respect to the fishwife portrait, Benjamin singles out dynamics that he regards as defining characteristics only of early portrait photographs. Agamben, in contrast, deduces what he regards as a universal characteristic of portrait photography from Benjamin's discussion. Closely conjoining the notion of the photograph's presence and demand with the ethical, he interprets Benjamin's commentary on the portrait of the Newhaven fishwife as representative of a universal demand made by photographic portraiture. The photograph's exigency, Agamben argues, is neither factual nor aesthetic. Rather, it constitutes an ethical demand that encapsulates the notion of historical redemption, as the title of Agamben's aphoristic essay, 'Judgement Day', suggests. Writing with reference to Benjamin's comment on the profoundly felt demand for the sitter's name, Agamben states that this applies to every portrait photograph and highlights the idea that

> even if the person photographed is completely forgotten today, even if his or her name has been erased forever from human memory – or, indeed, precisely because of this – that person and that face demand their name; they demand not to be forgotten.[35]

Thus, the naming of the unknown or dead sitter, whose absent presence or present absence are photographically inscribed, entails a saving of this person to the extent that the uniqueness of his or her life and death are affirmed.[36] Agamben further adds that the photographic exigency is a 'demand for redemption';[37] a redemption that only the later beholder is able to grant. Following the Italian philosopher, every portrait photograph may be seen as potentially analogous to what Benjamin in the ninth thesis of his historico-philosophical manifesto, 'Über den Begriff der Geschichte' ['On the Concept of History'], describes as historical 'Trümmer' ['wreckage'], the dead and the 'Zerschlagene' ['smashed'] (GS, I, 697; SW, IV, 392). Together this is the catastrophe that the 'Engel der Geschichte' ['angel of history'] would want to assemble and revive (ibid.). The complex imagery of the angel, in Benjamin's text, is related to Paul Klee's *Angelus Novus* (1920), a small painting

35 Agamben, *Profanations*, 25.

36 The death is individualized both by the face and name, as could be argued following Maurice Blanchot (*L'Espace littéraire* (Paris: Gallimard, 1955), 163–4).

37 Agamben, *Profanations*, 26.

of great importance for Benjamin.[38] In Agamben's reading, this angel becomes the 'angel of photography', demanding redemption:

> Photography demands that we remember all this, and photographs testify to all those lost names, like the Book of Life that the new angel of the apocalypse – the angel of photography – holds in his hands at the end of all days, that is, every day.[39]

In light of the analogy between the 'angel of history' and the 'angel of photography', the historical as well as ethical aspect of Agamben's argument concerning the beholder's granting of redemption becomes clear. In both cases, the angel is the allegorical figure of a particularly ethical understanding of history, as it brings hope in relation to the apocalyptic 'judgment day'. In this respect, Agamben's 'angel of photography' is the secularization or 'profanation' of Benjamin's messianic angel of history.[40] This link established by Agamben between photography and ethics will serve us as a starting point for a reflection on the ethics of photography in relation to the viewer (see Chapter Three).

The Dauthendey Self-Portrait

In the 'Kleine Geschichte der Photographie', Benjamin's discussion of the fishwife portrait by Hill/Adamson is closely connected to another portrait with which it must be seen in tandem. This is a self-portrait by the German photographer Karl Dauthendey with his future (second)

38 See Gershom Scholem's account of how the painting came into Benjamin's possession and of its key role in the context of his thought, *Walter Benjamin und sein Engel. Vierzehn Aufsätze und kleine Beiträge*, ed. Rolf Tiedemann (Frankfurt a.M.: Suhrkamp, 1983), 35–72. For a detailed discussion of the angel in the ninth thesis, see Sigrid Weigel, *Entstellte Ähnlichkeit. Walter Benjamins theoretische Schreibweise* (Frankfurt a.M.: Fischer, 1997), 62–7.

39 Agamben, *Profanations*, 27. Similarly, in Stiegler's interpretation of Vilém Flusser's *Philosophy of Photography*, the role of photography in the apocalyptic history of humankind is said to be the 'Trompetenstoß des Engels' ['call of the angel's trumpet'], ultimately proclaiming redemption and freedom (*Theoriegeschichte der Photographie*, 396).

40 It has often been argued that in Benjamin's 'Über den Begriff der Geschichte' concepts rooted in the Jewish-mystical tradition resurface. With respect to redemption, therefore, the emphasis is on its messianic, as well as revolutionary, nature, as Heinrich Kaulen states in his entry on 'Rettung' in Michael Opitz and Erdmut Wizisla (eds.), *Benjamins Begriffe*, 2 vols. (Frankfurt a.M.: Suhrkamp, 2000), vol. 2, 654-6.

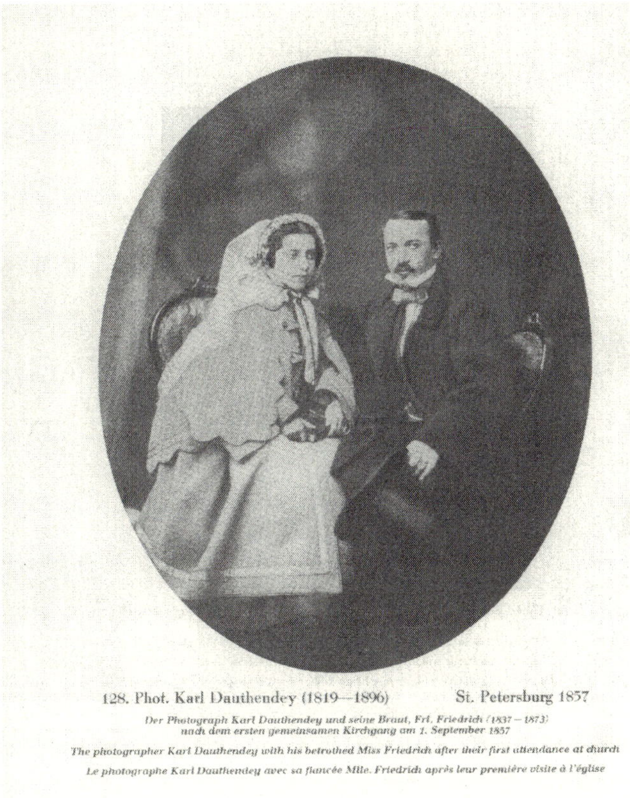

PLATE 6 Karl Dauthendey, Self-portrait with his future second wife, Miss Friedrich, 1857, in Bossert and Guttmann, *Aus der Frühzeit der Photographie.*

wife, a photograph which Benjamin takes from Bossert and Guttmann's catalogue of early photography.

Benjamin's commentary on this double portrait shows a number of imaginative modifications and misattributions. These speak to the presence (and, from an objective perspective, fallibility) of the complex processes of perception, imagination, affect and interpretation rooted in prior knowledge, which, as Benjamin argues, are all at work in the beholder's encounter with a photographic portrait and the reality it presents. Ironically, given Benjamin's emphasis in relation to the fishwife portrait, his misattributions also concern the identity of the photographed woman. In addition to confusing St Petersburg, where the photograph was actually taken (as the labelling clearly indicates), and Moscow, Benjamin also mistakes the depicted female person, Dauthendey's second wife, for his first one. As a result, he interprets the 'unheilvolle

Ferne' (GS, II, 371) ['ominous distance' (SW, II, 510)] towards which, he suggests, the depicted woman's gaze is directed as foreshadowing the suicide of the woman who was in fact Dauthendey's first wife.[41] By 1857, the wife who had taken her life in 1855 could of course no longer be photographed. André Gunthert has rightly pointed out that Benjamin superimposes the episode of the suicide that he had learned about from Max Dauthendey's biography of his father Karl (relating to a different photograph) with the photograph from Bossert and Guttmann, and hence views it as foreshadowing a tragic death.[42] Although Benjamin directly quotes from Dauthendey's biography elsewhere in the 'Kleine Geschichte der Photographie', it is clear that he draws on his memory of the text when seeing the photograph. Together with the reference to Moscow rather than St Petersburg, this underscores that the text-image interplay in Benjamin's essay corresponds to a play of memory and imagination on the author's part, as much as to factual and historical juxtaposition.

Despite their formal differences, for Benjamin, the Hill/Adamson and Dauthendey portraits are linked by their exemplification of the psychological effects of photography on the viewer as a result of the medium's relation to the reality it captures and preserves. Anticipating Bazin's arguments in his 1945 essay 'Ontologie de l'image photographique' ['Ontology of the Photographic Image'], on this psychological basis Benjamin further distinguishes between painting and photography and argues that to immerse oneself in this kind of portrait is to experience a 'magic' unique to photography by virtue of the image's automatic generation.

> Hat man sich lange genug in so ein Bild vertieft, erkennt man, wie sehr auch hier die Gegensätze sich berühren: die exakteste Technik kann ihren Hervorbringungen einen magischen Wert geben, wie für uns ihn ein gemaltes Bild nie mehr besitzen kann. Aller Kunstfertigkeit des Photographen und aller Planmäßigkeit in der Haltung seines Modells zum Trotz fühlt der Beschauer

41 This mislabelling has often attracted scholarly interest, not without leading to new misunderstandings. For instance, Krauss contends that Benjamin misread the labelling of the double portrait in Bossert and Guttmann, which is, however, clearly not the case, as the caption does not allude to the suicide (*Benjamin und der neue Blick*, 22, n. 53).

42 André Gunthert, 'Le Complex de Gradiva. Théorie de la photographie, deuil et résurrection', *Études photographiques*, 2 (1997), 115–28: 119–20. The story which Benjamin retells here, and the description of the photograph of Dauthendey and his first wife, can be found in Max Dauthendey, *Der Geist meines Vaters. Aufzeichnungen aus einem begrabenen Jahrhundert* (Munich: Albert Langen, 1912), 177–9; 180.

> unwiderstehlich den Zwang, in solchem Bild das winzige Fünkchen Zufall, Hier und Jetzt, zu suchen, mit dem die Wirklichkeit den Bildcharakter gleichsam durchgesengt hat, die unscheinbare Stelle zu finden, in welcher, im Sosein jener längstvergangenen Minute das Künftige noch heut und so beredt nistet, daß wir, rückblickend, es entdecken können. (GS, II, 371)
>
> Immerse yourself in such a picture long enough and you will realize to what extent opposites touch, here too: the most precise technology can give its products a magical value, such as a painted picture can never again have for us. No matter how artful the photographer, no matter how carefully posed his subject, the beholder feels an irresistible urge to search such a picture for the tiny spark of chance, of the here and now, with which reality has (so to speak) seared the subject, to find the inconspicuous spot where in the immediacy of that long-forgotten moment the future nests so eloquently that we, looking back, may rediscover it. (SW, II, 510)

What is notable about this passage is that it is less a description of the image than of the effect of the photograph on the viewer or, vice versa, his or her experience of it. The expressions 'spark' and 'spot' suggest that the photographic image is penetrated by a reality detail – something like Barthes's *punctum* detail, as numerous critics and theorists have suggested – that escapes all intentionality, be it that of the photographer, the sitter or, potentially, the viewer. But it is always present in the image as a potential waiting to be actualized in experience. This is what, in a different context, Derrida calls the 'beyond of art' in the photographic image.[43] Benjamin's account of photographic portraiture points to this 'beyond' as a singular, unrepeatable experience resulting from the meeting between image and subject wherein both are historically situated. Their coming together represents a 'fusion of temporal horizons' in something akin to Hans-Georg Gadamer's famous sense of this phrase.

Benjamin defines the photograph as a temporally and spatially complex image by acknowledging that the reality it pictures is always already a past moment, which is, in turn, linked to the present, the here and now of the act of looking. As has often been noted, Benjamin's characterization of the viewing experience of a photograph along these lines evokes his first attempted definition of aura as a 'strange weave of space and time',[44] which appears somewhat enigmatically in the 'Kleine Geschichte der Photographie'

43 Jacques Derrida, *Copy, Archive, Signature. A Conversation on Photography*, trans. Jeff Ford, ed. Gerhard Richter (Stanford: Stanford University Press, 2010), 9.

44 See, for example, Carolin Duttlinger, 'Imaginary Encounters: Walter Benjamin and the Aura of Photography', *Poetics Today*, 29 (2008), 79–101: 84–6.

not in relation to nineteenth-century portraiture, characterized as auratic, but in his discussion of the lack of aura in later photography (notably in Atget's images). Thus, from one perspective, in this essay at least, the main discursive value of aura is a 'negative' one, that is, as a concept introduced to indicate what is absent from many photographs rather than something that some seem to positively possess. However, in considering the first full definition of aura in Benjamin's writing,[45] we can begin to construct a more positive account of what may provide for the auratic dimension of certain images on Benjamin's general view as related to an affective, spatio-temporal immersion on the viewer's part.[46]

In the 'Kleine Geschichte der Photographie', aura is described as a complex phenomenon of perception:

> Ein sonderbares Gespinst von Raum und Zeit: einmalige Erscheinung einer Ferne, so nah sie sein mag. An einem Sommermittag ruhend einem Gebirgszug am Horizont oder einem Zweig folgen, der seinen Schatten auf den Betrachter wirft, bis der Augenblick oder die Stunde Teil an ihrer Erscheinung hat – das heißt die Aura dieser Berge, dieses Zweiges atmen. (GS, II, 378)
>
> A strange weave of space and time: the unique appearance of distance, no matter how close it may be. While at rest at a summer's noon, to trace a range of mountains on the horizon, or a branch that throws its shadow on the observer, until the moment or the hour become part of their appearance – this is what it means to breathe the aura of those mountains, of that branch. (SW, II, 518–19)

The *Denkbild*[47] used by Benjamin to introduce this quality or affect appears at first to have little to do with photography in being instead

45 Although Benjamin uses the term aura in the more esoteric and occult context of his experiments with drugs (see GS, VI, 588), there is a common consensus that the 'Kleine Geschichte der Photographie' provides the first definition of it in relation to cultural phenomena. See Josef Fürnkäs's entry on 'Aura', in Opitz and Wizisla (eds.), *Benjamins Begriffe*, vol. 1, 109. For two classic discussions of aura, see Burkhardt Lindner, 'Benjamins Aurakonzeption: Anthropologie und Technik, Bild und Text', in Uwe Steiner (ed.), *Walter Benjamin (1892–1940) zum 100. Geburtstag* (Frankfurt a.M.: Peter Lang, 1992), 217–48 and Michael Wetzel, 'Il y aura. Über die Kunst, die Herzen schneller schlagen zu lassen', *Fotogeschichte*, 9 (1982), 11–20.

46 Birgit Recki has made a similar point with regard to Benjamin's aura, emphasizing the subjective aspects over the object's particular properties, albeit in the context of the tradition of Kantian aesthetics (*Aura und Autonomie. Zur Subjektivität der Kunst bei Walter Benjamin und Theodor W. Adorno* (Würzburg: Königshausen & Neumann, 1988), 13–26).

47 Rather than a metaphor or concept, the *Denkbild* (literally 'thought-image') is a constellation of language through which an idea is evoked. Benjamin's

an image of directly witnessed natural phenomena. (This evocation of aura by way of nature allows Benjamin to keep the phenomenon distinct from artistic intentionality and even aesthetic experience despite the fact that it can be a property of cultural artefacts.)[48] Yet, as tied to an act of vision, this imagistic description of aura has clear photographic connotations. This formulation of aura by way of nature imagery recurs in subsequent texts, including in the essay on the 'Kunstwerk' (see GS, I, 479). The reference to the 'moment' and 'hour' as part of the perception of objects or phenomena, however, appears only in the essay on the history of photography, where it can be associated with the pronounced temporal duration of the image-production process in nineteenth-century portraiture with its long exposure times. The evocation of the sun as related to the passage of time connotes photography's use of light to arrest the passage of time in the form of an image.

Therefore, it would seem that Benjamin's imagistic definition of aura here has nolens volens a strong affinity with defining characteristics of photography, despite the fact that this seems to contradict his later attempt to strictly divorce aura from photography (see Chapter Three). However, although otherwise thoroughly visual, Benjamin's choice of the verb 'to breathe' ('atmen') rather than 'to see', in this passage, suggests that, unlike a look, or an arrow whose movement stops when it reaches its target, aura is not a one-way experience but rather a circular or reciprocal movement in which closeness and distance are dialectically interrelated, as is characteristic of those life experiences marked by a pronounced imaginative immersion. This sense of aura anticipates Benjamin's last definition of aura, associated with an object returning the gaze of the subject.

Benjamin's discussion of the Newhaven fishwife portrait and the self-portrait by Dauthendey, then, testifies, in the ways that have been noted, to aura as related to an active and involved experience with the photograph on the part of the beholder. However, this experience is not incidental to photographs' physical being and the circumstances of their creation. For Benjamin, the psychological impact of mid-nineteenth-century photographs, such as the two portraits, and the imaginative experiences

Denkbilder are nearly impossible to translate, and indeed often disappear in translation, as Weigel has argued (*Walter Benjamin*, 213–27).

48 Although Costello problematically equates the experience of aura with an aesthetic one, he is right in highlighting that Benjamin is here interested in the form rather than content of the experience ('Aura, Face, Photography', 172–3). Cf. also Wetzel, 'Il y aura', 18.

they provide, are inescapably related to the historical and technological facts of their production. Thus, to the extent that aura is here clearly rooted in objective properties of the image, it is distinct from his later definition of it as primarily the product of a reciprocal gaze, whereby the object is figuratively transformed into a seeing subject.

Auratic Features of Nineteenth-Century Portraiture

With respect to his understanding of all cultural phenomena, Benjamin's emphasis on the specific conditions of nineteenth-century photographic production is strongly informed by Marxist-dialectical reasoning which, to some degree at least, regards changes at the level of cultural life as corresponding to changes in the means of technological production. While there is a great deal of ambiguity surrounding Benjamin's various conceptions of aura, which certainly extends to their often apparently contradictory applications to photography in various texts, it is clear that the aura of nineteenth-century photographs is the result of a complex bond between several elements, which must coincide for it to manifest itself. These include the available photographic technology, the use the photographer makes of it, his or her craftsmanship more generally and the sitter's nature and behaviour. For Benjamin, this confluence occurs only in the mid-nineteenth century.

Benjamin reminds us that at this early stage in the development of photographic technology, the relatively low-light sensitivity of the photographic plate made long exposure times inevitable. Establishing a strong link between photographic technology as a mode of production and the style of photographic images, Benjamin argues that there was a unique and historically unparalleled accord between the skills of early photographers and the operations of their cameras. Agreeing with Freund and Kracauer that the craftsmanship of the first artist photographers was necessarily superior to that of later generations,[49] Benjamin sees the fact that many were trained painters as a major contributor to the artistic exceptionality of their images. In contrast to Baudelaire's view of photography as a refuge for failed painters,[50] Benjamin contends that the

49 See Freund, *Photographie et société*, 35–49 and Kracauer, *Das Ornament der Masse*, 27–8.

50 Baudelaire, *Écrits sur l'art*, 364. The failed painter turned photographer was also a popular topic of many satirist caricatures of the 1840s and 1850s, as Aaron Scharf has shown (*Art and Photography* (Harmondsworth: Penguin, 1974), 39–49).

first generation of photographers, including Nadar, Ferdinand Stelzner, Pierre-Louis Pierson and Hippolyte Bayard alongside Hill,[51] produced images to high aesthetic standards precisely by needing to adapt to a new and profoundly difficult medium which seemingly limited artistic freedom and expression as traditionally understood. In this way they followed their artistic instincts and training in a medium as yet unaffected by mass industrialization.[52] The very facts that limited early photography's commercial exploitation – relatively unsophisticated technology, resulting in long exposure time, and the need to balance this with the short-lived light sensitivity of the wet plate – positively contributed to the creation of auratic images.

Benjamin focuses on a series of portraits taken by Hill and Adamson at Edinburgh's Greyfriars cemetery, to illustrate how aesthetic choices were determined by technical circumstances, especially the setting, motif and posing of sitters. The cemetery not only provided a secluded and peaceful plein-air setting, allowing for long, undisturbed exposure in direct sunlight but also affected the sitters, whom Benjamin imagines to be in a state of quiet and even shy concentration, resulting in their particularly composed and concentrated expression, which both entices and challenges the viewer. He writes that 'während der langen Dauer dieser Aufnahmen wuchsen sie [die Modelle] gleichsam in das Bild hinein' (GS, II, 373) ['during the long period of exposure, the subject grew, as it were, into the picture' (SW, II, 514)]. From the point of view of photographic technology, the sitter's image 'growing into the photograph' can be taken almost literally: Hill and Adamson used the paper-based calotype process, in which the light-sensitive silver solution is absorbed into the paper rather than sitting on a copper plate, as was the case in daguerreotypes, a technique of early photography which Benjamin only touches on.[53]

However, more figuratively, Benjamin contends that a feeling or sense of the extended temporal duration of the photograph's exposure finds its way

51 Works by all photographers mentioned by Benjamin figure prominently in Bossert and Guttmann's richly illustrated *Aus der Frühzeit der Photographie*. Pierson, one of the leading nineteenth-century society photographers in Paris, and Bayard, a rival of Daguerre, who invented the direct positive printing process in 1839, both appear in Nadar's illustrious list of nineteenth-century photographers in his memoir *Quand j'étais photographe* (Paris: L'École des Lettres/Seuil, 1994), 229.

52 Schwarz makes the same point in relation to Hill (*David Octavius Hill*, 34; 46).

53 For an account of the formal differences between daguerreotypes and calotypes, see Scharf, *Art and Photography*, 28–31.

into the image by way of the contemplative attitude of the sitter needing to pose for an extended period before the lens. This results, in Benjamin's account, in the overall impression that 'alles an diesen frühen Bildern war angelegt zu dauern' (GS, II, 373) ['everything about these early pictures was intended to last' (SW, II, 514)]. The aura of early photographs, their 'strange weave of space and time' is apparently a consequence of their simultaneously time-defying yet deeply durational quality or 'Dauer' (suggesting both of these meanings). In the case of these images, then, there is a mirroring and interplay between the actual time of their registration – the picture-taking event as an interaction between subject, camera and photographer – and the durational immersion these photographs encourage or prompt on the part of the viewer.[54] If aura is largely defined in relation to these dynamics, it is apparent why the emergence of 'instantaneous' photography in the late 1870s as well as other technological developments resulted in a decline or even absence of its photographic manifestation.[55]

The complex temporality of early photography is further linked to the formal qualities of these images. Despite his earlier distinction between traditional and photographic portraiture, Benjamin compares Hill/Adamson's photographs to the art of the mezzotint, the first method of engraving that allowed for tonal graduation. 'Wie auf Schabkunstblättern', Benjamin writes, 'ringt sich bei einem Hill mühsam das Licht aus dem Dunkel' (GS, II, 376) ['as in mezzotint, light struggles out of darkness in the work of Hill' (SW, II, 517)].[56] Benjamin rather cryptically suggests that the continuum from brightness to darkness is the manifestation of aura seen from a technical point of view since, presumably, it creates a feeling of duration of the image for the viewer. Although this argument about the formal feature of Hill and Adamson's portraits and the similarity with

54 This implicitly Marxist-dialectical reasoning is somewhat problematic and has attracted criticism. See, for example, Snyder's comments in Elkins (ed.), *Photography Theory*, 164–6.

55 It is clear that in this historical account and from Benjamin's twentieth-century perspective, aura is necessarily related to a period of photographic history that is already past; by extension, the recognition of the phenomenon of aura in nineteenth-century photography is inherently retrospective. Cf. Marleen Stoessel, *Aura. Das vergessene Menschliche. Zu Sprache und Erfahrung bei Walter Benjamin* (Munich: Carl Hanser, 1983), 15.

56 Not fortuitously for Benjamin's argument, calotypes were stylistically akin to lithography and, at the time of their first appearance, were compared to the work of Rembrandt. See Stevenson, *Hill and Adamson's The Fishermen and Women*, 32.

engravings is taken directly from Schwarz,[57] in stressing their experiential temporality Benjamin forges a link with aura. In a similar vein, Thierry de Duve writes of the use of chiaroscuro in photography as an example of how it 'endeavours to regain some of the features through which painting traditionally enacts time'.[58] In other words, through the use of 'softening techniques', such as chiaroscuro or blurring, such photographs metaphorically evoke the passage of time, in opposition to freezing one moment of it, through suggesting the fading in and out of details and objects.[59] In these ways, the auratic qualities of early portraiture, such as the aesthetic value and interest they possess, are considered by Benjamin, to some degree, to be inherent properties of the image itself. Thus, although for Benjamin aura is necessarily an experiential dynamic, it is not 'subjective' in the sense of being a quality (or relating to one) that is merely projected onto a photograph or any other object by a viewer. Even more importantly in relation to themes and subjects we will later address, aura is not, in this context, a function of the beholder's prior knowledge of, or relationship to, the sitter. What is potentially auratic about these early photographs is built into the image at the time of their creation.

The Decline of Aura and Family Photographs

The early artistic peak of photography that Benjamin identifies in its mid-nineteenth-century manifestation, and to which most of the photographs associated with aura belong, was followed, in his view, by a period of artistic and auratic decline. According to Benjamin, Disdéri's invention of the *carte-de-visite* and the ensuing commercialization and standardization of portraiture resulted in the proliferation of more superficial, contingent and taste- and fashion-bound turn-of-the-century images. Given the somewhat problematic and overdetermined materialist-dialectical reasoning of his 'Kleine Geschichte der Photographie' and the designation of aura as a phenomenon belonging to a bygone age, it is not surprising that Benjamin viewed certain socio-cultural changes in early post-industrial society, together with the evolution of photographic technology itself, as triggering decisive changes in the history

57 See Schwarz, *David Octavius Hill*, 38–9.

58 Thierry de Duve, 'Time Exposure and Snapshot. The Photograph as Paradox', in James Elkins (ed.), *Photography Theory* (New York and London: Routledge, 2007), 109–23: 119.

59 Ibid.

of the medium towards the end of the nineteenth century. In contrast to Michel Foucault's heralding of the playful fusion of photography and painting during this pictorialist period between 1860 and 1880,[60] Benjamin regarded this period as one of a 'jäher Verfall des Geschmacks' (GS, II, 374) ['sharp decline in taste' (SW, II, 515)].[61] As we have seen, the decline was related, in his opinion, to the appropriation of the camera by the masses, which, by the 1880s, had become increasingly smaller, lighter and easier to handle; together with a much simplified image-development process and higher-sensitivity emulsion material, this significantly aided the medium's new-found accessibility to the amateur. These technological advances and greater accessibility led to the introduction and popularity of bound family photo albums, a phenomenon, which marks an important moment in photographic history, especially in Benjamin's history of photography.[62]

For Benjamin, who was born in 1892, the turn-of-the-century family album portrait evoked memories of having his picture taken as a child. The writing of the autobiographical *Berliner Chronik* [*Berlin Chronicle*] in 1931, during the same year as the 'Kleine Geschichte der Photographie', can be seen as an important inter-text here, informing Benjamin's more autobiographical comments in the latter text.[63] That the commercialization of photography through the *carte-de-visite* portrait from the late 1850s onwards contributed to a general decline in the artistic quality of portraiture

60 Michel Foucault characterizes this period positively as a 'frénésie neuve de l'image' ['new image frenzy'] ('La Peinture photogénique', in *Dits et écrits 1954-1988* (Paris: Gallimard, 1994), vol. 2, 707–15: 707). Cf. also Bernd Stiegler, 'Medienphilosophie der Photographie', in Mike Sandbothe and Ludwig Nagl (eds.), *Systematische Medienphilosophie* (Berlin: Akademie Verlag, 2005), 253–71: 261.

61 Cf. Berg's comments on Benjamin's argument on taste, in *Die Ikone des Realen*, 100.

62 It is important to remember in this context that the various uses of photography were shaped by larger epistemic shifts, such as a new obsession with cataloguing human knowledge and classifying social classes. Cf. Peter Hamilton and Roger Hargreaves's socio-cultural study on nineteenth-century photography, *The Beautiful and the Damned. The Creation of Identity in Nineteenth Century Photography* (exhibition catalogue) (Aldershot: Lund Humphries, 2001), 57–8. In his *Passagen-Werk*, Benjamin focuses on such wider considerations of photography's history (see GS, V, 824–46).

63 Molderings even contends that Benjamin's interest in Atget and Bloßfeldt, two nineteenth-century photographers, is coloured by his personal memories to an extent that their aesthetic innovations are overlooked (*Die Moderne der Fotografie*, 168).

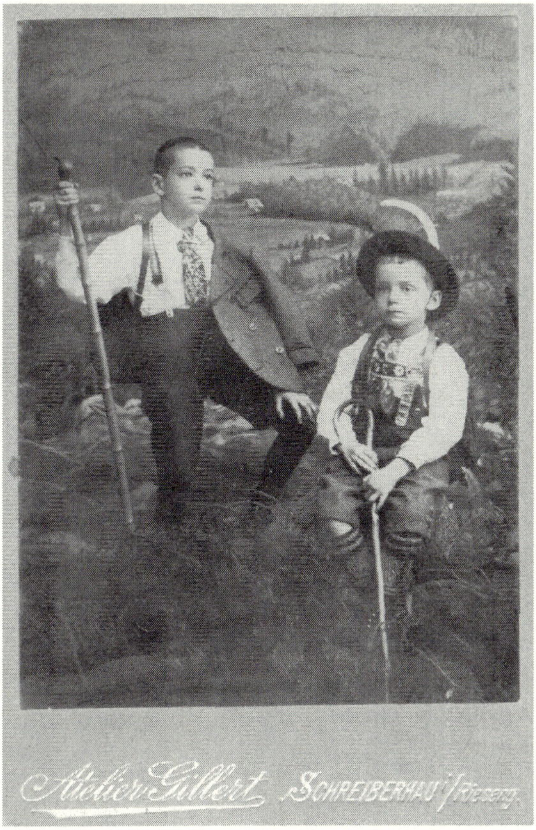

Plate 7 *Carte-de-visite* photograph of Walter and Georg Benjamin in Schreiberhau, 1902.

is a common theme in the history of photography. Yet it is Benjamin's personal memory that renders his critique of photographic production from this period particularly fierce and poignant. As a consequence, his history of photography fully reveals itself to be an evaluation of the medium viewed through the lens of his life experience as much as through that of aesthetics, cultural history or Marxist dialectics.

Like Max Dauthendey in the biography of his father, Benjamin describes the commonplace leather-bound family photograph albums.[64] But while Dauthendey praises the photographs contained in them for bringing back precious memories, Benjamin ridicules such posed family images for their seemingly contrived sentimentality. Not sparing his own family, he cites various portraits of himself, in which as a child he is seen

64 See Dauthendey, *Der Geist meines Vaters*, 363.

as a 'Salontiroler, jodelnd, den Hut gegen gepinselte Firnen schwingend, oder als adretter Matrose, Standbein und Spielbein, wie es sich gehört, gegen den polierten Pfosten gelehnt' (GS, II, 375) ['parlour Tyrolean, yodelling, waving the hat before a painted snowscape, or as a smartly turned-out sailor, standing rakishly with the weight on one leg, as is appropriate, leaning against a polished post' (SW, II, 515)]. Indeed, were it not for the autobiographical inter-texts and evidence of existing pictures that closely resemble Benjamin's evocative description of these theatrical images, these allusions could be taken as manufactured examples in support of the historical evolution – and decline of taste – traced in his history of photography. The 1902 *carte-de-visite* photograph of Benjamin in Schreiberhau with his younger brother Georg, for example, does indeed show the two as 'parlour Tyroleans' in front of a painted background, highlighting the very aspects Benjamin cites as evidence of the clichéd theatricality and artifice of portrait photography during this period.

The boys seem to have been dressed up especially to match the idealized landscape in the background, representing the mountainous region around Schreiberhau (in present-day Poland). Yet, at odds with Benjamin's text, neither of them is waving a hat in the photograph nor indeed looks as if he is singing. There are other studio portraits that resemble Benjamin's description, though they do not entirely match it. They include a second *carte-de-visite* portrait, depicting Benjamin with his younger brother and sister in sailor suits.

In the attempt to create an idyllic, bourgeois family picture, the three children, who were clearly dressed up to have their picture taken in a Berlin studio, pose in front of another artificial backdrop.[65] The pictorial coherence of the background screen and the posing children is belied by the carpet and upholstered furniture around which they are grouped. Together with the then-fashionable sailor suits worn by Walter and Georg, everything about the portrait strongly resonates with Benjamin's evocation of family album photographs in the 'Kleine Geschichte der Photographie'. However, the juxtaposition of text and corresponding (albeit not entirely matching) image shows that his account is not a straightforward factual description of what is seen in the existing photographs, but is, rather, a more allusive

65 Cf. Geoffrey Batchen's compelling analysis of *carte-de-visite* photographs and 'bourgeois imagination', in 'Dreams of Ordinary Life. Cartes-de-visite and the Bourgeois Imagination', in Martha Langford (ed.), *Image and Imagination* (Québec: McGill-Queen's University Press, 2005), 63–74.

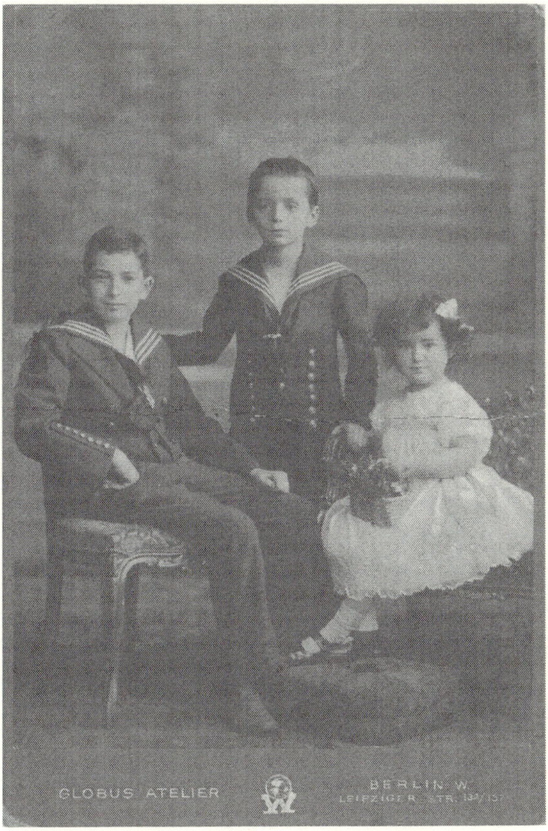

PLATE 8 *Carte-de-visite* photograph of Walter, Georg and Dora Benjamin, around 1904.

and imaginative extrapolation from them.[66] This underscores Benjamin's playful and mnemonic engagement with certain photographs, in spite of his and other early-twentieth-century theorists' championing of photography as a medium of great representational exactitude. These images are charged with emotion and can be related to what, in his essay on 'Das Kunstwerk

66 There is another very faded and time-worn photograph that Benjamin might have had in mind when writing his history of photography. It shows Benjamin as a four-year-old boy, dressed in a sailor suit and wearing a large hat. This picture was taken outside, however, and he is posing together with his cousin, Gertrud Kolmer, and their grandmother, Hedwig Schoenflies. A reproduction of the photograph can be found in Rolf Tiedemann, Christoph Gödde and Henri Lonitz (eds.), *Walter Benjamin 1892–1940* (exhibition catalogue) (Marbach: Deutsche Schillergesellschaft, 1990), 18.

im Zeitalter seiner technischen Reproduzierbarkeit', Benjamin calls a 'cult of remembrance'.

In this essay, photography is portrayed as a key contributor to a wider displacement of values that effect our understanding and experience of artworks. This is a shift from 'Kultwert' ('cult value'), based on the object's inaccessibility, to 'Ausstellungswert' ('exhibition value'), relating to its wide access (GS, I, 485).[67] Against the background of this cultural shift, Benjamin's argument is squarely focused on the many implications of an artwork's visual reproducibility via photography. He argues that, from a historical point of view, the traditionally ceremonial context from which the autonomous artwork emerged not only grants a particular spatio-temporal place to it but also guarantees its uniqueness, which, here at least, is seen as equivalent to aura (see GS, I, 480). According to Benjamin, photography dispels aura by reproducing the artwork and making it available to a large number of viewers in a multitude of places. It promotes the public exhibition of the work, as opposed to its private and exclusive viewing, harkening back to past ritualistic experiences that are somehow partly retained in the work. Even though this is never explicitly acknowledged, photography is understood here in a very narrow sense indeed, namely as a means of the reproduction and dissemination of images of artworks.[68] One near-contemporary of Benjamin, André Malraux, sees this as a cultural gain – for the mobility of reproduced artworks in both space and time allows for a novel diachronic and cross-cultural understanding of art. The reproduced artwork can travel in the form of a two-dimensional image and is thus constitutive of an 'imaginary museum' where images of European paintings sit alongside those of Indian, Japanese or Byzantine sculptures.[69] By contrast, and despite the fact that reproducibility and related easy dissemination may also grant anti-elitist and democratic access to artworks (or, at least,

---

67 From an empirical point of view, during the same time, the New Yorker Museum of Modern Art recreated the 'cult value' that Benjamin associates with painting for photography by presenting it in large-scale exhibitions formerly reserved for painting, as Christopher Phillips has argued ('The Judgment Seat of Photography', in Annette Michelson et al. (eds.), *October. The First Decade, 1976–1986* (Cambridge, MA: MIT Press, 1987), 257–93).

68 The arguments forwarded in the 'Kunstwerk' essay have often been erroneously generalized, resulting in the simplistic opposition of all aura and photography.

69 See André Malraux, *Le Musée imaginaire* (Paris: Gallimard, 1965), 15–16 (originally published in 1947).

their images),[70] Benjamin's theme is primarily one of loss. However, and crucially for our main focus, Benjamin does acknowledge that the shift from cult to exhibition value (and the corresponding loss of aura) is not a straightforward one with respect to photographic portraiture.

All four versions of the 'Kunstwerk' essay include one chapter devoted to how aura may still dwell in later photographs even if the mass development and use of the medium at large contributes to its disappearance.[71] Reminiscent of his earlier arguments concerning nineteenth-century portraiture in the 'Kleine Geschichte der Photographie', Benjamin describes the human face in photographs as the last residuum of aura: 'Im flüchtigen Ausdruck eines Menschengesichts winkt aus den frühen Photographien die Aura zum letzten Mal' (GS, I, 485) ['In the fleeting expression of a human face, the aura beckons from early photographs for the last time' (SW, IV, 258)]. Rather than emphasizing the technological and formalistic foundation of aura as he did in relation to mid-nineteenth-century photographs, where it is at least closely related, if not identical, to their aesthetic value as physical artefacts, Benjamin now emphasizes the connection between aura and the viewer's relation to the photographic referent, i.e. the sitter. Aura is thus bound to the 'Kult der Erinnerung an die fernen oder die abgestorbenen Lieben' (GS, I, 485) ['cult of remembrance of dead or absent loved ones' (SW, IV, 258)]. This in turn provides for a potentially auratic quality to the more personal family photographs that Benjamin dismissed in 1931 as being negligible in these terms, in light of their contrived and stereotypical trappings. Such images now become the locus for a new form of photographic aura even more closely bound to the identity of the photographed subject, an aura which has become wholly separable from the art and craft of the medium and any aesthetic considerations.

In addition, the theme of absence and death, emphasized by Benjamin in relation to the portrait of the Newhaven fishwife, and more strongly with respect to the self-portrait by Dauthendey with his future wife, takes on a new significance in relation to family-album-type portraits. Their nostalgic and commemorative appeal to the attentive viewer that

70 This view seems particularly appropriate in the age of digital reproduction and dissemination via the internet. For discussions of Benjamin's 'Kunstwerk' essay in this contemporary context, see Hans Ulrich Gumbrecht and Michael Marrinan (eds.), *Mapping Benjamin: The Work of Art in the Digital Age* (Stanford: Stanford University Press, 2003).

71 The passage can be found in GS, I, 445-6 (first version), GS, VII, 360–1 (second version), GS, I, 718 (French version) and GS, I, 485 (third and canonical version).

Benjamin acknowledges is related to Kracauer's idea that a photographic portrait harbours the depicted person's history under a layer of snow ('Schneedecke' is the word used by Kracauer), a poetic notion Benjamin was familiar with (which replaces a more conventional expression of the dust or sands of time).[72] Applied to Benjamin's argument, it can be said that in the case of a portrait of a family member or a loved one, the hidden story is known to the viewer and hence the photograph speaks to him or her in a much more personal and existential way; as a result, its demand is more strongly felt. In sum, Benjamin thus exempts the family photograph from the wider shift from cult value to exhibition value and the concurrent decline of aura, to which photographic technology significantly contributes.

To return to the 'Kleine Geschichte der Photographie', in it Benjamin draws attention to one particular family-album photograph from the late 1880s which transcends the contrived and artificial studio setting characteristic of the genre. This is the child portrait of Franz Kafka depicted in what Benjamin describes as a kind of a winter garden in 1888/89. Benjamin regards this portrait as an equivalent of early portraiture in which 'die Menschen noch nicht abgesprengt und gottverloren in die Welt sahen' (GS, II, 376) ['people did not yet look out at the world in such an excluded and godforsaken manner' (SW, II, 515)].[73] Carolin Duttlinger succinctly argues that for Benjamin the Kafka portrait thus 'remains associated with a phenomenon [aura] whose decline it simultaneously illustrates'.[74] This is disconcertingly at odds with Benjamin's historical taxonomy of early auratic portraiture, less auratic, turn-of-the-century photographs, and the modern, avant-garde images (or Atget's documentary

72 Kracauer, *Das Ornament der Masse*, 26. Besides directly quoting Kracauer in his 'Kleine Geschichte der Photographie' (see GS, II, 373), Benjamin announces the upcoming publication of his friend's famous article on photography (which appeared in 1927) in a letter from Paris, where Kracauer apparently visited him around that time (see GB, III, 291). Schöttker, similarly contends that Benjamin here builds on Kracauer's ideas (Benjamin, *Das Kunstwerk*, 143).

73 Interestingly, Benjamin unequivocally models this argument on Goll's introductory remarks to Recht's book on early photography, where the effect and quality of early portraits is described as related to a 'menschliche Atmosphäre' ['human atmosphere'] (*Die Alte Photographie*, 14). It is clear that Benjamin changed Goll's terminology into his own, adding another source for his concept of aura, some of which Werner Fuld attempts to locate ('Die Aura. Zur Geschichte eines Begriffs bei Benjamin', *Akzente*, 3 (1979), 352–70).

74 Duttlinger, 'Imaginary Encounters', 88.

photography) that completely lack aura. Rather than neatly fitting into these classifications, the Kafka portrait exemplifies a kind of experience akin to the 'cult of remembrance' described in the essay on the 'Kunstwerk' which in this sense provides a belated explanation for what the 'Kleine Geschichte der Photographie' performs and enacts in relation to the Kafka portrait. Namely, it associates an auratic quality as an experiential phenomenon with the beholder's interaction with the individual picture rather than one period or style of photographic production.

In sum, the Kafka portrait represents the culminating photograph of Benjamin's history of photography as centred on the viewing subject. Despite continuing to be associated with aura, but in a new form, Benjamin's provocatively affective response to this singular image can more precisely be aligned with a novel concept of *photographic singularity*. As we will see in the following chapter, Benjamin's engagement with the childhood portrait entails psychological and emotional responses, and an existential investment in the image, which go well beyond any of the aspects encompassed in his many definitions of aura.

Chapter 2

Alter Ego: The Childhood Portrait of Franz Kafka

The portrait of Kafka seems to fall outside of the general historical, socio-cultural and technological arguments of the 'Kleine Geschichte der Photographie'. As we have seen, these trace the decline of photographic aura and authenticity as photography evolved from a specialist art and craft to an industrialized mass medium driven by commercialization and instrumentality. Yet, in phenomenological and psychological terms, focused on the concrete relation between viewer and image – and, by extension, the human subject of the portrait photograph – and the corollary ethical dimension of its presence, the childhood photograph of Kafka is at the heart of Benjamin's writings on photography. However, the full significance of this portrait emerges only through its recurrence in other texts, where Benjamin's subsequent discussions of the image not only shed new light on its first description in his photography essay but also establish a complex network of compounding relations between text and image, theory and autobiography, within his larger body of work. The emotive importance of the Kafka photograph for Benjamin is most notable in his *Berliner Kindheit um Neunzehnhundert*.[1] Here the image is part of a series of associative superimpositions of various photographs whereby it transforms into Benjamin's own childhood portrait. The Kafka portrait thus comes to exemplify the affective, imaginative and existential investment in a photograph more generally, as bound to the singularity of the viewer's encounter with what is presented.

Let us first turn to the issue of why, in the 'Kleine Geschichte der Photographie', the Kafka portrait is an exception within the clichéd genre of turn-of-the-century family photographs, complete with artificial decor and atmosphere, to which it belongs. It is highly significant that unlike the portraits by Hill/Adamson and Dauthendey, which as reproduced in the text can be directly compared with Benjamin's commentary on them, the

1 Although this text does not deal directly with photography from a theoretical or historical perspective, there is a general affinity between it and the medium, as has been highlighted by Adorno who, in his afterword to the first edition from 1950, refers to the text as consisting of 'Märchenphotographien' ['fairytale photographs'] (*Über Walter Benjamin*, 32). Cf. also Gerhard Richter's interpretation of the *Berliner Kindheit* as an 'act of self-portraiture', in *Benjamin and the Corpus of Autobiography* (Detroit: Wayne State University Press, 2000), 204.

Kafka photograph is absent from the essay. This is despite the fact that it was in Benjamin's possession until his death[2] and that he certainly had some input in the choice of illustrations for his essay.[3] Beyond the possible practical reasons for why it is not included (which we may never know) the visual absence of the portrait – which strikingly mirrors the absence of the crucial portrait of Barthes's mother in *La Chambre claire* – provides the platform for the aforementioned imaginative juxtapositions, which its literal inclusion may have hampered. Its absence may thus reflect either a highly deliberate strategy on Benjamin's part or a less conscious but no less revealing impulse. Benjamin provides a detailed description of the portrait, highlighting the contrasting relation between the setting and the sitter:

> Damals sind jene Ateliers mit ihren Draperien und Palmen, Gobelins und Staffeleien entstanden, die so zweideutig zwischen Exekution und Repräsentation, Folterkammer und Thronsaal schwankten und aus denen ein erschütterndes Zeugnis ein frühes Bildnis von Kafka bringt. Da steht in einem engen, gleichsam demütigenden, mit Posamenten überladenen Kinderanzug der ungefähr sechsjährige Knabe in einer Art von Wintergartenlandschaft. Palmenwedel starren im Hindergrund. Und als gelte es, diese gepolsterten Tropen noch stickiger und schwüler zu machen, trägt das Modell in der Linken einen unmäßig großen Hut mit breiter Krempe, wie ihn Spanier haben. Gewiß, daß es in diesem Arrangement verschwände, wenn nicht die unermeßlich traurigen Augen diese ihnen vorbestimmte Landschaft beherrschen würden. (GS, II, 375)
>
> This was the period of those studios – with their draperies and palm trees, their tapestries and easels – which occupied so ambiguous a place between execution and representation, between torture chamber and throne room, and to which an early portrait of Kafka bears pathetic witness. There the boy stands, perhaps six years old, dressed up in a humiliating child's suit overloaded with trimming, in a kind of winter-

2 The exact circumstances whereby Benjamin came into the possession of this photograph are not known. Since Benjamin never met Kafka, Detlev Schöttker assumes that Kafka's friend Hugo Bergmann, whom Scholem met in Bern in 1919, was part of the channel through which the image ended up in Benjamin's possession ('Benjamins Bilderwelten. Objekte, Theorien, Wirkungen', in Detlev Schöttker (ed.), *Schrift Bilder Denken. Walter Benjamin und die Künste* (Frankfurt a.M.: Suhrkamp, 2004), 10–29: 21, n. 28).

3 Benjamin was a friend of Willy Haas, the publisher and editor of the *Literarische Welt* between 1925 and 1933, where the essay appeared, and he also incorporated two of his own photographs by the German photographer Germaine Krull into his text. See Schöttker's commentary in Benjamin, *Das Kunstwerk*, 158 and the annotations by the editors of the *Gesammelte Schriften*, GS, II, 1141.

> garden landscape. The background is thick with palm fronds. And as if to make these upholstered tropics even stuffier and more oppressive, the sitter holds in his left hand an inordinately large broad-brimmed hat, such as Spaniards wear. He would surely be lost in this setting were it not for his immeasurably sad eyes, which dominate this landscape predestined for him. (SW, II, 515)

Historically speaking, the painted background, together with artificial columns and potted plants, which Benjamin mentions, had come to replace the plain screen and simple settings of earlier portraiture and were ubiquitous by the 1860s.[4] Originally an expression of the new sense of identity and solidarity among the emerging middle class, which sought to lend their photographic likeness an added importance and grandeur through the use of such props,[5] this fashion continued well into the twentieth century. Its iconographic tradition was firmly established during the childhoods of both Benjamin and Kafka. Beyond the historical accuracy of Benjamin's description, however, his in-depth treatment of the absent Kafka-as-child portrait – no other post-1880s photograph is afforded such careful attention – strongly suggests that, for him, it was more than a mere historical document of bourgeois taste.

Diametrically opposed to the evocative natural settings of the cemetery portraits by Hill and Adamson, which encourage and support the sitter's collected expression, as Benjamin argues, the clichéd and overdetermined pictorial arrangement here is like a trap, holding and observing the boy as if he were a prisoner. Although the child's contrived and formal pose eschews the expression of individual identity in favour of signifying bourgeois social and class membership or aspiration,[6] for Benjamin, it more significantly underscores the specific melancholy of the portrait and the boy's unique vulnerability in this alienating setting. This impression is further accentuated by Kafka's costume, which is not unlike the suits that Benjamin and his

---

4 See Beaumont Newhall, *The History of Photography* (New York: The Museum of Modern Art, 1982), 70–1. Benjamin likewise glosses this phenomenon as a development of the 1860s (see GS, II, 375).

5 Batchen argues that the *carte-de-visite* portraits signified 'the political victory of the bourgeoisie' and that they hence functioned as a 'social device' as much as a portrait ('Dreams of Ordinary Life', 65; 68). For a more detailed historical argument surrounding bourgeois portraiture, especially in relation to the pose and studio setting, see Bernd Busch, *Belichtete Welt. Eine Wahrnehmungsgeschichte der Fotografie* (Munich and Vienna: Carl Hanser, 1989), 311–14.

6 See Busch's account of the function of the pose as a 'Schutzschild' ['protective shield'] of social distinctions (ibid., 311).

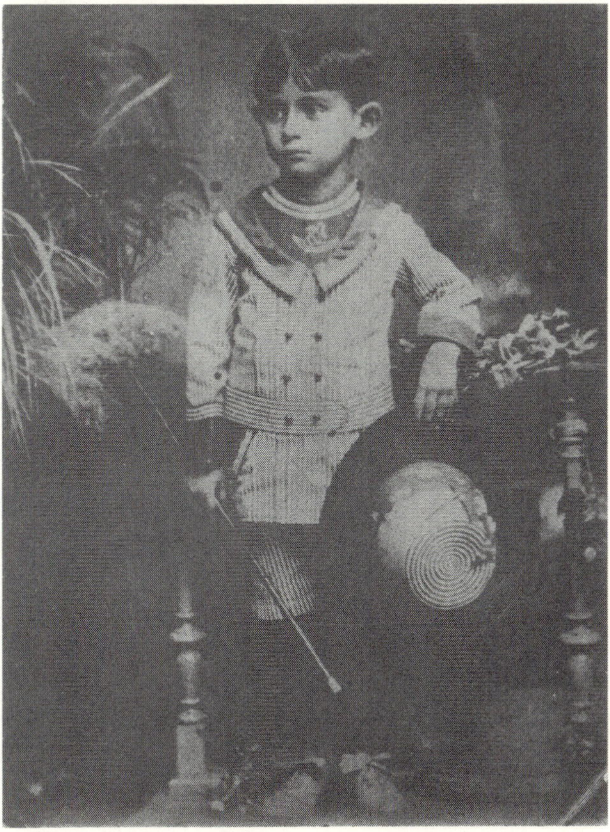

PLATE 9 Childhood portrait of Franz Kafka, 1888/89.

brother wear in a different childhood photograph (see Plate 8). Moreover, when he describes Kafka's dress as 'humiliating', Benjamin is undoubtedly recalling his own sittings in the studio in fancy dress.

Although the winter-garden photograph of Kafka is first cited in relation to Benjamin's own family photographs, including portraits of himself as a child which are offered as prime examples of a decline in photographic taste in the late 1880s, as we have seen, the Kafka portrait disturbs him by virtue of one detail in relation to the image as a whole, namely the boy's 'immeasurably sad eyes'. As in the interrelation between setting and sitter in the portraits by Hill/Adamson, the child's melancholic gaze interacts with the surrounding 'landscape'. In contrast to those early photographs, however, the value of this particular childhood portrait emerges from the perception of the incongruent rather than harmonious nature of this relation. In the midst of the conventional and stifling banality of this then standard portrait iconography, the child's sad gaze challenges its intended sentimental function and bestows upon it a deeper affective quality in some ways similar to that of mid-nineteenth-century portraiture, despite the fact that as an image it lacks their formal and artistic qualities and overall atmosphere with which aura is associated. The child's incongruent relationship with the theatrical studio surroundings, in sum, results in a sense of alienation that sharply contrasts with the symbiosis between sitter and environment in the portraits by Hill/Adamson.

Thus the true significance and value of the childhood portrait of Kafka and its appeal for Benjamin are not rooted in any of the formal features that he and others praised in earlier photography, which are there to be seen on the surface of the images when they are reproduced (as in the 'Kleine Geschichte der Photographie') even without Benjamin's accompanying commentary on them. For it is this formal value and interest as images which such clichéd studio portraits precisely lack on his analysis. Nor does its value reside in the temporal and material process of the photograph's generation, which also defined the exceptionality of mid-nineteenth-century portraiture, for, again, as early as the 1860s, developments in technology had considerably shortened the duration of the image's creation, leading towards the era of instantaneous picture taking. Rather, the significance of the Kafka portrait is a function of the individual viewer's (Benjamin's) relation to the represented content of the photograph, which in this instance is rooted, paradoxically, in the very lack of any original, formal-aesthetic features of the image. Interestingly, in this context, Geoffrey Batchen suggests with respect to the *carte-de-visite* image as a genre that 'the more banal the photograph, the greater its capacity to induce us to exercise our imaginations'.[7] This clearly also applies to Benjamin's response to the Kafka-as-child portrait, although, characteristically for Benjamin, it is only part of a more complex dialectic with respect to this image.

The particular tension between the setting of the portrait and Kafka's bearing and gaze comes to the fore only in and through Benjamin's highly

7 Batchen, 'Dreams of Ordinary Life', 74. Jean-Paul Sartre refers to a similar 'phenomenological paradox' whereby 'des images extrêmement pauvres et tronquées . . . peuvent avoir pour moi un sens riche et profond' ['extremely poor and truncated images . . . can have a rich and profound sense for me'] (*L'Imaginaire. Psychologie phénoménologique de l'imagination* (Paris: Gallimard, 2005), 29; *The Imaginary. A Phenomenological Psychology of the Imagination*, trans. Jonathan Webber (London and New York: Routlegde, 2006), 11).

impressionistic description of it. Thus, while in one sense the inclusion of the photograph in the 'Kleine Geschichte der Photographie' would have made his observations concerning it more literally persuasive, in another, the fact of its absence further reinforces the idea that its deepest meanings are ultimately personal, subjective and affective – not simply there to be directly perceived. We can appreciate the sadness expressed in Kafka's eyes, with or without Benjamin drawing our attention to it. However, lacking the multivalent personal connections and associations with the image that Benjamin possesses, its affective depth and full poignancy are forever inaccessible, for they are a property of a unique historical and personal confluence. Benjamin's consideration of what is most authentic and positive in photography thus shifts here from aspects of the photographic image in itself, as a perceptual object, to the photograph as the locus of a profound and singular life event for the beholder. And it is the task of the writer who has had such an experience to convey the sense of this singularity to others, despite its seeming impossibility.

This tension between what anyone may see in the Kafka portrait and what only Benjamin sees, implicit in the 'Kleine Geschichte der Photographie', and which may be extrapolated to apply to potentially any portrait photograph and any 'privileged' viewer of it (that is to say, the viewer with such an existential relation to its represented content) is more directly suggested in Benjamin's overtly autobiographical writings.

The Kafka Portrait and Benjamin's Childhood Memories

Shortly after writing the 'Kleine Geschichte der Photographie', Benjamin started working on a personal childhood memoir, also intended to be a reflection of turn-of-the-century Berlin life. Known as the *Berliner Kindheit um Neunzehnhundert*, it was published as a whole only posthumously.[8] Neither the first draft of this text, titled *Berliner Chronik* (from 1931) nor its last version (from 1938) include any direct reference to the Kafka portrait by name. Only the 1932 version of the *Berliner Kindheit* contains a key passage in which, as Anna Stüssi has pointed out,

8 During Benjamin's lifetime only separate chapters appeared in various newspapers (the *Frankfurter* and the *Vossische Zeitung*, for example) and after August 1933 Benjamin used pseudonyms (Detlef Holz and C. Conrad) to do so. See Anja Lemke's entry in Burkhardt Lindner (ed.), *Benjamin-Handbuch. Leben, Werk, Wirkung* (Stuttgart and Weimar: Metzler, 2006), 654.

Benjamin's account of his memory of being photographed as a child, in the 'Mummerehlen' chapter, merges and blends with the description of the Kafka portrait in the essay on photography, quoted above, wherein he imaginatively reconstructs the scenario of its creation and the young Kafka's experience.[9] As has often been acknowledged in the wake of Stüssi's finding, Benjamin's description of the portrait in the *Berliner Kindheit* is nearly identical to his previous discussions of the Kafka image in both the 'Kleine Geschichte der Photographie' and his essay 'Franz Kafka' from 1934 (see GS, II, 416).[10] Yet in the *Berliner Kindheit* he changes the personal pronouns when referring to the sitter, replacing 'he' (Kafka) with 'I' (Benjamin). The passage reads as follows:

> Wohin ich blickte, sah ich mich umstellt von Leinwandschirmen, Polstern, Sockeln, die nach meinem Bilde gierten wie die Schatten des Hades nach dem Blut des Opfertieres. Am Ende brachte man mich einem roh gepinselten Prospekt der Alpen dar, und meine Rechte, die ein Gemsbarthütlein erheben mußte, legte auf die Wolken und Firnen der Bespannung ihren Schatten. Doch das gequälte Lächeln um den Mund des kleinen Älplers ist nicht so betrübend wie der Blick, der aus dem Kinderantlitz, das im Schatten der Zimmerpalme liegt, sich in mich senkt. Sie stammt aus einem jener Ateliers, welche mit ihren Schemeln und Stativen, Gobelins und Staffeleien etwas vom Boudoir und von der Folterkammer haben. Ich stehe barhaupt da; in meiner Linken einen gewaltigen Sombrero, den ich mit einstudierter Grazie hängen lasse. Die Rechte ist mit einem Stock befaßt, dessen gesenkter Knauf im Vordergrund zu sehen ist, indessen sich sein Ende in einem Büschel von Pleureusen birgt, die sich von einem Gartentisch ergießen. Ganz abseits, neben der Portiere, stand die Mutter starr, in einer engen Taille. Wie eine Schneiderfigurine blickt sie auf meinen Samtanzug, der seinerseits mit Posamenten überladen und von einem Modeblatt zu stammen scheint. (GS, IV, 261)
>
> Wherever I looked, I saw myself surrounded by folding screens, cushions and pedestals which craved my image much as the shades of Hades craved the blood of the sacrificial animal. In the end, I was offered up to a crudely painted prospect of the Alps, and my right hand, which had to brandish a kidskin hat, cast its shadow on the clouds and snowfields of the backdrop. But the tortured smile on the lips of the little mountaineer is not as disturbing as the

9 See Anna Stüssi, *Erinnerung an die Zukunft. Walter Benjamins 'Berliner Kindheit um Neunzehnhundert'* (Göttingen: Vandenhoeck & Ruprecht, 1977), 189–92.

10 The ekphrastic account included in the 'Kafka' essay is introduced in a passage entitled 'Ein Kinderbild' ['A Childhood Photograph'] which, for Benjamin, is an emblem of an '"arme kurze Kindheit"' (GS, II, 416) ['"poor, brief childhood"' (SW, II, 800)], as he quotes from Kafka's novella 'Josefine'. Cf. Carolin Duttlinger's interpretation of the passage in Benjamin's essay, *Kafka and Photography* (Oxford: Oxford University Press, 2007), 21–30.

> look I take in now from the child's face, which lies in the shadow of a potted palm. The latter comes from one of those studios which – with their footstools and tripods, tapestries and easels – put you in mind of both a boudoir and a torture chamber. I am standing there bareheaded, my left hand holding a giant sombrero which I dangle with studied grace. My right hand is occupied with a walking stick, whose curved handle can be seen in the foreground while its tip remains hidden in a cluster of ostrich feathers spilling from a garden table. Over to the side, near the curtained doorway, my mother stands motionless in her tight bodice. Like a tailor's dummy, she stares at my velvet suit, which for its part is laden with braid and other trimming and looks like something from a fashion magazine. (SW, III, 391–2)

The Kafka portrait is here increasingly experienced and presented by Benjamin as an image of himself. Whether this is a simple confusion and unintended similarity, perhaps resulting from a wider identification with Kafka, or a more deliberate strategy on Benjamin's part to blur the identity of the children alluded to,[11] or indeed something between these scenarios, it is the clearest indication of Benjamin's quasi phenomenological approach to the photographic image to date. This entails describing aspects of the viewing subject's encounter with photographs in the concrete form of his own experience.

There is, however, another specific inspiration for this passage apart from the Kafka portrait, namely the aforementioned Schreiberhau *carte-de-visite* photograph of Benjamin and his brother, also referred to in the 'Kleine Geschichte der Photographie'. Undoubtedly, the commonly held view that Benjamin drew on both the double portrait taken in Schreiberhau and the Kafka photograph for this description derives much of its persuasiveness from the documented existence of the two photographs.[12] In contradistinction, Detlev Schöttker has pointed out that Benjamin might have had another, and now lost, photograph in mind when writing this passage,[13] an assumption that can be sustained by a written testimony. In 1933, Benjamin wrote to Gretel Karplus, Adorno's future wife, asking her whether she remembered the 'Mummerehlen' chapter in which he wrote of a 'Kinderbild von mir, dessen Original ich Ihnen einmal gezeigt

11 See Linda Haverty Rugg's analysis of Benjamin's staging of a 'plurality of selfhood', in *Picturing Ourselves: Photography and Autobiography* (Chicago and London: University of Chicago Press, 1997), 187.

12 Indeed, it is often exclusively these two images that accompany critical commentaries on the passage. See, for example, Rugg, *Picturing Ourselves*, figs. 3.4 and 3.5 and, more recently, Nitsche, *Benjamins Gebrauch der Fotografie*, figs. 41 and 42.

13 See Schöttker, 'Benjamins Bilderwelten', 21.

habe' ['childhood photograph of myself, the original of which I have shown you once'].[14] He adds that in this photograph he stands in front of a palm tree, dressed in a rather ridiculous costume. Enclosed in this letter Benjamin sent a more recent passport photograph of himself, from the early 1930s, which he describes as being a similarly contrived portrait as the one from 35 years before. This dates the possible, missing picture at around 1898 when Benjamin was six years old and thus corresponds to both the date of the Kafka portrait and Kafka's age in the photograph.

However, the detailed resemblance between the description in the *Berliner Kindheit* and the Kafka portrait still raises substantial doubts as to whether Benjamin is describing an unknown or lost portrait of himself. The description matches the two existing (and possibly lost third) photographs in certain respects, yet never fully coincides with any of them. Except for the missing hat in his right hand and the omission of his younger brother, the first half of Benjamin's account evokes the double portrait of Walter and Georg Benjamin (see Plate 7). On the other hand, the second half of the passage seems to describe the Kafka portrait. This conflation (together with the suggested presence of the mother) highlights the imaginary and mnemonic character of Benjamin's ekphrasis. Its allusive nature comes to light only with the benefit of a comparison between the two actual photographs and the text, which reveals a subtle and complex ekphrastic superimposition of mental images on photographic ones. Neither the actual Kafka portrait nor the various Benjamin childhood portraits are included in the *Berliner Kindheit*, which presumably was not intended to be illustrated, unlike his 'Kleine Geschichte der Photographie', where the absence of these images is thus more striking. This fact, in turn, underscores the sense of Benjamin's highly emotional, affective and self-identificatory response to the Kafka portrait, noted in relation to his first discussion of it in his essay on the history of photography.

On the subject of written descriptions of images more generally, the American media-theorist William Mitchell has critiqued John Hollander's distinction between two types of ekphrasis, a 'notional' one of imaginary or lost artworks and an actual ekphrasis of familiar and well-known ones. Mitchell is surely correct in arguing that all ekphrasis is notional insofar as it 'seeks to create a specific image that is to be found only in the text'.[15] In

14 Gretel Adorno and Walter Benjamin, *Briefwechsel 1930–1940*, eds. Christoph Gödde and Henri Lonitz (Frankfurt a.M.: Suhrkamp, 2005), 68.

15 William J.T. Mitchell, *Picture Theory: Essays on Verbal and Visual Representation* (Chicago and London: University of Chicago Press, 1994), 157, n. 19.

his criticism he touches on the central problem of ekphrasis as the verbal mimesis of an artistic image and on the question of what happens to the image in its transformation from one medium to another. Comparing the possible photographic counterpieces to Benjamin's text, it is clear that the 'images' in his autobiographical writing are notably enriched by imagination and fabulation. The photograph here is not simply perceived as an image already replete with the real. Rather, its reality is actualized and animated by the viewer in serving only as the starting point for a flight of creative imagination, resulting in superimposition,[16] which is, paradoxically perhaps, rooted in the portrait's factual and indexical representation of a reality before the camera. Similar to the photographic technique of multiple exposure of one photographic plate or negative, resulting in a composite image, Benjamin's ekphrasis in his *Berliner Kindheit* is like a memory plate that as been exposed to several images as seen and remembered.[17] This speaks to the fact that Benjamin's engagement with the Kafka portrait is not only an 'imaginary encounter'[18] with a person and writer to whom Benjamin felt a close cultural and intellectual affinity, despite their never having met each other, but the occasion for a self-reflexive dynamic of affect and projection/identification drawing Benjamin back into his own childhood.[19]

Although Benjamin's complex engagement with this photograph is fully discernible only in interpretative juxtaposition between the 'Kleine Geschichte der Photographie' and the later *Berliner Kindheit*, it

16 I prefer the concept of 'superimposition' to Stiegler's 'montage' for the reason that superimposition creates a new image by fusing several other ones, without drawing attention to its 'montage' nature (*Theoriegeschichte der Photographie*, 277). More recently, Nitsche has used the term 'Doppelbelichtung' ['double exposure'] in this context (*Benjamins Gebrauch der Fotografie*, 231–3).

17 Benjamin himself suggests an analogy between the gradual developing of memory in consciousness and the developing of an image on a photographic plate in his *Berliner Chronik* (see GS, VI, 516).

18 This expression is borrowed from the title of Duttlinger's article, 'Imaginary Encounters', where she discusses Benjamin's description of the Kafka portrait (86–91).

19 Benjamin's identification with Kafka has often been highlighted. See, for example, André Gunthert, 'Le Temps retrouvé. Walter Benjamin et la photographie', in Marie-D. Garnier (ed.), *Jardins d'hiver. Littérature et photographie* (Paris: Presses de l'École Normale Supérieure, 1997), 43–54: 53 and Berg, *Die Ikone des Realen*, 102. For an account of Benjamin's more intellectual identification with Kafka, see Young-Ok Kim, *Selbstporträt im Text des Anderen. Walter Benjamins Kafka-Lektüre* (Frankfurt a.M.: Peter Lang, 1995), 321–68.

is experienced and presented as exceptional already in the former. The young boy's sadness overpowers the studio landscape and invests its then fashionable generic formula with a singular individuality, transcending the conventions of bourgeois portraiture. The photograph's 'uferlose Trauer' (GS, II, 375) ['boundless sadness'], as perceived by Benjamin, cannot be accounted for by any general historical or aesthetic categories applied to photography. Although on one level the suggested winter-garden setting calls to mind a suspension or freezing of the natural progression of seasons, and therefore the passage of time, for Benjamin this background also constitutes a reference to passing and contingent bourgeois taste, which is here preserved. Nonetheless, Kafka's sad eyes endow the image with a poignant sadness, recalling the romantic association of time-worn objects with melancholy.

Relating to its iconography, the central characteristics of both the childhood photograph of Kafka described in the 'Kleine Geschichte der Photographie' and its double described in the *Berliner Kindheit* – namely, theatricality and melancholy – align it with aspects of allegory as defined in Benjamin's *Ursprung des deutschen Trauerspiels* [*Origin of German Tragic Drama*]. This book is of importance for the present argument to the extent to which it sheds light on certain aspects of photography that are also reflected in Benjamin's engagement with the Kafka portrait, even if in submerged or implicit fashion. Benjamin critiques the dominant, classical notion of allegory and attempts to develop a new understanding of it based in the baroque genre of *Trauerspiel*.[20] The central notion here is an arresting of time through mimetic representation. Although the writing of the *Ursprung des deutschen Trauerspiels* (between 1916 and 1925) predates Benjamin's work on photography in the late 1920s, Hubertus von Amelunxen has argued that Benjamin's reflections on the relation between allegory and melancholy cast a potentially sharper light on the nature of the medium than the writings he actually devotes to it.[21] And what it reveals significantly overlaps with Barthes's later discussion of photography, time and mortality.

20 For a comprehensive summary of the complex philosophical issues addressed in this book, see Bettine Menke's entry, in Lindner (ed.), *Benjamin-Handbuch*, 210–29.

21 See Hubertus von Amelunxen, 'Skiagraphia – Silberchlorid und schwarze Galle. Zur allegorischen Bestimmung des photographischen Bildes', in Willem van Reijn (ed.), *Allegorie und Melancholie* (Frankfurt a.M.: Suhrkamp, 1992), 90–108: 96. The connection between photography and Benjamin's reflections on allegory has also been highlighted by Busch (*Belichtete Welt*, 333–5).

Von Amelunxen begins with Barthes's idea concerning the kinship between photography and theatre by virtue of their common and traditional relation to the cult of the dead (see CC, 56). Comparing the theatrical *tableau vivant* and the photograph, von Amelunxen argues that they both paradoxically represent life by symbolically mortifying it, doing so in allegorical fashion: 'Die Photographie und das *tableau vivant* verbindet ihre allegorische Kontur: beide vermitteln jene *fausse apparence du présent*, sie denunzieren den falschen Schein der Gegenwart, indem sie den Abschied von der Gegenwart zur Darstellung bringen'[22] ['Photography and the *tableau vivant* are related through their allegorical contour: both convey that *false appearance of being present*; they denounce the false appearance of the present by representing the departure from presence']. In other words, photography and the *tableau vivant* represent a dialectics of life and death inasmuch as both depart from presence by stopping and thereby mortifying a passing instance of life. The French expression used by von Amelunxen is taken from both Derrida's discussion of mimesis with respect to Plato and, more importantly, in relation to the conjunction of photography with theatre – Stéphane Mallarmé's short text on art as mimesis titled 'Mimique' (from 1886). In this text on Paul Margueritte's pantomime *Pierrot assassin de sa femme* [*Pierrot Murderer of His Wife*], Mallarmé writes of the ability of the mime to present actions of the past and future while they appear to be in the present. Thus the mime's act creates an '*apparence fausse de présent*' ['*false appearance of the present*'].[23] In von Amelunxen's view, this suspension of time is precisely what links the photograph to the *tableau vivant*: both are mortified fragments of the continuum of life and are therefore similar to the allegorical object according to Benjamin's definition of it.

Indeed, there is no denying the remarkable similarity between photography and what Benjamin describes as the allegorical transformation from life to death in the context of the *Trauerspiel*. He writes how the melancholic gaze contributes to allegorization and mortification of the object: 'Wird der Gegenstand unterm Blick der Melancholie allegorisch, läßt sie das Leben von ihm abfließen, bleibt er als toter, doch in Ewigkeit

22 Von Amelunxen, 'Skiagraphia - Silberchlorid und schwarze Galle', 96.

23 Stéphane Mallarmé, *Œuvres complètes*, 2 vols., ed. Bertrand Marchal (Paris: Gallimard/Bibliothèque de la Pléiade, 2003), vol. 2, 178–9. Derrida, in his interpretation of Mallarmé, adds the critical notion that the mime, rather than mimicking presence, in fact imitates nothing ('La Double séance', in *La Dissémination* (Paris: Seuil, 1972), 199–317: 221).

gesicherter zurück, so liegt er vor dem Allegoriker, auf Gnade und Ungnade ihm überliefert' (GS, I, 359) ['If the object becomes allegorical under the gaze of melancholy, if melancholy causes life to flow out of it, it remains behind dead, but eternally secure, then it is exposed to the allegorist, it is unconditionally in his power' (OG, 183–4)]. Just as the object becomes lifeless and allegorical under the 'gaze of melancholy', so too does the photographic image fix a person or object under the gaze of the lens, thereby mortifying them.[24]

Benjamin, however, does not fail to see the significance of the positive safeguarding or embalming aspect that goes hand in hand with mortification. He draws attention to the fact that the mortified object may act as a passage to something else, something alive: 'In seiner [des Allegorikers] Hand wird das Ding zu etwas anderem . . . und es wird ihm ein Schlüssel zum Bereiche verborgenen Wissens, als dessen Emblem er es verehrt' (GS, I, 359) ['In his hands the object becomes something different; . . . for him it becomes a key to the realm of hidden knowledge, as the emblem of which he reveres it' (OG, 184)]. For Benjamin, the object becomes a 'fixiertes Bild' (GS, I, 359) ['fixed image' (OG, 184)], thus allowing for the discovery of a 'realm of hidden knowledge'.

The conceptual affinity with photography here, together with the notion of unlocking a hitherto inaccessible realm, is strongly echoed in Benjamin's 'Mummerehlen' chapter of the *Berliner Kindheit*.[25] In the autobiographical text, it is the fixed image of photography that leads to the affective 'inside' of a lived past (see GS, IV, 261). Moreover, it is through these complex interrelations that the connection between the perceived sadness of Kafka's gaze in his childhood portrait and its allegorical and fragmentary character come to the fore. While the Kafka portrait is closely associated with melancholy and the arrest of chronological time, it is simultaneously evocative of a hidden story of the past. In fact, it is perhaps by virtue of this very freezing of time, suggestive of a 'false totality',[26] that the image triggers a flight of imagination. In other words, the viewer integrates the photograph into a new continuum of time, that is to say, his own (life-) story.

24 Cf. Duttlinger, *Kafka and Photography*, 29.

25 The connection between Benjamin's autobiographical writings and his book on German tragic drama is not fortuitous. Scholem has highlighted that, especially in relation to melancholy, the study on the *Trauerspiel* has indeed an autobiographical subtext (*Walter Benjamin und sein Engel*, 37–8).

26 This expression is borrowed from Busch, *Belichtete Welt*, 334.

Benjamin's engagement with the childhood portrait of Kafka, then, is a manifestation of his attempt to lift the 'layers of snow' from the photograph, to use Kracauer's metaphor, and to unearth the hidden story of the sitter that is mutatis mutandis also his own past, which this photograph of the other unlocks. Its evocation of a lost time is thus equivalent to what Benjamin in his 'Kleine Geschichte der Photographie' calls the 'magic' of the photograph. In the following section we shall examine the ways in which this applies to the Kafka portrait in particular, and how the magical effect of certain photographs in Benjamin's account is related to the subject-centred orientation of his reflections on photography by way of language, childhood and memory.

Language, Magic and Photography

Benjamin's account of the Kafka-as-child photograph in the *Berliner Kindheit* is interwoven with a complex interplay of present and past, self and other, actuality and imagination. In the 'Mummerehlen' chapter, these themes are related not only to photography in general, and the arresting childhood portrait in particular, but also to Benjamin's concept of language and magic. These two subjects can be provocatively linked to the temporal aspects of the photographic portrait, on the one hand, and to the sitter's identity and past reality, on the other. Magic is central to Benjamin's reflections on the nature of language[27] and also underscores a conceptual affinity with Proust. Winfried Menninghaus has argued that *À la recherche du temps perdu* served Benjamin as a model for his autobiographical writings, particularly with regard to the suggested magic quality of (proper) names.[28] Benjamin's 'theory of the magic of language' – to borrow

27 This relation is especially pronounced in his 1916 'Über Sprache überhaupt und über die Sprache des Menschen' ['On Language as Such and on Language of Man'], which forms part of his philosophy of language during the late 1910s and 1920s. For a concise overview of Benjamin's complex conceptualization of language, see Michael Bröcker's entry on 'Sprache' in Opitz and Wizisla (eds.), *Benjamins Begriffe*, vol. 2, 740–73.

28 Winfried Menninghaus, *Walter Benjamins Theorie der Sprachmagie* (Frankfurt a.M.: Suhrkamp, 1995), 184–5. For a concise contrasting between Benjamin's and Proust's childhood memoirs in relation to their understanding of time experience, see Peter Szondi, 'Hoffnung im Vergangenen. Über Walter Benjamin', in *Schriften II* (Frankfurt a.M.: Suhrkamp, 1978), 275–94: 282–8.

the title of Menninghaus's study – overlaps with his conception of the unique magic of photography, with both being closely related to childhood experience and remembrance. While Benjamin's complex theory of language cannot be explicated here, we can trace some suggestive connections between language, magic and photography as prompted by the narrative of the *Berliner Kindheit*.[29]

The title of the chapter in question, 'Die Mummerehlen', is a reference to a children's nursery rhyme, with the opening line referring to a character named Muhme Rehlen, translating into English as Auntie Rehlen, 'Muhme' being an archaic German word for aunt, and Rehlen a surname. The child – in his narrative the young Benjamin – upon hearing the rhyme but not knowing the meaning of these two new obscure words creates a non-existent compound word, 'Mummerehlen'. This is then erroneously taken by the child to refer to ghosts, via the phonetic similarity with the German 'mummen' (GS, IV, 261), literally to be wrapped up in a covering, as in a death sheet or shroud.[30] Benjamin describes the words that result from such creative if unintentional transformations as bridging the realm of the child's life world and that of adult meaning: 'Worte, die auf der Grenze zweier Sprachbereiche, dem der Kinder und der Älteren stehen' (GS, VI, 495) ['words that exist on the frontier between two linguistic regions, that of children and that of adults' (SW, II, 617)]. However, as his text and his own childhood confusion concretely show, such expressions may also be a vehicle between two other realms, namely past and present, as traversed by memory, since these words remain potent reminders of a magical period of childhood for the adults who recall them.[31] Throughout his life, Benjamin had a continual fascination with children's pre-literacy perception and language acquisition.[32] It is

29 In the context of Benjamin's theory of language, the 'Mummerehlen' chapter is often regarded as an extrapolation of his theoretical concepts. Werner Hamacher states that Benjamin's memoirs are a 'radicalization' of his theoretical programme ('The Word Wolke – If It Is One', in Rainer Nägele (ed.), *Benjamin's Ground. New Readings of Walter Benjamin* (Detroit: Wayne State University Press, 1988), 147–76: 166). Cf. for a 'photographic' reading of the 'Mummerehlen' chapter Rugg, *Picturing Ourselves*, 167–71 and Richter, *Walter Benjamin*, 219–25.

30 Cf. Hamacher's extrapolation of a whole array of such distortions and resonances in the *Berliner Kindheit*, 'The Word Wolke', 161–3.

31 In the *Berliner Chronik* Benjamin declares that these sorts of words inspired the writing of his childhood memoirs (see GS, VI, 495).

32 It is not only his autobiographical writings which testify to this interest but also his considerable collection of children's books (which he started

not surprising, therefore, that he partly builds his so-called philosophy of language (*Sprachphilosophie*) on children's creative misunderstandings and distortion of words, often resulting in inadvertent punning. In poetry, of course, this may be a highly deliberate strategy, where it is termed *paronomasia*, the creation of unexpected meaning through words that sound familiar.

In Benjamin's case, 'Mummerehlen' serves as the entrance to a bygone reality founded on a specific perception of the world that only a child could have. Extrapolating from his experience, Benjamin describes such words as possessing a 'magische Gewalt' (GS, VI, 518) ['magical power' (SW, II, 634)]. We can recall here his reference to the 'magical value' of early photographs in the 'Kleine Geschichte der Photographie' in relation to the Dauthendey self-portrait with his future wife, where it is associated with the uncanny presence of a past reality. The association of magic and photography is a common one that stretches back to the time of the medium's invention. For instance, in 1840, in a short newspaper article on the appearance of the daguerreotype, the American writer Edgar Allan Poe, no stranger to uncanny presences, praised the magical quality of photographic images.[33] However, in light of Benjamin's childhood memories, the relation between magic and photography is more concrete, not only based on the fascination for a new technology, as in Poe's case. Both the Kafka childhood portrait and Benjamin's childhood portrait(s) (or the composite reality they create), and the privileged word, bring back the past in a particularly powerful manner. The magic of photographs and the word 'Mummerehlen' render an absence present. Of course, not just any word serves this function but only one that is related to the particular child's (Benjamin's) reality-shaping expression. Likewise, it is not any photograph that possesses the magic power of bringing the past in the form of an image but only those that may speak to the beholder in a particularly powerful fashion via the channel of personal memory, and which cast their own transformative spell.

---

assembling together with his wife Dora as early as 1918), to which can be added his compilation of postcards of Russian toys and his documenting of the development of his son, Stefan. For an illustrated article in relation to the first point, see Margarethe Gerber, 'Die Kinderbuchsammlung Walter Benjamins', in *Bucklicht Männlein und Engel der Geschichte. Walter Benjamin, Theoretiker der Moderne* (exhibition catalogue) (Giessen: Anabas-Verlag, 1990), 84–91.

33 See Trachtenberg (ed.), *Classic Essays on Photography*, 37.

More abstractly and theoretically, the 'Mummerehlen' chapter explores the themes of childhood language, magic and photography in relation to the concepts of 'Entstellung' ['distortion'][34] and 'Ähnlichkeit' ['similarity' or 'resemblance'], which can be extended to encompass visual mimesis in the form of representation such as photography. Benjamin suggests that distortion, as *Entstellung*, such as the above-noted linguistic distortion, is a mimetic activity through which the child creates a meaningful relation between himself or herself and the surrounding world by creating a picture of that world, even if a distorted or inaccurate one from the adult's point of view.[35] Benjamin views this process of distortion in positive terms, as aiding in the child's construction of self-identity. Indeed, it is, as he writes, an instinctive and necessary process, part of the child's adaptation to the otherwise alien environment in which he or she is immersed.[36] In this context, *Entstellung* actually complements, rather than opposes, mimesis or resemblance conceived as a process of imitation.

Benjamin writes that words unknown to the child, such as 'Muhme Rehlen', have a certain effect on it, namely 'ähnlich zu werden und sich zu verhalten' (GS, IV, 261) ['to become similar and to behave mimetically' (SW, III, 390–1)]. As we have seen, he describes how, as a child, when

34 The first part of the 'Mummerehlen' chapter is an almost playful display of semantic variations of the verb 'stellen' by adding different prefixes: 'ver-stellen', 'ent-stellen' and 'um-stellen' (GS, IV, 260–1).

35 Cf. Hubertus von Amelunxen, 'D'un état mélancolique en photographie. Walter Benjamin et la conception de l'allégorie', *Revue des Sciences Humaines*, 81 (1988), 9–23: 9.

36 The child's inadvertent punning on 'Muhme Rehlen' creates what Benjamin, in his 'Lehre vom Ähnlichen' ['Doctrine of the Similar'] and 'Über das mimetische Vermögen' ['On the Mimetic Faculty'], calls an 'unsinnliche Ähnlichkeit' or 'nonsensuous similarity' (GS, II, 207; SW, II, 696), a term that describes a language concept that simultaneously denotes the mimetic correspondences between language and the world and the arbitrary representational link between the two. This is, in effect, the child combining what the theorist would describe as a pre-modern, magical/mimetic use or understanding of language with a modern one rooted in conventional representation, by creating an 'unsinnliche Ähnlichkeit' between language and the world. As Irving Wohlfarth has argued, however, Benjamin's language theory ultimately refutes the notion of pure arbitrariness and in this sense is anti-Saussurean ('Walter Benjamin's Image of Interpretation', *New German Critique*, 17 (1979), 70–89: 74). For an in-depth discussion of Benjamin's complex understanding of mimesis, see Tilman Lang, *Mimetisches oder semiologisches Vermögen? Studien zu Walter Benjamins Begriff der Mimesis* (Göttingen: Vandenhoeck & Ruprecht, 1998), 25–101.

encountering unfamiliar words, he created meaningful correspondences between himself and his surroundings by establishing links of resemblance between the two where none previously existed. Yet for the six-year-old Benjamin, this mimetic process of apprehension collapsed when faced with the self-reflexive circularity inherent in being the subject/object of a portrait photograph, which left him bewildered: 'Und darum wurde ich so ratlos, wenn man Ähnlichkeit mit mir selbst von mir verlangte' (GS, IV, 261) ['And that is why I was at such a loss when someone demanded of me a resemblance with myself' (SW, III, 391)]. The request to 'be oneself', or resemble oneself, the axiom of traditional portraiture, founded on a concept of iconic resemblance as the guarantor of psychological identity, is alien to the child's instinctive desire to imitate what is other, external and different, and thereby to make it similar, part of one-self, one's life world.[37] Thus Benjamin stresses that the reality of photographic depiction, certainly when it is the self that is represented, is fundamentally different from the reality of the child's perception and comprehension of the world around it. Bearing in mind that Benjamin emphasizes the necessity of the child's distortion of names as part of the creation of a self-identity, there exists an incompatibility between the world imaged by photography and the world perceived and imaginatively created by the child. For photography captures the objective surface of physical reality with an undeniable exactitude. Therefore, what has often been praised as being the achievement of photographic technique, its ability to produce a precise record,[38] separates the child's imaginary mimesis based on creative distortion of the other from photography's iconic mimesis rooted in resemblance and near identity.[39]

---

37 Cf. Eduardo Cadava's compelling reading of the 'Mummerehlen' chapter, which emphasizes the relation between self and alterity, in *Words of Light: Theses on the Photography of History* (Princeton: Princeton University Press, 1997), 106–15.

38 Therein lies the reason for André Bazin's apotheosis of photography in relation to the Western history of representation that he, problematically perhaps, describes as striving for exact mimesis ('Ontologie de l'image photographique', in *Qu'est-ce que le cinéma?* (Paris: Éditions du Cerf, 1999), 9–17: 13–17).

39 From a wider perspective, the relation between photography and language, and autobiography in particular, is complex and requires closer critical analysis of issues such as representation and referentiality. See, for example, Timothy Dow Adams, *Light Writing and Life Writing: Photography in Autobiography* (Chapel Hill and London: University of North Carolina Press, 2000).

Yet although photography resists the distortion or misunderstanding operable in language and thus is not amenable to the creative magic of *Entstellung*, the privileged childhood photograph, in this case, can nonetheless convey something of this magic in a particularly poignant way. The beholder of the portrait, the adult (Benjamin), facing the image of himself as a child, can still regain something of the child's world through its experience. For now, as an adult, the image from childhood is that other, 'not self', which must be mimetically regained through an immersive and mnemonic engagement, one leading back into the 'Inneres' or inside of the child's world (GS, IV, 261). There is, therefore, a parallel implicit here between the magic of certain special words and that of singular portrait photographs.

The Photographic Return of the Self as Other

Against the outlined backdrop of a complex interaction between linguistic and photographic resemblance and distortion, the description of the Kafka-as-child portrait, despite Benjamin's narrative alterations, appears, after all, to be a reasonably truthful ekphrasis of the existing image. The discrepancies between the portrait and its description, as we have seen, bring to light the highly emotive interplay between self and other, or between the self and the 'other self', which is both a central Benjaminian theme and also a psychological and existential dynamic inherent in the experience of portrait photography.[40] In the 'Mummerehlen' chapter Benjamin concludes his description of the image with the seemingly paradoxical claim that he is 'entstellt vor Ähnlichkeit mit allem, was hier um mich ist' (GS, IV, 261) ['distorted by resemblance with all that surrounds me here' (SW, III, 392)]. When applied to photography, the child's otherwise successful mimetic ability fails, as we have seen. In Benjamin's case, he can no longer generate a meaningful correspondence between himself and the world via language. Instead, when the photographer demands of the boy that

40 Gerhard Richter has analysed similar dynamics in relation to what he calls Benjamin's 'confessional and literary writings', arguing that they 'reveal a self that can come into its own only in, and as, another, an alterity', which results in the notion of a 'constantly shifting self' ('Acts of Self-Portraiture: Benjamin's Confessional and Literary Writings', in David S. Ferris (ed.), *The Cambridge Companion to Walter Benjamin* (Cambridge: Cambridge University Press, 2004), 221–37: 221–2).

he 'resemble himself', the boy has a sensation of being distorted in such as way as to resemble the artificial studio surroundings, which are also, if implicitly, associated with the only superficial mimesis of the photograph on the level of appearance. This, in turn, corresponds to the superficial bourgeois identity such generic portraits are intended to convey. The fact that, for Benjamin, Kafka's portrait expresses so much more is a function of his particular mnemonic-affective engagement with the image, rather than of what lies on its perceptual surface as an artefact. This is not only the inverse of Benjamin's suggestions concerning the inherent auratic qualities of mid-nineteenth-century portraiture but also signals his even more radical move away from an ontology and aesthetics of the photographic image to an existential phenomenology of its experience – anticipating Barthes's similar endeavour about half a century later.

Notwithstanding the alienation previously described by Benjamin in relation to Kafka, the evocation of his own portrait allows Benjamin to compare and contrast the external and physiognomic identity of the sitter with the internal and remembered one. In looking back at his childhood as a whole and the photographic portrait simultaneously, he has the benefit of comparing and contrasting his memories with what the image depicts. It is in hindsight that his false resemblance with the studio setting as a boy is diametrically opposed to his authentic resemblance with the imagined and remembered world. The distinction drawn here is similar to Kracauer's distinction between 'Gedächtnisbilder' ['memory images'] and photographic images.[41] In Kracauer's view, photography merely depicts an 'Oberflächenzusammenhang' [a 'surface coherence'] of external phenomena, without providing any clue for the truth and meaning of a lived life.[42] To use the metaphors Benjamin deploys in the 'Mummerehlen' chapter, the relation between the photographic portrait and the lived childhood is analogous to the relation between a 'shell' ('Muschel') and a 'mollusc' ('Weichtier') (GS, IV, 261). The shell represents external aspects of the nineteenth century, just as the photograph depicts the prevalent taste of its time of production. The mollusc represents the sedimented personal history Benjamin recalls as far back as his early childhood around 1900. To us as viewers of the Kafka photograph and readers of Benjamin's *Berliner Kindheit* the photograph is the shell, presenting us

41 Kracauer, *Das Ornament der Masse*, 25–7.

42 Ibid., 27. Both Kracauer and Benjamin are clearly writing in the wake of Proust's contrastive juxtaposition of photographic images and involuntary memory (see Chapter Three).

with a document of bourgeois portrait iconography, whereas Benjamin's reflections on his childhood animate the image and reveal its larger truths, through layers of a mediated life-story.

It could be no other way, as only Benjamin possesses the knowledge, experience and memory of both this collective and personal history. Thus he both knows and feels the discrepancy between what the photograph shows as past and what he remembers as past. The sitter's resemblance with his image could be recognized by any viewer who knew the child, whereas the mental images of memory can be recaptured only by the beholder who was the child.[43] Indeed, the relevant discrepancy between lived reality and photographic reality is perceivable only if sitter and beholder are one, if they are the same person, albeit at different stages of life. This constitutes what can be understood as the photographic return of the alter ego.

In Benjamin's specific encounter with the Kafka-as-child photograph, the return of the alter ego begins with his identification with Kafka as a child. Although of course bound to the admiration of one great writer and thinker for another, all the ways in which Benjamin rediscovers his childhood through Kafka go well beyond an affinity rooted in an artistic, intellectual or religious tradition and lineage.[44] Rather, this rediscovery attaches itself to a moment of past personal and historico-cultural time that is imaginatively shared between the two, with all the poignancy that actual childhood bonds of friendship often entail. While Benjamin's discourse on photography in his *Berliner Kindheit* does not explicitly develop any of his previously articulated theoretical and historical arguments on photography, as noted, the 'Mummerehlen' chapter nonetheless sheds a new light on his phenomenologically oriented engagement with photographic images by virtue of this personal investment in the special portrait. While these dynamics, whereby one recognizes and re-experiences a lived past through the mediation of the present, are clearly not reducible to the photograph as a material and perceptual object, they are still occasioned not only by the singular photograph in question but also by the unique nature of any photographic image's particular presence-in-absence via both the fact and affects of its indexicality, the physical-causal link between the image and the world it pictures.

43 Cf. Michael Opitz's entry on 'Ähnlichkeit', in Opitz and Wizisla (eds.), *Benjamins Begriffe*, vol. 1, 44–5.

44 This is similar to Barthes's existential identification with Proust that he self-consciously dwells on in his lecture 'Longtemps, je me suis couché de bonne heure' (see OC, V, 459).

Despite the fact that the juxtaposition of the Kafka photograph and Benjamin's ekphrasis of it in the *Berliner Kindheit* result in a suspension of the literal identification of the sitter – constantly oscillating between himself as a child and Kafka as a child – the particular poignancy of the encounter described nonetheless hinges on the nature of the photographic referent, perceived as the other self of the beholder. Following the formulation forwarded by Derrida in his text on the 'deaths' of Barthes, the word-and-image dynamic in the 'Mummerehlen' chapter testifies to an encounter with the 'singularité absolue de l'autre' ['absolute singularity of the other'],[45] allowed by the photograph's 'mummification' of past time, to quote Bazin.[46] That is to say, through the photographic referent, the beholder is confronted with the other as much as with the past and present self, in an encounter mediated by the photograph – as a perceptual object bearing a trace of the real in the form of the past existence of the sitter – through which its beholder enters into a relation with the represented other.

Benjamin's encounter with, and frequent return to, the childhood portrait of Kafka, then, is a testimony to the singularity of photography. But they are also closely aligned with the crucial theme of redemption. When Benjamin, in his childhood memoirs, writes that the child portrait shows him a false resemblance, it is visible to him, as it were, only by virtue of the fact that the sitter and the later beholder are the same person. Yet, it is not only the temporal discrepancy between the remembered situation of the picture-taking and its viewing that co-constitutes the perceptibility of the child subject's alienation, but the fact that the sitter was presumably not Benjamin but Kafka. When Benjamin's identification with Kafka thus merges the child Kafka with the child Benjamin, it is not an attempt to 'cancel out individual features' of the children, as Linda Haverty Rugg has proposed,[47] in order to speak of all children's experience, but first and foremost to preserve the unique individuality of the child as other in relation to the viewing 'me'. Benjamin's reflections on the photographic image here underscore the irreducibility of the other, and his experience, by virtue of the fact that even a portrait of the viewing self presents the self as not-self, as alter ego.[48]

---

45 Derrida, 'Les Morts de Roland Barthes', 272; 'The Deaths of Roland Barthes', 39.

46 See Bazin, 'Ontologie de l'image photographique', 14.

47 Rugg, *Picturing Ourselves*, 170. Cf. also Richter, *Walter Benjamin*, 220.

48 In *La Chambre claire*, Barthes describes the photographic portrait of the self as an 'avènement de moi-même comme autre' (CC, 28) ['advent of myself as

The singularity of the privileged photograph in these respects begs the question of its and all other photographs' reproducibility, with which Benjamin's critical writings are associated. Is this not a contradiction? Not necessarily, because clearly the singularity in question remains largely unaffected by the photograph's easy replication as a material object,[49] since it is not a necessary function of that object alone. Rather, it is the consequence of a relational event that occurs in the moment of viewing the photograph, a contingent meeting of the specific image, the individual viewer and the unique referent or sitter. In short, this is an experiential singularity rather than merely physical or material uniqueness. The greatest truth and value of the Kafka portrait in Benjamin's possession, a precious token of the writer whom he so admired, unlike the aura of a painting, does not reside in its physical uniqueness as an image on paper but rather in the 'idealization' of its indexical and iconic features, which are given a new, greater life in the consciousness of a unique subjectivity. In other words, while the experiential dynamic in question is prompted by the photograph's facticity, as a material trace of the real, in the beholder's response it quickly passes beyond all externally verifiable fact and appearance, just as the sitter's identity in the photograph is ultimately problematized, rather than proven, by any empirical mimetic fidelity. Such a response to a particular image of a particular person is more or less emotionally charged and revealing depending on who the depicted person is and what he or she represents to the viewer, which, in turn, determines the intensity of the portrait photograph's demand.

In meta-theoretical terms such experiential realities are clearly not wholly capturable in any traditionally detached, objective and impersonal scholarly account of photography. They call, instead, for a highly personal, even autobiographical, engagement with the medium and its potentials, one that proceeds by way of specific images and specific responses to them. This does not mean, however, that a more generally applicable truth cannot be extrapolated from such unrepeatable and subjective experience (as rooted in the felt as well

---

other' (CL, 12)]. Cf. Cadava, *Words of Light*, 113–15. In a different context, Hirsch has rightly pointed out that this dynamic between self and other in photographic portraiture is what Philippe Lacoue-Labarthe termed the 'allo-portrait', which also echoes with Lacanian notions of the 'mirror stage' in the formation of self-identity (*Family Frames*, 86–9).

49 In *The Singularity of Literature*, Attridge's only reference to photography draws out exactly this distinction, confirming that singularity can inhere in a photograph even if it is 'reproduced a million times' (64).

as known relation between past and present). For such experience may, in turn, lead to the development of a critical and/or narrative practice of writing that remains faithful to such experiences and also safeguards them in the wider context of cultural life, creating and maintaining a space where they are able to occur.

In this context the notion of a 'redemptive criticism' central to Benjamin's thought points the way towards such a practice.[50] This is usually understood as literary, cultural or historical criticism that studies cultural phenomena from a retrospective historical perspective.[51] More precisely, it is a criticism that pays more attention to phenomena at the moment of their disappearance, rather than that of their historical apogee or golden age, with the aim of rescuing or recovering them. Benjamin's engagement with photography, however, testifies to another form of redemptive criticism, centred on existential rather than historical or cultural realities, with which it nonetheless retains a dialectical connection.

The exceptional place of the Kafka-as-child portrait in Benjamin's writings on photography suggests that this particular photograph is both the particular object of, and the example for,[52] a redemption through writing. This photograph is, on the one hand, saved from the forgetfulness of time and also separated from other prosaic and commercialized images, that is to say, it is shown to be worth saving. On the other hand, it is redeemed by a type of writing that is a natural extension of the subjective and immersive response to a photographic image. Rather than redemption being granted by simply naming the nameless person depicted in the photograph, as Agamben suggests, Benjamin's frequent recourse to the Kafka-as-child portrait makes clear that redemption is here also closely intertwined with the viewer's affective engagement with it. In this respect, it is precisely the theme and reality of singularity vis-à-

50 As I have argued in the Introduction, the expression 'rettende Kritik' is attributable to Kracauer and Habermas. With respect to visual artefacts, Weigel explores Benjamin's 'Gestus einer rettenden Kritik' ['attitude of redemptive criticism'] in direct relation to photography ('Das Detail in Benjamins Theorie', 51), while Miriam Hansen looks at this particular critical practice with respect to film ('Benjamin, Cinema and Experience: The Blue Flower in the Land of Technology', *New German Critique*, 40 (1987), 179–224: 182, n. 4).

51 Heinrich Kaulen summarizes the various aspects of 'Rettung' in Benjamin's œuvre as entailing three major meanings: epistemological or philosophical, eschatological and literary cultural (in his entry on 'Rettung', in Opitz and Wizisla (eds.), *Benjamins Begriffe*, vol. 2, 629).

52 I borrow and slightly alter this formulation from Hansen ('Benjamin, Cinema and Experience', 182).

vis the portrait that ultimately fully justifies and explains what Agamben has described as the photograph's 'demand for redemption'.[53] The fact that Benjamin saves the Kafka childhood photograph from oblivion not only by writing about it but also by writing about it in the particular way he does, is thus in itself an expression of a profound sense of ethical responsibility towards the photographically represented other.

On the whole, photography as an object of discussion in Benjamin's œuvre is profoundly dualistic. The exceptional, self-affirming and potentially life-changing status of the Kafka-as-child portrait is a dialectical response to Benjamin's generally negative assessment of the medium (at least in its widespread use and effects). The theme of singularity, in fact, emerges only through this dynamic discord between the general and particular, collective and personal, which provides the necessary heuristic context for its recognition. These tensions are reflected and paralleled by Benjamin's problematization of photography and memory. The wider treatment of this subject sheds new light on the redemptive and ethical aspects of Benjamin's engagement with the childhood portrait of Kafka, and, potentially, of any portrait photograph.

53 Agamben, *Profanations*, 26.

Chapter 3

Photography, Memory and Redemption

The autobiographical context within which Benjamin addresses (childhood) memory and photography raises more general, complex issues as to the relations between them. They pertain, for instance, to the temporality inherent in the actual workings of the photographic medium (including the development process in the case of non-digital photography), the actual physical as well as mental storage and retrieval of photographs and the temporal and imaginative dynamics of their viewing. There is a long-standing tradition of comparing the camera's optics and the development process with the neuro-physiological mental processes of perceiving and remembering. At the beginning of the seventeenth century, the *camera obscura*, the precursor of the photographic camera, was thought to function in an analogous way to the human eye.[1] Both bundle the light rays and project them, upside down, onto a screen or retina thereby producing an image. In the wake of the invention of photography – that is, the discovery of how such evanescent light projections could be fixed chemically – the metaphorical analogy between the eye and the camera was extended to memory. The permanent storing and archiving of photographic images was thought to parallel the brain's storage of imagistic data for later access through memory images. In 1859, the American physician and man of letters Oliver Wendell Holmes articulated this connection by famously calling the daguerreotype a 'mirror with a memory'.[2] Such analogies and comparisons proliferated over subsequent decades of photographic history and theory and are also particularly prominent in Freudian psychoanalysis and in Proust's poetics of memory – two pivotal inter-texts for Benjamin's treatment of the subject. In Benjamin's work, the relation of photography to memory is closely connected not only to his personal biography, as we have seen, but also to his reflections on modernity and collective history.

Here, it is important to reiterate that, looked at as a totality, Benjamin's engagement with photography shifts from a cultural-historical and quasi-phenomenological one rooted in the viewing and description of specific images in the early 1930s, to a much more abstract, dialectical-materialist

1 See Stiegler, *Theoriegeschichte der Photographie*, 384 and, for a more detailed historical discussion, Busch, *Belichtete Welt*, 93–106.

2 Trachtenberg (ed.), *Classic Essays on Photography*, 74.

approach to photography as a mass medium, from the middle of the same decade onwards. The latter approach is also associated with the Frankfurt School's perspectives on culture, which developed in close dialogue with Benjamin's work.[3] The most notable consequence of this shift was a striking re-evaluation of the notion of photographic aura. Benjamin's change of emphasis, which should by no means be taken as a repudiation of his earlier writings on the unique power and value of specific photographs, must be seen against the backdrop of twentieth-century history and the rise of fascism in Europe and Germany. His assessment of the potential political role of photography when accompanied by text (heralded by the nature and presentation of Atget's images), in the 'Kleine Geschichte der Photographie' and other writings, indicates that Benjamin was now viewing the medium through the perspective of an unprecedented cultural and historical crisis.[4] In order to understand its occurrence and to respond to its challenges, Benjamin turns back to the nineteenth century to explore how and why the nature of human experience fundamentally changed with the rise of modernity. Before assessing photography's place in this seismic epistemic and experiential shift, it is first necessary to establish some key points of Benjamin's theory of modernity. This will in turn allow us to see how he adopts Proustian conceptions of memory and applies them to both the photographic medium and to portrait photographs, in particular, to negotiate his coexisting negative and positive assessments of photography's impact on memory.

Modernity, Experience and the Unconscious

Benjamin's 1939 'Über einige Motive bei Baudelaire' ['On Some Motifs in Baudelaire'] is a central text with respect to his theory of modernity. Here he draws explicitly on Freud's influential study 'Jenseits des Lustprinzips' ['Beyond the Pleasure Principle'] from 1920, and implicitly on Georg Simmel's 'Die Großstädte und das Geistesleben' ['Metropolis and Mental

---

3 For an in-depth account of the relations between Benjamin and the Frankfurt School, see Susan Buck-Morss's classic, *The Origin of Negative Dialectics. Theodor W. Adorno, Walter Benjamin, and the Frankfurt Institute* (New York: Free Press, 1977).

4 Vilém Flusser's philosophy of photography, written after the Holocaust in 1983, is complementary to Benjamin in this respect (*Towards a Philosophy of Photography*, trans. Anthony Mathews (London: Reaktion, 2000). For a comparison between them, see Stiegler, 'Medienphilosophie der Photographie', 259.

Life'] from 1903.[5] Against the conceptual frameworks provided by Freud and Simmel, Benjamin maps the emergence of a modern type of experience, *Erlebnis*, and opposes it to *Erfahrung*, its pre-modern counterpart.[6] He argues that the quintessential modern experience, *Erlebnis*, is rooted in the sort of throbbing, sensational stimuli found in the environment of a crowded, industrialized metropolis. Emanating from a city infrastructure featuring accelerated transport systems and resultant crowds, with large numbers of fast moving passersby, these stimuli are experienced by the human observer as an intermittent series of sensory 'shocks'. In this context of environmental and social change following on the heels of industrialization, photographic technology provides Benjamin with a compelling illustration for his characterizations of modern versus pre-modern experience, as it is one notable and concrete manifestation of myriad changes that not only alter human perception of the here and now but also fundamentally alter the processes of memory.

In 'Über einige Motive bei Baudelaire', in addition to Freud's and Simmel's theories, Benjamin draws on the literary reference points of Baudelaire's *Les Fleurs du mal* [*The Flowers of Evil*] but also Proust's *À la recherche du temps perdu*. Not least through his translations of substantial parts of their work into German, Benjamin had an in-depth familiarity with Baudelaire and Proust, who each exercised an important influence on his thought and whom he presents, to some degree, as artistic precursors of his critical-historical and philosophical concerns.[7] He

5 Benjamin attended Simmel's lectures at the Humboldt University in Berlin at the beginning of the last century and was quite familiar with his work. While he does not quote Simmel in relation to the passages here discussed, he does refer to the sociologist's theories on the modern metropolis elsewhere in his studies on Baudelaire (see GS, I, 539–40).

6 There is no literal translation of these two words into English. The translators of Benjamin suggest that *Erfahrung* is an 'experience over time', in opposition to *Erlebnis*, which is an 'isolated experience of the moment', highlighting the different durational aspects (SW, IV, 345, n. 11).

7 Proust's influence on Benjamin is complex and far-reaching and has attracted the attention of many scholars. See Ursula Link-Heer, *Benjamin liest Proust* (Cologne: Private Print of the German Proust Society, 1997); Robert Kahn, *Images, Passages: Marcel Proust et Walter Benjamin* (Paris: Éditions Kimé, 1998); Henning Teschke, *Proust und Benjamin. Unwillkürliche Erinnerung und dialektisches Bild* (Würzburg: Königshausen & Neumann, 2000); Johannes Bittel, *Proust-Benjamin, Benjamin-Proust: Traum, Rausch, Erwachen* (Frankfurt a.M.: Verlag Neue Wissenschaft, 2001); and Dominik Finkelde, *Benjamin liest Proust: Mimesislehre, Sprachtheorie, Poetologie* (Munich: Fink, 2003). However, except for Kahn's short discussion, none

regards these writers' work as expressions of essentially post-romantic experiences of nineteenth-century Paris, a city that had been a busy centre of modern life since the 1850s and serves Benjamin as the paradigmatic metropolis in his analysis of modernity. The main focus of the essay is on how the creation and reception of *Les Fleurs du mal* marks a transition point in these socio-historical transformations of human experience. The philosophical and literary treatment of memory in *À la recherche* is used to support Benjamin's interpretation of Baudelaire's work and its context, notably Proust's distinction between *mémoire volontaire* and *mémoire involontaire*. These are understood as the deliberate, active and intellectual recollection of the past versus the passive, unintentional and profoundly contingent recollection occasioned by unforeseen external triggers, such as, most famously, the taste of a madeleine dipped into tea, which brings back a lost world of childhood for Proust's hero.

In Benjamin's view, Proust's distinction corresponds to the historical shift from *Erfahrung* to *Erlebnis*, with the latter associated with a relative decline of the potential for experiences of involuntary memory and its powerful effects. In other words, modernity is seen to rob the individual of his or her deepest and most affecting connection to a personal and historical past. Coupled with his detailed knowledge of Proust, this perceived conceptual compatibility goes some way towards explaining why Benjamin turns to the French novelist's reflections on memory rather than to the more systematic treatment of memory and lived time in the philosophy of Henri Bergson.[8] In contradistinction to the then prevailing idea of a strong affinity between Bergson and Proust, Benjamin draws attention to the conceptual and philosophical differences between the two, critiquing the *Lebensphilosophie* [life philosophy] of the former. According to Benjamin, Bergson, in *Matière et mémoire* [*Matter and Memory*] (from 1896), defines the general nature of human experience in a way that is deeply incongruent with

of these studies addresses photography as a nexus between the two (*Images, Passages*, 93–8).

8 In contrast to Proust's, Bergson's possible influence on Benjamin's conception of memory has received little scholarly attention. See, however, Arno Münster, '"Eingedenken" – "mémoire pure" und "mémoire involontaire". Walter Benjamin im philosophisch-literarischen Spannungsfeld zwischen Henri Bergson und Marcel Proust', in Klaus Garber and Ludger Rehm (eds.), *Global Benjamin*, 3 vols. (Munich: Fink, 1999), vol. 2, 1135–46. Bergson's influence on Proust, on the other hand, is well documented. See, for instance, the important study by Joyce Megay, *Bergson et Proust. Essai de mise au point de la question de l'influence de Bergson sur Proust* (Paris: Vrin, 1976).

post-industrial experience. Benjamin criticizes Bergson's philosophy for its a-historical orientation and accuses him of neglecting the profound changes that mental life has undergone since the rise of industrialization. In Benjamin's dialectical-historical view, it is primarily these changes that are at stake in any truthful consideration of the subject, be it literary or philosophical.

Benjamin instead turns to Freud to buttress his interpretation of Proust's distinction between voluntary and involuntary memory, and the processes and effects of each, with reference to a more systematic conception of the psyche. Benjamin had linked Freud and Proust as early as 1930, in a journalistic article for the *Literarische Welt*, titled 'Pariser Tagebuch' ['Paris Diary']. Freud's 'Jenseits des Lustprinzips' is described here as the 'grundlegende Proust-Kommentar' (GS, IV, 580) ['fundamental commentary on Proust' (SW, II, 346)]; and in his 'Über einige Motive bei Baudelaire', Benjamin explores this relation in greater detail.

Freud's seminal treatise on the pleasure principle introduces a novel concept of the psyche's structure according to which it is divided into three main parts or systems: the conscious, the pre-conscious and the unconscious. Freud further developed this model in his later work, in 'Das Ich und das Es' ['The Ego and the Id'], one of his last major meta-psychological studies, where these three aspects are given their more famous labels of superego, id and ego. Based on the axiom of the psyche's functional division, in 'Jenseits des Lustprinzips', consciousness and memory are conceived as two systems which, albeit linked, operate largely independently of each other. The special function of consciousness is the registration of impressions and stimuli from the environment, whereas memory is responsible for the storing of such sensations. While the external impulse is registered consciously by consciousness, memory stores them in the form of unconscious marks: 'Dauerspuren' or 'permanent traces'.[9] Influenced by the then current view of the anatomical position of consciousness being in the outer layer of the brain, Freud defines its function as 'Reizschutz', that is, a protective shield of the psyche from potentially harmful external stimuli.[10] Put differently, consciousness processes stimulations from the external environment

9 Freud occasionally also calls them 'Gedächtnis'- or 'Erinnerungsspuren' ['memory traces'] (*Psychologie des Unbewußten* (Studienausgabe, vol. 3) (Frankfurt a.M.: Fischer, 1975), 235).

10 Ibid., 237.

without being itself affected or structurally changed by them.[11] Thus, the more conscious a sensual stimulation is experienced, the less permanent are the traces inscribed into memory.

The formulation of the proportional relation of consciousness to memory traces is one of the key notions that Benjamin borrows from Freud and juxtaposes with both Proust's two categories of memory and the *Erfahrung/Erlebnis* distinction. Benjamin applies Freud's concept of memory in general to Proust's specific notion of involuntary memory and states that 'Bestandteil der mémoire involontaire kann nur werden, was nicht ausdrücklich und mit Bewußtsein ist "erlebt" worden, was dem Subjekt nicht als "Erlebnis" widerfahren ist' (GS, I, 613) ['only what has not been experienced explicitly and consciously, what has not happened to the subject as an isolated experience (*Erlebnis*), can become a component of *mémoire involontaire*' (SW, IV, 317)]. Benjamin's emphasis on *Erlebnis* here is significant. As has been noted, in his historical understanding of experience, *Erlebnis* represents the kind of surface experience that, owing to a sensory overload of stimulation, predominates in the context of modern city life. It supersedes the deeper, more resonant and often more authentic one described as *Erfahrung* conjoined with Proust's more profound form of memory.[12]

For Benjamin, photography as well as cinematography (which he addresses in the 'Kunstwerk' essay) is not simply the product of a modernity marked by the change of experience but is itself seen as a major contributor to this historical transformation. To illustrate his point, Benjamin relates photography to a theory of 'shocks'. He draws on Freud's notion of consciousness as being a protective shield against external stimuli. This mechanism not only operates independently of

---

11 Freud writes: 'Das System *Bw* [Bewußtsein] wäre also durch die Besonderheit ausgezeichnet, daß der Erregungsvorgang in ihm nicht wie in allen anderen psychischen Systemen eine dauernde Veränderung seiner Elemente hinterläßt, sondern gleichsam in Phänomen des Bewußtwerdens verpufft' (ibid., 235). ['The system *Cs.* [consciousness] is characterized by the peculiarity that in it (in contrast to what happens in other psychical systems) excitatory processes do not leave behind any permanent change in its elements but expire, as it were, in the phenomenon of becoming conscious' ('Beyond the Pleasure Principle', in *On Metapsychology and the Theory of Psychoanalysis* (The Pelican Freud Library, vol. 11) trans. and ed. James Strachey (Harmondsworth: Penguin, 1982), 269–338: 297)].

12 For an interpretation that puts emphasis on the differences between Benjamin and Proust in this respect, see Krista R. Greffrath, 'Proust et Benjamin', in Heinz Wismann (ed.), *Walter Benjamin et Paris* (Paris: Cerf, 1986), 113–31: 122.

memory but even excludes the long-term storing of experience as mental data, which, as we have seen, makes memory possible. Benjamin applies this model of a protective mechanism to the decline of *Erfahrung* and suggests a causal relation between shock and *Erlebnis*:

> Je größer der Anteil des Chockmoments an den einzelnen Eindrücken ist, je unablässiger das Bewußtsein im Interesse des Reizschutzes auf dem Plan sein muß . . ., desto weniger gehen sie in die Erfahrung ein; desto eher erfüllen sie den Begriff des Erlebnisses. (GS, I, 615)
>
> The greater the shock factor in particular impressions, the more vigilant consciousness has to be in screening stimuli; . . . the less these impressions enter long experience (*Erfahrung*) and the more they correspond to the concept of isolated experience (*Erlebnis*). (SW, IV, 319)

In Freud's reasoning, the failure of consciousness to protect against an excess of stimulation leads to the psychological state of trauma.[13] By contrast, Benjamin posits shock not as the result but as the cause of *Erlebnis*. Significantly, Benjamin, following Simmel, also adds a socio-cultural and historical perspective to Freud's psycho-theoretical theses arguing that the modern metropolis, with its dense population and accelerated pace of life, is the epicentre of external stimulations, experienced as shocks.[14] Simmel's axiomatic assumption that the most general aspects of life are closely intertwined with the most individual and private ones serves Benjamin as a powerful model for his analysis of the relation between a post-industrial, urban environment and concomitant experiential, perceptual and psychological changes in peoples' lives.[15] Benjamin's proportional argument noted above can therefore be read as an application of Freud via Simmel: the consequence of life in big cities is an increase of *Erlebnis* owing to the constant alertness of consciousness, which in turn prevents the deep inscription of permanent traces of experience into memory.

Yet Benjamin's view of the interaction between the collective and the individual in this context is more pessimistic than Simmel's. Whereas Simmel emphasizes the levelling out of social hierarchies in the metropolitan environment and the freedom that this may entail for individual expression, Benjamin endorses Paul Valéry's verdict that

---

13 See Freud, *Psychologie des Unbewußten*, 239.

14 Georg Simmel analyses the interconnection between the particular characteristics of the metropolis and its impact on the mental, social and economic life of its inhabitants ('Die Großstädte und das Geistesleben', in *Aufsätze und Abhandlungen 1901–1908*, 2 vols. (Frankfurt a.M.: Suhrkamp, 1995), vol. 1, 116–31).

15 See ibid., 116–17; 125.

the modern mechanization of everyday life fundamentally isolates and impoverishes all human relations (see GS, I, 630). This gloomy prognosis is highlighted in Benjamin's vocabulary, with terms such as 'decline', 'loss' and 'disappearance' figuring prominently in his texts on modern experience.

In order to make photography, as *the* modern medium of visual representation, compatible with the concept of shock and the withering of *Erfahrung* (expressed as the main historical thrust of Benjamin's essay on Baudelaire), its technology must seemingly be dialectically related to both phenomena. Benjamin notes that in everyday modern life complex chains of causal actions, characteristic of manual manufacturing processes, are replaced by abrupt gestures. For example, the act of picking up the receiver of the modern telephone, in contrast to the previous winding mechanism, is a similar automated gesture experience to pressing the shutter release button of the automatic camera.[16] Projecting Freud's psychoanalytical terms onto a historico-cultural screen, Benjamin argues that picture taking is conjoined with shock by way of the ability to instantly record a non-mental image of a fleeting moment without any mental and durational reflection: 'Ein Fingerdruck genügte, um ein Ereignis für eine unbegrenzte Zeit festzuhalten. Der Apparat erteilte dem Augenblick sozusagen einen posthumen Chock' (GS, I, 630) ['Henceforth a touch of the finger sufficed to fix an event for an unlimited period of time. The camera gave the moment a posthumous shock, as it were' (SW, IV, 328)]. Despite the fact that its recording and archiving function is exactly that which traditionally links photography with memory (in ways that are akin to the functioning of involuntary memory, as we shall see), Benjamin sees in the camera's immediate operation and mechanical instrumentality a denial of *Erfahrung* and of involuntary memory by virtue of its mechanical triggering of shocks – akin to those which inhabitants of cities experience to a degree which effects their entire nervous and behavioural systems. In turn, the processes of memory become mechanical and perfunctory.

For Benjamin, the camera is not only a mechanical and mechanizing device, that is to say dehumanizing, but also bestows a retrospective shock upon the event it captures. While this argument bears a structural

16 Busch argues in a similar vein, suggesting that the photographic camera was the first portable machine that entered into people's everyday lives in the nineteenth century (*Belichtete Welt*, 321–2). This development was exponentially accelerated by George Eastman's invention of the Kodak camera and film roll in the 1880s, making picture taking accessible to amateur photographers.

resemblance to Freud's early theorization of trauma as a memory of an event that becomes traumatic only in retrospect (or 'nachträglich'),[17] exactly how this notion of 'posthumous shock' should be understood is not entirely clear.[18] Moreover, Benjamin's stress on the camera's *permanent fixing* of an event – echoing Freud's thesis concerning the inscription of a permanent trace into memory – does not sit easily with this conjunction of picture taking and *ephemeral shock*, triggered by an external stimulation, which consciousness is seen to efface or cancel out. Setting this ambiguity to one side, photography is unequivocally opposed to *Erfahrung* and, by extension, to involuntary memory, as it is part of the mechanization of human relations in the wake of the Industrial Revolution. It can be argued that Benjamin's commitment to a materialist dialectics between changes in the production processes and the mental structure of post-industrial society requires almost by necessity this conjunction of the emergence of photographic technology with the decline of the more purportedly authentic and truthful process of involuntary memory. Moreover, it must be remembered here that for Benjamin the contingent, pre-reflective nature of both *Erfahrung* and involuntary memory (as something which, although potentially profoundly affecting the subject, cannot be willed into existence), is the source of their power and cognitive value.

There is, nonetheless, a telling parallel between Benjamin's invocation of Freud's concept of the permanent trace of memory and the permanent capturing of an event through photographic technology. And beyond a general metaphorical affinity between psychoanalysis and photography,[19] what is thus meta-theoretically emphasized is a notable

---

17 Freud introduces this notion, which frequently recurs in his work with respect to sexual development, in an early text from 1895 ('Entwurf einer Psychologie', in *Aus den Anfängen der Psychoanalyse. Briefe an Wilhelm Fliess, Abhandlungen und Notizen aus den Jahren 1887–1902*, eds. Marie Bonaparte, Anna Freud and Ernst Kris (London: Imago Publishing, 1950), 371–466: 435). In his later, more historico-culturally oriented study on the origin of Jewish monotheistic religion, this notion is, in fact, related to photographic metaphors (*Fragen der Gesellschaft*, 571).

18 Cadava has also suggested that there is a link between Benjamin's formulation and Freud's notion of trauma (*Words of Light*, 102–4). Yet, beyond the Freudian analogy, if it is one, Benjamin's suggestion remains somewhat obscure.

19 Eric Downing suggests that photography influenced psychoanalysis in the formulation of its key concepts, including the unconscious (*After Images. Photography, Archaeology, and Psychoanalysis and the Tradition of Bildung* (Detroit: Wayne State University Press, 2006), 4–5). In 1912, Freud made an

tension between Benjamin's characterizations of the psychological and affective dynamics of the experience of specific photographic images and the socio-historical and psychoanalytic framework within which he discusses the photographic medium. In the latter context, photography is strongly opposed to the Proustian involuntary memory, whereas in the former, it is equally emphatically linked to the concept of latency and a belated recognition that constitutes precisely this kind of memory.

Between Baudelaire and Proust: Photography's Effects on Memory

In line with the broad sweep of its cultural-historical arguments, in 'Über einige Motive bei Baudelaire' photography is almost exclusively understood as a mass medium and a technology of reproduction, linked to larger changes in material production as a result of the Industrial Revolution.[20] From this vantage point, the basic capacity of the camera as a means of reproduction both transcends and eclipses consideration of any particular photograph's content.

In this wider context, the nature and quality of aura is radically reinterpreted. Benjamin addresses photography's impact on auratic experience with reference to Baudelaire's aforementioned Salon

---

analogy between the subconscious and the photographic negative and the conscious as the positive print (*Psychologie des Unbewußten*, 34). Similarly, he attempts to shed light on the origins of Jewish religion via psychoanalytical analogies coupled with photographic metaphors, such as latency and later development, in his study 'Der Mann Moses und die monotheistische Religion', in *Fragen der Gesellschaft*, 515–20; 571. For a concise analysis of Freud's ambivalent uses of photographic metaphors throughout his works, see Sarah Kofman, *Camera obscura, de l'idéologie* (Paris: Éditions Galilée, 1973), 37–46. A more comprehensive historical argument as to the interaction of photographic metaphors and psychoanalytic concepts can be found in Douwe Draaisma, *Metaphors of Memory. A History of Ideas about the Mind*, trans. Paul Vincent (Cambridge: Cambridge University Press, 2000), 7–23.

20 Weigel convincingly suggests that the camera here becomes a 'dialectical image' for the culture of modernity (*Walter Benjamin*, 339). Norbert Bolz even contends that photography figures in Benjamin's œuvre as an 'absolute Metapher historischer Erkenntnis' ['absolute metaphor for historical recognition'], which, in its generalization, is problematic, however, given the many facets of Benjamin's engagement with photography ('Der Fotoapparat der Erkenntnis', *Fotogeschichte*, 32 (1989), 21–7: 21).

review of 1859. While Benjamin's assessment of the artistic value of mid-nineteenth-century portraiture in the 'Kleine Geschichte der Photographie' was at odds with Baudelaire's famous critique of photography as art, here, in relation to photography from the late nineteenth-century onwards, he is in agreement with the poet and critic. Benjamin, like Baudelaire, sees photography as registering the ephemeral events of everyday life to store them in the 'archives de notre mémoire' ['archives of our memories'], as Baudelaire writes.[21] For Baudelaire, however, when this medium of the everyday impinges on the aesthetic realm of art and beauty, both are diminished. The image 'industry' that photography became in the wake of Disdéri's mass-produced *carte-de-visite* portraits, triggering an excessive 'cardomania' during the 1850s,[22] dulls the creative imagination, which he regarded as the 'reine des facultés' ['queen of faculties'].[23]

Affirming Baudelaire's opposition between photography and art, the mundane and the factual, the aesthetic and the creative, Benjamin also aligns Baudelaire's archival memory, associated with photography, with Proust's voluntary memory.[24] Whereas in the 'Kleine Geschichte der Photographie', certain photographic portraits, such as those of the Newhaven fishwife, were seen to possess a significance that the painted portrait could never have, Benjamin now laments the fact that the photograph as technical reproduction lacks what he calls the 'Tiefe der Zeit' of painting (GS, I, 646). This 'temporal depth' of the artwork is a sign of a 'Vorgeschichte' or artistic and socio-cultural tradition that Benjamin associates with aura in both his essay on the 'Kunstwerk' and on Baudelaire (GS, I, 643–4). The photograph's indexicality and its psychological effects, engendering an imaginative immersion via its reality quotient (i.e. the fishwife portrait) are now no longer seen to guarantee a value that a painting can never possess. Instead, photographs are unfavourably compared with paintings, as the former carry within themselves as material objects the physical marks of an artistic and cultural tradition in a way that photographs are not able to do.

21 Baudelaire, *Écrits sur l'art*, 365. Benjamin quotes this passage from Baudelaire's review (see GS, I, 644–5).

22 Newhall, *The History of Photography*, 64. See also Batchen, 'Dreams of Ordinary Life', 64.

23 Baudelaire, *Écrits sur l'art*, 366.

24 At the end of his novel fragment *Jean Santeuil*, Marcel Proust similarly quotes Baudelaire's photography critique, yet connects the 'archives of our memories' with involuntary memory (*Jean Santeuil*, ed. Pierre Clarac (Paris: Gallimard/Bibliothèque de la Pléiade, 1971), 897–8).

More generally, photographs are also seen to correspond only to the most inadequate and impoverished mental images in one's memory, those that fail to do justice to the past experience with which they are associated, rather than with those more powerful, evocative and truthful visual memories which truly re-capture the experience. Here again, Benjamin turns to Proust in support of his argument. He quotes a passage from *À la recherche* where the narrator compares the lifeless images of Venice, which his willed, voluntary memory provides, with photographs.[25]

> In dem Zusammenhange, da Proust die Dürftigkeit und den Mangel an Tiefe in den Bildern beanstandet, die ihm die mémoire volontaire von Venedig vorlegt, schreibt er, beim bloßen Wort 'Venedig' sei ihm dieser Bilderschatz ebenso abgeschmackt wie eine Ausstellung von Photographien vorgekommen. (GS, I, 646)
>
> Proust, complaining of the barrenness and lack of depth in the images of Venice that his *mémoire volontaire* presented to him, notes that the very word 'Venice' made those images seem to him as vapid as an exhibition of photographs. (SW, IV, 338)

Here and elsewhere Benjamin forwards the view that Proust's novel is anti-photographic, whereby the medium is seen to challenge or problematize the truthful capturing of the past through memory and imagination. Similarly, Kracauer, in the context of his film theory from 1960, interprets the encounters of the Proustian narrator with photography as predominantly alienating ones.[26] This 'negative' interpretation of photography in *À la recherche* was a prominent one among first- and second-generation Proust commentators with an interest in photography or visual phenomena. The reality, however, appears much less clear-cut, as has been highlighted by subsequent critics.[27] As we shall see, Barthes argues that there is in fact a significant affinity between photography and involuntary memory while at the same time demonstrating photography's kinship to voluntary

25 See Marcel Proust, *À la recherche du temps perdu*, 4 vols., ed. Jean-Yves Tadié (Paris: Gallimard/Bibliothèque de la Pléiade, 1987–1989), vol. 4, 444. It is interesting to note in passing that John Ruskin, who greatly influenced Proust's aesthetics in many ways, expressed his ambivalent appreciation of photography in relation to his drawings of Venice in particular. For a fuller discussion of Ruskin's changing views of photography, see Scharf, *Art and Photography*, 95–101.

26 See Siegfried Kracauer, *Theory of Film. The Redemption of Physical Reality* (Princeton: Princeton University Press, 1997), 14–16.

27 See Jean-François Chevrier, *Proust et la photographie. Avec des photographies de Pierre de Fenoyl et Holger Trülzsch* (Paris: Éditions de l'Étoile, 1982) and Brassaï, *Marcel Proust sous l'emprise de la photographie* (Paris: Gallimard, 1997).

memory in other respects (see Chapter Six), whether or not Proust or his narrator acknowledges it.[28] Moreover, as in so many other ways, what Benjamin denies here to photography in general, as a medium, is granted and even insisted upon in relation to privileged portrait photographs.

Photography, Aura and Gaze

With specific reference to aura, Benjamin further extrapolates from the passage from *À la recherche* where the narrator compares impoverished, lifeless memories with a series of photographs. He argues that 'wenn man das Unterscheidende an den Bildern, die aus der mémoire involontaire auftauchen, darin sieht, daß sie eine Aura haben, so hat die Photographie an dem Phänomen eines "Verfalls der Aura" entscheidend teil' (GS, I, 646) ['If the distinctive feature of the images arising from *mémoire involontaire* is seen in their aura, then photography is decisively implicated in the phenomenon of a "decline of aura"' (SW, IV, 338)]. While the thesis of a conjunction between the decline of aura and the emergence of photography is not new here, what is surprising is the extent to which photography itself is directly opposed to aura. Benjamin, in fact, reverses on his previous celebration of early photographic technology and reinterprets it.

> Was an der Daguerreotypie als das Unmenschliche, man könnte sagen Tödliche mußte empfunden werden, war das (übrigens anhaltende) Hereinblicken in den Apparat, da doch der Apparat das Bild des Menschen aufnimmt, ohne ihm dessen Blick zurückzugeben. Dem Blick wohnt aber die Erwartung inne, von dem erwidert zu werden, dem er sie schenkt. Wo diese Erwartung erwidert wird . . ., da fällt ihm die Erfahrung der Aura in ihrer Fülle zu. . . . Die Erfahrung der Aura beruht also auf der Übertragung einer in der menschlichen Gesellschaft geläufigen Reaktionsform auf das Verhältnis des Unbelebten oder der Natur zum Menschen. Der Angesehene oder angesehen sich Glaubende schlägt den Blick auf. Die Aura einer Erscheinung erfahren, heißt, sie mit dem Vermögen belehnen, den Blick aufzuschlagen. (GS, I, 646–7)

---

28 In the context of the Proustian influence on Benjamin and Barthes, Irene Albers rightly draws attention to the problem of applying Benjamin's as well as Barthes's reflections on the medium to Proust's novel, leading to a circular argument inasmuch as the ideas which Benjamin and Barthes partly extract from their readings of Proust are then applied back to Proust ('Proust und die Kunst der Photographie', in Wolfram Nitsch and Rainer Zaiser (eds.), *Marcel Proust und die Künste* (Frankfurt a.M. and Leipzig: Insel-Verlag, 2004), 205–39: 209).

> What was inevitably felt to be inhuman – one might even say deadly – in daguerreotypy was the (prolonged) looking into the camera, since the camera records our likeness without returning our gaze. Inherent in the gaze, however, is the expectation that it will be returned by that on which it is bestowed. Where this expectation is met . . ., there is an experience (*Erfahrung*) of aura in all its fullness. . . . The experience of aura thus arises from the fact that a response characteristic of human relationships is transposed to the relationships between humans and inanimate or natural objects. The person we look at, or who feels being looked at, looks at us in return. To experience the aura of an object we look at means to invest it with the ability to look back at us. (SW, IV, 338)

This passage, which echoes the description of aura as a phenomenon perceived by the sensitive viewer of nineteenth-century photographs in the 'Kleine Geschichte der Photographie', exemplifies Benjamin's late definition of aura as a two-way dynamic between object and beholder. In this new context, however, Benjamin argues that such a reciprocal dynamic communicated through the gaze is diametrically opposed to the act of picture taking. For the act of posing in front of a camera is now seen to have been experienced as 'inhuman', and even 'deadly', by the sitter, a notion that is dramatically at odds with Benjamin's earlier emphasis, in the essay on photography, on the quiet contemplation of the sitters in the portraits of Hill/Adamson, which, as captured in the image, is seen to express precisely their humanity.

The idea that being photographed somehow damages the human subject is certainly as old as the medium. Honoré de Balzac famously suggested that the camera takes away a layer of the portrayed person's essence,[29] and in the above-quoted passage, Benjamin is possibly referring to Balzac's view.[30] Yet the emphasis on the ways in which the technological and mechanical nature of picture taking threatens the auratic is not entirely incommensurate with the possibility of experiencing aura when looking at a photograph, even if Benjamin does not explicitly acknowledge this in 'Über einige Motive bei Baudelaire'.

Benjamin goes on to confidently state that Proust's views are identical to his own.[31] This congruency, he argues, pertains to the relation between

29 Nadar ascribes this superstitious belief to Balzac, which apparently did not prevent him, however, from sitting for a daguerreotype in 1848 (*Quand j'étais photographe*, 9–18; 284).

30 Benjamin knew Nadar's book and describes it as an important source for the study of nineteenth-century photography in his 'Pariser Brief II' (see GS, III, 500, n. 5).

31 I agree with Recki's contention that Benjamin uses a 'Rhetorik der souveränen Anerkennung' ['rhetoric of confident recognition'] to avoid contradictions

aura and the gaze in the sense of the reciprocal act of looking, as transposed from an instinctive reaction among humans observing each other to the artwork or inanimate object. Benjamin here cites another line from *Le Temps retrouvé* [*Time Regained*], the last volume of Proust's novel: '"Einige, die Geheimnisse lieben, schmeicheln sich, daß den Dingen etwas von den Blicken bleibt, welche jemals auf ihnen ruhten"' (GS, I, 647) ['"People who are fond of secrets flatter themselves that objects retain something of the gaze that has rested on them"' (SW, IV, 338–9). Benjamin comments on this quotation: 'Doch wohl das Vermögen, sie zu erwidern' (GS, I, 647) ['The objects, evidently, have the ability to return the gaze' (SW, IV, 339)].[32]

What Benjamin borrows from Proust, then, is the dialogical relation between the object that has been looked at and the one that has conserved the gaze (a Freudian trace, perhaps) and the subsequent return of the gaze.[33] The French verb 'regarder' aptly expresses this reciprocity as it has the dual meaning of 'to look at' and 'to concern'.[34] Following Valéry, Benjamin also associates such reciprocity of the gaze with the perception of objects in dreams. In Benjamin's interpretation, however, there is much greater emphasis on the beholder of the object who bestows it with the ability to look back than is found in Proust or Valéry.[35] This

---

that may otherwise arise in closely juxtaposing his own materialistic objectivism with Proust's notion of a more subjectively oriented auratic experience (*Aura und Autonomie*, 43).

32 See the original passage in Proust, *À la recherche*, vol. 4, 463. Ursula Link-Heer has argued that the common denominator between Proust and Benjamin here is the 'halluzinatorische Subjektivität des Objekts' ['hallucinatory subjectivity of the object'], a claim that highlights the link between aura and mid-nineteenth-century clinical investigations into phenomena of hysteria ('Aura hysterica oder das Blick-Aufschlagen des Objekts', *Kaleidoskopien*, 1 (1996), 78–87: 86). For a more in-depth historical account of this context, see Georges Didi-Huberman, *Invention de l'hysterie. Charcot et l'iconographie photographique de la Salpêtrière* (Paris: Macula, 1982), 84–112.

33 For an account of the reciprocity of looking more generally, see James Elkins, The *Object Stares Back. On the Nature of Seeing* (San Diego: Harcourt, 1996).

34 Georges Didi-Huberman makes a similar observation with respect to Benjamin's definition of aura, drawing attention to the ambiguity as to whether 'la proximité envisagée se rapporte à l'apparition, ou bien au lointain lui-même' ['the proximity in question refers to the appearance or to the distance itself'] (*Ce que nous voyons, ce qui nous regarde* (Paris: Éditions de Minuit, 1992), 103, n. 3). The title plays, of course, with the double meaning of 'regarder'.

35 Recki speaks of a 'produktive Erwartung des Betrachters' ['beholder's productive expectation'], similarly highlighting the beholder's active role (*Aura und Autonomie*, 24).

emphasis is of great importance given that it underlines the pivotal role of the individual perceiver in the appearance and experience of aura, and thereby problematizes Benjamin's argument concerning the clear-cut opposition between photography and aura here.

In fact, the relational and experiential nature of aura, as Benjamin defines it in his later work, corresponds in some respects to the implied theme of the singularity of photography because this understanding of the gaze links aura, if only indirectly, to the Kafka childhood portrait.[36] Animated by Benjamin's response to it, which draws attention to the depicted boy's sad gaze, the image is felt as having the power to return this attention back onto the beholder. I do not mean to suggest, however, that what I have referred to as photographic singularity is identical to aura. The singularity of the photograph, as it emerges in Benjamin's engagement with the Kafka portrait, cannot be subsumed into, or equated with, aura since the profound existential and ethical encounter with the photographic other that the experience of singularity entails transcends the auratic. That is to say, not every experience of aura (in the above sense) has this sort of potentially life- and self-altering effect, although every such special encounter with the other through the photographic portrait does possess this subject-object reciprocity.

Thus, when Attridge claims that what he conceives as 'singularity' is different from Benjamin's aura (which Attridge equates with material 'uniqueness'), he problematically adopts only Benjamin's narrower conception of aura as a feature of artworks, which their mechanical reproduction diminishes.[37] However, Benjamin's later view of aura as related to the gaze (developed through Proust), pertaining to the event character of an object's experience, significantly departs from the idea of aura simply as a unique quality that a painting, for instance, as a physical object possesses. It is precisely this alternative Benjaminian understanding of aura as what happens between subject and object that relates to the singularity of the photographic encounter as an ethical engagement with

36 Duttlinger has stressed the importance of the gaze in relation to the Kafka portrait ('Imaginary Encounters', 94–5).

37 See Attridge, *The Singularity of Literature*, 64. For an account of the difference between aura in the 'Kunstwerk' and 'Baudelaire' essays, see Samuel Weber, 'Mass Mediauras; or Art, Aura and Media in the Work of Walter Benjamin', in David S. Ferris (ed.), *Walter Benjamin: Theoretical Questions* (Stanford: Stanford University Press, 1996), 27–49: 44–9.

the represented other.[38] (And the ethical, unlike the aesthetic, is a relation between two subjects, or at least a subject and an object experienced as subject, rather than the one-directional perception of an object.)

In summary, then, in Benjamin's 'Über einige Motive bei Baudelaire', photography represents a technology that affects the very nature of human experience in a fundamental, universal and detrimental way. However, this view fails to acknowledge the fact that specific photographs may be perceived in a way that actually transcends or even opposes these historically determined effects, as Benjamin himself suggests in earlier texts (and specifically with respect to the role of photographs in a 'cult of remembrance'). As noted, it is not necessarily contradictory to view photographic technology as contributing to changes in perception and memory that result in the decline of the experience of aura and to consider specific photographs to be auratic. However, as articulated in Benjamin's writings, which in chronological terms move from consideration of the latter to the former, there is a tension here. This is one that Benjamin himself seems to have been aware of at some level, and which can be seen as largely attributable to his extra-photographic ideological and philosophical commitments, notably his allegiance to a Marxist-dialectic understanding of culture, history and modernity. The general shift in Benjamin's work from a nominalistic and phenomenological conception of photography to one that is highly abstract and impersonal, and where any discussion of specific images is avoided, is thus an indication of an inherent paradox: the concept of aura, initially developed in relation to photography, is subsequently defined in opposition to it. Yet because Benjamin retains certain aspects of his first definition of aura, rooted in mid-nineteenth-century portraiture, there remains something essential in the very concept that resists opposition even to subsequent 'non-auratic' photography. In other words, there remains something essentially 'photographic' in aura,[39] in all its definitions, related to the

38 Cf. Costello's analysis of the experience of aura as 'encountering others as others', which, in his view, is linked to all portrait photography and is particularly relevant for contemporary art photography, which functions in an analogous fashion to 'our relation to other persons' ('Aura, Face, Photography', 180–4).

39 Benjamin also frequently aligns aura and trace, which strongly echoes, of course, another photographic theme, as he himself acknowledges and explores in the context of his study on Baudelaire (see GS, I, 550). For an analysis of the conceptual relation between aura and trace, see Bettine Menke, *Sprachfiguren: Name, Allegorie, Bild nach Walter Benjamin* (Munich: Fink,

temporality and the reciprocity between subject and object,[40] which is potentially a part of any photograph's experience, regardless of historical or stylistic period, and even the specific processes of the image's creation.

Recollection and Redemption

Returning to the Proustian inter-text in Benjamin's late writings, as chiefly concerned with a socio-historical analysis of modernity in which photography is subsumed, it is important to call attention to the fact that there is one highly significant instance in Benjamin's œuvre where photography is aligned with the very type of memory – that is, involuntary memory – whose disappearance it is later seen to encourage. This is a fragmentary piece of writing in which Benjamin directly links his reflections on photographic images and childhood memories with involuntary memory. It was presumably written in the context of his 'Proust Papiere' ['Proust Papers'] comprising corrections and possible alternative material for his essay 'Zum Bilde Prousts' ['The Image of Proust'] from 1929, and is titled 'Aus einer kleinen Rede über Proust, an meinem vierzigsten Geburtstag gehalten' ['From a Little Speech on Proust Delivered on my Fortieth Birthday']. Dated around 1932, this short speech suggests a significant analogy between photographic images and involuntary memory, rooted in their nearly identical relation to time. Complementary to the consideration of the triggering of involuntary memory, the 'when' of the phenomenon explored in 'Über einige Motive bei Baudelaire', in this speech Benjamin discusses the actual mental form of its appearance or the 'how'.[41]

In addressing what he regards as the paradoxical nature of involuntary memory, Benjamin states that to fully understand it, one must acknowledge

---

1991), 360–9. For a detailed account of Benjamin's reading of photographs as traces, see Nitsche, *Benjamins Gebrauch der Fotografie*, 171–92.

40 Revealingly, the gaze has become a key concept in photographic theory, especially in a feminist or Lacanian context, suggesting an inherent or necessary affinity between the two that Benjamin here attempts to deny. See Margaret Iversen's comments on the gaze in 'What Is a Photograph?', *Art History*, 17 (1994), 450–63: 456–8.

41 Detlev Schöttker has pointed out that Benjamin here focuses on the 'Wesen' ['essence'] of involuntary memory in contrast to its 'Anlaß' ['occasion'] (*Konstruktiver Fragmentarismus: Form und Rezeption der Schriften Walter Benjamins* (Frankfurt a.M.: Suhrkamp, 1999), 226).

that 'ihre Bilder kommen nicht allein ungerufen, es handelt sich vielmehr in ihr um Bilder, die wir nie sahen, ehe wir uns ihrer erinnerten' (GS, II, 1064) ['not only do its images arrive without being called up; they are also images that we have never seen before remembering them']. This paradox is highly relevant to the photographic image as well, and Benjamin thus continues:

> Am deutlichsten ist das bei jenen Bildern, auf welchen wir – genau wie in manchen Träumen – selber zu sehen sind. Wir stehen vor uns, wie wir wohl in Urvergangenheit einst irgendwo, doch nie vor unserm Blick, gestanden haben. Und gerade die wichtigsten – die in der Dunkelkammer des gelebten Augenblicks entwickelten – Bilder sind es, welche wir zu sehen bekommen. Man könnte sagen, daß unseren tiefsten Augenblicken . . . – ein kleines Bildchen, ein Photo unsrer selbst – ist mitgegeben worden. Und jenes 'ganze Leben' das, wie wir oft hören, an Sterbenden oder an Menschen, die in der Gefahr zu sterben schweben, vorüberzieht, setzt sich genau aus diesen kleinen Bildchen zusammen. (Ibid.)
>
> This is especially evident in those images in which we see ourselves as we do in certain dreams. We stand before ourselves as once we stood, albeit never in front of our own gaze, in some distant past. And it is exactly the most important images, the ones developed in the dark room of the lived moment, which we get to see. One might say that we are granted a little image . . ., a photo of ourselves, to accompany our deepest moments. And that 'whole life', which, as we often hear, passes in front of the eyes of dying people or those in danger of dying, is composed precisely of such little images.

According to Benjamin, then, the remembered images of oneself that were never seen before are like photographic self-portraits, inscribed as memory traces in the unconscious.[42] Unlike the painted portrait, a photograph indisputably testifies to the sitter's past presence, to the fact that he or she was there, in front of the camera, and not just in the painter's imagination. By virtue of the latent preservation of the exposure in the form of a light trace, only the photographic portrait literally bears witness

42 In Benjamin's œuvre more generally, the notion of a not yet consciously actualized past experience is of pivotal importance and recurs in various contexts during the 1930s. For instance, as Samuel Weber has shown, with regard to awakening or 'Erwachen' in the *Passagen-Werk*, Benjamin employs a similar phrasing of the 'Noch-nicht-bewußtes-Wissen vom Gewesenen' (GS, V, 491) ['not-yet-conscious knowledge of what has been' (AP, 389)]. ('Das Erwachen bei Benjamin und Proust oder Wie Verrenkung erfahren wurde', in Thomas Amos et al. (eds.), *Les Mots de la Tribu: Für Gerhard Goebel* (Tübingen: Stauffenburg, 2000), 387–94: 389). For a fuller analysis of how Benjamin's notion of the 'dialectical image', which also entails this dynamic, may relate to photography, see Cadava's important study, *Words of Light*.

to the paradox of a memory of an unconscious or forgotten moment and confronts us with our own self and gaze in this past moment; an image of a moment in our life of which we have no direct consciousness because only the photographer has seen it through the camera lens in the now of experience.[43]

Rather than seeing this dynamic as a case of simple forgetting, the suggestion that the most important images are developed 'in the dark room of the lived moment' indicates a certain period of latency during which the lived visual experience is stored for (potential) later development. Moreover, from the vantage point of Sartre's phenomenology of imagination, Benjamin's analogy between involuntary memory and photographic images can be said to all but erase the difference between imagination and perception. For, following Sartre, the structure of the imaginary is different from the structure of perception to the extent that the former cannot surprise us: while we can discover something new in an object through perception, the object in imagination is only what we imagine it to be.[44] Directly counter to Proust, Benjamin suggests that the mental images of spontaneous recollection are like photographs, a simile that links back to his earlier discussions of the viewer's affective and emotional response to certain photographic portraits in the 'Kleine Geschichte der Photographie',[45] since what is highlighted here is not the factual and objective nature of the photograph as a purely perceptual object but instead its imaginative dimension. This is rooted in what Bernd Busch refers to as the 'phantasmagorical excess' of photographic technology, akin to the magical properties of the photograph for Benjamin, which allows for the beholder's flight of affective imagination bridging past and present.[46]

---

43 Following Freud, the memory trace is unconscious, as we have seen. By contrast, Adorno suggests that the latent memory is forgotten rather than unconscious, and in fact criticizes Benjamin on his vagueness in this respect (*Über Walter Benjamin*, 158–60).

44 See Sartre, *L'Imaginaire*, 23–5. Barthes similarly aligns the Proustian involuntary memory with the perception of photographs (see Chapter Six).

45 In Benjamin's work, this inherently private and intimate experience is dialectically related, as one might expect, to a more collective and historical experience, which he calls *Eingedenken*. Cf. Jürgen Link and Ursula Link-Heer, 'Synchronische Diachronie. Von Benjamins "Kleiner Rede über Proust" zu den Aphorismen "Über den Begriff der Geschichte"', in Harald Hillgärtner and Thomas Küpper (eds.), *Medien und Ästhetik. Festschrift für Burkhardt Lindner* (Bielefeld: Transcript Verlag, 2003), 16–33.

46 Busch speaks of an 'imaginären Überschuß', *Belichtete Welt*, 214.

The complex connections between photographic images and involuntary memory, which we have now traced, allow us to conceive the childhood portrait of Kafka and the theme of singularity from a new angle. They further highlight how the Proustian inter-text in Benjamin's writings works in support of a redemptive criticism or narrative, one which, in turn, foregrounds the ethical consideration implied in Benjamin's analysis.

The suggestion at the end of Benjamin's 'Rede über Proust' that often the most profound moments of a life are recalled in a form akin to photographic images recurs, albeit slightly reworded, in the last chapter of the 1932 version of the *Berliner Kindheit um Neunzehnhundert*; that is to say, the version which includes the 'Mummerehlen' chapter and the ekphrasis of the portrait of Kafka. Thus, we read in the last chapter: 'Ich denke mir, daß jenes "ganze Leben", von dem man sich erzählt, daß es vorm Blick der Sterbenden vorbeizieht, aus solchen Bildern sich zusammensetzt' (GS, IV, 304) ['I think that this "whole life", which, as we often hear, passes in front of the eyes of dying people, is composed of such images']. Although Benjamin here evokes photography only implicitly, as images that anticipate cinematography in the form of little flipbooks, this inter-textual relation testifies to the closeness between the 1932 version of the *Berliner Kindheit* and the 'Rede über Proust' from the same year. Therefore, even if the suggested relationship between photographs and involuntary memory is generally one of analogy only, the autobiographical context of Benjamin's engagement with the subject reminds us of the actual relation between the two as rooted in the specific dynamic between photograph, sitter and beholder – a dynamic concretely instantiated in Benjamin's relation to the Kafka portrait as a mediated encounter with his own childhood self-image.

In this respect, the recurring evocation of the Kafka photograph is analogous to the Freudian notion of the belated effect of trauma, as a 'nachträgliche' or belated realization of the significance of a 'prime event'.[47] It entails two forms of belatedness: on the one hand, in spite of the exceptional place that it already occupies in the 'Kleine Geschichte der Photographie', the winter-garden set photograph can be said to acquire its full significance only belatedly in the mirror of Benjamin's own childhood memories, written some time after the 1931 text. In fact, to apply Weigel's idea that images seen by Benjamin remained essentially

47 See Freud's remarks on latency and belated effects of trauma in 'Der Mann Moses und die monotheistische Religion', in *Fragen der Gesellschaft*, 521–8.

latent until their development into a *Denkbild*,[48] the Kafka portrait similarly remained an imaginary alter ego before Benjamin generated a story into which he integrated it. On the other hand, the 'Mummerehlen' chapter of Benjamin's *Berliner Kindheit* is also an example of the paradoxical dynamic of forgetting and remembering which, according to his speech on Proust, constitutes the similarity between the photographic self-portrait and involuntary memory. The fact that Benjamin describes the involuntary memory in terms that are akin to the photographic portrait of an earlier or other self, who is looking at a forgotten image of himself or herself, validates this assumption.

While the Kafka portrait can thus be seen as inextricably conjoined with Benjamin's personal remembrance in that Freudian process of latency and belatedness that he explicates (as previously discussed), on an inter-textual level, the ethical dimension of his engagement with the photograph is more Proustian in nature. For there is no doubt in Proust's novel, especially the final volume, *Le Temps retrouvé*, that involuntary memory shows itself to be redemptive.[49] This type of memory has the power to save a lost past, owing to its time- and death-defying potential. Benjamin surely brings his specific conceptual aims and argumentative strategies to bear on Proust's literary rendering of involuntary memory as an ecstatic experience that lifts the self out of the passage of time in which he or she is otherwise swept up. The Proustian dichotomy between voluntary and involuntary memory nonetheless provides Benjamin with a convenient and powerfully suggestive framework within which to address the time-defying nature of certain photographs, like the Kafka portrait, which is saved from time and forgetting by being associatively interwoven with *mémoire involontaire*, retrospectively narrated.[50]

---

48 Weigel discusses the role of actual paintings that Benjamin saw and how they influenced his particular 'Bilddenken' (*Walter Benjamin*, 276–7). Her vocabulary, however, can be characterized as essentially photographic.

49 The narrator of Proust's *À la recherche* unequivocally describes this redemptive quality of the experience of a *mémoire involontaire*: 'on comprend que le mot de "mort" n'ait pas de sens pour lui; situé hors du temps, que pourrait-il craindre de l'avenir?' ['one can understand that the word "death" should have no meaning for him; situated outside of time, why should he fear the future?'] (*À la recherche*, vol. 4, 451; *In Search of Lost Time*, 6 vols., trans. Scott Moncrieff and Terence Kilmartin, revis. D. J. Enright (London: Vintage, 1996), vol. 6, 225).

50 This weaving is comparable to what Benjamin in his essay on Proust calls a 'Penelopearbeit des Eingedenkens' (GS, II, 311) ['Penelope work of recollection' (SW, II, 238)].

If, as I have argued, the winter-garden photograph is both the object of, and the example for, a redemptive criticism, this is in part through its links, albeit implicit, with Proust's canonical narrative of the successful recapturing of the past. Seemingly paradoxically, yet in analogous relation to the Proustian memory seen via the lens of Freud, this emotional and existential value of the childhood photograph – that is the composite reality of the Kafka portrait and one or more images of Benjamin as a child – remained forgotten or unconscious until Benjamin's autobiographical writing provided a framework within which it could be addressed and contextualized. In sum, Benjamin's complex engagement with the Kafka portrait in various writings works against a process of 'disintegration', which, as Kracauer believes, starts once the sitter of a photographic portrait has disappeared, highlighting the fact that the truth of a photograph – its 'Wahrheitsgehalt' ['truth-content'] – is bound to time.[51] In other words, if it is not actualized, its content appears to us only in the form of an external truth (like Benjamin's 'shell') and, in Kracauer's view, will then be abandoned like a piece of old clothing, which merely testifies to a past fashion.[52] In Benjamin's ekphrasis of the childhood portrait, by contrast, the boy withstands being swallowed up by the taste-bound, contingent surroundings and is saved from becoming a mere document of the period's conventions of fashion or photography, through Benjamin's affective and intellectual investment in it. In short, the core truth content of the image is saved from forgetfulness, amounting to disintegration, as a result of being integrated into Benjamin's writing of his life story.

Benjamin's complex and multifaceted assimilation of the Kafka portrait into both his autobiographical narrative and photographic theory can be read simultaneously as an expression and extension of his 'responsible response'[53] to the image. This response, in turn, is rooted in the felt demand that the childhood photograph made on Benjamin. As we have

---

51 Kracauer, *Das Ornament der Masse*, 30. His example is also a family photograph, one of a grandmother, which evokes the famous scene in *À la recherche* where the narrator compares his detached observation of his grandmother with a photographer taking a picture. See Proust, *À la recherche*, vol. 2, 438–40. Kracauer uses this episode in his *Theory of Film* to highlight the alienating aspects of photography (14–16).

52 See Kracauer, *Das Ornament der Masse*, 30. With reference to these ideas by Kracauer, Arlette Farge convincingly suggests that there is nonetheless a 'future to come' that nests in the 'déjà fini' ('Le Temps logé en la photographie. À partir de Barthes et de Kracauer', *Intermédialités/Intermedialities*, 7 (2006), 205–13: 206–7).

53 Attridge, *The Singularity of Literature*, 124.

seen, Agamben associates the redemptive power of photography with the actual naming of the depicted person, which the portrait photograph, lacking this identifying gloss, demands. Against the background of Benjamin's personal engagement with the privileged photograph, however, it is possible to highlight another, albeit related, form of the photograph's 'demand for redemption'.[54] Even if the photograph's demand on the beholder might always *exist*, it is *felt* with more or less force, depending on the individual viewer as well as his or her relation to the photographic other depicted in the image. The full extent of the beholder's crucial role is revealed in relation to Benjamin's encounter with the childhood portrait, and it is with respect to this central image that his writerly gesture of redemption is realized. Given that the irreducible other, which the childhood photograph represents for Benjamin, is the already dead other, or former self, the photograph's demands can be more specifically coupled with a certain responsibility that we, the living, have towards the dead.

This kind of commitment to the photographic other is, as Attridge argues in a different context, an essentially ethical attitude.[55] Rather than simply trying to name the other, it is a particular type of writing about the encounter with the other in relation to the specific photograph from which redemption ensues. In discussing Benjamin's ideas about the coupling of photographs with the written word to effect political and social changes, Sontag counts Benjamin among the 'moralists who love photographs' who 'always hope that words will save the picture'.[56] While Sontag touches on the key issue of redemption here, Benjamin's writing on the Kafka-as-child photograph and the singularity that this encounter evokes, is ethical rather than 'moral', for it is an expression of a duty towards the other, ultimately stemming not from arbitrary law but a shared human condition. The written testament to the photograph that captures and preserves the encounter with it as a singular one is what promises the redemption of the life and memory of the person represented in the image and represents the fulfilment of the ethical obligation towards the other demanded by the portrait photograph. This also represents a profound extension and amplification of what is already apparent in existing discussions of photographic ethics.

54 Agamben, *Profanations*, 26.

55 As Attridge rightly points out, this ethical responsibility is quite distinct from morality (*The Singularity of Literature*, 126–7).

56 Sontag, *On Photography*, 107.

The ethical dimension of photography is traditionally associated with the image's factual authenticity and 'truth', especially in a documentary and photo-journalistic context. It is a question therefore of how the reality or event before the camera is documented and how the resulting image is subsequently presented in the context of communicating this reality or event.[57] Benjamin's call for the coupling of photographs with captions and descriptions to convey an authentic socio-political meaning or message is the recognition (as Sontag also notes) that the photographic image alone is seldom ever capable of constituting an ethical position. Instead, it necessitates an accompanying discursive description and gloss, which draws attention both to particular features of the image (which might otherwise remain invisible) and the historical circumstances of the image's production, which ipso facto are the circumstances of the concrete reality it pictures – that is, the historical and personal narrative that lies behind every image. In the case of the Kafka childhood portrait, the ethical demand of the image is met in Benjamin's writing about it, which provides the singular photograph with a specific form of 'Beschriftung'; that is, an autobiographical and existential discourse in dialectical exchange with a theoretical and historical one. More generally, the extent of Benjamin's emphasis on the concrete, affective and imaginative experience of the viewing subject, unprecedented in any previous theory of photography, adds a new and vital component to its conceptualization. And it is this potential ethical relation between the viewer and the photographically represented person, in an encounter between past and present, as this is revealed through the first-person description of this encounter juxtaposed with autobiographical narrative, which profoundly links Benjamin's and Barthes's writings on photography. In addition, and more specifically, many of the key terms and concepts that have now been introduced and discussed in the preceding chapters – including indexicality, the nature and presence of the photographic referent, transformational magic and involuntary memory – all prominently feature in Barthes's texts on photography, most notably *La Chambre claire*.

57 Not surprisingly, in the more contemporary context of the ubiquity of digital image manipulation technologies, this aspect of photographic ethics has once more come under scrutiny. Cf. William J.T. Mitchell, *The Reconfigured Eye: Visual Truth in the Post-photographic Era* (Cambridge, MA and London: MIT Press, 1992), 52–5. For an account that foregrounds the viewer's anxiety in relation to the potentially unsettling effect of post-production image manipulation, one that implicitly calls for a responsible use of computer technology in a journalistic context, see Fred Ritchin, *In Our Own Image. The Coming Revolution in Photography: How Computer Technology Is Changing Our View of the World* (New York: Aperture, 1990).

Part II

Photography and Subjectivity

Roland Barthes was and still remains one of the most influential figures in photographic theory. His diverse writings on photography have introduced a number of concepts that have shaped subsequent discussions of the medium in a profound way. These include, most notably, a semiotic definition of the photograph as a 'message without a code' and the well-known distinction between *studium* and *punctum*. The latter distinction is rooted in an overtly subjective and affective approach to the photographic image that can also be aptly characterized as phenomenological. There is some irony, however, in the fact that Barthes can be credited with one of the most significant phenomenological treatments of photography (in *La Chambre claire* from 1980), given that his earlier semiotic and structuralist work was part of a wave of critical theory that in the 1960s eclipsed the phenomenological orientation of a good deal of French philosophy and criticism associated with the work of Sartre, Merleau-Ponty, Bazin and others. The subject-centred framework of *La Chambre claire* dovetails with the general orientation of Barthes's late, post-semiotic thought, which is marked by an increasing attention to the highly personal and existential experience of cultural artefacts. Indeed, this approach finds its ultimate object in certain photographs, especially in a childhood portrait of Barthes's mother.

With regard to Barthes's œuvre as a whole, his engagement with photography can be divided into two distinct periods, although the actual point of transition between them is less straightforward. Stretching from the mid-1950s to the mid-1960s, the first is anchored in a linguistic and semiotic paradigm, whereas the later period, from the late 1970s onwards, is in keeping with the aforementioned phenomenological turn. This division is reflected in the types of photographs that Barthes discusses and, in some cases, reproduces in his texts; for example, advertisement and journalistic images (in *Mythologies* and 'Le Message photographique') and art-photography portraits and personal family photographs in his autobiographical writings and *La Chambre claire*. As we have seen, there is a similar general methodological transition in Benjamin's theory of photography, but one which goes in the chronologically reverse direction. However, in contrast to Benjamin's pronounced shift from exploring the aesthetic and emotive effect of particular photographs to a more abstract and collective assessment of the role of the photographic medium in the emergence of modernity, Barthes's overriding focus remained more local and contained, even when he was investigating the semiotic construction of meaning in the image and its ideological and social implications for mass consumer society. That is, it was centred on close analysis of specific images and clearly defined types of photographic production. Unlike Benjamin's later historical arguments, Barthes's analysis is therefore less prone to the charge of unwarranted over-generalization with respect to the nature and effects of the medium.

If this concrete grounding in actual photographic practice is one consistent feature of Barthes's writings on photography, another even more significant one is that he held firm to a realist view of the medium. This entails a stress on the indexical nature of the photographic image as an inscription of light on a material base, for example, paper, which bears a physical trace of the reality it represents and the comparative elevation of the effects of this mechanical and optical-chemical generation on the viewer over other, more formal considerations. As will be discussed, in Barthes's earlier work especially, this ontological realism is not incompatible with a focus on the cultural and ideological construction of the photographic image and its interpretation, as one might prima facie assume. Of course, on the subject of a continuity between Barthes's semiotic and phenomenological investigations, it must also be noted that, as Wolfgang Kemp has pointed out, semiotic theories of photography and the notion of the viewer's 'reading' of images they entail represented the first systematic attention to the individual and collective reception of photographs in critical and theoretical debates about the medium.[1] Reception thus became a supplement, if not necessarily an alternative, to ontological and technological considerations from which they were previously divorced in discussions of photography, with the notable exception of some of Benjamin's arguments. The critical point here is that in Barthes's writings, unlike in other past and current theories of photography, the ontological and technological nature of the photographic image, on the one hand, and the reception, affect and interpretation of it, on the other, are always coexisting, although the relation between them is highly variable. Within the systematic confines

1 See Kemp (ed.), *Theorie der Fotografie*, vol. 3, 24–5.

of his and others' semiotic theories, however, the beholder remains an abstract, socio-historical subject at the mercy of ideological manipulation through images. In Barthes's later, post-semiotic account, by contrast, the viewer is radically individuated and becomes a full, concrete subjectivity engaging in affective, emotional and imaginative ways with photographs. And it is in this context of interactions that cannot be empirically or systematically codified, and thus cannot be accounted for by semiotics, that the crucial theme of the singularity of the photographic encounter in Barthes's writings emerges most clearly – nowhere more so than in his much analysed discussions of the childhood portrait of his late mother.

In Benjamin's case, there is a pronounced tension between the particular photograph – which occasions an experience of singularity as partly rooted in the encounter with the represented other – and all other photographs, or the photographic medium as such. Whereas Barthes preserves this distinction, his understanding admits of more nuanced degrees, in suggesting an implicit hierarchy among valuable, perceptual and imaginative relations between the beholder and the image, and the process of affective memory they trigger. In contrast to his predecessor, Barthes traces such singularity in a self-reflexive manner, presenting it as part of a dialectical relation between the specific and the general, between the personal and the universal. Such a dialectic is seen at work in relation to the psychologically unsettling potential of photographic images, the status of the photographic referent and the poignancy of the relation between time and the image. Thus, despite notable differences, Barthes's discussion of photography can be seen as a continuation, and perhaps radicalization, of Benjamin's pioneering departure from purely ontological, technological and aesthetic concerns and towards photography's psychological, existential and ethical dimensions.

In order to further draw out and explain these relevant similarities and differences between Benjamin and Barthes, and to provide a new perspective on Barthes's central concepts and the place of photography within his larger theoretical projects, in Chapter Four I will first map Barthes's evolving engagement with photography against a wider theoretical and historical background. The decisive shift from semiology to phenomenology will be emphasized by highlighting the implications of considering the photograph as a sign, that is, as part of a larger signifying system endowed with ideological and political meaning, as distinct from what certain photographs may mean for the individual viewer, as a result of his or her unique experience and life history. Barthes's analysis of a number of stills from the films of Sergei Eisenstein in 'Le Troisième sens' ['The Third Meaning'] will be shown to represent a movement on his part from a more abstract concept of a general viewer guided by the cognitive apprehension of a communicated message to an individuated, 'feeling' viewer whose encounter with the photograph is guided by desire and emotion. With respect to the latter, the photographic referent or sitter is notably foregrounded as a key element of the photographic experience and thus contributes decisively to the classification of photographs along the phenomenological *studium–punctum* binary.

Chapter Five will explore the ways in which this general phenomenological framework provides Barthes with a theoretical context within which to address the experience of the singularity of photography. It will be shown that the Winter Garden photograph of the mother actually exists, despite some suggestions to the contrary, and that the acknowledgement of its existence is central to a full understanding of what is at stake in Barthes's conception of photography. In relation to his discovery of this portrait, singularity emerges in his essayistic narrative against the backdrop of an exploration of the magical and alchemical nature of photography, which is, in turn, linked to a figurative immortalization of the mother via the medium's recording capacity.

Following on from a discussion of how Barthes's writing on the photographic encounter with the mother as a child is connected to the theme of redemption, Chapter Six will focus on the strong Proustian inter-text of this encounter. The mournful and melancholic aspects of Barthes's engagement with photography are seen to be anchored in his borrowing from *À la recherche du temps perdu*. Echoing Benjamin's interpretations of Proust, the tension between the photograph-in-general and the photograph-in-particular is closely related to the conjunction of photography with the two different processes of memory Proust describes. Barthes's discourse will thus be examined with respect to his oscillating account of a suggested antithesis between involuntary memory and the photograph-in-general, and the Winter Garden photograph's profound association with involuntary memory. Finally, the close affinity between Barthes's *punctum* and Proust's *mémoire involontaire* will be shown to contribute to the creation of a narrative and conceptual design within which the mother as represented in the photograph is saved from time and forgetfulness.

Chapter 4

From Semiology to Phenomenology

When Barthes first began to write about photography in the mid-1950s, the medium was marked by a high degree of functional differentiation. It was being used in a myriad of cultural, social and scientific contexts, from art to advertising, education to astronomy, medicine to journalism. The amateur use of photography to document family life in this era of the snapshot had exploded,[1] compared even to the turn-of-the-century ubiquity of family portraiture Benjamin notes in the 'Kleine Geschichte der Photographie'. At the same time, by the mid-twentieth century, photographic theory and criticism were already increasingly characterized by the pronounced plurality of methodologies and approaches that still marks the discourse today and makes it a natural bedfellow of cognate discourses in art history and theory, film studies, media theory, cultural studies and semiotics. One feature that all of these discourses and disciplines notably share is their reference, in one way or another, back to Benjamin's rich critical and historical writings.

As if in external and symbolic confirmation of the entrenchment of photography as a mass medium in Western and some non-Western societies by mid-century, 1955 saw the famous *The Family of Man* photography exhibition, reputedly seen by some nine million people. The dominant theme of the exhibition was photography as a universal language, capable of transcending historical, cultural, linguistic and political boundaries and barriers. This utopian vision of photography's humanistic ability to unite people and cultures was, however, also contested. Indeed, Barthes's first significant discussion of photography is a highly critical assessment of the governing concept of the exhibition that, as we shall see, he damningly characterizes as both intellectually misleading and ideologically corrupt. *The Family of Man* exhibition coincided with a growing interest in linguistics as a structural model for the study of cultural phenomena, including mass media. In France especially, this was the period of the rise of structuralist semiotics. While the film theorist Christian Metz, for instance, was initiating a groundbreaking semiotic study of 'film language' in the early 1960s, Barthes, then working at the Centre for the Study of Mass Communication at the École Pratique des Hautes Études,

---

1 Cf. Bourdieu's study on the social uses of photography in post-war France, *Un Art moyen*.

published his first semiotic texts on photography. However, almost a decade earlier, Barthes had already made a decisive contribution to the analysis of so-called 'vernacular' – that is, non-artistic – photography, in the larger context of showing how and why the products of mass consumer culture and the images used to sell them could be worthy objects of intellectual study. Although not exclusively devoted to it, Barthes's seminal *Mythologies* nonetheless represents the first theoretical engagement with photography in the French theorist's œuvre.

Photographic Myths

Between 1954 and 1956, Barthes wrote monthly 'mythology' columns for the French left-wing journal *Les Lettres nouvelles*, which were eventually assembled to form *Mythologies* published in 1957. Focused on discourses that surround everyday objects or iconic artefacts of French popular culture, including cars, food, films and photographs, the aim of the short essays was to critique bourgeois ideology and its mode of address or speech, i.e. 'myth', which, according to Barthes, hides its ideology by making it appear self-evident or 'natural'. When Barthes discusses photography in *Mythologies*, in the majority of cases, he refers to images reproduced in journalistic, political or ideological contexts, most notably in popular print magazines, such as *Elle*, *Paris-Match* and the *Nouvel Observateur*.[2] In the concluding essay, 'Le Mythe, aujourd'hui' ['Myth Today'], which is more systematic than the others, Barthes specifies the role of photography in the creation and promotion of this mythological discourse. According to the text's Saussurean premise, myth is defined as speech, i.e. 'une parole' (OC, I, 823), and thereby as a binary system of communication, consisting of signs, understood as conjunctions of formal signifiers and signified objects. In this context, the photograph is a sign, a vehicle for the communication of an ideologically inflected message. It is this message, Barthes suggests, that must be demystified to reveal the latent and contingent cultural and political content beneath its naturalistic guise and false sense of necessity. In the case of photographs

2 Jaqueline Guittard traces nine articles in *Mythologies* back to photographs that appeared in *Paris-Match* ('Impressions photographiques: les *Mythologies* de Roland Barthes', *Littérature*, 143 (2006), 114–34: 116). In the 2010 edition of Barthes's book, much of the visual material, photographs and otherwise, has been included to document the sources that he used (Roland Barthes, *Mythologies*, ed. Jacqueline Guittard (Paris: Seuil, 2010)).

of candidates for parliamentary elections, for example, which Barthes discusses in one of the pieces, the message in question centres on the upstanding lifestyle and implied moral virtue of the candidates as conveyed through dress and posture, which are foregrounded at the expense of their political programmes. The photograph is here used to establish a seemingly direct personal link between candidates and voters based on an ostensibly shared 'manière d'être' (OC, I, 796) ['manner of being' (M, 91)], which is quite possibly an illusion.

One might expect, given this cultural-critical perspective, that Barthes's laying bare of the myth of some photographs' apparently naturalistic and objective representation also entails a repudiation of the photographic medium's conveyance of objective 'truth', as articulated, for instance, in Bazin's 1945 essay on the 'Ontologie de l'image photographique'.[3] However, Barthes's main concern here is with the semiotic and ideological content of the photographic image, rather than with its form, or the medium per se. He thus avoids the loaded question of whether there is something inherent in the visual medium of photography that lends itself to ideological use in such a powerful and persuasive way – that is to say, its being to some degree an objective inscription of reality – and also the related issue of the psychological effects following on from it.

In *Mythologies*, there are two essays that deal directly with photography exhibitions. In them, Barthes analyses the parasitical or 'second-order' messages that both the exhibitions and the photographs within them convey. With regard to an exhibition of confrontational images held at the Parisian Galerie d'Orsay, which included a photograph juxtaposing a crowd of soldiers with a field of dead bodies and another photograph of a young military man contemplating a human skeleton, Barthes ironically titles his critical analysis 'Photos-chocs'. He condemns the photographers' apparent intent to create images designed mainly to shock the viewer in ways which Barthes perceives as a distortion of what – in a formulation that becomes clearer in subsequent writings – he calls the 'first-order message' of the photograph. According to Barthes,

3 As noted, Bazin viewed photography and cinema as the apotheosis of Western history of visual representation, arguing that the invention of perspective in the fifteenth century, for instance, was driven by men's psychological need for ever-more life-like depictions of the visual world. Implicitly distinguishing between a formal-aesthetic and psychological realism, he argues that the automatic production of the photograph has a powerful psychological effect that satisfies the need for a mimetic realism, even if the image is also constructed in some respects ('Ontologie de l'image photographique', 13–17).

the photographs actually fail to shock by virtue of the photographers' careful formal presentation of the content of each image using effective contrast, juxtaposition and conventional iconography.[4] For Barthes, the recognizable intentionality that follows from one's perception of the photographs' artifice weakens, rather than strengthens, their emotional or affective impact. He describes what he believes is a key mistake of photographers in relation to the attempted cultivation of psychological impact in such non-shocking 'photo-choc' images, suggesting that this sort of image

> ne résonne pas, ne trouble pas, notre accueil se referme trop tôt sur un signe pur; la lisibilité parfaite de la scène, sa *mise en forme* nous dispense de recevoir profondément l'image dans son scandale; réduite à l'état de pur langage, la photographie ne nous désorganise pas. (OC, I, 752)
>
> does not resound, does not disturb, our reception closes too soon over a pure sign; the perfect legibility of the scene, its *formulation* dispenses us from receiving the image in all its scandal; reduced to the state of pure language, the photograph does not disorganise us. (ET, 72)

Yet, if the perceived intention in this case reduces the photographic image to language, and thereby to a linguistic message that can be more easily grasped (and with some critical distance, demystified), Barthes also acknowledges that there is something essential to the photograph that resists this conventionalizing appropriation. The photograph may indeed possess the power to truly disturb the viewer, but owing to a quality of the image that bypasses all intentionality and mediation on the part of the photographer. This potential of the photographic portrait, especially, would be a main topic in Barthes's later reflections on photography, beginning in the 1970s, and is directly related to the concept of the *punctum* in *La Chambre claire*.

The second photography exhibition critiqued in *Mythologies* is Edward Steichen's aforementioned *The Family of Man*. After its opening in the Museum of Modern Art in New York in January 1955, precisely one

4 A similar critique of photography, in relation to the iconography of portraiture, is to be found in his essay on the myth created by the famous Parisian Harcourt portrait studio. Founded in 1934, this studio can be seen as the twentieth-century successor of Nadar's celebrated nineteenth-century studio and was highly frequented by Parisian celebrities. While Barthes praises Nadar not only as one of the greatest photographers but also as a great 'mythologue' of the French bourgeoisie in *La Chambre claire* (CC, 61), he critiques the Harcourt portraits for their conscious photographic deceit through which actors, for instance, are transformed into God-like creatures (see OC, I, 688).

hundred years after the *Exposition Universelle* in Paris, which prominently included photography for the first time in France, *The Family of Man* successfully toured the world for several years. Even if Barthes did not happen to see it in person when it was on display in Paris in 1956, as Jacqueline Guittard has suggested,[5] he nonetheless had much to say about it. Unlike subsequent critics of this exhibition, who regarded it as Cold-War propaganda and a display of US American hegemony,[6] in his essay entitled 'La Grande famille des hommes' ['The Great Family of Man'], Barthes attacks the problematic 'naturalization' of history underlying Steichen's intention to depict mankind as a 'family'.[7] The exhibition was presented as a milestone in cultural diversity, with more than 500 images on display taken by 273 different photographers from 68 different countries. This apparent diversity is belied by the fact that many of the photographers were affiliated with the American photojournalistic weekly magazine *Life* (a fact that, had Barthes noted it, would further have supported his arguments). The exhibition, Barthes argues, problematically suggests that these images can be understood in the same way by every viewer due to the universality of 'photographic language', a notion Barthes rejects.[8]

The Family of Man's rhetoric of photography as a 'universal language' and its power to reconcile and unify the otherwise fragmented Babel-like plurality of cultures, associated with chaos and confusion, was an already popular theme in photographic criticism and theory, going back to the nineteenth century.[9] It peaked at the beginning of the twentieth century, with August Sander's 1931 radio broadcast entitled 'Die Photographie als Weltsprache' ['Photography as a Universal Language'] a testimony to its widespread currency and rhetorical appeal.[10] In *Mythologies*, and

5 See Guittard, 'Impressions photographiques', 130.

6 See, for example, Allan Sekula, 'The Traffic in Photographs', *Art Journal*, 41 (1981), 15–25: 19–21.

7 Steichen writes in the introduction to the catalogue that the exhibition 'was conceived as . . . a mirror of the essential oneness of mankind throughout the world' (*The Family of Man* (exhibition catalogue) (New York: The Museum of Modern Art, 1955), 4).

8 However, while Barthes strongly questions the assumption as to the cultural universality of photographic language, the idea that photography is a kind of language is, of course, retained, as this is axiomatic to his and any other semiotic analysis of photographic images.

9 For a concise discussion of this idea, see Bernd Stiegler, *Bilder der Photographie. Ein Album photographischer Metaphern* (Frankfurt a.M.: Suhrkamp, 2006), 209-15.

10 The radio lecture, the fifth in a six-part series, was broadcast by the Westdeutscher Rundfunk in Cologne and has recently been re-published in August

in the wider context of semiotic and Marxist critique of right-wing and bourgeois dogma in the form of a totalizing and difference-eradicating humanism (which Barthes was certainly not alone in questioning), the founding rhetoric of *The Family of Man* predictably comes under fierce attack. It is critiqued for its failure to acknowledge the profound extent of socio-cultural differences with respect to both the people represented in the photographs and the exhibition's viewers.[11] Instead, it propagates the myth of a single homogenous human culture: 'Nous voici tout de suite renvoyés à ce mythe ambigu de la "communauté" humaine . . . . L'homme naît, travaille, rit et meurt partout de la même façon' (OC, I, 806) ['We are at the outset directed to this ambiguous myth of the human "community" . . . . Man is born, works, laughs and dies everywhere in the same way' (M, 100)]. For Barthes, not only does this monolithic concept of the human 'oneness', as Steichen calls it,[12] implicitly introduce a Western concept of God into the exhibition, but it transforms contingent human history into nature, thereby glossing over and excusing injustice as a natural part of the conditio humana or even divine providence. With respect to the photographic images themselves, he argues that once history is removed from them, they become tautological in simply re-presenting birth, life and death without inviting critical reflection as to their particular significance in individual cases. In sum, if the photographs in the Orsay Gallery exhibition disappoint Barthes due to their failure to authentically affect and disturb the viewer in a way which would prompt some novel understanding of the issues they address, and/or cultivate a new form of feeling, *The Family of Man* exhibition is both a failure and repudiation of photography's critical potential to reaffirm existential singularity and difference – a potential which is implicitly regarded in *Mythologies* (and more explicitly stressed in Barthes's much later writings) as the true calling of a modern medium rooted in the concrete representation of individual realities.

In opposition to these two exhibitions, which intentionally or unintentionally furthered reactionary mythological discourse, Barthes aligns a successful photographic questioning of dominant ideology with

---

Sander, *Sehen, Beobachten und Denken* (Munich: Schirmer/Mosel, 2009), 25-31. For a more detailed discussion of this little-referenced text, see Sekula, 'The Traffic in Photographs', 17–18.

11 In a more contemporary context, however, Hirsch has shown that the idea of photography as a universal language persists with respect to family photographs (*Family Frames*, 48–77).

12 *The Family of Man*, 4.

Brechtian aesthetics, recalling Benjamin's promotion of the critical, anti-fascist photomontages by Heartfield. In Barthes's illustrated essay, 'Préface à Brecht, "Mère Courage et ses enfants"' ['Preface to Brecht: "Mother Courage and her Children"'] from 1960, where he refers to Benjamin's analysis of the gesture in Brecht's theatre (see OC, I, 1075),[13] he writes that Roger Pic's photographs, taken during the Berliner Ensemble's performance of *Mutter Courage und ihre Kinder* in Paris in 1957, 'sont véritablement critiques: elles n'illustrent pas, elles aident à découvrir l'intention profonde de la création' (OC, I, 1064) ['are truthfully critical: they do not illustrate, they help to discover the profound intention of the creation']. For Barthes, rather than simply illustrating an event by tautologically representing it, the photographs in question help the viewer to understand the principle of Brecht's politically motivated 'distancement', that is, his well-known technique of spectatorial *Verfremdung* ('estrangement' or 'distanciation'). Barthes pits this strategy against the photographic 'mystification' and intoxicating false humanism characterizing *The Family of Man* exhibition (OC, I, 1079). Pic's photographs exemplify distanciation, Barthes argues, in drawing attention to specific details that, given the temporal transience of the theatrical work, might otherwise go unnoticed. In short, although Barthes does not use Benjamin's famous phrase in this context, despite its clear applicability, these images reveal an 'optical unconscious', one which in this case serves a progressive, critical-ideological function.

As these descriptions indicate, Barthes's primary interest in photography during the 1950s, as typified by *Mythologies*, concerns the ideological context within which images are encountered in everyday, public life. At least with regard to its explicit arguments, this text remains ambivalent on the issue of the specificity of the photographic image in comparison with all other types of visual representation. The photograph is seen as a sign onto which the mythological signifier is attached, as in the

13 For a more detailed comparison on this point, see my 'Die Photographien "zu ihrem Rechte kommen lassen"', 24–5. Geoffrey Batchen has pointed out that Barthes echoes a quotation from Brecht that Benjamin uses in his 'Kleine Geschichte der Photographie' (see GS, II, 384), which concerns the problematic aspect of photographs that merely reflect reality rather than saying anything substantial or critical about it ('Palinode. An Introduction to *Photography Degree Zero*', in Geoffrey Batchen (ed.), *Photography Degree Zero. Reflections on Roland Barthes's Camera Lucida* (Cambridge, MA: MIT Press, 2009), 3–30: 6). More directly, Barthes refers to this Brechtian critique in *La Chambre claire* in relation to Sander (see CC, 63–5).

case of the linguistic sign, creating a second-order system of signification. Additionally, myth, for Barthes, is a matter of a message that, contra Marshall McLuhan, transcends, and in some cases obscures, the basic nature or condition of the medium that delivers it. Thus, photography is subsumed in a larger signifying system, and even when his arguments challenge semiotic orthodoxy, allegiance to a semiotic framework shaped Barthes's reflections on photography up until the early 1970s.

The Semiology of Photography

In *Mythologies*, as we have seen, Barthes combines a general formalistic/linguistic conception of photography with a left-wing socio-critical perspective informed by Marxism. A few years later, he began to pursue in earnest a more systematic line of semiotic inquiry, informed by structuralism, which was coming to dominate cutting-edge French intellectual discourse.[14] In 'Le Message photographique' from 1961 and 'Rhétorique de l'image' from 1964, Barthes again focuses on journalistic and advertising imagery. But unlike *Mythologies*, explicit socio-political critique is now muted and replaced by a more academic observation and analysis of the impersonal and formal processes of cultural signification and meaning production.

Elaborating and refining the notion that the photograph is a sign, in 'Le Message photographique' Barthes treats it as a structurally autonomous entity that may function independently of language. However, his focus on photojournalism, where the photograph is accompanied by the written word, calls for a contrasting analysis of the photographic and the linguistic sign (see OC, I, 1121). Barthes's oft-quoted semiotic definition of the photograph as '*un message sans code*' (ibid.) ['*a message without a code*' (IMT, 17)] derives from this analysis.[15] From a strictly semiotic perspective, Barthes's claim is self-contradictory, given that for a message to be a message, it must be the product of conventional codes. However, the starting point for this definition is the particular causal relationship between photographic representation and the reality it pictures, that is, its indexicality. All mimetic representation entails denotation and

14 See Ffrench, *The Time of Theory*, 17–18.

15 Although most studies on Barthes and photography focus on *La Chambre claire* as the central text, this definition is frequently referenced and often taken as a concise summary of his early views. See, for example, Stiegler, *Theoriegeschichte der Photographie*, 347.

connotation.[16] In the case of painting, for example, not only the connoted (the metaphorical, allegorical, etc.) but also the denoted (i.e. the basic 'what' of the image, its literal representation) carry with them a coded message, as a result of being always mediated by an artistic and historical style (e.g. not apples, but Cézanne's apples; not bodies, but Cubist bodies). In the case of photography, however, the denoted – as an indexical impression of reality – largely bypasses such cultural, aesthetic and psychological mediation. The conventional signification that photographs do undoubtedly partake in is thus confined to supplementary, second-order connotations that come *on top* of the reality content of the image, as it were (see OC, I, 1122–3).

From this perspective, every photograph has two coexisting messages: the denoted sense of the reality it captures and the connoted, cultural (or 'coded') meaning that surrounds this 'reality-effect'.[17] This latter connotation is the concrete product of both *actual* language – that is, any text physically accompanying the image as well as language used to describe and interpret the image – and the visual *meta-language* of photography. Borrowing from painting in some cases, the latter includes 'truquage, pose, objets' or 'photogénie, esthétisme, syntaxe' (OC, I, 1124) ['trick effects, pose, objects' or 'photogenia, aestheticism, syntax' (IMT, 21)] and can potentially be found in all photographs (and which is, of course, the focus of Barthes's critique of the 'Photos-chocs' exhibition). In other words, every photograph as an image has a conventional aesthetic and ideological grammar and syntax to some degree, but also in principle a 'purer' significance, for which there is no conventional code, as it is by definition as unique as the reality before the camera.

Barthes argues that in most cases, the connoted dimension of the photographic image, the fact that it tends to be instinctively viewed through language – when it is 'saisie immédiatement par un méta-langage intérieur' (OC, I, 1131) ['grasped immediately by an inner meta-language' (IMT, 28)] – tends to obscure or bury the reality message.

---

16 Connotation, as opposed to denotation, is akin to what Barthes, in *Mythologies*, calls 'méta-langage' (OC, I, 829), except that the latter is attached to the sign, whereas the former pertains to systems, as Michael Moriarty has pointed out (*Roland Barthes* (Stanford: Stanford University Press, 1991), 88).

17 I borrow this term from Barthes's famous structuralist analysis of Flaubert's short story 'Un Cœur simple' ['A Simple Heart'] as exemplifying nineteenth-century realist literature's 'effet de réel' through meticulous description of details that, from a strictly narratological perspective, are superfluous (OC, III, 25–32). While the reality-effect of photography is, of course, different in nature, the expression can aptly be applied to it.

This is unless, owing to the content of the image and the individual viewer's relation to it, the photograph's reality-effect breaks through the layers of cultural mediation, at which point the true potential of photographic representation emerges, at least in part. Shifting from semiotic to psychoanalytic vocabulary, this is the case, Barthes suggests, in relation to those photographs he characterizes as truly 'traumatic', which escape codification: 'le trauma, c'est précisément ce qui suspend le langage et bloque la signification' (OC, I, 1132) ['trauma is precisely what suspends language and blocks meaning' (IMT, 30)]. Ronald Berg has rightly pointed out that, as the above summary demonstrates, Barthes here only retrospectively provides the full theoretical explanation for why the 'Photos-chocs' images were not affecting in a truly photographic way, that is, owing to their over-reliance on conventional codes and iconic traditions, which dilutes rather than maximizes the force of the disturbing realities they picture.[18] More generally, trauma is thus rendered an important concept in understanding what makes photographic images potentially unique, in experiential terms, in comparison with other forms of visual representation.

Yet, trauma, as rooted in the irrefutable certainty of the past reality of the depicted scene, is an aspect of photography that, as Barthes admits, semiotic analysis simply cannot account for, since the traumatic photograph does not signify in any conventionally meaningful way. Bringing the concept of 'myth' into 'Le Message photographique', he suggests a proportional relation between the photograph's conventional signification associated with myth and its trauma-effect: 'l'effet "mythologique" d'une photographie est inversement proportionnel à son effet traumatique' (OC, I, 1133) ['the "mythological" effect of a photograph is inversely proportional to its traumatic effect' (IMT, 31)].[19] The photographs that are the least meaningful, from a semiotic point of view, are often the most troubling and significant from a psychological perspective. The logical conclusion here is, perhaps, that only through renunciation of semiotic theory, rather than its continued application, can the materiality of the

18 See Berg, *Die Ikone des Realen*, 203.

19 De Duve calls this photography's 'built-in trauma effect' ('Time Exposure and Snapshot', 120). Although Benjamin also refers to trauma in relation to modernity and picture-taking, as we have seen, his interpretation of this link is quite different from Barthes's, who is more interested in the effect of the image on the individual viewer. Moreover Barthes, unlike Benjamin, follows Lacan when he stresses that trauma is 'outside meaning', rather than Freud, as Andrew Brown has argued (*Roland Barthes. The Figures of Writing* (Oxford: Oxford University Press, 1992), 241).

photograph as a physical artefact, its indexicality and its affective impact on the viewer be adequately accounted for. However, while admitting that significant aspects of photography fall outside of a semiotic-structuralist paradigm, as still firmly entrenched within it, Barthes is here – for the historical moment at least – content mainly to demarcate the boundaries of what can ever be objectively and systematically studied with respect to the photograph, rather than question such would-be scientific paradigms. But, it remains true, of course, that it is through semiology that Barthes's insights as to what escapes its conceptual net are discovered.

A subsequent text, 'Rhétorique de l'image', also seeks to understand photography in semiotic terms. Like 'Le Message photographique', it was published in *Communications*, and here photography is seen first and foremost as a mass medium. Pierre Bourdieu's *Un Art moyen* [*A Middlebrow Art*], a nearly contemporaneous text from 1965, is a classic example of a sociological approach to photography, one which examines various uses of the medium, including amateur family photography, photojournalism and artistic practices. Whereas Bourdieu's study is sociological-empirical, Barthes's approach is linguistic-structuralist. 'Rhétorique de l'image' attempts to develop the heuristic tools for a systematic understanding of how photography produces meaning. The specific commercial photograph that Barthes takes as an example, a newspaper advertisement for Italian pasta products by Panzani, is seen as a complex sign, featuring three sorts of messages: a linguistic message, a coded iconic message and a non-coded iconic one. Although Barthes often alters his terminology in the text,[20] it is clear that the latter two are purely visual meanings, characteristic of the photographic sign, which, in advertisement, is generally coupled with a third, written message.

Barthes's juxtaposition of textual and visual messages in this piece provides insight into his view of the relation between word and image. In contrast to Benjamin's politically motivated contention that the textual supplementation of photographic images became necessary (with the emergence of Atget's photographs of a depopulated Paris) to promote the photograph's crucial potential function as historical evidence, Barthes's perspective is historically much broader. He traces the relation between photography and language back to that between image and text that has persisted since the advent of the book, wherein the template is set for the visual to play a supplementary role as illustration

20 He also refers to the coded iconic message as simply 'iconique', 'symbolique' and 'connoté' and to the non-coded iconic as 'message sans code', 'message littéral' and 'dénoté' (OC, II, 576–7).

of text (see OC, II, 578). Barthes nevertheless concludes that Western civilization in the second half of the twentieth century remains a culture of the written word. Despite the exponential proliferation of images following in the wake of photographic production and reproduction on an industrial scale, it is language rather than the image itself that conveys meaning.[21] Rather than rooted in the natural state of things, however, this reality is a cultural and historical construction, a product of the dominant uses of text and image and their coupling. In 'Rhétorique de l'image', Barthes critiques this linguistic appropriation of the photograph on the basis that, according to the framework introduced in 'Le Message photographique', the photographic sign consists of both a connotative (coded) and a denotative (non-coded) message. The attempted fixing or 'anchoring'[22] of this latter polysemantic message, whereby conventional connotation obscures or challenges concrete photographic denotation (of reality), is, for Barthes, both ideologically motivated and repressive, an attempt to restrict meaning and suppress the ambiguity of reality. As Sabine Kriebel has noted, this is in contrast to Benjamin, who sees the restriction of the photograph's meaning via language as offering vital conceptual guidance to the viewer, especially in a complex social and political environment.[23]

Barthes views the detrimental effects of the ideologically motivated linguistic coding of photographs as operating most clearly in contemporary photo-based advertising culture. And yet, he insists, although processes of signification and interpretation subsume 'pure' photographic denotation, usurping its indexical reality, wholly non-mediated objectivity and transparency remains an ideal, even if a utopian one: 'débarrassée utopiquement de ses connotations, l'image deviendrait radicalement objective, c'est-à-dire en fin de compte innocente' (OC, II, 581) ['cleared utopically of its connotations, the image would become

21 Since the so-called 'iconic turn' of the 1990s, art historians and theorists, especially in a German-speaking context, have been preoccupied with the vexed question of how images as such produce meaning. See, for example, Gottfried Boehm, *Wie Bilder Sinn erzeugen. Die Macht des Zeigens* (Berlin: Berlin University Press, 2007).

22 Barthes defines two ways of text-image relation: 'ancrage' and 'relais' (OC, II, 578). The former is at once the more repressive and more frequently used one (in opposition to 'relais', describing the more complementary relation between text and image, as can be found in films or comic strips).

23 See Sabine T. Kriebel, 'Theories of Photography. A Short History', in James Elkins (ed.), *Photography Theory* (New York and London: Routledge, 2007), 3–49: 14–15.

radically objective, or, in the last instance, innocent' (IMT, 42)]. This is an astonishingly 'realist' position for a semiotician to adopt. And, despite Barthes's suggestion that such an uncultured 'image littérale à l'état pur' (OC, II, 581) ['literal image in a pure state' (IMT, 42)] is utopian, it is not surprising that the mere suggestion of its possible existence was, and remains, controversial. For this goes against the grain not just of semiotics but of so much cultural studies (from the early 1980s onwards), especially in an Anglo-American context, as influenced, for example, by Foucault's analysis of power and ideology. In relation to photography, this discourse is marked by a pronounced movement away from questions of photography's direct relation to some unmediated reality to the nature of the complex network of heterogenic cultural codes – in which every image is caught up – and its effects.[24] The idea that there might be some 'essential' feature of a photograph that (co-)determines its meaning, and that, moreover, is un-coded, is difficult to square with this approach to photography as a 'practice of signification'.[25] From a more doctrinal semiotic perspective, Umberto Eco strongly rejected the notion of a 'pure' message that escapes codification, arguing that even the perception of a photograph is always culturally coded and informed by learned conventions.[26] More explicitly targeting the argument of 'Rhétorique de l'image', Allan Sekula questioned the distinction between a connoted and a denoted photographic message and denied that a purely denoted image ever existed in the 'real world'.[27]

A powerful counter-argument to this anti-realist position, and one indebted to Barthes's early writing on photography, is Philippe Dubois's 1983 study *L'Acte photographique* [*The Photographic Act*]. The Belgian theorist's starting point is the notion of a denoted or un-coded message, which he couples with Peirce's pragmatic semiotics.[28] Dubois affirms

---

24 See, representatively, Victor Burgin's introduction in *Thinking Photography* (London: Macmillan, 1982), 1–14. This collection is, to some extent, a critical response to Barthes.

25 Ibid., 2.

26 See Umberto Eco, 'Critique of the Image', in Victor Burgin (ed.), *Thinking Photography* (London: Macmillan, 1982), 32–8.

27 Sekula, 'On the Invention of Photographic Meaning', in Victor Burgin (ed.), *Thinking Photography* (London: Macmillan, 1982), 84–109: 87. Cf. for an overview of these debates Peter Geimer, *Theorien der Fotografie. Zur Einführung* (Hamburg: Junius, 2009), 89–92.

28 Together with Dubois, Van Lier and Schaeffer, in 1983 and 1987, respectively, also develop a semiotic approach to photography with reference to Barthes (see Henri Van Lier, *Philosophie de la photographie* (Paris and Bruxelles:

Barthes's brand of photographic realism and argues that at least in the brief moment when the camera's shutter opens, there is 'un instant d'oubli des codes, un index quasi pur' ['an instance without codes, a quasi pure index'].[29] While for Dubois this indexicality is constitutive of photography, he goes on to suggest that the medium can best be understood not from an ontological or materialist perspective alone but from a more 'pragmatic' one, which takes into account all the potential *effects* of this fundamental indexicality. As will become clear, this dual emphasis on the ontology of the photographic image and its psychological and phenomenological effects is, in fact, the keynote of Barthes's post-semiotic *La Chambre claire*.

Barthes's thesis concerning the denoted message of the photograph in 'Rhétorique de l'image' shows the extent to which he was beginning to substantially break from some aspects of the semiotic framework. For him, what is unique and radically new about photographic representation, as arrived at via the concept of a non-coded message, is its ability to present the viewer with a new form of knowledge, relating to the photograph's '*avoir-été-là*' (OC, II, 583) ['*having-been-there*' (IMT, 44)]. The experientially novel, indeed revolutionary, temporal-spatial dynamic of the photograph,[30] as a paradoxical combination of an 'unnatural, yet nature-determined' sign, as de Duve puts it,[31] is most clearly stated in the following passage from 'Rhétorique de l'image':

> C'est donc au niveau de ce message dénoté ou message sans code que l'on peut comprendre pleinement *l'irréalité réelle* de la photographie; son irréalité est celle de *l'ici*, car la photographie n'est jamais vécue comme une illusion, elle n'est nullement une *présence*, et il faut en rabattre sur

---

Les Impressions Nouvelles, 1983) and Schaeffer, *L'Image précaire*). In contrast to their reliance on Peirce's semiotics, Barthes was largely influenced by contemporary linguists, including Louis Hjelmslev and A.J. Greimas as well as Saussure. A more extensive semiotics of photography based on the work of Hjelmslev is René Lindekens's *Essai de sémiotique visuelle* from 1976. Unlike Barthes, however, Lindekens assumes all aspects of photography to be coded.

29 Philippe Dubois, *L'Acte photographique* (Paris: Nathan, 1983), 47.

30 Hans Belting has argued that Barthes's particular experience of photography is not in line with this claim because he tends to look for portraits of people he knew in order to compare the photographic image with his mental image of them, a test of fidelity to the real which is applicable to painting and drawing, and predates photography (*Bild-Anthropologie. Entwürfe für eine Bildwissenschaft* (Munich: Fink, 2001), 213). Belting seems to underestimate, however, that indexicality and not just iconicity remains a decisive factor in Barthes's various theories of photography.

31 De Duve, 'Time Exposure and Snapshot', 113.

> le caractère magique de l'image photographique; et sa réalité est celle de *l'avoir-été-là*, car il y a dans toute photographie l'évidence toujours stupéfiante du: *cela s'est passé ainsi*. (OC, II, 583)
>
> It is thus at the level of this denoted message or message without code that the *real unreality* of the photograph can be fully understood: its unreality is that of the *here*, for the photograph is never experienced as illusion, is in no way a *presence* (claims as to the magical character of the photographic image must be deflated); its reality is that of the *having-been-there*, for in every photograph there is the always stupefying evidence of *this is how it was*. (IMT, 44)

Barthes here touches on concepts that would be of paramount importance in his later reflections on photography, including the peculiar 'past presence' the photographic image represents, its unique relation to reality and the photograph's ostensible 'magical' character. With respect to the last of these, while it is here dismissed, the photograph's profound relation to magic is one of the prominent themes of *La Chambre claire*. But, if these elementary characteristics of the photographic image can be theoretically grasped on the level of the denoted message only, as Barthes suggests, the question arises as to whether it helps us understand the actual encounter with specific images. In short, does a photograph ever exist in such a 'pure' state? As Barthes hints, away from the world of advertising and other socio-cultural contexts and uses of the medium, it may be possible to find such an 'innocent' photograph, free of ideological and semiotic coding. And it is such an image and the realist utopia it represents that Barthes pursues in *La Chambre claire*, where he ponders the difficulty of escaping one's enculturation and laments: 'face à certaines photos, je me voulais sauvage, sans culture' (CC, 20) ['looking at certain photographs, I wanted to be a primitive, without culture' (CL, 7)]. However, before Barthes, in the late 1970s, embarked on the book that sought to do full justice to what he labelled the traumatic effect of certain photographs, rooted in their expression of the real, his engagement with photography first passed through an intermediary period, one marked by the transition from a focus on the photograph's objective signification to its subjective affects. One text in particular, 'Le Troisième sens', marks the start of this turn.

The Third Meaning and the Viewing Subject

First published in 1970 in the re-oriented post-Auteur-theory *Cahiers du cinéma*, when the legendary French film journal moved in a more theoretical, left-wing ideological direction and began to open its doors to writers like Barthes, 'Le Troisème sens' also occupies an intermediary position with respect to the particular type of images Barthes investigates, namely, film stills as opposed to photographs, taken from Eisenstein's *Battleship Potemkin* (1925) and *Ivan the Terrible I* (1944).[32] As pieces of a film, stills are neither photographs nor, given the lack of duration, cinematic, and Barthes writes that the still actually belongs to its own category, which he calls the 'filmique' (OC, III, 503).[33]

Eisenstein, one of the great theorist-directors in the history of cinema, founded both his early film theory and practice on the 'third meaning' produced by the editing techniques of dialectical montage (or the 'montage of film attractions').[34] This entails a third mental image resulting from the juxtaposition of, and dialectical collision between, two film shots, as used most powerfully in *Battleship Potemkin* and *October 1917* (1928). Thus, for Eisenstein, the meaning that matters most in cinema is a function of the relation between images in sequence, rather than the contents of any one, a visually stimulated meaning intended to be collective, that is, more or less the same for every viewer. This allows for montage to affect a mass audience 'known and selected in advance for its homogeneity', as Eisenstein writes, and fulfil its initially intended role as Soviet propaganda, 'concentrating the audience's emotions in any direction dictated by the production's purpose'.[35] In diametrical contrast to Eisenstein, Barthes considers individual film stills in isolation from the narrative sequence and gauges their impact on the viewing subject as realities in themselves.[36] Despite his familiarity with some of Eisenstein's

32 For a more detailed film-theoretical analysis of this text, see Winfried Pauleit, *Filmstandbilder. Passagen zwischen Kunst und Kino* (Frankfurt a.M. and Basel: Stroemfeld Verlag, 2004), 135–47.

33 Barthes's repeated search for a third term that escapes binary oppositions, the theme of his second Collège de France seminar series dedicated to *Le Neutre*, is examined by Marielle Macé in relation to the 'romanesque' ('Barthes Romanesque', in Alexandre Gefen and Marielle Macé (eds.), *Barthes, au lieu du roman* (Paris: Desjonquères-Nota Bene, 2002), 173–94).

34 Sergei M. Eisenstein, 'The Montage of Film Attractions', in *Selected Works*, 4 vols., trans. and ed. Richard Taylor (London: BFI Publishing, 1988), vol. 1, 39–58: 43.

35 Ibid., 41.

36 It is well known that Barthes frequently stressed his dislike for cinema in contrast to photography, as in *La Chambre claire* where he writes on the first page that he loves 'la Photo *contre* le cinéma' (CC, 13) ['Photography *in opposition to* Cinema' (CL, 3)]. Martin Jay's contention that the discovery of the photograph's *avoir-été-là* marked the beginning of Barthes's strict

film-theoretical writings (translated and published in the *Cahiers du cinéma*), Barthes puts forward a very different conception of a third meaning, which evidences his burgeoning interest in the highly variable and subjective perception of photographic images. This is a supplemental meaning or message that falls outside any given semiotic system, of the sort Barthes now flatly states no longer concerns him (see OC, III, 485), and that would include Eisenstein's suggested cinematic grammar, created on the basis of the film-maker's manipulation of conventional signs.

Barthes quickly passes over what he regards as the 'first meaning' of the film still, which pertains to its literal representation and, in this case, narrative or diegetic importance, conceived as its most basic level of communication. Instead, he focuses on the second and third meanings, that is, the '*sens obvie*' ['*obvious meaning*'], in the Latin sense of *obvius* as something coming before or ahead of something else, and the '*sens obtus*' (OC, III, 488) ['*obtuse meaning*' (IMT, 54)], respectively. The second meaning is the non-literal, symbolic and intentional significance of the image and its contents (the level of metaphor and analogy). The third, or obtuse meaning, is akin to what Barthes in *Mythologies* and 'Le Message photographique' characterizes as the traumatic aspect of photographic images that cannot be discursively articulated or formalized. Despite not being reducible to any one feature of content, this affecting and suggestive characteristic of certain stills is commensurate with the subject of the specific image through which Barthes apparently discovers the third meaning of the photographic still: a still from *Battleship Potemkin* of a woman mourning for the dead sailor, Vakulinchuck, leader of the uprising on board the eponymous ship. In this still, as in others from the same sequence, Eisenstein employs all the classical iconography of mourning (bowed head, lowered eyes, hands on heart, etc.) that constitutes its *sens obvie*. And yet, for Barthes, it also possesses something beyond it that can never be fully intended. Although it is retrospectively seen to be located in the expression produced by a certain constellation of features (in this case, the relation between the woman's hair and scarf), it is a *Gestalt* property of the image that always transcends or escapes satisfactory attribution to this or that element. Barthes refers to this property as a 'signifiant sans signifié' ['signifier without a signified'], which causes his reading of it to be 'suspendue entre l'image et sa description, entre la définition et

---

separation of photography and cinema is convincing in this context (*Downcast Eyes: The Denigration of Vision in Twentieth-Century French Thought* (Berkeley: University of California Press, 1993), 443–4).

l'approximation' (OC, III, 500) ['suspended between the image and its description, between definition and approximation' (IMT, 61)].

It has been rightly noted by a number of scholars that Barthes's third or obtuse meaning anticipates the photographic *punctum* elucidated in *La Chambre claire* and, by extension, that the obvious or symbolic meaning is the predecessor of what Barthes will later call the *studium*.[37] In line with the general shift in Barthes's writings on photography from semiology to phenomenology, 'Le Troisième sens' indeed testifies to the emergence of the individual viewing subject whose feelings and perceptions are described from the standpoint of the writing or theorizing 'I'. The 'third meaning' applies not to the intended and, in a given cultural context, transparent message of the image – in the case of the Potemkin stills, the representation of shock or mourning in the image that expresses the emotion to the viewer in mediated fashion through symbolization. Rather, it pertains to a meaning (that which Julia Kristeva calls '*signifiance*') that elicits a more associative affective response, inextricably linked to the specific experience of an individual beholder (see OC, III, 487–8). Indeed, as Berg has aptly suggested, the Barthesian third meaning does not reside in the image at all but in the highly variable and contingent relation between the image and the beholder,[38] similar to Benjamin's emphasis in at least one of his major definitions of aura.

Barthes thus defines the obtuse meaning in relation to affect: 'je crois que le sens obtus porte une certaine *émotion*; . . . c'est une émotion qui *désigne* simplement ce qu'on aime, ce qu'on veut défendre; c'est une émotion-valeur, une évaluation' (OC, III, 493) ['I believe that the obtuse meaning carries a certain *emotion*. . . . It is an emotion which simply *designates* what one loves, what one wants to defend: an emotion-value, an evaluation' (IMT, 59)]. This stress on an emotion with a particular value that is unique to the individual viewer with regard to the photographic image is indeed further developed in *La Chambre claire*, partly in the form of the *punctum*. One difference, however, is that Barthes conceives of this *sens obtus* as a fundamentally communicable aspect of the image, one that can be trans-subjectively agreed upon. He suggests the following:

---

37 See, for example, Marty, 'Présentation', in OC, III, 17. By contrast, Shawcross argues that 'Le Troisième sens' ends in closer alignment with Barthes's literary theories, especially *S/Z*, rather than his writings on photography (*Roland Barthes on Photography*, 21).

38 See Berg, *Die Ikone des Realen*, 216.

> Car si vous regardez ces images que je dis, vous verrez ce sens: nous pouvons nous entendre à son sujet, 'par-dessus l'épaule' ou 'sur le dos' du langage articulé: . . . grâce à ce qui, dans l'image, est purement image (et qui à vrai dire est très peu de chose), nous nous passons de la parole, sans cesser de nous entendre. (OC, III, 500)
>
> For if you look at the images I am discussing, you can see this meaning, we can agree on it 'over the shoulder' or 'on the back' of articulated language. . . . Thanks to what, in the image, is purely image (which is in fact very little), we do without language yet never cease to understand one another. (IMT, 61)

The return of the notion of the 'pure' image is here accompanied by the idea that the 'troisème sens' possesses a certain universal value insofar as it is potentially perceivable, at least in the discussed stills, by any viewer. In contrast to the concept of the *punctum*, there is also a sense in which the obtuse meaning is an objectification of Barthes's interpretative construct offered to the reader for, and implicitly requiring, his or her assent. Whereas the *punctum* of the photograph, as we shall see, designates a detail of the image with a subjective value beyond all rationalization and argument: it simply is.

It is perhaps ironic that the subjective and particularly photographic first-person dynamic between image and beholder, which calls for a more phenomenological description, and which is in part a function of the photograph's resistance to narrative, embryonically emerges in Barthes's writings in relation to film stills, created as part of a narrative sequence that was intended to convey a universal, ideological content (and with which Barthes has no directly personal connection). Unsurprisingly, it fully flowers when Barthes instead turns to photographs that do have a highly personal significance for him and that in themselves lack a narrative context – save a subjective one provided by the viewer. This conceptual and methodological shift is reflected in the form and presentation of the texts themselves: while the majority of the hitherto discussed texts were published without photographic illustrations (the texts on Brecht and Eisenstein are exceptions here), all of his later writings on photography are abundantly illustrated with images carefully chosen by Barthes.[39] This is again the direct

39 Derek Attridge has suggested that the reproductions in Barthes's later texts provide the reader with a potentially similar experience to the ones Barthes seeks to describe ('Roland Barthes's Obtuse, Sharp Meaning and the Responsibilities of Commentary', in Jean-Michel Rabaté (ed.), *Writing the Image after Roland Barthes* (Philadelphia: University of Pennsylvania Press, 1997), 77–89: 81). Cf. also Ann Jefferson's analysis of the distinct phases of Barthes's engagement with photography in relation to writing each of which

inverse of the progression noted in relation to Benjamin, where there is an opposite movement with regard to photography: from the more personal and local to the more collective and general. In Benjamin's case, this goes hand in hand with a gradual diminishment and then a complete loss of the rich text-image dynamics of the 'Kleine Geschichte der Photographie'.[40] *La Chambre claire*, while possessing such inter-medial interests, is, however, like Benjamin's essay, marked by the absence of the most significant image, one which so much of its arguments explicitly or implicitly turns on and which serves Barthes as an emotive and affective guide through what he calls the photographic labyrinth (see CC, 114).

The Return of the Referent

Although *La Chambre claire* is Barthes's major work on photography and has become one of his best-known texts, in an interview from 1977, he insisted on calling it 'un livre modeste' (OC, V, 934) ['a modest book' (GV, 357)] and stated that he lacked an expert's knowledge of photographic history and theory. Barthes was, however, clearly familiar with a number of canonical works in the field, including the writings of Freund and Newhall, Bourdieu and Sontag, as well as, of course, Benjamin's 'Kleine Geschichte der Photographie', published in French in the *Nouvel Observateur*. In the same conversation with Angelo Schwarz, Barthes notes the precarious nature of photographic theory as caught between two methodological poles corresponding to seeing the photograph as an artistic image (albeit a special kind) and a direct impression of the real. Barthes's distinction generally, if not precisely, maps onto the still dominant opposition in photographic theory (paralleling classical film theory) between aesthetic constructivism/formalism and ontological realism. In spite of the fact that Barthes's own contributions to the photographic discourse are more in keeping with the latter realist

---

is constructed 'as the Other to the other' ('Roland Barthes: Photography and the Other of Writing', *Journal of the Institute of Romance Studies*, 1 (1992), 293-307: 296).

40 Nancy Shawcross argues that the 'filter' of culture leads Barthes (and also Benjamin) to condemn certain photographs while celebrating others 'without culture' ('The Filter of Culture and the Culture of Death. How Barthes and Boltanski Play the Mythologies of the Photograph', in Jean-Michel Rabaté (ed.), *Writing the Image after Roland Barthes* (Philadelphia: University of Pennsylvania Press, 1997), 59-70: 60).

position, in important respects he rightly suggests that this ostensibly either/or choice is a false one, since

> la photo ne peut pas être transcription pure et simple de l'objet qui se donne comme naturel, ne serait-ce que parce qu'elle est plate et non en trois dimensions; et d'autre part, elle ne peut pas être un art, puisqu'elle copie mécaniquement. (OC, V, 933)
>
> a photo cannot be a pure and simple transcription of the object that presents itself as natural, if only because it is flat and not three-dimensional; and on the other hand, photography cannot be an art, because it copies mechanically. (GV, 355–6)

For Barthes, the challenge for any theory of photography is to escape both reductive determinations, associated with 'art' and 'reality', through what he calls, in the context of an aphoristic essay on the French photographer Daniel Boudinet, a 'recherche difficile' (OC, V, 317). If *La Chambre claire* is taken as the major statement of Barthes's mature theory of photography, we may ask how it extends, disavows or negotiates between the two poles of this fundamental duality, to what extent it represents such a 'difficult search' and what it discovers.[41]

In his then almost contemporary seminar delivered at the Collège de France between 1978 and 1979, *La Préparation du roman I*, Barthes introduces some of the ideas that he later develops more thoroughly in *La Chambre claire*. He suggests, for example, that the specificity of the photograph 'ne peut être la "structure" (perceptive) de l'Image' (PR, 114) ['can't be the (perceptive) "structure" of the Image' (PN, 71)], for it is not rooted in an objectively significant structure as in the case of painting or other traditional artworks. Lacking such an inherent aesthetic foundation, there is no a priori standard of artistic classification and judgement with respect to photography. Even if there were one, it would, almost by definition, fail to account for the specificity of photography, which must to some extent be rooted in the properties of the medium rather than its formal use or any artistic intentionality.[42] At the same

41 Elkins, in his recent book *What Photography Is*, which is explicitly written 'against' *La Chambre claire* (ix), while imitating the layout of the English translation, attempts to similarly move away from the dominant discourses surrounding photography, which view it relationally, that is, with respect to other media, art forms and socio-cultural issues, proposing instead that photography is 'essentially solitary' and incomparable (vii–viii).

42 Although in *La Chambre claire* Barthes discusses certain photographs that can be and are classified as art (those by Richard Avedon, André Kertész or Robert Mapplethorpe, for instance), their inclusion does not reflect any

time, Barthes's position is also at odds with Bourdieu's sociology of photography almost solely tied to the photographer's intentions (albeit not aesthetic).[43] On this latter point, the theoretical thrust of this position is comparable to Barthes's infamous manifesto 'La Mort de l'auteur' ['The Death of the Author'] from 1968, in which he rejects the idea that the meaning and uniqueness of any literary text are rooted in its author's intentions, posing that meaning is not given and fixed but continually produced and reproduced by the text and its reader. On Barthes's view of the photograph as a camera-produced record of a perceptual reality, however, there is no author, in the strong sense, to 'kill off'.

The first problem that Barthes addresses in his pursuit of photography's 'essence'[44] in *La Chambre claire* is the fact that photography cannot be classified: 'la Photographie est inclassable' (CC, 15). Echoing his earlier semiotic work, he maintains that the 'unclassifiable' nature of photography is a result of the fact that the image is only denoted rather than connoted, because the relationship between a photograph and its referent is what Barthes calls an 'analogon' rather than a transformation. In contrast to painting, where the referent is necessarily mediated through, and determined by, the painter's individual choice of lines, shapes, colours and juxtapositions, that is, through style, governed by cultural and ideological conventions and traditions, Barthes insists that the photograph's referent remains unmediated and untouched in this sense. As Sontag has similarly argued, the photograph is as contingent and under-determined, in a sense, as reality itself.[45]

---

general aesthetic criterion or reputation but their personal meaning for Barthes.

43 See Bourdieu (ed.), *Un Art moyen*, 108.

44 *La Chambre claire* can be characterized as a double search for 'essence': on the one hand, it is a search for the phenomenological essence of photography (predominantly in the first part of the book), and, on the other, it is a search for the essence of the mother's identity (mainly in its second part). Even if phenomenology rejects the idea of 'essence' in an ontological sense, Barthes here relates it to the defining features of an experience. On the issue of essence and phenomenology, see Maurice Merleau-Ponty, 'What Is Phenomenology?', in *The Essential Writings of Merleau-Ponty*, ed. Alden L. Fisher (New York: Harcourt, Brace and World, 1969), 27–43: 27.

45 See Sontag, *On Photography*, 77-80. Neither in Barthes's nor in Sontag's view does the acceptance of this axiom entail the naïve assumption that the presentation of the referent in photography is not mediated by the camera or choices on the part of the photographer; however, this mediation is of a different kind and order than in painting or drawing, to the extent that in the case of the latter two the referent itself is always separable from this constructed presentation.

Whereas painting is always an addition to reality, the photograph, for Barthes, again like Sontag, is *experienced* as a piece torn from reality. In a short text on the phenomenology of the photographic image, Damisch has called this photography's 'ontological deception'.[46] Photography's ontology, its origins in a physical contact with reality, determines the perception of the image as a direct adjunct to it. But, for Damisch, this ontological deceit is complemented by a 'historical deceit' rooted in the mechanical process of the camera, which makes us forget the highly constructed nature of the images it produces (most significantly in relation to its in-built perspective, which is, in fact, a culturally determined optical-spatial construct, rather than a perceptual given).[47] Barthes's strong realism, pertaining to the psychological reality-effect of the photograph, has attracted criticism from subsequent photography theorists, as a result of both the profound anti-realist nature of cultural and media studies at the time of the publication of *La Chambre claire* in 1980 and the fact that many more contemporary theorists understandably view its arguments through the lens of digital image-making or manipulation.[48] From such a retrospective standpoint, photographic indexicality, and the faith in the truth of the reality of what is pictured, is undoubtedly problematized. However, this perspective can also distort Barthes's argument and a number of relevant theoretical issues. That said, if in both content and the terms of their expression some of Barthes's claims about the transparency of the photograph to reality seem overstated to the point of deliberate provocation in the context of media and cultural studies, as well as his past affiliation with semiotics, this must be seen as part and parcel of both his self-consciously naïve and, as Barthes himself suggests, 'archaic'

---

46 Hubert Damisch, 'Five Notes for a Phenomenology of the Photographic Image', in Alan Trachtenberg (ed.), *Classic Essays on Photography* (New Haven: Leete's Island Books, 1980), 287–90: 289.

47 Damisch regards these characteristics of photography as rendering it a problematic object for successful phenomenological description and, he later implies, for Barthes's position (ibid., 288–9). In an article published two years after Barthes's death, Damisch wonders if Barthes had ever read his notes on the phenomenology of the photographic image ('L'Intraitable', *Critique*, 38 (1982), 681–7: 683).

48 See, for example, Joel Snyder, 'Picturing Vision', *Critical Inquiry*, 6 (1980), 499–526. At a time when photography theory was by and large moving away from notions such as 'trace' and 'impression', associated with realist positions, Barthes's approach was regarded as outdated by some critics. Schaeffer, on the other hand, maintains that the incontrovertible fact that the photograph is an image based on the imprinting of photons is the 'arché' or fundamental condition of photography (*L'Image précaire*, 27).

methodologies of his book (see CC, 147). This methodology amounts to his particular version of a 'phenomenological reduction' whereby some intellectual background knowledge and context concerning the object under investigation is bracketed in order for one's direct conscious experience of it to be seen in a new and potentially revealing light.[49] Mainly, however, his realist orientation strongly corresponds to his full discovery and acknowledgement of the nature of the inviolable presence and the significance of the uniqueness of the photographic referent.

At the outset of *La Chambre claire*, Barthes states that a decisive difference between the photograph as perceptual object and the object/person as represented in the image is the former's reproducibility and the latter's spatio-temporal uniqueness as a matter of a lived moment: 'ce que la Photographie reproduit à l'infini n'a eu lieu qu'une fois: elle répète mécaniquement ce qui ne pourra jamais plus se répéter existentiellement' (CC, 15) ['what the Photograph reproduces to infinity has occurred only once: the Photograph mechanically repeats what could never be repeated existentially' (CL, 4)]. Photographic representation produces a paradoxical image inasmuch as it is the reproduction of something irreproducible.[50] The image, for Barthes, does nothing more or less than deictically indicate that this is the captured scene or person: '*ça, c'est ça, c'est tel!*' (CC, 16) ['*that, there it is, that's it!*' (CL, 5)]. This uniqueness-within-the-reproducible that is the photograph is at the very heart of Barthes's attempt to conceptualize existential singularity, a '*Mathesis singularis* (et non plus *universalis*)' (CC, 21) ['a *mathesis singularis* (and no longer *universalis*)' (CL, 8)], within the context of a wider theory of photography.[51] The utopian character of this project harkens back to the quest for the purely denotative or 'innocent' photograph in 'Rhétorique de l'image'.[52] Although the uniqueness of the

---

49 See Merleau-Ponty, 'What Is Phenomenology?', 32. As Dudley Andrew has argued with respect to film theory, a phenomenological approach does not get us closer to an object's 'truth' but closer to our experience of it ('The Neglected Tradition of Phenomenology in Film Theory', in Bill Nichols (ed.), *Movies and Methods. An Anthology*, 2 vols. (Berkeley: University of California Press, 1985), vol. 2, 625–32: 632).

50 This aspect of photography has often been related to singularity as a synonym for uniqueness. See, for example, Jean Delord, *Roland Barthes et la photographie* (Paris: Créatis, 1981), 75 and Dubois, *L'Acte photographique*, 73.

51 For a similar interpretation, see Stiegler, *Theoriegeschichte der Photographie*, 353.

52 For a concise account of Barthes's wider concerns with utopia with respect to literature and writing, see Diana Knight, 'Roland Barthes in Harmony: The Writing of Utopia', *Paragraph*, 11 (1988), 127–42.

photographic referent is cast as a property of all photographs, only some images draw attention to it and only for some viewers. In these cases, with respect to portrait photographs, the experiential affect of the referent transcends the image's symbolic nature, a sign pointing to what is absent, to become a lived presence.

What is more, for Barthes, the photograph and its referent are not only analogues but nearly tautological. This near identity between the represented person or thing and its photographic image is understood as photography's raison d'être, which Barthes expresses in his famous claim that 'le référent adhère' (CC, 18) in the photographic image.[53] In the second part of *La Chambre claire*, this nature of the referent's 'adherence' in the image is more strongly associated with the essence of photography and what distinguishes it from all other systems of representation, in which the link between signifier and signified is contingent (if not always wholly arbitrary). The author declares, 'j'appelle "référent photographique", non pas la chose *facultativement* réelle à quoi renvoie une image ou un signe, mais la chose *nécessairement* réelle qui a été placée devant l'objectif, faute de quoi il n'y aurait pas de photographie' (CC, 120) ['I call "photographic referent" not the *optionally* real thing to which an image or sign refers but the *necessarily* real thing which has been placed before the lens, without which there would be no photograph' (CL, 76)]. However, not only is the event or object in front of the camera necessarily real but also necessarily past: thus, Barthes's well-known definition of the experiential essence of the photographic image as the '*ça-a-été*' (CC, 120) ['*that-has-been*' (CL, 77)], where the unique and contingent moment of reality (*ça*) rendered necessary by the image is conjoined with the past (*a été*).[54] This objective fact of photography becomes an existentially and psychologically felt one when the referent is an absent beloved person,

53 Barthes's formulation of this particular 'sticky' relation between referent and photographic image is often cited and attacked by later theories of photography. See, for instance, Kriebel, 'Theories of Photography', 21. Having revitalized the notion of indexicality in relation to painting, Rosalind Krauss points out that Joel Snyder and Michael Fried pour scorn upon Barthes's (and her own) supposed naivety with respect to their understanding of photographic representation. See her introductory note to the 'Art Seminar', in Elkins (ed.), *Photography Theory*, 125–7.

54 Even though this definition has attracted criticism, particularly from a more rigorously semiotic perspective (such as Van Lier's, for example, in *Philosophie de la photographie*, 156–7), the *ça-a-été* persists as a valid and much-used formulation in photographic theories addressing the relation between image and reality.

when, in Benjamin's words, a photograph takes its place in a 'cult of remembrance'.

Derrida's reading of *La Chambre claire* sheds further light on the photographic referent as both real and past, while adhering to the image. He points out that where the referent is gone, and hence absent, 'disparu dans l'unique fois passée de son événement' ['vanished into the unique past time of its event'], the 'référence à ce référent, disons le mouvement intentionnel de la référence . . . implique aussi irréductiblement l'avoir-été d'un unique et invariable référent' ['reference to this referent, call it the intentional movement of reference . . . , implies just as irreducibly the having-been of a unique and invariable referent'].[55] Following what is implicit in Barthes's analysis, Derrida not only rejects a simplistically realist understanding of the referent, which is instead understood as a 'reference to a referent' (and thus a symbolic mediation of a sort), but affirms that this type of referentiality is uniquely inscribed in the photograph, no matter how often it has been reproduced. Even if it is a defining characteristic of the medium, Barthes had previously already rejected the notion of reproducibility as the most significant fact about photography from an experiential standpoint in the *La Préparation du roman* seminar (see PR, 114). Photography's experiential essence is instead identified with the potential of a specific photograph to both embody and give rise to an experience of singularity, which may take on a particularly profound and existential cast in some special instances.

Studium and *Punctum*

In seeking photography's essence in *La Chambre claire*, Barthes rejects traditional, would-be objective and overtly general taxonomies related to photographic history, style or genre. He also, as has been noted, avoids direct intervention in the polarized debate between realism and formalism, which he regards as a dead end. Instead, he takes an unapologetically subjective and personal approach rooted in a passionate affirmation of a Nietzschean '"antique souveraineté du moi"' (CC, 21) ['"ego's ancient sovereignty"' (CL, 8)].[56] He does so in the most concrete way possible,

55 Derrida, 'Les Morts de Roland Barthes', 283; 'The Deaths of Roland Barthes', 53.

56 Barthes's use of Nietzsche as a reference point for his subjectivism is in line with his 'La Mort de l'auteur', where he alludes to Nietzsche in order to reject a particular, God-like author-figure (see OC, III, 44). For a detailed

with reference to his own body, the body, which, since Barthes's *Le Plaisir du texte* [*The Pleasure of the Text*] from 1973, represents the source of all knowledge, desire and pain.[57] Accordingly, when Barthes ponders as to what his body 'knows' of photography, it is clear that the subjectivity introduced here is not that of the purely intellectual Cartesian cogito, that aspect of the self which engages in abstract and disinterested philosophical inquiry, but rather an existential subjectivity rooted in affective and emotional certainties.[58] Hence, the primary distinctions he does propose in relation to photography are rooted in the concrete physical acts: 'faire, subir, regarder' (CC, 22) ['to do, to undergo, to look' (CL, 9)], describing the basic activities of photographer (or '*Operator*'), sitter (or '*Spectrum*') and viewer of the image (the '*Spectator*') (CC, 22), respectively. Barthes identifies the first act as uninteresting or irrelevant for his project, claiming that he knows nothing about picture-taking and signals his focus on the latter two activities. In characterizing the photographer as a mere *Operator*, he immediately distances his approach adopted in *La Chambre claire* from those that begin with the photographer's intentions or motivations. Moreover, although Barthes devotes one chapter to the *Spectrum*, in relation to photographic self-portraiture, he is undoubtedly most interested in the *Spectator*, in the actual viewing of photographic images. Not only does this correspond to his own experience as the author of the text, whose feelings and judgements are deliberately, and as a matter of principle, not separated from the text's more objective concepts and arguments, as scholarly tradition would dictate, but this perspective of the viewing subject also serves as the guiding criterion for Barthes's selection of the specific photographs reproduced in the text. For all these reasons, Barthes rightly associates his subjectivism with a kind of phenomenology, one he describes, perhaps in order to dissociate his project from the highly abstract and formal phenomenological analysis of Edmund Husserl and other philosophers, as a 'phénoménologie vague, désinvolte, cynique même' (CC, 40) ['vague, casual, even cynical phenomenology' (CL, 20)].[59]

---

comparison between Barthes and Nietzsche on the theme of subjectivity, see Daniela Langer, *Wie man wird was man schreibt. Sprache, Subjekt und Autobiographie bei Nietzsche und Barthes* (Munich: Fink, 2005).

57 In *Roland Barthes par Roland Barthes*, he highlights that 'corps' is his 'mot-mana' ['mana-word'] (OC, IV, 704). For a concise account of the role of the body in Barthes's œuvre, see Moriarty, *Roland Barthes*, 186–94.

58 Cf. Langer, *Wie man wird was man schreibt*, 308.

59 See Merleau-Ponty's account of the difference between his existential phenomenology and Husserl's more 'genetic' or 'constructive' one, 'What Is Phenomenology?', 27–8.

Given all of these larger considerations, it is not surprising that, as has been pointed out on many occasions, the categories of *studium* and *punctum*, introduced in the first half of *La Chambre claire*, describe the viewer's individual response to the photographic image. In fact, scholarly interpretations have oscillated between defining *studium* and *punctum* as objective properties of photographs that engender particular effects, and seeing them as purely responsive categories, expressing different attitudes towards images, on Barthes's part.[60] It is, however, important to defend this ambiguity in order to appreciate the to-ing and fro-ing from the photograph-in-general to the photograph-in-particular, and the viewer's (i.e. Barthes's) subjective response to it, as well as the implicit hierarchy of photographic images following from it, which is constitutive of *La Chambre claire* on a number of levels.

Barthes argues that the *studium* corresponds to culturally determined aspects of the image, including its theme, content and presentation. It thus resembles the connoted message of the photograph, as defined in his earlier semiotic works. But, here, in the case of the *studium*, there is a stronger emphasis on the individual viewer's interest in uncovering a more collective significance in a given image, which Barthes aligns with cultural tastes: 'C'est par le *studium* que je m'intéresse à beaucoup de photographies, soit que je les reçoive comme des témoignages politiques, soit que je les goûte comme de bons tableaux historiques' (CC, 48) ['It is by *studium* that I am interested in so many photographs, whether I receive them as political testimony or enjoy them as good historical scenes' (CL, 26)]. With hindsight, the *studium* can be said to have determined the types of photographs discussed in Barthes's earlier semiotic texts, as those that attracted his more distanced intellectual attention and curiosity. The photographs that now attract him, however, according to the personal narrative of *La Chambre claire*, are images in which the *studium* coexists with the emotional *punctum*.

This second term, the *punctum*, is characterized as an unsettling disturbance of the *studium* that cannot be 'tamed' by the cultural aspects of the photograph, to use a metaphor employed by both Benjamin and Barthes. It defies naming and classification and hence evades

60 Representing these two extreme positions (which occur in various degrees in other critical commentary), Patrizia Lombordo argues that *studium* and *punctum* are 'effects of photography' (*The Three Paradoxes of Roland Barthes* (Athens and London: University of Georgia Press, 1989), 114), whereas Brown calls them 'qualities of attention' (*Roland Barthes*, 278).

ideological, systematic or indeed semiotic interpretation. It cannot a priori be analysed, because it occurs involuntarily. Emphasizing the viewer's passivity in relation to the *punctum*, Barthes writes the following:

> Le second élément vient casser (ou scander) le *studium*. Cette fois, ce n'est pas moi qui vais le chercher (comme j'investis de ma conscience souveraine le champ du *studium*), c'est lui qui part de la scène, comme une flèche, et vient me percer. (CC, 48–9)
>
> The second element will break (or punctuate) the *studium*. This time it is not I who seek it out (as I invest the field of the *studium* with my sovereign consciousness), it is this element which rises from the scene, shoots out of it like an arrow, and pierces me. (CL, 26)

The *punctum* breaks through the *studium* – almost violently and certainly disruptively. Barthes speaks of it as 'blessure', 'piqûre' and 'marque faite par un instrument pointu' (CC, 49) ['wound', 'prick' and 'mark made by a pointed instrument' (CL, 26)]. These words echo his formulation of the traumatic effects of certain photographs in 'Le Message photographique', those images that suspend language and signification by virtue of their authenticating power.[61] Highlighting the intention-less aspect of the *punctum*, Barthes further defines it as follows: 'Le *punctum* d'une photo, c'est ce hasard qui, en elle, *me point* (mais aussi me meurtrit, me poigne)' (CC, 49) ['The *punctum* of a photograph is that accident in it which *pricks me* (but also bruises me, is poignant to me)' (CL, 27)]. In contrast to the *studium*, which is partly a result of the photographer's intentional creation of a culturally coded effect of the image, the *punctum* is the detail that is captured and preserved in the photograph by chance, as a result of the camera's relatively indiscriminate and objective recording function.[62] Its experiential subjectivity notwithstanding, the *punctum* is firmly rooted in the ontology of the photographic image, as being first and foremost an optical-mechanical recording. For this reason, Barthes's *punctum* is

61 For a critique of Barthes's connection between trauma and *punctum*, see Serge Tisseron, *Le Mystère de la chambre claire. Photographie et inconscient* (Paris: Champs arts, 1996), 158–66.

62 On the surface at least, this would seem to suggest an affinity between *punctum* and Benjamin's 'optical unconscious'. However, there are numerous differences, not least the fact that the optical unconscious pertains primarily to formalistic and highly stylized images, a kind of photography Barthes dismisses as uninteresting (see CC, 58). Cf. Berg's suggestion as to the affinity between *studium* and optical unconscious, in *Die Ikone des Realen*, 240–1.

not easily applicable, if applicable at all, to traditional artistic images, despite theorists' attempts to move in this direction.[63]

But if the *punctum* has this necessary mediumistic foundation in the particular ontology of the photographic image as a qualitative feature, it is certainly not reducible to it. For Barthes leaves us in no doubt as to the personal and subjective effect of the *punctum*, as an experiential phenomenon, which for him bestows the photograph with an added, superior value: 'une valeur supérieure' (CC, 71), as he makes clear. The *punctum* thus relates to the photograph's 'imaginary surplus',[64] one which is activated differently by every viewer. By necessity, given the highly evaluative fashion in which *studium* and *punctum* are defined from the outset, Barthes imposes a hierarchy on photographs, whereby what he refers to as *studium*-photographs are less valuable or interesting than *punctum*-ones. This is a fundamentally a posteriori classification, or, better put, description, since it is rooted in the actual experience of a given photograph. As Barthes suggests in an interview with Guy Mandery, the images reproduced in *La Chambre claire* are a direct illustration of this hierarchy in practice, as their choice was based on whether or not they 'touchent mon affect' (OC, V, 935) ['affect me' (GV, 358)].[65] Summarizing the apparently paradoxical and dual nature of the *punctum*, and putting his finger on where his realist ontology of photography meets his 'naïve' phenomenology – as well as why and how the two are inseparable in Barthes's mature theory of photography – Barthes affirms, following Derrida, that the *punctum* is 'un supplément:

63 Michael Fried has attempted to align the *punctum* with the aesthetic tradition of eighteenth-century French painting, which he sees in the context of his theories of 'antitheatricality' (*Why Photography Matters as Art as Never Before* (New York and London: Yale University Press, 2008), 102). In response to Fried, James Elkins has pointed out (rightly, I believe) that the *punctum* in Fried's reading becomes another instance of *studium* ('What do We Want Photography to Be? A Response to Michael Fried', in Geoffrey Batchen (ed.), *Photography Degree Zero. Reflections on Roland Barthes's Camera Lucida* (Cambridge, MA: MIT Press, 2009), 171–85: 171). For a more nuanced reflection on the paradoxes concerning Barthes's subjectivism and the question of art photography, see Philippe Ortel, '*La Chambre claire* ou le refus de l'art', *Les Cahiers de la photographie*, 'Roland Barthes et la photo: le pire des signes' (Paris: Contrejour, 1990), 32–9.

64 See Busch, *Belichtete Welt*, 214.

65 Batchen, by contrast, has suggested that *La Chambre claire* represents 'another little history of photography', given that Barthes's photographic illustrations cover almost every decade of photographic history from the 1820s to the 1970s ('*Camera Lucida*: Another Little History of Photography', 79).

c'est ce que j'ajoute à la photo et *qui cependant y est déjà*' (CC, 89) ['a supplement: it is what I add to the photograph and *what is nonetheless already there*' (CL, 55)].[66] The *punctum* thus describes a reciprocal relationship between a detail of a photograph – be it the large belt of a sitter in a family photograph by James van der Zee, the bad teeth of a young Italian-American boy recorded by William Klein or the dirty fingernails of Tristan Tzara in a portrait taken by André Kertész (see CC, 73–4) – and its perception and effect.[67] It describes something that happens between the photograph and its perceiver and that cannot be reduced to either party alone, or indeed to a simple phenomenon of cause and effect.

The dynamic of the *punctum*-detail described here then is structurally analogous to Benjamin's last conception of aura as a reciprocal dynamic between object and beholder, even if it is explicitly dissociated from photography in his 'Über einige Motive bei Baudelaire'. But there is also an even closer link between *punctum* and Benjamin's description of the auratic in photography, possibly rooted in Barthes's direct engagement with his predecessor's text. This pertains to Benjamin's reflections on the viewer's response to the self-portrait by Karl Dauthendey, described as a compulsion to look for the coincidental detail, which, as has often been remarked, is akin to Barthes's understanding of *punctum* as an accidental element of the image with a potentially profound effect.[68] Moreover, Benjamin's account of the peculiar spatio-temporal 'spot' or 'spark' with which an image as a whole is saturated is likewise similar to Barthes's *punctum*, but mainly on his second, differently oriented formulation of it, introduced in the second part of *La Chambre claire*, namely, the *ça-a-été* of photography that relates to time as encapsulated in the image.

66 Derrida, in his reading of *La Chambre claire*, draws on Barthes's *punctum* as 'supplément', giving rise to a certain mise-en-abyme with respect to this notion ('Les Morts de Roland Barthes', 272–4).

67 Taking such details as a starting point for his discussion of *La Chambre claire*, Antoine Compagnon suggests that it is 'un livre sur les mains' ['a book about hands'] ('L'Objectif déconcerté', *La Recherche photographique*, 'Roland Barthes, une aventure avec la photographie', 12 (1992), 73–7: 77).

68 In the scholarship on both Benjamin and Bathes, and in relation to photography, the conjunction between aura and *punctum* has become a commonplace and examples are too numerous to list here. In many cases, however, these comparisons fail to specify which of Barthes's two formulations, or definitions, of *punctum* is being compared to aura.

Time, Affect and Mortality

In the second part of *La Chambre claire*, the photograph's most significant form of experiential temporality is identified with the nature of the photographic referent, which transcends the medium's artistic or communicative function, and is the essence of the photograph as perceived by the beholder, or its 'noème' (CC, 120).[69] This is in keeping with the fact that the second half of the book is presented as Barthes's search for his late mother's identity or essence as captured in a photograph. And, consequently, the image's more general expression of *avoir-été-là*, underlining that something existed at another place and time, as forwarded in 'Rhétorique de l'image', changes into the more specific *ça-a-été*. The replacement of the infinitive with a demonstrative pronoun draws greater attention to the specificity of the referent. It is in light of photography's *ça-a-été* that the *punctum* is alternatively defined – in the mode of a typical Barthesian *glissement* – as relating first and foremost to time: 'Ce nouveau *punctum*, qui n'est plus de forme, mais d'intensité, c'est le Temps, c'est l'emphase déchirante du noème ("*ça-a-été*"), sa représentation pure' (CC, 148) ['This new *punctum*, which is no longer of form but of intensity, is Time, the lacerating emphasis of the *noema* ("*that-has-been*"), its pure representation' (CL, 96)].[70]

This new emphasis on the temporal aspect of the *punctum* brings to the fore the relation between photography, mortality and mourning that is not only a recurring theme in photographic theory, in general, but of paramount importance in Barthes's discourse on the medium. In *La Chambre claire*, the poignant link between the portrait photograph and death is first established in relation to an image of Lewis Payne, one of the conspirators in the assassination of Abraham Lincoln. Payne was photographed by Alexander Gardner in what looks like his prison cell in 1865, just days before his execution.

69 As the *Oxford English Dictionary* indicates, 'noema' was first used by Husserl to describe the object of a thought or perception. Barthes's use of it is rather vague and implies an abstracted characteristic of photography. The genesis of photography's *noema* in Barthes's work goes back to his seminar, *La Préparation du roman*, in which he formulates the more tentative hypothesis that the 'cela a été' or the 'ça a été' is the 'noème' of photography (PR, 114-15).

70 For a detailed analysis of the Proustian references here, see my 'Barthes et Proust: La *Recherche* comme aventure photographique', *Fabula LHT* (*Littérature, histoire, théorie*), 4 (2008), paragraphs 22–3.

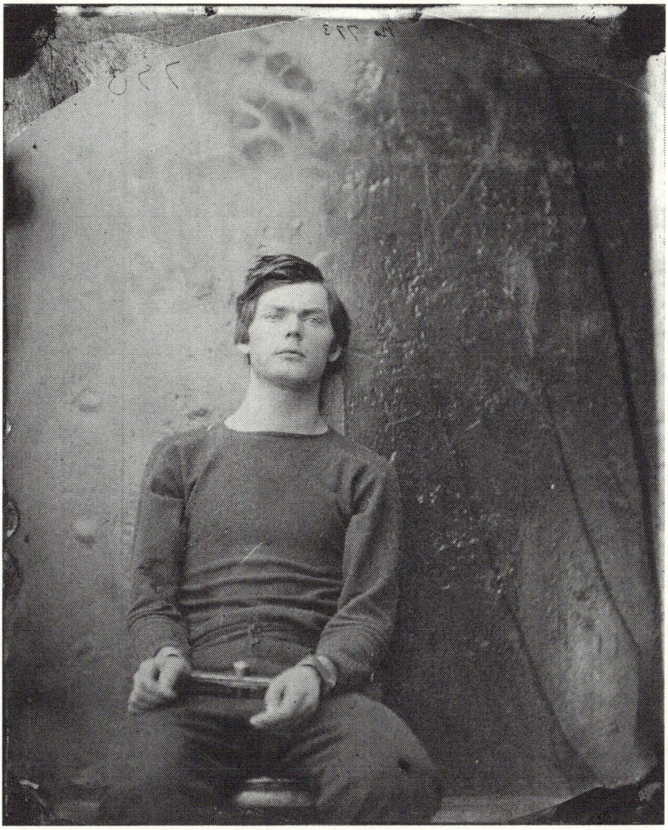

PLATE 10 Alexander Gardner, Lewis Payne, 1865.

This portrait, which is part of a larger series of photographs of Payne and other conspirators, fascinated commentators on photography before Barthes, and indeed before the editors of the *Nouvel Observateur* included it in the second special number on photography (see Plate 2). Iwan Goll had described another Payne portrait by Gardner in the context of his wider discussion of nineteenth-century portraiture in Recht's *Die Alte Photographie*, which Benjamin used as a source for his 'Kleine Geschichte der Photographie'.[71]

Barthes's fascination with the portrait is, by contrast, more personal. What he perceives to be both the photograph's and the sitter's physical beauty is characterized as a *studium* (see CC, 148–50), one quickly eclipsed by the felt intensity of the portrait's paradoxical temporality. This

71 See Goll's preface, in Recht, *Die Alte Photographie*, xv.

is related to Payne's impending death, which the photograph represents as simultaneously already past (from the point of view of the beholder) and in the future (from the point of view of the subject and photographer), hence Barthes's caption: '*Il est mort et il va mourir*' (CC, 149) ['*He is dead and he is going to die*' (CL, 95)]. Barthes learned of Payne's fate after the photograph was taken from the text that accompanied the publication of this image in the special photography issue of the *Nouvel Observateur*. This extra-image knowledge, which the photograph in itself does not and cannot provide, subsequently becomes a major part of Barthes's experience of the image and his emotive response to it; just as the knowledge of the tragic death of Dauthendey's first wife (which Benjamin learned from the photographer's biography) inescapably coloured Benjamin's experience and description of Dauthendey's self-portrait with his future, second wife.[72] Unlike Benjamin, however, Barthes acknowledges that, apart from these dramatic instances in which a documented tragic narrative surrounds the image, every portrait photograph speaks (of) the death of every sitter. Now especially attuned to this fact by the loss of his mother, Barthes writes that he simultaneously perceives: '*cela sera et cela a été*; j'observe avec horreur un futur antérieur dont la mort est l'enjeu. . . . Que le sujet en soit déjà mort ou non, toute photographie est cette catastrophe' (CC, 150) ['*this will be and this has been*; I observe with horror an anterior future of which death is the stake. . . . Whether or not the subject is already dead, every photograph is this catastrophe' (CL, 96)]. As Benjamin's and Barthes's writing on particular portraits demonstrates, this past presence of future death, constituting the catastrophic or traumatic dimension of the photographic portrait, may of course be felt and experienced with more or less intensity depending on the particular nature of the real or imagined relationship between the sitter and the beholder, and range from intellectual fascination and poignancy to a profound grief and sadness.[73]

Against this background, the pressing problem that both Benjamin and Barthes face in their theories of photography is foregrounded, namely, the necessarily unresolved discord or friction between a critical enquiry into the nature of the photographic medium and the question as to what particular photographs mean to each writer and viewer and why. In one

72 Mary Price has similarly stressed the narrative quality of Benjamin's description of the Dauthendey double portrait and compares Benjamin's narrative investment with Barthes's account of the Payne photograph (*The Photograph. A Strange Confined Space* (Stanford: Stanford University Press, 1994), 93-6).

73 De Duve makes a similar, more general point in 'Time Exposure and Snapshot', 120–1.

respect, this amounts to the tension between the photograph-in-general and the particularity of the individual image, which corresponds to the universalist and nominalist poles of their respective discourses. While Barthes, in *La Chambre claire*, self-reflexively addresses this tension by juxtaposing *studium*-photographs with *punctum*-photographs, Benjamin's 'Kleine Geschichte der Photographie' projects the problem into a historical dimension, through the attribution of aura to some nineteenth-century photographs, which ensures their experiential uniqueness, and its dissociation from the vast majority of twentieth-century images, which are viewed through the prism of technological and cultural evolutions that work against such specificity. In Barthes's case, not only the presence of this tension but also its necessity, as getting to the very heart of photography, has often been neglected by those who object to the perceived naïve realism, personal sentimentalism or existential absolutism of *La Chambre claire*.[74] On the other hand, it has been widely acknowledged that both Barthes's *punctum* and Benjamin's aura are like conceptual placeholders for deeply personal experiences that possess a unique poignancy in relation to specific portrait photographs.[75]

Whether or not these similarities between aura and *punctum* can be traced to Barthes's first-hand reading of Benjamin's French version of the 'Kleine Geschichte der Photographie', it has certainly influenced subsequent interpretations of Benjamin's concept. When reading the two authors together, this may lead to the impression that 'the tyranny of time [is] almost overturned' and that Barthes is here '*imitated by his ancestor*', to borrow from Harold Bloom's phraseology,[76] which is particularly appropriate with respect to the temporal paradoxes of the photograph. Be this as it may, with respect to the theme of singularity, it is essential to acknowledge that neither Benjamin nor Barthes directly applies aura or *punctum*, respectively, to the privileged winter-garden photographs of

74 See for instance Van Lier, *Philosophie de la photographie*, 110 and John Tagg, *The Burden of Representation. Essays on Photographies and Histories* (Basingstoke and London: Macmillan Education, 1988), 3–4.

75 Rather than suggesting one should better not speak of aura, as has been done by Josef Fürnkäs ('Aura' in Opitz and Wizisla (eds.), *Benjamins Begriffe*, vol. 1, 143), or proposing that it is a definition of the indefinable, as Stoessel does (*Aura. Das vergessene Menschliche*, 43–6), I agree with Elkins, who argues that both aura and *punctum* introduce 'something ineffable, private, or even sublime – something that couldn't otherwise be put into a book or essay' and hence function as indicators, or placeholders, for those subjectively perceived phenomena (*Photography Theory*, 159).

76 Bloom, *The Anxiety of Influence*, 141.

Kafka as a child and Barthes's mother as a child. These two portraits represent the most personal and existential pole of each author's engagement with photography. And even if their narratively mediated experiences conform to Benjamin's and Barthes's various definitions of aura and *punctum* in certain respects (as many scholars have stressed in various ways), the felt meaning of these images exceeds these conceptual categories. As the ne plus ultra manifestation of the particular versus the general, the experience of these images cannot be confined to, and/or captured within, any detached and objective scholarly analysis. Their significance emerges, instead, only where theory and criticism, and the categories and distinctions it entails, partly give way to autobiographical narrative.

Chapter 5

Lost and Found: The Winter Garden Photograph

La Chambre claire has often been read as Barthes's attempt to come to terms with the death of his mother on 25 October 1977 – with whom he was particularly close until the end of her life – and to pay tribute to her memory.[1] The recent publication of Barthes's *Journal de deuil* [*Mourning Diary*], which covers a period of mourning from his mother's death up until September 1979, provides a new impetus for biographical interpretations. Bringing together 330 poignant notes, this diary is like a blueprint for the autobiographical aspects of *La Chambre claire*, underlining the notion that Barthes's exploration of photography is inextricably intertwined with the death of his mother and the desire to create a 'monument' for her (JD, 245).[2] These autobiographical considerations aside, Barthes's reflections on photography in relation to death and mourning are certainly in line with major themes in photographic theory.[3] In the wake of more general romantic notions of the melancholy of transience prompted by time-worn objects, such as the fragmentary ruin of a church, castle or sculpture, the emergence of photography in the 1820s and 1830s coincided with a heightened desire to hold on to a physical token of past time, especially as related to the absence of a family member or friend. This commemorative function is no doubt partly responsible for the popularity of portraiture in the mid-nineteenth century and is also reflected in the then widespread practice of photographing the dead.[4]

1 See, for example, Marty, 'Présentation', in OC, V, 17.

2 In 'L'Œuvre et l'espace de la mort', which Barthes would certainly have been aware of, Blanchot discusses the relation between writing and death in similar terms (*L'Espace littéraire*, 103–209). Gunthert has suggested that the death of Barthes's mother served as a starting point for the writing of *La Chambre claire* ('Le Complexe de Gradiva', 122). Cf. also on this issue of origin Jean-Louis Calvet, *Roland Barthes. 1915–1980* (Paris: Flammarion, 1990), 281–2. For a more general analysis of photography's relation to loss with respect to Barthes, see Jay Prosser, *Light in the Dark Room. Photography and Loss* (Minneapolis: University of Minnesota Press, 2005), 19–52.

3 For an anthropologically oriented account of the relation between photography and death, see Belting, *Bild-Anthropologie*, 143–88. Also the Latin *imago* was used to refer to death masks, thereby establishing an etymological link between image and death.

4 For a more in-depth socio-historical discussion of these issues in relation to new social orders in industrialized society, see Hamilton and Hargreaves, *The Beautiful and the Damned*, 10–14.

Death and mourning are linked to the photograph not only on a functional level – that is to say, with respect to the image's use as a token of the absent one, or indeed as a *memento mori* for the beholder's own death[5] – but also owing to the photograph's immanent temporal nature. As we have seen, Benjamin, together with Kracauer, was among the first theorists to more systematically articulate the complex spatio-temporal structure of the photographic image of a person as a past present. For Kracauer, in relation to Victorian photographs, this is associated with a historical alienation between the depicted person and the viewer, one which, he argues, works against a genuine emotional identification between the two owing to the photograph's function as an objective, historical document, which trumps all other affective and subjective engagements.[6] For Benjamin, on the other hand, this temporality always primarily relates to mortality and melancholy, as evidenced in his contemplation of both the portrait of the Newhaven fishwife and, especially, Dauthendey's self-portrait with his future wife. Although it is not explicitly related to death, Benjamin's emphasis on the sad eyes of Kafka's childhood portrait similarly exemplifies a specific melancholy associated with the passage of time, as prompted by the photographic portrait. The contrastive juxtaposition of Kracauer's and Benjamin's arguments, here, rooted in their very different understanding of photographic portraiture, highlights that although photography may be the 'only image-producing technique that has a mourning process built into its semiotic structure', as de Duve has asserted,[7] not every photographic portrait affects every viewer with the same intensity in this respect. In Barthes's case, this can be seen with reference to portraits that illustrate his 1970 book *L'Empire des signes* [*Empire of Signs*], a reflection on Japanese life, society and art, based on his personal experience with this culture. He acknowledges the general affective relation between photography and death in commenting on the images of General Nogi and his wife, who, having already decided to commit suicide after the death of their emperor, pose in front of a camera for a last time.[8] In *La Chambre claire*, however, in the wake of

5 See Sontag, *On Photography*, 15.

6 See Kracauer, *Das Ornament der Masse*, 30–2.

7 De Duve, 'Time Exposure and Snapshot', 120. In this essay, de Duve considers photographic portraiture as principally funerary, placing him in the general tradition referred to here.

8 Similar to his captioning of the Payne portrait in *La Chambre claire*, Barthes here subtitles the photographs: '*Ils vont mourir, ils le savent et cela ne se voit pas*' (OC, III, 422–33) ['*They are going to die, they know it, and it does not show*' (ES, 92–3)]. Shawcross rightly regards the view of photography

his mother's death and the concrete loss of a singular being for him – the kind of loss which is 'chaque fois unique' ['each time unique'] to quote the title of Derrida's collection of commemorative essays[9] – this relation is not only expressed in highly personal terms but seen as the root of the portrait image's affective power as a singular encounter with the photographic other.

Reproduction, Description and Superimposition

If the first half of *La Chambre claire* is predominantly a search for the phenomenological essence of photography, its second is primarily a Proustian search for the essence of the mother's identity. Reflecting this double-sidedness, Barthes in his *Journal de deuil* simply calls what was to become *La Chambre claire* the 'livre *Photo-Mam.*' (JD, 148) ['*Photo-Maman* book' (MD, 136)].[10] As we have seen, the first part of the book deals with phenomenological classifications, notably *studium* and *punctum*, based on the viewer's response to certain photographs. Coinciding with the articulation of a different sense of the *punctum*, which transforms into the more temporally oriented concept of the *ça-a-été*, presented as the essence of photography, in the second part, the general *studium-punctum* dichotomy fades into the background. In terms of the narrative progression of *La Chambre claire*, the catalyst for this change is Barthes's discovery of the childhood portrait of the mother at the age of five, taken in a winter-garden setting. It is in relation to this specific portrait that the singularity of photography – beyond that which the *studium-punctum* distinction can accommodate – comes to the fore. The childhood portrait of the mother conveys singularity as rooted in the self-acknowledged unique and privileged relationship between the beholder, the depicted person and the photograph. As will become clear, after we have first established how the loss of the mother concretely impacts on Barthes's conceptualization of the photographic

this implies as a turning point in Barthes's writings (*Roland Barthes on Photography*, 16–18).

9 See Jacques Derrida, *Chaque fois unique, la fin du monde*, eds. Pascale-Anne Brault and Michael Naas (Paris: Galilée, 2003).

10 Elissa Marder has suggested that Barthes's book, like Baudelaire's sonnet 'À une passante' ['To a Passerby'], represents an 'impossible address to a female figure who has . . . "passed away"', which she interestingly links with Benjamin's interpretation of the poem in his essay on Baudelaire ('Flat Death: Snapshots of History', *Diacritics*, 22 (1992), 128–44: 128).

referent, this singularity is expressed through writing that moves towards an existentially and ethically motivated redemption of the other.

In the second part of *La Chambre claire*, Barthes recounts how, in the midst of mourning her, he attempts to find a photograph of his mother which truly captures a sense of her identity for him, a search that in both the book and his diary he characterizes as a Sisyphean task (see CC, 104; JD, 151). After what is described as a painful and disappointing hunt, he does find an image, which conjures her essence in a unique way. The fact that the photograph in question is not reproduced in *La Chambre claire* has given rise to much speculation as to whether it really exists. The predominant views among Anglo-American Barthes scholars are that the Winter Garden photograph of the mother is likely a fiction and/or that it simply does not matter whether it exists.[11] In a French-speaking context, in contrast, the prevalent assumption is that the photograph did or does exist, and – rightly, I would argue – that it is the photograph's actual existence that gives genuine meaning to its absence from the text.[12] Since the publication of the *Journal de deuil*, in 2009, together with previously available photographs of Barthes sitting in his study, which clearly show a photograph like the one he describes, it can be said fairly conclusively that not only did the Winter Garden portrait exist, but that it was also likely found in the accidental manner suggested in *La Chambre claire*. In June 1978, approximately one year before he began writing his book on photography, Barthes mentions coming across the portrait in his diary: 'ce matin, à grand peine, reprenant les photos, bouleversé par une où mam. petite fille, douce, discrète à côté de Philippe Binger (Jardin d'hiver de Chennevières, 1898)' (JD, 155) ['this morning, painfully returning to the photographs, overwhelmed by one in which *maman*, a gentle, discreet little girl beside Philippe Binger (the Winter garden of Chennevières, 1898)' (MD, 143)]. The diary further documents that some months later he had this portrait enlarged, although it was then still too painful for him to place it on his desk as he would later do (see JD, 231).

In the context of my research with respect to the Winter Garden photograph, Éric Marty, a former student and friend of Barthes, and one of the foremost specialists on his life and work, pointed me towards Daniel Faunières's portrait of Barthes in his study.

---

11 See, representatively, Diana Knight, *Barthes and Utopia. Space, Travel, Writing* (Oxford: Clarendon Press, 1997), 265–6 and Olin, 'Touching Photographs', 108; 112.

12 See, for example, Chantal Thomas, 'La Photo du jardin d'hiver', *Critique*, 38 (1982), 797–804.

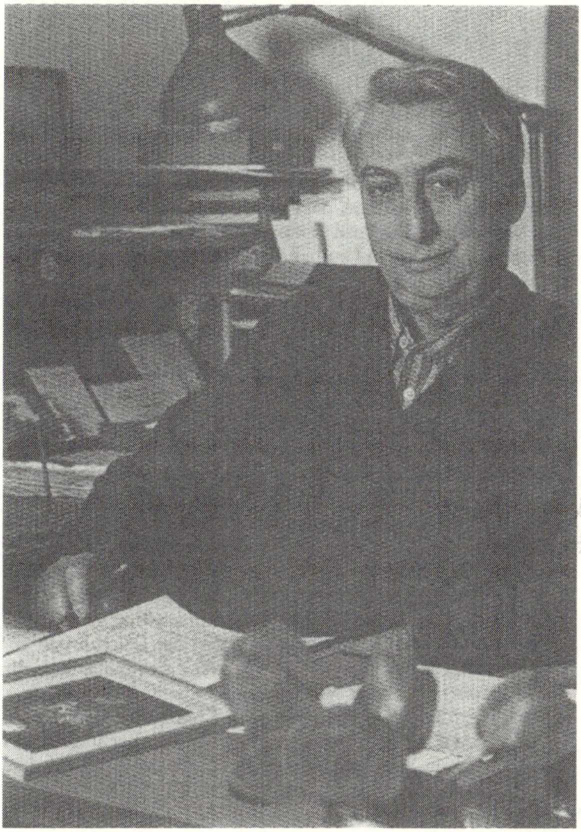

PLATE 11 Daniel Faunières, Roland Barthes at his desk in Paris, 1979 (original in colour).

Taken in early 1979, this photograph appeared on the cover of the 1981 edition of *Le Grain de la voix* [*The Grain of the Voice*], a collection of interviews with Barthes. It is reasonable to assume that the framed photograph lying on the desk is the portrait of the mother as a child, as it is a black and white image that appears to depict a winter-garden setting. Indeed, this portrait of Barthes is a kind of re-enactment of his writing of *La Chambre claire*: pen in hand and the manuscript of the text, together with the photograph of his mother in front of him, it can be seen as at least figuratively representing the moment of the book's genesis.[13] A slightly

13 There is an entire series of portraits of Barthes at his desk at various stages of his career. He includes four in his photographic preface to *Roland Barthes par Roland Barthes* (see OC, IV, 617–19). See Ette's more detailed interpretation of them as a self-reflexive expression of Barthes as a writer, *Roland Barthes*,

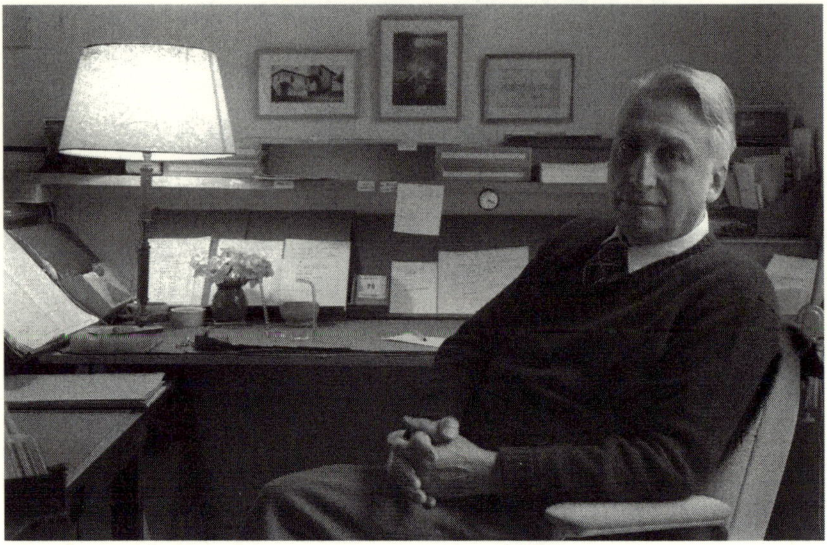

Plate 12 François Lagarde, Roland Barthes at his desk in Paris, 25 April 1979.

later portrait of Barthes, taken in April 1979, the same month when the process of writing *La Chambre claire* began, confirms that although Barthes was reluctant to reproduce the Winter Garden photograph in his book, he did not object to having his picture taken with it.

The portrait can be seen on the wall behind Barthes's desk between two other photographs.[14] His detailed ekphrasis of the Winter Garden photograph, which replaces its actual reproduction in *La Chambre claire*, matches what is discernable in both portraits by Faunières and Lagarde. Barthes describes the portrait of the two children, his mother standing next to her brother, and imagines the photographer's interaction with her, recalling Benjamin's imaginative speculations as to the inter-personal dynamics between his childhood self and the photographer while his portrait was being taken in the *Berliner Kindheit um Neunzehnhundert*.

> La photographie était très ancienne. Cartonnée, les coins mâchés, d'un sépia pâli, elle montrait à peine deux jeunes enfants debout, formant groupe, au bout d'un petit pont de bois dans un Jardin d'Hiver au plafond vitré. Ma

---

392–6. Interestingly, Ette even comments on the Faunières portrait, which is reproduced in his book (fig. 10), without, however, linking it to the missing photograph in the text that Barthes was writing at the time (ibid., 400–2).

14 The portrait by Lagarde has recently been included in the English translation of *Journal de deuil*, where the photograph on the wall is identified as the Winter Garden portrait of the mother (see MD, fig. 9).

> mère avait alors cinq ans (1898), son frère en avait sept. Lui appuyait son dos à la balustrade du pont, sur laquelle il avait étendu son bras; elle plus loin, plus petite, se tenait de face; on sentait que le photographe lui avait dit: 'Avance un peu, qu'on te voie'; elle avait joint ses mains, l'une tenant l'autre par un doigt, comme font souvent les enfants, d'un geste maladroit. Le frère et la sœur, unis entre eux, je le savais, par la désunion des parents, qui devaient divorcer peu de temps après, avaient posé côte à côte, seuls, dans la trouée des feuillages et des palmes de la serre (c'était la maison où ma mère était née, à Chennevières-sur-Marne). (CC, 106)
>
> The photograph was very old. Paper-backed, the corners blunted, the sepia print had faded and barely showed two young children standing together at the end of a little wooden bridge in a glass-roofed Winter Garden. My mother was five at the time (1898), her brother seven. He was leaning against the bridge railing, along which he had extended one arm; she, shorter than he, was standing a little back, facing the camera; one could tell that the photographer had said to her: 'Step forward a little so one can see you'; she was holding one finger in the other hand, as children often do, in an awkward gesture. The brother and sister, united, as I knew, by the discord of their parents, who were soon to divorce, had posed side by side, alone, under the arched leaves and palms (it was the house where my mother was born, in Chennevières-sur-Marne). (CL, 67–9)

This description of the real yet absent photograph, as meticulous as Benjamin's account of the Kafka-as-child portrait in the 'Kleine Geschichte der Photographie' and the *Berliner Kindheit*, similarly fuses the actual image with the beholder's imaginary projections. In this case, Barthes experiences and describes the image by way of his mother's life story, creating a mise-en-abyme of parent-child relations over two generations. The similarities do not end here, because, as is also the case with respect to Benjamin's ekphrastic account of his childhood portrait, the visual absence of this central image in *La Chambre claire* has led to the suggestion that it is, in fact, an imaginary composite of a number of images. Diana Knight has pointed out that the description of the Winter Garden photograph partly matches a different childhood portrait of the mother, titled by Barthes *La Souche* [*The Stock*],[15]

15 See Knight, *Barthes and Utopia*, 265–6. There is also another *carte-de-visite* photograph of the two children with their mother, which confirms that it is indeed Barthes's mother, her brother and their grandfather pictured in *La Souche*. See Marianne Alphant and Nathalie Léger (eds.), *R/B Roland Barthes* (exhibition catalogue) (Paris: Seuil/Centre Pompidou/IMEC, 2002), 230, fig. 5. The presence of this image answers Liliane Weissberg's speculation as to the relationship between Barthes and the girl in the *La Souche* photograph ('Bilderwechsel: Barthes, Benjamin, Freud und der Exkurs der Photographie', in Ortrud Gutjahr (ed.), *Kulturtheorie* (Würzburg: Königshausen & Neumann, 2005), 217–40: 225).

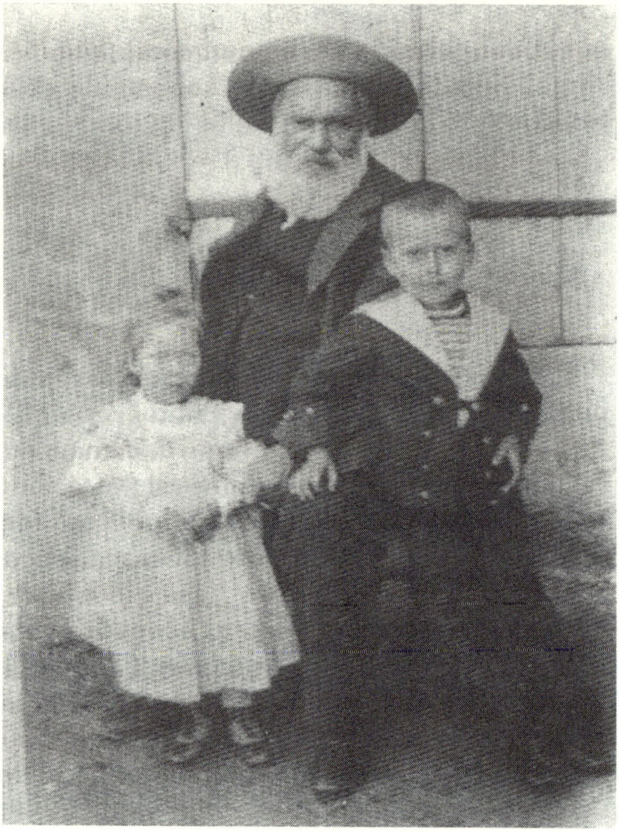

PLATE 13 *La Souche*: Philippe and Henriette Binger with their grandfather, 1895/96.

which is the only image of his family Barthes reproduces in *La Chambre claire*.

This 'avatar' of the absent Winter Garden image, as Marty calls it,[16] depicts Henriette and Philippe Binger with their grandfather against a bare wall. It is indeed noteworthy that aspects of Barthes's description of the Winter Garden portrait also match this particular image, including the position of sister and brother and the childlike gesture the girl makes with her hands. This seems evidence enough for a possible superimposition of the two images, one reproduced and one only described, analogous to Benjamin's merging of the Kafka-as-child portrait with (at least) one

16 Éric Marty, *Roland Barthes, la littérature et le droit à la mort* (Paris: Seuil, 2010), 44.

portrait of himself as a child in the *Berliner Kindheit* (with the difference that in Benjamin's texts neither is reproduced).

Going further, it is even tempting to see Benjamin's description of these images in his slightly earlier essay on photography as directly contributing to this associative collage in *La Chambre claire*. Margaret Olin has speculated that Barthes may have associated the large hat worn by the grandfather in the *La Souche* portrait with Benjamin's description of the Kafka-as-child photograph in the 'Kleine Geschichte der Photographie', which mentions Kafka's large hat, thereby reminding Barthes of this family image when he read Benjamin's text in preparation of *La Chambre claire* in the *Nouvel Observateur*.[17] However, it is documented that other childhood portraits taken around 1900 reminded Barthes of portraits of his mother.[18] One at least apparently unambiguous similarity between the childhood portrait of Kafka and the mother as a child is their winter-garden setting.[19] Yet as is typical within the ekphrastic labyrinth of Benjamin's and Barthes's texts, although Benjamin refers to the Kafka portrait as a 'kind of winter-garden landscape' (see GS, II, 375), the actual image is rather non-committal on this point, as only the foliage behind Kafka indicates this setting (see Plate 9).[20] By contrast, the wider angle of the portrait of Barthes's mother – in reality and as described – pictures a full winter-garden landscape setting. Although Barthes draws attention to the palm trees in the background of the sitters, just as Benjamin does, whether this similarity is an intentional signpost to Benjamin on Barthes's part, or,

17 See Olin, 'Touching Photographs', 108–9.

18 In his last seminar, 'Proust et la photographie', Barthes comments that he is particularly moved by two portraits of children taken by Paul Nadar, by virtue of their evocation of his mother's childhood (see PR, 444; 447).

19 This link has attracted many scholars' attention. See, for example, Patrizia Lombardo, 'Le Leurre d'une recherche', *La Recherche photographique*, 'Roland Barthes, une aventure avec la photographie', 12 (1992), 53–7: 55–6. An essay collection on photography and literature which takes its starting point from Benjamin and Barthes is aptly titled 'Winter Gardens', see Marie-D. Garnier (ed.), *Jardins d'hiver. Littérature et photographie* (Paris: Presses de l'École Normale Supérieure, 1997).

20 Olin has rightly commented that the French translation of the 'Kleine Geschichte der Photographie' in the *Nouvel Observateur* unequivocally places the child in a winter garden ('Touching Photographs', 108). However, this first French translation also erroneously ages Kafka, describing him as a 16 (!) rather than six-year-old boy (Walter Benjamin, 'Les Analphabètes de l'avenir', trans. Maurice de Gandillac, *Le Nouvel Observateur*, *Spécial Photo*, 2 (1977), 7–20: 16).

much more likely, simply a reference to a stock element of this turn-of-the-century portrait iconography remains open to interpretation.

Knight has also forwarded the thesis that the childhood photograph of the mother is 'displaced' by the Nadar photograph of an elderly woman,[21] which is reproduced in *La Chambre claire* immediately after Barthes's description of his rediscovery of the Winter Garden photograph. He compares the two images on the basis of their affective surplus, rooted in, yet also transcending, what the camera objectively recorded, which, he observes, provides their greatest value for him. In a suggestive fashion, Barthes captions the photograph '*Mère ou femme de l'artiste*' (CC, 108) ['*The artist's mother or wife*' (CL, 68)], perhaps blending this image of a paralysed old woman with his memory of his mother towards the end of her life. The portrait by Nadar, which is in fact of his wife Ernestine and not his mother,[22] may in this sense represent an imagined counterpiece to the Winter Garden photograph, in the form of an imagined visual juxtaposition.

For the most part, in contrast to Benjamin's wholly textual fusion of different photographic images, which would perhaps go unnoticed were it not for the accessibility of the actual photographs in question (allowing them to be compared with the descriptions), the superimposition in *La Chambre claire* is primarily visual and associative. But as a result of both Benjamin's and Barthes's strategy of visual and textual superimposition, combined with the withholding of key images, the readers and critics of their works are compelled to embark on an interpretative and speculative search that parallels the two writers' own subjective and associative probing of the images in question.

It is, however, important to reiterate here that although the explicit or implicit assumption that the Winter Garden portrait of Barthes's mother is imaginary may have encouraged Barthes scholars to forward a number of

---

21 Diana Knight, 'Roland Barthes, or The Woman Without a Shadow', in Jean-Michel Rabaté (ed.), *Writing the Image after Roland Barthes* (Philadelphia: University of Pennsylvania Press, 1997), 132–43: 139.

22 The portrait of Ernestine Nadar is from 1890. Nadar's mother, Thérèse Tournachon, died in 1860. See the recent biography of the photographer which includes the image Barthes discusses, Stéphanie de Saint Marc, *Nadar* (Paris: Gallimard, 2010), fig. 11. Following Snyder, Mitchell has suggested that Barthes knowingly added a misleading caption (*Picture Theory*, 305, n. 20). However, Newhall misdates the image around 1853 and Barthes, who saw it in his *History of Photography* (68), from which he also takes the cover illustration for *La Chambre claire*, might have been misled by Newhall's mistake.

interesting and insightful interpretations (as well as ones that for this very reason potentially misunderstand Barthes's view of the relation between photograph, viewer and textual description),[23] the substantial evidence pointing to its reality, as explicated above, should now put the issue to rest. [24] Future investigations are best to proceed on the assumption of the existence of the Winter Garden portrait and all that follows from this assumption, as I shall attempt to further trace with continual reference to Benjamin.

In light of the documented existence of both winter-garden photographs, their absence in each case is all the more striking, especially given that other images, also central to Benjamin's and Barthes's arguments – such as the early portraits by Hill/Adamson and Dauthendey, and the Gardner portrait of Payne – are not only described but also reproduced in the relevant texts. The preference given to ekphrasis over image reproduction implies not only the exceptionality of the winter-garden images in comparison with others but also something in or about them that would defy general recognition on the part of the reader/viewer and hence the pronounced relativity of their significance. As previously suggested with respect to the absence of Benjamin's childhood portrait(s) and the Kafka portrait from the 'Kleine Geschichte der Photographie', visual reproduction of the images would automatically absorb them into more general theoretical and historical arguments. Textual description alone, however, suggests that their true importance exists in the 'mind's eye' of the authors, who recognize something in the childhood portraits that is perceptually inaccessible in the images by anyone but them, even if coupled with a linguistic description of their effects. Barthes makes this

---

23 Cf. Richard Stamelman's contention that the Winter Garden photograph 'must be read *as writing* and not seen *as image*' (*Lost Beyond Telling. Representations of Death and Absence in Modern French Poetry* (Ithaca: Cornell University Press, 1990), 265). Cf. also Erin Mitchell's analysis of Barthes's Winter Garden photograph as 'virtual photography', in 'Writing Photography: The Grandmother in *Remembrance of Things Past*, the Mother in *Camera Lucida*, and especially, the Mother in *The Lover*', *Studies in Twentieth-Century Literature*, 24 (2000), 325–39: 325.

24 In January 2011, Michel Salzedo, Barthes's half-brother, transferred Barthes's estate from the Institut Mémoire de l'Édition Contemporaine (IMEC), where it had been held since 1996, to the Bibliothèque Nationale de France. The Winter Garden portrait, however, and indeed other photographs, are not part of this collection and therefore remain a 'family secret', to borrow Annette Kuhn's title (*Family Secrets. Acts of Memory and Imagination* (London and New York: Verso, 1995)).

point unmistakably clear when he addresses the reader and argues that he cannot reproduce the photograph of the mother as a child because for us it would represent nothing but 'une photo indifférente, l'une des mille manifestations du "quelconque" . . . ; tout au plus intéresserait-elle votre *studium*: époque, vêtements, photogénie; mais en elle, pour vous, aucune blessure' (CC, 115) ['an indifferent picture, one of the thousand manifestations of the "ordinary"...; at most it would interest your *studium*: period, clothes, photo genius; but in it, for you, no wound' (CL, 73)]. Benjamin, in contrast, does not directly tackle the discrepancy between the expressed significance of the Kafka photograph and its visual absence in the 'Kleine Geschichte der Photographie' and, to a lesser degree, the *Berliner Kindheit*. Together this illuminates the much more self-reflexive nature of Barthes's writing, which could be traced to numerous historical and intellectual contexts and influences as well as the autobiographical dynamics of *La Chambre claire*. Yet this does not negate the functional – and possibly intentional – similarities between these withholding strategies and their effects, on Benjamin's and Barthes's part.

If these multilayered commonalities between the two writers' engagements with their respective winter-garden photograph cannot be reduced to Barthes's direct reception of Benjamin in the form of his reading of the 'Kleine Geschichte der Photographie', there is another important conceptual connection here that may represent the clearest, most direct trace of Benjamin's influence on Barthes. This concerns Barthes's notion of the portrait's '*air*' (CC, 167), which he associates with his preference for portrait photography, over any other genre of image, a preference shared by Benjamin as foregrounded in his essay on photography.[25] For Barthes, all photographs indexically and, in most cases iconically, authenticate reality. In the case of images of objects as well as people, this takes the form of a superficial perceptual resemblance, which he refers to in alternating fashion as 'likeness', 'analogy' and 'platitude,' connoting both lack of physical depth and banality or triviality (see CC, 166–7). This must be understood as Barthes's means of emphasizing the no-more-and-no-less quality of the photograph in relation to the visual

25 Cf. Krauss, *Benjamin und der neue Blick*, 168. In Barthes's case, this almost exclusive focus on portraiture has prompted objections from photographic theorists, who argue that this leads to a one-sided view of the medium, as construed mainly in relation to so-called vernacular, family photographs, which de-emphasizes or excludes fine-art photography, and also entire genres: the landscape photograph, the still life, the abstract image and so on. See, for example, Elkins, *What Photography Is*, 43–4.

scene before the camera, when it is conceived purely as a visual or surface reality duplicated by the camera.

In the case of most portraits of loved ones such superficial likeness, or platitude, can be painful, the literal and symbolic indication of a deeper lack, that is, everything about the person one knows and loves that cannot be perceptually captured or displayed (no matter how visually accurate the representation): 'la platitude de la Photo devient plus douloureuse' ['the Photograph's platitude becomes more painful'] when it depicts 'un être aimé' (CC, 166) ['a beloved person' (CL, 107)]. Some rare portrait photographs, however, possess a deeper form of likeness, associated with markers of the photographed person's irreducible individuality, which is always more than 'skin deep', whose existence such images also authenticate and preserve. This feature, which Barthes terms *air*, is an immediately felt yet fundamentally incommunicable aspect of a portrait that mirrors the irreducible and incommunicable nature of the personality and identity of any human being. Thus, only some portraits (and only portraits, as this is a fundamentally human dynamic) possess and express *air*, further defined as 'cette chose exorbitante qui induit du corps à l'âme – *animula*, petite âme individuelle' (CC 167) ['that exorbitant thing which induces from body to soul – *animula*, little individual soul' (CL, 109)]. Those that do, lift the image out of the realm of physical and perceptual 'platitude', and bring the beholder, even if often only momentarily, into contact with something far more affective and immersive because the true object of the image's *air* is a non-physical quality, as Barthes's recourse to the term 'soul' indicates. He describes both the nature of *air* and its discovery as the end of all explanatory or analytical language, resonating with his description in earlier texts of the traumatic quality of some photographs as similarly resisting language. Recognition of *air*, Barthes suggests, can only be expressed in a quasi-tautological and evidential exclamation: '*C'est ça!*'(CC, 167) ['*That's it!*'].[26]

Distinguishing thus between the perception of mere resemblance and the recognition of something more in the image, Barthes remembers the discovery of the childhood photograph of his mother as an 'éveil brusque, hors de la "ressemblance", *satori* où les mots défaillent' (CC, 168) ['a sudden awakening, outside of "likeness", a *satori* in which words fail' (CL, 109)]. In relation to painted portraiture, Nancy has highlighted the important difference between resemblance and recognition, arguing that most viewers never see the living subject of paintings and thus have no

26 Marielle Macé traces this figure throughout Barthes's œuvre in her essay '"C'est ça!" Expérience esthétique et pensée de l'effet, à propos de Barthes'.

basis (outside of photographs, if and when they exist) to judge visual likeness.[27] This is, mutatis mutandis, also true for the photograph. For in Barthes's case, even if he contemplates a photograph of his mother, he has never actually seen the girl depicted in the image. Yet the Winter Garden photograph conveys the essential identity of the mother and hence provides him, against all the odds, with an 'image juste', in Barthes's citation of Jean-Luc Godard's slogan and play on words ('a just image' and 'just an image') (CC, 109). Thus, this portrait simultaneously reveals the essence of photography as perceived, the *ça-a-été*, and the essence of the mother, the *c'est ça!*. It is therefore at this point in *La Chambre claire* that the essence of the photograph-in-general and the essence of Barthes's exceptional photograph coincide, reflecting the dialogical dynamic between the general and particular in his writing on photography. In line with this dynamic, the *air* of a photographic portrait can potentially be recognized even if the depicted person is not known to the viewer.

Barthes describes *air* in relation to the portrait of Philip Randolph, the leader of the North-American Labour movement, taken by Richard Avedon, as 'l'ombre lumineuse qui accompagne le corps' (CC, 169) ['luminous shadow which accompanies the body' (CL, 110)]. This formulation is remarkably close to Benjamin's definition of aura as a 'Hauchkreis' or halo surrounding the sitters in nineteenth-century photographic portraiture (GS, II, 376). As Berg has pointed out, aura and *air* resemble each other in a semantic as well as etymological sense.[28] Both terms entail the notion of a light breath of air and perhaps an allusion to the fourth atmospheric element in ancient thought. Both derive from the Greek *aêr* or *aeros* and the Latin *aer*; the latter also connotes 'glimmer of light' and thereby adds a visual dimension, as Schöttker has noted.[29] Aura and *air* further relate to 'halo': the German *Aura* connotes aureole and nimbus and the French for the Latin *halos* or Greek *halôs* is *halo*, which relates to *aire* in the sense of a luminous circle around the moon or the sun.[30] Although much less frequently cited in critical studies on Benjamin and Barthes than the connections between aura and *punctum*, those between *air* and aura bear out a similar commonality between the two

27 See Nancy, *Le Regard du portrait*, 40.

28 See Berg, *Die Ikone des Realen*, 291. Cf. also on this similarity Ferguson, *Developing Clichés*, 190.

29 See Schöttker's commentary in Benjamin, *Das Kunstwerk*, 139.

30 Didi-Huberman even collapses the two terms when he writes that 'l'aura, c'est l'air, l'air qui court sur un visage' ['the aura, that is the air, the air which flows over a face'] (*Invention de l'hysterie*, 98).

writers' conceptions of photography, namely, emphasis on the concrete dynamic between photograph and beholder via something specific and observable in relation to the photographic referent, which is, at the same time, irreducible and outside of linguistic articulation. This is anchored in an active and attentive as well as affective and emotional response to particular photographs.

Besides indicating what is perhaps Barthes's most direct borrowing from Benjamin in relation to photography, both aura and *air* – and the sort of experiences they entail – correspond to an animation or vivification of both the portrait photograph and, figuratively, the person it represents, which (in those privileged cases in which aura and *air* are present) counters photography's mortification of its subjects. This idea of giving life to what is lifeless (i.e. to the photograph as a static, inanimate object), or returning life to one that has lost it (i.e. the dead or absent sitter), corresponds to the consideration of the magical and alchemical that represents yet another prominent conceptual current running through *La Chambre claire*.

Magic, Alchemy and Immortalization

Rendering the combined amazement and bewilderment that the new image-production technology triggered among the first generation that experienced it, the discourses of magic, alchemy and the supernatural continue to surround discussions on photography and, in a contemporary context, on other media. From the beginning of the medium's existence, 'magic' was a placeholder for the unknown or inexplicable in photography, especially in cases where the technology in question was not understood by the photographed person, the viewer of the image or even, later, with the arrival of the instant camera and mail-order development in the late nineteenth century, by the photographer. With these developments one did not have to understand photography's technology and optical-chemical functioning to use it, recalling Arthur C. Clarke's profound and oft-quoted suggestion that at a certain level of complexity technology is 'virtually indistinguishable' from magic. Much earlier, however, Benjamin expressed a similar notion, specifically in relation to photography, in the 'Kleine Geschichte der Photographie', suggesting that the difference between magic and technology is primarily historical (see GS, II, 371–2). Testimonies as to photography's emergence and rapid spread during the second half of the nineteenth century, including Max Dauthendey's account of the uncomprehending reactions which his father's production of 'Wunderbilder' ['magic images'] encountered, are full of references to magic, the supernatural and the occult.[31] As we have seen, Benjamin also refers to the magical quality of the photographic portrait, as rooted in its indexicality, and contrasts it with the painting's lack thereof. Likewise, when Barthes makes use of this theme and imagery in *La Chambre claire*, it is in order to best capture the unique effects of the photographic portrait on the viewer (in direct opposition, therefore, to his earlier claim in 'Rhétorique de l'image' that the association of photography with magic only hinders discovering the true nature of the medium and should therefore be resisted).[32]

As a corollary to his general unwillingness to credit the photographer with being an artist but instead an *Operator* (with emphasis on the technical craft as opposed to artistic creativity, imagination and intentionality), Barthes de-emphasizes the perceptual-optical, theatrical and fine-art pre-history of photography as rooted in painting, the magic lantern show or the *camera obscura*.[33] Instead he highlights the pivotal role played by chemical discoveries in the invention of photography. Apart from its literal aspects and implications, focusing on photography as a primarily physical and chemical process (involving the transference of light from an object to a chemically treated ground) provides Barthes with a 'rich mythological and symbolic field', as Nancy Shawcross argues, one that is inescapably tied to magic and alchemy.[34] He describes a photograph as 'littéralement une émanation du référent' (CC, 126) ['literally an emanation of the referent' (CL, 80)]. This emanation moves both physically (via optical perception) and metaphorically between the sitter and the viewer, as Barthes continues: 'D'un corps réel, qui était là, sont

---

31 Dauthendey, *Der Geist meines Vaters*, 50–1.

32 See, on this inter-textual relation, Guittard, 'Jardin d'hiver: formation d'une relique', 150. Stiegler describes Barthes as the 'last alchemist' in twentieth-century photographic history (*Bilder der Photographie*, 127). For a more in-depth historical account of the relation between alchemy and photography, see Busch, *Belichtete Welt*, 157–77.

33 This is in contradistinction to Bazin, for instance, who stresses the importance of such optical refinements as part and parcel of the move towards greater 'realism' in Western art ('Ontologie de l'image photographique', 15–17). Colin MacCabe has pondered why Barthes does not acknowledge Bazin's work on photography in *La Chambre claire* ('Barthes and Bazin: The Ontology of the Image', in Jean-Michel Rabaté (ed.), *Writing the Image after Roland Barthes* (Philadelphia: University of Pennsylvania Press, 1997), 71–6: 74–5).

34 Shawcross, *Roland Barthes on Photography*, 31.

parties des radiations qui viennent me toucher, moi qui suis ici' (CC, 126) ['From a real body, which was there, proceed radiations which ultimately touch me, who am here' (CL, 80)]. This formulation of photography as light inscription recalls Talbot's description of his invention of the camera-less process called 'photogenic drawing', in his programmatically titled book *The Pencil of Nature* (published between 1844 and 1846), which is not only the founding text of photographic history and theory but the first articulation of a realist conception of the medium.[35] However, it also, of course, relates to a much earlier history and the Greek etymology of *photo-graphia* as light-writing. Didi-Huberman gives a witty account of the invention of the verb 'to photograph' by the hermit Philotheos who purportedly exposed his body to the strong sunlight of his region so that he might become an image visible to God and, noting how the light imprinted itself onto him, referred to this process as 'to photograph'.[36] However, Barthes, who refers to Sontag as a predecessor with respect to the conception of photography as inscription, adds a twist to this view in suggesting, as in the above-quoted lines from *La Chambre claire*, that the light rays that impact the body of the object and move outwards to the light-sensitive ground, producing the image, later strike the image's viewer.

In the context of this exchange of light, and by extension life, of which the sun is the source, Barthes further elaborates on the nature of the relation between sitter and beholder and describes it as a 'sorte de lien ombilical [qui] relie le corps de la chose photographiée à mon regard: la lumière, quoique impalpable, est bien ici un milieu charnel, une peau que je partage avec celui ou celle qui a été photographié' (CC, 126–7) ['sort of umbilical cord [that] links the body of the photographed thing to my gaze: light, though impalpable, is here a carnal medium, a skin I share with anyone who has been photographed' (CL, 81)]. It is not insignificant that Barthes refers to an umbilical cord in a book centring on a photograph of his mother.[37] He does not, however, hesitate to generalize to include all photographic portraits and the description of this relation as skin-like

35 William Henry Fox Talbot, 'Introductory Remarks', in *The Pencil of Nature* (New York: Da Capo Press, 1969) (no pagination).

36 See 'Celui qui inventa le verbe "photographier"', in Georges Didi-Huberman, *Phasmes. Essais sur l'apparition* (Paris: Éditions de Minuit, 1998), 49–56.

37 Cf. Elissa Marder's psychoanalytic reading, according to which the 'photograph is a palpable fetish of the maternal body' ('Nothing to Say: Fragments on the Mother in the Age of Mechanical Reproduction', *L'Ésprit Créateur*, 40 (2000), 25–35: 31). See Schaeffer's critique of this metaphor from a semiotic point of view, *L'Image précaire*, 115.

chimes with the superstitions of some nineteenth-century portrait sitters who believed that instead of merely recording and imprinting their image, the camera took away a layer of bodily tissue, as noted in our discussion of Benjamin. Bernd Stiegler remarks that this belief was far from limited to occult and esoteric circles, although it was later exploited in this way in the context of early twentieth-century spiritual photography.[38] In fact, as Didi-Huberman has shown, there was also a widespread notion during the mid-to-late nineteenth century that the luminous 'aura' of a person could be captured on the photographic plate, a phenomenon associated with the photographic experiments of the French doctor Hippolyte Baraduc.[39] By the same token, in his famous essay on photography from 1859, Holmes argued that perception involves a connection between object and perceiver that is based on thin membranes which can be captured by the camera,[40] an idea echoed (most likely unintentionally) in Barthes's definition of the sitter as *Spectrum*. Coupled with the idea that the photograph either robs or records something emanating from the human body is the belief that the camera takes away a layer of the portrayed person's 'essence' or soul, as Balzac (who disliked being photographed for that reason) believed, according to Nadar, an idea which is also, of course, associated with the beliefs of some pre-modern tribal societies.

Barthes makes nuanced use of these traditions of belief. He shifts the negative connotation of photography as subtracting something from a human being's essence or body to a positive emphasis of a union between sitter and the camera, preserving him or her in form of an image. Moreover, Barthes focuses on the relation between the sitter and the viewer of the photograph rather than that between the sitter and the camera. The sitter and viewer are united via a bond of light transforming into a skin or covering. This moves Barthes's argument concerning the 'milieu charnel' towards bodily conjunction or osmosis, associated with human life and organicity more generally, as opposed to the alienation or separation of life from the body that Benjamin emphasizes in the context of his last definition of aura in his 'Über einige Motive bei Baudelaire', where the relation between camera and sitter is described as inhuman and deadly (also recalling the common identification of the camera with a gun that 'kills' the subject). The relation between the body of the sitter and that of the perceiver as sharing a mutual skin, in this attenuated and metaphorical

38 See Stiegler, *Bilder der Photographie*, 121–3.
39 See Didi-Huberman, *Invention de l'hysterie*, 90–8.
40 See Trachtenberg (ed.), *Classic Essays on Photography*, 72–3.

sense, suggests that both bodies also share the same state of existence, as it were. It implies that the photographed body is alive or, at least, that it is perceived and felt as being alive by the viewer. It is in this connection that Barthes refers to alchemy in relation to the photograph of the mother as a child, who is depicted in a time-arresting winter-garden setting, and suggests that the sitter is immortalized through the photographic/alchemic transformation: 'le corps aimé est immortalisé par la médiation d'un métal précieux, l'argent (monument et luxe); à quoi on ajouterait l'idée que ce métal, comme tous les métaux de l'Alchimie, est vivant' (CC, 127) ['the loved body is immortalized by the mediation of a precious metal, silver (monument and luxury); to which we might add the notion that this metal, like all the metals of Alchemy, is alive' (CL, 81)]. The body of the person photographed, that is, the mother, is alchemically transformed by photography. This is not a matter of literally bringing the dead person in the photograph back to life, for what is animated is not the represented person but the mediator, or photograph, which is, like the alchemist's metal, seen to be alive.[41] Although Barthes does not mention it, metal – a silver-coated copper plate – was the ground material of the daguerreotype, perhaps the type of photograph which in process, product and affect (as a kind of magic mirror) comes closest to the magical and alchemical.

The particular photograph of the dead mother is perceived to be more intense and more alive than other images, which, by contrast, only conjure death as opposed to life. In other words, the psychological and emotional effect/affect of the Winter Garden portrait on Barthes transcends the photograph's symbolic relation to death, whereas in the case of other photographs the latter predominates over the former. Barthes also explores the symbolic relation between photography and death from a more explicitly anthropological standpoint. In concert with Jean Baudrillard's nearly contemporary thesis concerning the exclusion of death from modern consumer society,[42] and with direct reference to Edgar Morin's earlier study on *L'Homme et la mort* [*Man and Death*] (from 1951), Barthes conceives of photography as the locus for death in twentieth-century secular society:

---

41 Barthes is aware of the provocative and perhaps archaic nature of his claim in the context of a disenchanted world (see CC, 127), an admission that Tagg glosses over in his materialist criticism of Barthes's coupling of photography and alchemy (see *The Burden of Representation*, 3).

42 See Jean Baudrillard, *L'Échange symbolique et la mort* (Paris: Gallimard, 1976), 193–201.

> Car la Mort, dans une société, il faut bien qu'elle soit quelque part; si elle n'est plus (ou est moins) dans le religieux, elle doit être ailleurs: peut-être dans cette image qui produit la Mort en voulant conserver la vie. (CC, 144)
>
> For Death must be somewhere in a society; if it is no longer (or less intensely) in the sphere of religion, it must be elsewhere: perhaps in this image, which produces Death while trying to preserve life. (CL, 92)

Barthes's supposition here is particularly intriguing since photography is seen not simply as the conservatory of death but as assisting it through a misguided attempt to preserve only a superficial likeness of life. This is also part and parcel of Barthes's generally critical attitude towards the attempt to make the photograph more 'life-like' by way of formal and stylistic means (colour and posture, for instance). Such efforts are fundamentally different from the sort of 'Pygmalion effect'[43] his own hallucination in front of the Winter Garden photograph entails, understood as the coming to life of an inanimate substance. As Victor Stoichita's study of the Pygmalion myth in Western art and art history highlights, it is not a matter of art trying to present life more accurately, as is sometimes thought, but of the work *coming alive*, that is, not imitation but *incarnation*, and it is thus particularly relevant to Barthes's descriptions. Through this affective-magical and imaginative, as opposed to perceptual and formal, vivification, the Winter Garden photograph is felt as being almost identical with the mother. If, like all art, photography in its more consciously artistic uses always necessarily draws attention to its representational and symbolic character, photography as magic hides and denies it. For the latter exhibits the reality authenticating power of the medium to substitute the referent for the referential object through the actual causal relation between the two. This relation is a literalization and technological fulfilment of all sorts of magical substitutions, such as the wine for blood in the transubstantiation of Christian tradition.

The near identity of the photographed person and the photograph itself (related to the near breakdown of the semiotic distinction between signifier and signified) is always, however, tempered by the nature of the image as irrevocably past. That is to say, it is always both a picture and piece of the past, no matter how immediate and animated the momentary life-presence it instigates. Barthes hence returns to his thesis as to the emanation of the referent which the photograph captures and re-emphasizes that it is not only a trace of the real but of a reality

43 See Victor I. Stoichita, *The Pygmalion Effect. From Ovid to Hitchcock*, trans. Alison Anderson (Chicago: University of Chicago Press, 2008).

now past, 'une émanation du *réel passé:* une *magie,* non un art' (CC, 138) ['an emanation of *past reality*: a *magic*, not an art' (CL, 88)], like a ghostly apparition. The magic and alchemic discourses surrounding photography provide Barthes with a framework within which to explore the potential of the photograph's 'mediating' power, which connotes the camera serving the role of spiritual medium, as a channel, link or go-between, bridging the realm of the living and the dead, the present and the past. And like the medium at a séance whose identity disappears when channelling and incarnating the spirit of the dead, so too does the camera or photographer recede in this dynamic, leaving the viewer and sitter in more direct experiential relation. This potential, however, is realized only by the Winter Garden photograph, which provides Barthes with a sense of the mother's true identity. In this sense, *La Chambre claire* is the *mise-en-œuvre* of the magical photographic encounter with the irreducible singularity of the other.

Singularity and the Encounter with the Other

As should now be clear, for Barthes, the Winter Garden photograph is fundamentally different from all others, be they other portraits of his mother, family photographs or any public portrait images. This particular portrait of the mother as a child is distinct in being seen and felt to convey the essence of the mother – that is to say, her irreducible singularity – and, secondly, the photograph itself is experienced as a magical object or token, not by virtue of its objective, formal or perceptual properties as an image but through the viewer's (Barthes's) affective and imaginative engagement with it. Rooted in the viewer's knowledge of, and relation with, the referent, this dynamic finds a natural correspondence in some technical-chemical and alchemical facts of the image's actual physical-material generation as shared by all analogue photographs. The singularity of the photographic encounter, comprising all these related aspects, is experienced by Barthes as a recognition of the mother's essence and her 'bonté' (CC, 107) ['kindness' (CL, 69)] as expressed in the image. Such singularity occurs, therefore, when three unique realities – the (past) being of the person in the photograph, the specific image (which is materially as well as representationally unique) and the present existence of the beholder – converge in a precise historical moment in time and enter into an unpredictable interrelation. In all of these ways, this dynamic experience is justly theorized as powerfully and emphatically singular, just as it is felt to be so by the viewer.

In *La Chambre claire*, the singularity of the Winter Garden photograph is expressed most basically in Barthes's capitalization of it within the text.[44] Remarking on this fact, Jean-Claude Milner has pointed out that the practice of capitalization of French words that would conventionally be written in lower case 'arrache le mot à son usage courant' ['removes the word from its common usage']; this conveys a strong sense of uniqueness, which Milner, like others, relates to Benjamin's aura, as the opposite of what is reproducible and repeatable.[45] By the same token, as Milner continues, 'la majuscule . . . distingue un référent unique et en souligne l'identité à soi' ['the capital letter designates a unique referent and emphasises its self-identity'].[46] Applied to the mother-as-child photograph, by capitalizing 'Jardin d'Hiver' and hence transforming the general portrait setting into a proper name for it, Barthes draws attention to its uniqueness. Yet given that he deduces a number of more generally applicable ontological and temporal features of photography from his example of this singular image, which in some respects, at least, do transcend Barthes's unique experiences and biography, the important question arises as to how exactly singularity relates to the *punctum* and the photographic referent.

In line with Derrida's reflections on Barthes's *punctum*, I wish to argue that photographic singularity is indeed closely linked to an encounter with the 'singularity of the other', as acknowledged by the viewing subject. In contrast to Derrida, however, who in this context equates or identifies this singularity with the *punctum*, I maintain that the experience of singularity marking Barthes's encounter with the Winter Garden photograph exceeds that which is defined as the *punctum* in a profound way. Although the concept of the *punctum* makes speaking of the singular possible to some degree, for it paradoxically introduces into the more general theory of photography that which escapes any objective, a priori definition, the singularity of the photograph as expressed in Barthes's writing is not identical to it.

44 In the *Journal de deuil*, by contrast, 'Jardin d'hiver' is not, or only partly, capitalized (JD, 155).

45 Jean-Claude Milner, *Le Pas philosophique de Roland Barthes* (Lagrasse: Verdier, 2003), 12. He writes that 'Barthes, eût-il [Benjamin] dit, projette autour du mot une *aura*' ['Barthes, he [Benjamin] would have said, creates an *aura* around the word'] (ibid.). Although my emphasis on singularity is at odds with his juxtaposition of aura and reproducibility, which indeed perpetuates a common misunderstanding of Benjamin's theories of photography which this study opposes, Milner nonetheless proposes a number of interesting points of convergence between Benjamin and Barthes.

46 Ibid., 17.

To first establish Derrida's interpretation of Barthes's *punctum*, in 'Les Morts de Roland Barthes', Derrida sets out to find a detail through which to access the multifaceted œuvre of his late friend, one that 'interrupts' the established trajectory of Barthes's thought to cast it in a new and different light. Derrida appropriately turns to Barthes's notion of *punctum* in this context. In emphasizing the *punctum* as a significant detail in an image, Derrida privileges the definition given in the first part of *La Chambre claire*, as opposed to the differently oriented, later one. Bearing in mind that what is 'punctuated' is the culturally coded surface of the photograph (that is, the reproducible), in Derrida's account the *punctum* is associated with the singular, that is to say, the unrepeatability of the photographed moment.[47] Following Barthes's sense of the *punctum* as entailing a reciprocal dynamic between photograph and viewer, Derrida states that the *punctum* 's'adresse à moi, c'est dans sa définition' ['its very definition is that it addresses itself to me'].[48] He further links the *punctum* not only to the specific viewing subject but to the 'singularité absolue de l'autre' ['absolute singularity of the other'], that is, the other in the photograph.[49]

Following Derrida's reading of *La Chambre claire*, the *punctum* is a recognition of the particular detail in a photograph through which the irreducible otherness of the photographic referent is manifested, which, in turn, enables it to be spoken of. This point of absolute singularity that addresses the viewer is the absolute other, the other which cannot be reduced to 'the same'. However, the other in the photograph paradoxically appears at the very moment of its absence, which indicates the precarious and even ghostly status of presence in photographic representation. Derrida elaborates on the absent presence of the referent and explains that its '"présence" se dérobe à jamais . . . , il est déjà enfoncé dans le passé' ['"presence" forever escapes me, having already receded into the past'].[50] The presence of the referent, in other words, is ghostly insofar as it is a presence of the absent. It is exactly this paradox, in Derrida's view,

---

47 On this point, Derrida suggests a fundamental compatibility between Benjamin's and Barthes's conceptualization of the referent in the age of technological modernity, rooted in an understanding of the *punctum* as a unique detail which challenges 'la reproduction . . . des analogies, des ressemblances, des codes' ['the reproduction . . . of analogies, likenesses, and codes'] ('*Les Morts de Roland Barthes*', 272; 'The Deaths of Roland Barthes', 39).

48 Ibid.

49 Ibid.

50 Ibid.

that is at the heart of Barthes's writing on the mother and her childhood photograph. In spite of the photograph's construed power to resurrect and evoke the beloved person, the mother ultimately remains absent; in the words of Derrida: 'Ici, là, l'autre unique, sa mère, paraît, c'est-à-dire sans paraître, car l'autre ne peut paraître qu'en disparaissant' ['Here, there, the unique other, his mother, appears, that is to say, without appearing, for the other can appear only by disappearing'].[51] The *punctum* is the appearance of the photographic referent, an appearance that is both absent and past (he or she appears through disappearing) and hence coupled with death.

It is necessary to observe here that for Derrida the temporal structure of the photograph, this deferral or suspension of the referent, which he develops out of his understanding of *punctum*, is applicable to other non-photographic and non-visual phenomena as well. In 'Les Morts de Roland Barthes', Derrida's example is the proper name, which similarly speaks of the bearer's present absence. In a later interview, he also adds his particular conceptions of the 'archive' and the 'signature' to that of the proper name and the photograph as examples of this inherently temporal signifying structure.[52] As this indicates, Derrida wishes to see the role of the referent in the context of the *punctum* in more general semiotic terms as one type of referential relationship, neither specific to the photograph nor centred on the subject's unique existential and affective relation to the referent. Therefore, for Derrida, the absolute singularity of the other in the photograph which addresses itself to 'me' is the singularity of *any* other.[53] Whereas, as we have seen, for Barthes, and implicitly for any viewer, the absolute singularity in question is always that of one special individual and one particular photographic image.

The demand of the Winter Garden photograph, like that demand for redemption that Agamben draws out of Benjamin's analysis of nineteenth-century photographic portraiture, is felt by Barthes in a uniquely powerful way that far surpasses the felt impact of a *punctum* in the other photographic images he discusses. It is not any 'other' that this photograph represents but the beloved mother and her unique essence,

51 Ibid., 279; 48.

52 See Derrida, *Copy, Archive, Signature*, 3–4.

53 See Derrida, 'Les Morts de Roland Barthes', 272. Following Derrida, Eduardo Cadava and Paola Cortés-Rocca similarly align the *punctum* with irreducible singularity, which is somewhat at odds with the notion of singularity presented here ('Notes on Love and Photography', in Geoffrey Batchen (ed.), *Photography Degree Zero. Reflections on Roland Barthes's Camera Lucida* (Cambridge, MA: MIT Press, 2009), 105–39: 112–18).

as only Barthes could have recognized. This existential confrontation with the absent mother renders this encounter with the photograph particularly poignant. It is now fully clear why it is necessary to accept and acknowledge that Barthes's discourse on photography in *La Chambre claire* is centred on an actually existing photograph, as this kind of existential confrontation between the self and the other can only be triggered by an actual photograph, felt and perceived as external to oneself, as opposed to an only imaginary one which is by nature never outside of the self. The imaginary photograph would not be an encounter with radical otherness but instead an encounter with (only) the self's image of the other.[54] And while imaginative immersion is central to the dynamic of photographic singularity, it is an imaginative and affective engagement which is, and must be, preceded by the direct perception of an actual image object.

To turn to Derrida's more general commentary on *La Chambre claire*, he views Barthes's distinction between *studium* and *punctum* as the only way of speaking of the singular (the *punctum* or photographic referent) within a study (or *studium*) of the general. The latter is taken as photography in general, as a stable, external corpus of innumerable images and facts about the medium which Derrida associates with the 'same' or the endless and identical reproducibility of the photograph. Barthes himself draws attention to the fact that such a project is utopian and would ultimately be doomed to failure, were it not for the Winter Garden photograph. He poignantly writes that 'la Photographie du Jardin d'Hiver, elle, était bien essentielle, elle accomplissait pour moi, utopiquement, *la science impossible de l'être unique*' (CC, 110) ['the Winter Garden Photograph was indeed essential, it achieved for me, utopically, *the impossible science of the unique being*' (CL, 71)]. This impossible science, which Barthes also calls '*Mathesis singularis*' (CC, 21), describes the impossibility of speaking (of) the singular, as Attridge has noted in the wake of Derrida.[55] Being aware of the impossibility of the task, however, and the attempt that is nonetheless made, ultimately

54 By contrast, in Attridge's account of literature as the 'other', the encounter with it results in the other no longer being entirely other ('Innovation, Literature, Ethics', 21). The ethical implications of Barthes's and Benjamin's engagements with the childhood photographs as related to the other (or 'Autrui') are closer to Levinas's ethics than to Derrida. Röttger-Denker convincingly outlines the relation between desire and ethics with respect to Barthes and Levinas (see *Roland Barthes*, 130–3).

55 See Attridge, 'Roland Barthes's Obtuse, Sharp Meaning', 82.

grants its success. In this sense, *La Chambre claire* as a whole moves towards redemption by seeking to re-enact the experience of singularity in relation to the Winter Garden photograph. It is this particular quixotic process of conveying experiential singularity through writing about it that ultimately saves the mother and her memory from time and forgetting. In the attempt to write (about) the singular encounter with the specific photograph, Barthes expresses a duty towards the dead, a 'devoir' that Derrida speaks of feeling when writing on Barthes on the occasion of the latter's death.[56]

As previously noted with respect to Benjamin's critical-historical project which finds its focus in the Kafka-as-child photograph, the Winter Garden photograph in *La Chambre claire* is both the object of, and the example for, a redemptive criticism. Each portrait and the experience it triggers for Benjamin and Barthes is saved from the passage of time – just as the winter garden arrests the passage of the seasons – by their respective phenomenological descriptions of their encounters with it in the context of a larger, supplementary autobiographical narrative. The ethical movement towards redemption is the tertium comparationis between both authors' projects, and the specifically photographic aspect of their redemptive criticism is rooted in the particularly powerful material and psychological connection to (past) reality possessed by every photograph. In contrast, the relevant dynamics of identification and recognition are unique to a particular photograph and to the beholder's unique response to it, as bound to personal experience and memory.

56 See Derrida's pondering on the fact that writing on the dead is simultaneously a wound and a duty, 'Les Morts de Roland Barthes', 284. Prior to Derrida, Emmanuel Levinas put forward the argument that our connection to death manifests itself via a responsibility to the other in the unknown (*Dieu, la mort et le temps*, ed. Jacques Rolland (Paris: Grasset, 1993), 20–4).

Chapter 6

Photography and Memory: Barthes's Proustian Quest

Barthes's reflections on photography and memory are concerned with how photographic images operate as tokens of a personal past in both direct and indirect ways. As we have seen in relation to Benjamin's use of photographic metaphors and analogies, Proust's *À la recherche du temps perdu*, from which Benjamin cherry-picks suggestive passages, is a natural precedent and authority in this respect. Barthes, however, refers not only to the poetics of memory present in the novel but also to its autobiographical foundation, aspects of which he sees reflected and refracted in his own life story. Indeed, to the extent to which it juxtaposes the experience of loss with a related desire to write, *La Chambre claire* can aptly be described as a Proustian search for the lost mother in the form of a photograph and for the meaning of photography more generally,[1] despite the fact that Barthes's and Proust's conceptions of photography also considerably diverge, as we shall see.[2]

The parallel between *À la recherche* and *La Chambre claire* with respect to their origin and their process-centred self-reflexivity is emphasized by Barthes through what Marty rightly regards as a double temporality in the form of a simultaneous 'pas encore' and 'déjà'.[3] Although in *La Chambre claire* the seminal photograph is represented as not yet found until the midway point of the book, its discovery is also the book's point of origin, that is, what was already known to the author, this being comparable to the narrative of *À la recherche*, which is represented as yet to be completed, although it has been written already.[4] More generally,

1 Philippe Roger has suggested that *La Chambre claire* is written 'à l'ombre de Proust' ['in the shadow of Proust'] (*Roland Barthes, roman* (Paris: Bernard Grasset, 1986), 221).

2 In the wake of Chevrier's early study on photography in *À la recherche* (*Proust et la photographie*), this topic has attracted much scholarly attention. For two concise accounts, see Roxanne Hanney, 'Proust and Negative Plates: Photography and the Photographic Process in *A la Recherche du Temps Perdu*', *Romanic Review*, 74 (1983), 342–54 and Angela Cozea, 'Proustian Aesthetics: Photography, Engraving, Historiography', *Comparative Literature*, 45 (1993), 209–29.

3 Éric Marty, 'L'Assomption du phénomène', *Critique*, 38 (1982), 744–52: 745–7.

4 This circularity is based on the assumption that Proust's finished book and the narrator's yet-to-be-written one are the same. However, this interpretation

mirroring the influence that Proust exerted on Benjamin's writings decades before, Barthes, throughout his career, and on a number of personal and professional levels, saw Proust as the exemplary writer and *À la recherche* as the paradigmatic novel.[5] The literal, as opposed to only figurative, Proustian nature of Barthes's post-1970s œuvre, which encompasses a myriad of texts, seminars, interviews, radio programmes and diaries in part devoted to the novelist, corresponds to Barthes's own desire to write a literary work partly inspired by Proust's example. Barthes's evocation of Proust as his '*souvenir circulaire*', in *Le Plaisir du texte* (OC, IV, 241) – that is, an instinctive, always present inter-text rather than a convenient literary authority or point of reference – is borne out in *La Chambre claire*, his Proustian book on photography, where this 'circular memory' is closely interrelated with the author's memory of his mother. Barthes's modelling his search for the mother on aspects of *À la recherche* and Proust's concept of *mémoire involontaire* are most evident in the second part of the book, which Barthes retrospectively calls 'une réflexion plus douloureuse sur un deuil' ['a more painful reflection on an episode of mourning'], in contrast to the first part, devoted to the 'plaisir de l'image' (OC, V, 930) ['pleasure of the image' (GV, 352)].[6]

In a 1978 lecture, programmatically entitled 'Longtemps, je me suis couché de bonne heure' ['For a long time I would go to bed early'], Barthes strongly identifies with Proust and the writing of *À la recherche* (see OC, V, 459). Jean-Louis Lebrave has highlighted the link between this lecture and *La Chambre claire* as revealed in the handwritten draft manuscript of the latter. Clearly evoking the incipit of *À la recherche*, the beginning of *La Chambre claire* in this draft reads: 'Depuis longtemps, je m'intéressais à la Photographie' ['For a long time, I have been interested

has been challenged, see, for instance, Joshua Landy, 'Proust, The Narrator and the Importance of the Distinction', *Poetics Today*, 25 (2004), 91–135: 111–27. Nonetheless, *À la recherche* remains highly self-reflexive in this respect as in others.

5 For two concise discussions of Barthes's engagement with the life and work of Proust, see Malcolm Bowie, 'Barthes on Proust', *Yale Journal of Criticism*, 14 (2001), 513–18 and Antoine Compagnon, 'Proust et moi', in Mary Donaldson-Evans et al. (eds.), *Autobiography, Historiography, Rhetoric: Essays in Honour of Frank Paul Bowman* (Amsterdam: Rodopi, 1994), 59–73.

6 Cf. Macé who, with regard to the presence of Proustian allusions and resonances, strongly affirms the pronounced difference between the first and the second parts of *La Chambre claire*, in her article 'C'est ça!'. Similarly, Marty, in his Proustian reading of Barthes, suggests that the first part of *La Chambre claire* represents the 'temps perdu' and the second the 'temps retrouvé' ('Présentation', in OC, V, 18–19).

in Photography'].[7] It appears as if Barthes, like the Proustian hero Marcel, attempts to compensate for a personal loss through writing *La Chambre claire*, or through writing *tout court*, that is *écriture*,[8] which Barthes disarmingly declares (in the published version of the text) to be the only goal left in his life (see CC, 113). Unlike the hero of *À la recherche* and perhaps its author, however, Barthes is not able to thereby overcome death, which, for him, is undialectical in this sense: 'Je ne pouvais plus qu'attendre ma mort totale, indialectique' (ibid.) ['From now on I could do no more than await my total, undialectical death' (CL, 72)].[9] According to Barthes's autobiographical reading of Proust, the loss of Proust's mother in 1905, only a few years before he started writing his opus magnum in 1909, is, at least partly, transformed and overcome by the creative process of writing. Barthes, on the other hand, ultimately remained overwhelmed by the death of his mother, and his own death, shortly after the publication of *La Chambre claire*, perhaps arrived too soon for a similar dialectical overcoming of mourning through writing to take place.[10]

In the narrower context of photography, however, there is an even more important difference between the respective projects of Proust and Barthes. For the narrator of *À la recherche*, the past is first and foremost imaginatively regained through the mental image, that is, mainly by virtue of involuntary memory. It is helpful here to recall that imagination, as Sartre stresses in his phenomenology of it, is a particular functioning of consciousness without necessary reference to an object external to it.[11] With respect to Proust, the beloved people, towns and

7 Jean-Louis Lebrave, 'La Genèse de *La Chambre claire*', *Genesis*, 19, 'Roland Barthes', (2002), 79–107: 83–5.

8 For Barthes, this is writing in an intransitive sense, that is, not the writing of a novel or essay, but writing itself. See his 1966 'Écrire, verbe intransitive?' (OC, III, 617–26). For Barthes's later return to this notion, see PR, 35.

9 In Barthes's *Journal de deuil*, there are at least a dozen references to his own death and mortality. With regard to the writing projects of Barthes and Proust, Éric Marty speaks of a negative and positive mise-en-abyme structure, respectively ('Marcel Proust dans "la chambre claire"', *L'Ésprit Créateur*, 46 (2006), 125–33: 130). Lawrence D. Kritzman similarly insists on Barthes's 'failure to master grief' ('Barthes's Way: *Un Amour de Proust*', *Yale Journal of Criticism*, 14 (2001), 535–43: 541).

10 In 'L' Œuvre et l'espace de la mort', Blanchot shows that Proust wanted to make death less bitter through writing, which also applies to Barthes, even though on his own account he fails (*L'Espace littéraire*, 115).

11 See Sartre, *L'Imaginaire*, especially the chapter titled 'L'image mentale', 108–12. Marty draws an interesting parallel between Barthes's exclusion

landscapes belonging to the past are imaginatively conjured owing to the rare and epiphanic memory of the hero. In other words, there are no external, perceptual objects of his engagement with the past, as they are no longer directly accessible or even no longer exist. Barthes's pursuit of lost time, on the other hand, is the attempt to find a truthful photographic representation of his mother. While involving imaginative, and even hallucinatory, processes of 'resurrection', this is anchored in an actual image, a photograph as a perceptual object that bears a direct material trace of the past.[12] In *À la recherche*, the profound and past-recapturing memory, that is, *mémoire involontaire*, is often distinguished from visual perception – traditionally associated with factual knowledge and truth – and is instead aligned with the less rational, mimetic and more impressionistic four senses of smell, taste, touch and hearing, as Benjamin has hinted in 'Zum Bilde Prousts' (see GS, II, 323). In *La Chambre claire*, by contrast, although its reader does not see the image of the mother, Barthes's rediscovery of her in the form of an encounter with her irreducible otherness is inextricably bound to an act of sight and the visual medium of photographic representation, which literally and metaphorically has much in common with human vision. From this perspective, Barthes's dedication of *La Chambre claire* to Sartre's *L'Imaginaire*, while in keeping with their shared phenomenological orientation, is also at odds with the book's perceptual, as opposed to imaginary, subject and genesis. Yet, seen in relation to the processes of memory, the dedication is also an indication of the larger Proustian dimension of *La Chambre claire*, since for Barthes, although beginning in visual perception, the experience of the pivotal portrait photograph, and certain others, is conjoined with a highly imaginative and affective engagement with the referent, which in some cases is inseparable from the workings of memory. And, of course, neither Barthes nor Proust seeks the reality of the past in the form of some objective-historical truth, unmediated by subjective imagination.

Instead, both authors search for a past reality that is real for them, that is to say, truthful to their own lived experience and memory. In

---

of any discourse on the 'hidden' or 'unconscious' in *La Chambre claire* and Sartre's phenomenological focus on what is conscious as opposed to unconscious ('L'Assomption du phénomène', 748–9).

12 According to Sartre, in opposition to perception, the content of mental images does not have any external reference point; hence his statement that 'on ne *voit* pas une image mentale' (*L'Imaginaire*, 109) ['one does not *see* a mental image' (*The Imaginary*, 52)].

the case of Barthes, this subjective reality is apparently at odds with his understanding of photography as a trace of the real and the factual evidence of the existence of what is photographed. But, as the discussion of Barthes's distinction between *studium* and *punctum* has shown, together with the phenomenological nature of his study, his reactions to photographs, despite being intellectually rooted in the concept of the indexicality of the medium, cannot be limited to it. In other words, the truth of reality that the photograph conveys by virtue of the nature of the medium is fundamentally distinct from the truth for the self arrived at via the specific photograph, even though the two are complexly interrelated. As Kracauer has argued, Proust's characterization of photographic representation as coldly objective and alienating by virtue of being hidebound to visual likeness and external perception serves to contrastively foreground the hero's rich, vivid and affective inner imaginative life as it is portrayed in the novel.[13] For Barthes, however, the relevant contrast with respect to the power to authentically re-present the past is not between all photography and memory/imagination (i.e. as external perception versus internal re-presentation). Rather, it is a contrast between those photographs of a person that do encourage a certain truthful recognition of him or her, through setting in motion an immersive process of memory and imagination, and those that inhibit this process, falsifying rather than authenticating memory and the past.

The Photograph as 'Contre-Souvenir'

As we have seen, in the late 1930s, Benjamin employed *À la recherche* in support of the idea that the photographic medium contributed to a pronounced decline in authentic experience, or *Erfahrung*, which he also associated with the most valuable form of memory, that is, Proust's *mémoire involontaire*, and instead argued that it fostered *Erlebnis*, a more superficial mode of experience endemic to modern, industrialized life. In *La Chambre claire*, Barthes also explicitly states that the photograph does not trigger memories in a Proustian fashion: 'La Photographie ne remémore pas le passé (rien de proustien dans une photo)' (CC, 129) ['The Photograph does not call up the past (nothing Proustian in a photograph)' (CL, 82)]. Barthes here implicitly regards memory as supplementing the present by the past. In the case of the memorial object, it is thus an imaginary addition to what is actually there. Owing to the

13 See Kracauer, *Theory of Film*, 15.

density and effect of its indexical reality, however, combined with its anti-narrative freezing and isolation of a single moment from a larger spatio-temporal continuum, the photograph, as a '*Tout-Image*' (CC, 139) ['*Total-Image*'], resists such imaginative supplementation.[14] Unlike a necessarily incomplete literary description of an object or scene, or even a realist painting, the photograph lacks perceptual-imaginative gaps or lacunae for the viewer to fill in because everything that gives the image its identity is already there: 'L'image photographique est pleine, bondée: pas de place, on ne peut rien y ajouter' (ibid.) ['The photographic image is full, crammed: no room, nothing can be added to it' (CL, 89)]. In symbolic terms, for Barthes, the photographic image resists metaphor, which is also an addition and supplementation, that is, of a literal meaning with a figurative one.

The perceptual plenitude that repels the viewer's supplementary imagination is borne out by Barthes in his description and analysis of a number of photographs in which their reality, signifying power and completeness surpass their memorial potential – as Kracauer had earlier suggested when, *contra* Benjamin, he discounted the affective memory function of family photographs that is countered by the image's objective, historical facticity. Barthes writes of an image by Kertész that it only affirms the past reality of the scene, rather than evoking a memory somehow related to it on the part of the viewer: 'ce que je vois, ce n'est pas un souvenir, une imagination, une reconstitution . . . , mais le réel à l'état passé: à la fois le passé et le réel' (CC, 130) ['what I see is not a memory, an imagination, a reconstitution . . . , but reality in a past state: at once the past and the real' (CL, 82)]. In one sense, here Barthes does little more than reaffirm that the image's indexicality determines, or over-determines, its reception. More interesting is what this suggests with respect to memory. Barthes implies that the certainty as to the past moment represented, to which every photograph testifies, thwarts memory, which, on some level of visual representation at least, is rooted in the fact that the past can never be recaptured in complete, accurate detail. In other words, memory not only functions in the gap between the perception of an object or event in the present and a later, always incomplete mental representation of it, but in a sense it is this gap: the mimetic fallibility of the memory-image makes it what it is and often guarantees its value. This is a fallibility never granted to a photograph, which is too wedded

14 The photograph here functions in a similar fashion to the 'texte lisible' or readerly text in Barthes's study of Balzac, in *S/Z*, since this kind of text is immune to productive readerly responses (see OC, III, 121–3).

to the past, in one sense, and never true to it, in another. The specifically photographic arresting of time is a kind of '*contre-souvenir*' (CC, 142, my emphasis) ['counter-memory' (CL, 91)], blocking imaginative access to the past.

Barthes's remarks on the ways in which most photographs present the viewer with nothing more or less than a stark, objective fact of what was before the camera, leaving little room for imaginative additions, are in keeping with the very beginning of the second part of *La Chambre claire*. It starts with an essentially anti-photographic citation from Proust's novel, recalling Benjamin's use of the Proustian narrator's dismissive comment on the sterility of both photographs and images arising from wholly voluntary remembrance (of Venice) that the narrator relates in order to second this notion. Flipping through some old photographs of his late mother, Barthes casually notes that 'je n'attendais rien de "ces photographies d'un être, devant lesquelles on se le rappelle moins bien qu'en se contentant de penser à lui" (Proust)' (CC, 99) ['I expected nothing from "these photographs of a being before which one recalls less of that being than by merely thinking of him or her" (Proust)' (CL, 63)].[15] Barthes begins his search for an authentic photograph of his mother in the same way as he theorizes photography in general, that is, with a strong scepticism as to photography's potential to match or authenticate one's most valuable and truthful memories. For Proust and Barthes, then, a portrait photograph is – generally speaking – inimical to the authentic recollection of the human being it represents rather than an aid to it. Such truthful recollection is instead associated with, and largely reserved for, the mental memory-image, as Barthes argues in both *La Chambre claire* and his later seminar, 'Proust et la photographie' ['Proust and Photography'].[16]

And yet, Barthes's discussion of the Winter Garden photograph seems to contradict these observations or suggests that it is once again exceptional in this respect, as in so many others. Although it is not (yet) related to features of this image or its experience, in its mirroring of settings, situations and imagery from *À la recherche*, the narrative Barthes constructs around his finding of the portrait is associated with the

15 The original passage, quoted by Barthes, can be found in Proust, *À la recherche*, vol. 4, 464.

16 In this seminar, Barthes reaffirms that the photograph irritates imagination, here involved in the process of reading (see PR, 397). See my 'Reading Through Photography: Roland Barthes's Last Seminar "Proust et la photographie"', *French Forum*, 32 (2009), 97–112: 105–9.

recapturing of the past through authentic involuntary memory. Barthes describes the loneliness of his quest and how it ended as follows:

> J'allais ainsi, seul dans l'appartement où elle [la mère] venait de mourir, regardant sous la lampe, une à une, ces photos de ma mère, remontant peu à peu le temps avec elle, cherchant la vérité du visage que j'avais aimé. Et je la découvris. (CC, 105–6)
>
> There I was, alone in the apartment where she [the mother] had died, looking at these photos of my mother, one by one, under the lamp, gradually moving back in time with her, looking for the truth of the face I had loved. And I found it. (CL, 67)

This concise, almost short-hand description compellingly echoes the beginning of *À la recherche* when the lonely Proustian hero is waiting for his mother to kiss him goodnight. Barthes adds to this association in suggesting that this event took place on a November night (see CC, 99), when the lamp functions like a searchlight in the dark, whereas his (most likely) more factual account in the *Journal de deuil* indicates that he found the mother-as-child portrait on the summer morning of 13 June 1978 (see JD, 155). The *La Chambre claire* version, however, echoes the first scene in *À la recherche*, the *camera obscura*-like situation in which the hero projects mental images of the past in the dark bedroom.[17] If the *camera obscura* is the predecessor of photography, Proust's narrative can analogously be considered the precursor for Barthes's search.[18] However, in *La Chambre claire*, the lonely 'narrator' does not contemplate fleeting mental images like the Proustian hero, but rather photographic ones, and Barthes is not only waiting in vain for his mother to return to him that particular night, but every night since her death. This testifies to the inescapably melancholic tone of *La Chambre claire*, steeped in the recognition that even if he discovers the truth of the mother's face in the Winter Garden photograph, the image is a token of her irrevocable

---

17 Of course, a *camera obscura* does not actually involve capturing and preserving images. However, a number of critics have made this connection from the episode in the novel to photography, as well as cinema, including Cadava, who calls the room described at the beginning of *À la recherche* a 'dark room' and compares the narrator to a 'spectator in the dark projection hall of a cinema' (*Words of Light*, 76).

18 Katja Haustein has analysed the reversal of light-dark metaphors in Proust and Barthes ('"La Vie comme œuvre": Barthes with Proust', in Peter Collier, Anna Magdalena Elsner and Olga Smith (eds.), *Anamnesia. Private and Public Memory in Modern French Culture* (Oxford: Peter Lang, 2009), 175–91: 186–7).

absence.[19] The mental images of the Proustian hero, by contrast, and specifically those originating in involuntary memory, are those that bring the past back into present life – at least as the narrator of *À la recherche*, as opposed to its author, makes us believe (whereas in Barthes's text, the author and narrator are much more closely conjoined, if not completely identical).[20]

Even if the promise of the future success of his project, on the part of the Proustian hero-as-writer, is based upon fragile and uncertain memories that occur only involuntarily, the end of *À la recherche* optimistically looks forward to the writing of the work. Barthes's life, by contrast, since the death of his mother 'n'arrive pas à se constituer en *souvenir*' (JD, 247) ['has not managed to constitute itself as *memory*' (MD, 236)], and although Barthes makes reference to his own Proustian epiphany of a '*Vouloir-Écrire*' in *La Préparation du roman* (PR, 32), his planed autobiographical work, *Vita Nova*, remained unwritten.[21] However, rather than undermine or call into question the Proustian echoes and resonances in *La Chambre claire*, some no doubt intended, these important 'meta-level' differences between Barthes's book and his unwritten novel and Proust's *À la recherche* and his hero's projects allow them to be viewed and appreciated in a more nuanced fashion.

The Photographic Resurrection of the Mother

In *La Chambre claire*, Barthes refers to a number of photographs of his mother, some of which were reproduced in *Roland Barthes par Roland*

19 This is why, in turn, *La Chambre claire* has become a touchstone for subsequent discussion of the wider relation between photography and melancholy, death and mourning. See, for example, Prosser, *Light in the Dark Room*.

20 Clearly, even if one wishes to distinguish between 'Barthes' the narrator of *La Chambre claire* and Barthes the author, as some scholars have, this is nowhere near as pronounced as between the narrator, hero and author of *À la recherche*. See Olin, 'Touching Photographs', 99. For a more in-depth account of the 'rhetoric of subjectivity' in Barthes's book, see Johnnie Gratton, 'The Subject of Enunciation in Roland Barthes's *Camera Lucida*', in Diana Knight (ed.), *Critical Essays on Roland Barthes* (New York: G.K. Hall, 2000), 266–78: 269.

21 There has been much speculation on this planed project by Barthes, of which we only have some preliminary notes and outline drafts (see OC, 994–1001). For a discussion of this project, see Diana Knight, 'Vaines pensées: la *Vita Nova* de Barthes', *Revue des Sciences Humaines*, 268 (2002), 93–107.

Barthes from 1975. These include a holiday snapshot, depicting Henriette Barthes walking on the beach of Biscarosse in les Landes in the early 1930s, which was the frontispiece image of the photographic preface to Barthes's unconventional autobiography.

Barthes refers to this image in *La Chambre claire* in a way that sheds light on his evolved understanding of photography, especially in comparison with that found in the earlier *Roland Barthes par Roland Barthes*, a difference that seems inseparable from intervening events in his personal and professional life. The photographs in Barthes's autobiography are, by and large, seen to correspond with his fascination with a time predating his career as a published author, his 'vie productive' (OC, IV, 582) ['productive life' (RB, 4)], and the pleasure he takes in recalling that period. The personal photographs described or reproduced

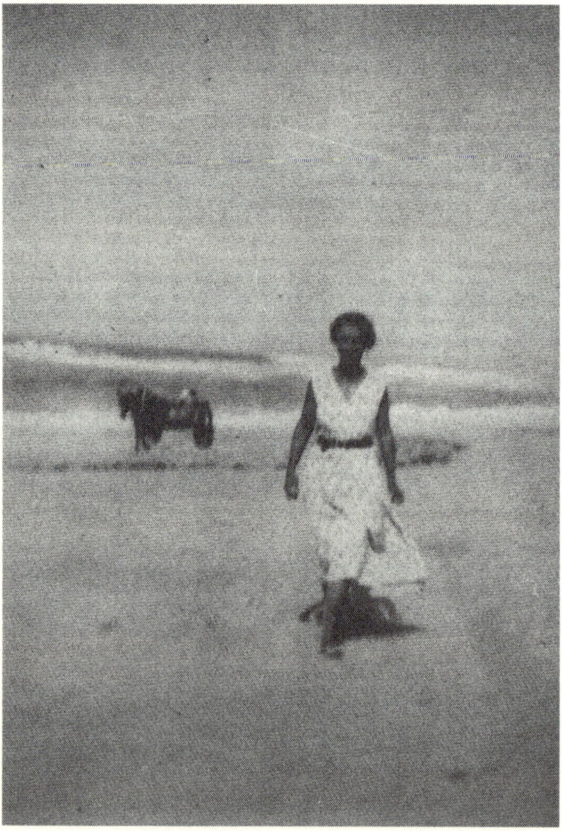

PLATE 14 Henriette Barthes on the beach of Biscarosse, South-West France, around 1932.

in *La Chambre claire* – the Winter Garden portrait and the *La Souche* photograph – are, by contrast, embedded in a dedicated phenomenology of photography that takes on the form of a personal search for the essence of his late mother from the standpoint of the present, and this self-observed last stage of his writing career.[22] The cataclysmic event of his mother's death fundamentally alters Barthes's response to the photograph of his mother on the beach. Although the image has obviously not changed, it now appears to be lacking something that was not felt with the same intensity before.

In *La Chambre claire*, Barthes stresses that his experience of the relative authenticity of every photograph of his mother is focused on her face. And he writes that even if he finds certain defining characteristics of her in the beach photograph, 'sa démarche, sa santé, son rayonnement' (CC, 100) ['her gait, her health, her glow' (CL, 63)], he does not find her face: 'mais non son visage' (CC, 100). In this instance, the fact that the image is out of focus, so that the mother's face is not wholly perceivable in a literal way (owing to her distance from the camera) – deficiencies that did not, however, prevent him from including the image in his autobiography before her death – now symbolically stands for the fact that neither in this image nor in others in which her face is directly and clearly visible does he 'find' it. That is, in the sense of recognizing its essence, a recognition or discovery Barthes associates with resurrection: 'aucune ne me paraissait vraiment "bonne": ni performance photographique, ni résurrection vive du visage aimé' (ibid.) ['none seemed to me really "right": neither as a photographic performance nor as a vivid resurrection of the beloved face' (CL, 64)]. Together with its Christian theological connotations, this striking recourse to the idea of resurrection in the context of photography resonates with Barthes's treatment of the alchemic and magical properties

22 For a concise juxtaposition of the photographs of the mother in both works, see Mounir Laouyen, 'L'Imago maternelle dans *Roland Barthes par Roland Barthes*', *Revue des Sciences Humaines*, 268 (2002), 129–41. Another pronounced difference between the two works is that the first one integrates the photographs of his mother in a series of private snapshots characteristic, as Kuhn has argued, of family albums (*Family Secrets*, 17). With respect to the Winter Garden portrait, this is clearly not the case, highlighting the unequalled status it has in Barthes's life story. From this perspective, *La Chambre claire* is also hardly only a sequel to *Roland Barthes par Roland Barthes*, as Herta Wolf has suggested ('Das, was ich sehe, ist gewesen. Zu Roland Barthes' *Die helle Kammer*', in Herta Wolf (ed.), *Paradigma Fotografie. Fotokritik am Ende des fotografischen Zeitalters* (Frankfurt a.M.: Suhrkamp, 2002), 89–107: 107).

of the photograph, which have been discussed in relation to what he regards as the physical-chemical immortalization of the photographed person via the indexical generation of the image. On this interpretation, the photograph thus preserves some physical aspect or trace of the subject ('mummifying' it, in Bazin's terms) in order that it may in some instances, and as a second step, lead to a figurative resurrection of the identity of the photographed person actualized in the viewer's affective experience of the image. This resurrection is also, however, a Proustian signpost.

Barthes's emphasis on the face as the privileged site of the manifestation of his mother's essence, which he finds only in the Winter Garden photograph, is in line with the Proustian hero's evocation of his grandmother's face, shortly after her death, and his subsequent recognition of her essence.[23] In *À la recherche*, this recognition is explicitly rooted in the involuntary memory of the hero. Yet, for Proust's protagonist an accidental memory leads to a more truthful realization of the lost and beloved being's essence, whereas in Barthes's case this insight is transferred from the memory-image to the photographic one. The key passage from the *Sodome et Gomorrhe* volume of *À la recherche* that Barthes turns to in this context is the famous 'Intermittences du cœur' ['Intermittences of the Heart'] episode. Having arrived in Balbec for the first time after his grandmother's death, the hero slowly bends down to take off his shoes and experiences a powerful involuntary memory that makes him fully realize the irrevocability of her death for the first time. This is the passage from the novel:

> Je venais d'apercevoir, dans ma mémoire, penché sur ma fatigue, le *visage* tendre, préoccupé et déçu de ma grand-mère, telle qu'elle avait été ce premier soir d'arrivée ; le *visage* de ma grand-mère, non pas de celle que je m'étais étonné et reproché de si peu regretter et qui n'avait d'elle que le nom, mais de ma grand-mère véritable dont, pour la première fois depuis les Champs-Élysées où elle avait eu son attaque, *je retrouvais dans un souvenir involontaire et complet la réalité vivante*. . . . Et ainsi, dans un désir fou de me précipiter dans ses bras, ce n'était qu'à l'instant . . . que je venais d'apprendre qu'elle était morte.[24]
>
> I had just perceived, in my memory, stooping over my fatigue, the tender, preoccupied, disappointed *face* of my grandmother, as she had been on that first evening of our arrival, the *face* not of that grandmother

23 Barthes, in a short text from 1966 on George Painter's Proust biography, expresses his incomprehension at the fact that Proust, in writing *À la recherche*, substitutes his actual mother's death with the fictional death of his grandmother (see OC, II, 811).

24 Proust, *À la recherche*, vol. 3, 153 (my emphasis).

> whom I had been astonished and remorseful at having so little missed, and who had nothing in common with her save her name, but of my real grandmother, of whom, for the first time since the afternoon of her stroke in the Champs-Elysées, *I now recaptured the living reality in a complete and involuntary recollection*. . . . And thus, in my wild desire to fling myself into her arms, it was only at that moment . . . that I became conscious that she was dead.[25]

In line with the proverbial notion that the face is the bodily manifestation of a human being's innermost essence, with the eyes being windows to the soul, both Proust in this passage and Barthes in *La Chambre claire* emphasize the face as the privileged locus for their epiphanic recognition. It is the face of the hero's grandmother that appears at the moment of involuntary remembrance and becomes the source for a sudden recognition of the lived reality as recreated in his mind. Likewise, in Barthes's book, it is the truth of the face in the Winter Garden photograph of his mother to which Barthes attaches utmost importance and which apparently determines its exceptional significance.

Apart from the literal differences between memory and photography that Barthes notes, as rooted in that lacuna between the creative imagination and the perception of the 'real', he nonetheless aligns the coincidental discovery of the Winter Garden photograph with Proustian memory by constructing a successive process of 'retrouver' and 'souvenir'. Barthes thus writes: 'J'observai la petite fille et je retrouvai enfin ma mère' (CC, 107) ['I observed the little girl and at last rediscovered my mother' (CL, 69)]. This unlikely rediscovery of the essence of the dead mother in her childhood face is perhaps even more Proustian than Barthes acknowledges. Following Marty's interpretation of these intertextual dynamics, whereas Proust creatively transforms the death of his actual mother in 1905 into the death of the hero's grandmother, Barthes, through the photograph, inversely transforms his predominant mental image of the mother from that of an ill, old woman to a young girl, imaginatively rejuvenating her in the literal sense of the word.[26]

Of course, the childhood photograph shows someone that Barthes could not possibly have known and thus 'recognized' as his mother, as

25 Proust, *In Search*, vol. 4, 180 (my emphasis).

26 Marty, *Roland Barthes, la littérature et le droit à la mort*, 45. In his *Journal de deuil*, Barthes quotes a passage from a 1907 article by Proust in which he compares the tears of the grandmother to the tears of a '*petite fille*' (JD, 199).

Anselm Haverkamp has noted.[27] Barthes acknowledges that the Winter Garden portrait is a photograph of the mother that 'ne lui ressemble pas, celle d'une enfant que je n'ai pas connue' (CC, 160) ['does not look like her, the photograph of a child I never knew' (CL, 103)]; it does not physically look like her as the adult he knew. This is again the paradox of photography, whereby in a medium of such mimetic fidelity, those portraits that most authentically resemble their subjects in a deeper sense of 'resemblance' – as truth to the lived being and experience of the person and their memory – are often not the most visually accurate or detailed likenesses. In this sense, at least, photographic portraiture and the painted portrait are alike. And yet, in this context, it is only the photographic image and its authenticating force, rooted in a particularly powerful coalescence of indexicality and iconicity, which make this unlikely 'recognition' beyond resemblance more surprising and more powerful. To put it in Benjamin's terms, the photograph has the power to make us 'remember something we have never seen before' to a greater degree than any other form of representation, as he suggests in his 'Rede über Proust' (see GS, II, 1064).

The rediscovery of his mother's irreducible being as reflected in her kindness, in turn triggers a sensation that Barthes aligns with an involuntary memory. He states:

> Pour une fois, la photographie me donnait un sentiment aussi sûr que le souvenir, tel que l'éprouva Proust, lorsque se baissant un jour pour se déchausser il aperçut brusquement dans sa mémoire le visage de sa grand-mère véritable, 'dont pour la première fois je retrouvais dans un souvenir involontaire et complet la réalité vivante'. (CC, 109)
>
> For once, photography gave me a sentiment as certain as remembrance, just as Proust experienced it one day when, leaning over to take off his boots, there suddenly came to him his grandmother's true face, 'whose living reality I now recaptured for the first time in a complete and involuntary recollection'. (CL, 70)

The hitherto dominant discourse on the 'anti-Proustian' nature of photography, reflected in the fact that other photographs of his mother did not bring back the beloved person, is suddenly ruptured, in a *punctum*-like gesture: the Winter Garden photograph has the power to offer him the same emotive reassurance of his mother's essence that the

27 See Anselm Haverkamp, 'The Memory of Pictures: Roland Barthes and Augustine on Photography', *Comparative Literature*, 45 (1993), 258–79: 271.

mémoire involontaire provides for the Proustian narrator in relation to his grandmother's identity.

The description of the discovery of the Winter Garden photograph in *La Chambre claire* is thus undoubtedly modelled on the pivotal 'Intermittences du cœur' scene in *À la recherche*, from which Barthes quotes. What is more, in the Proustian episode, the hero, after fully comprehending that his grandmother is irrevocably gone, looks at her portrait photograph in an attempt to reconcile himself with this reality, and notes that the woman in the image 'avait un air de condamnée à mort' ['had an air of being under sentence of death'].[28] The loss of the (grand-) mother is the most evident link between *À la recherche* and *La Chambre claire*, one that Barthes creatively exploits. But, although he shares this 'moment de souffrance' ['moment of suffering'], as Antoine Compagnon puts it,[29] with the protagonist of *À la recherche*, just like the Proustian hero, Barthes also insists on the 'originalité de ma souffrance' ['originality of my suffering'],[30] given his mother's uniqueness, 'ce qu'il y avait en elle d'absolument irréductible' (CC, 118) ['what was absolutely irreducible in her' (CL, 75)]. For the hero of the novel, the unique nature of his suffering was pitted against the temptation of using the photograph as a consolation, as he prefers to tolerate the pain of an intense involuntary memory rather than the false illusion of presence that the photograph evokes, as the former is at least seen to be an experience worthy of the depth of his grief. Barthes, however, uses the photograph of his mother as a vehicle to express his own suffering so as, from a wider perspective, to save her memory for posterity by writing about it in a way that also attempts to do justice to the external nature of the medium that has enabled his testament. In other words, Proust's redemption of lost time and death lies in his writing a literary work with all the expression

28 Proust, *À la recherche*, vol. 3, 176; *In Search*, vol. 4, 207. The mother of the narrator cannot bear to look at the photograph of the grandmother for this reason.

29 Compagnon, 'Proust et moi', 73.

30 Proust, *À la recherche*, vol. 3, 156; *In Search*, vol. 4, 184. Barthes directly quotes this expression (see CC, 118). In *La Chambre claire*, Proust serves Barthes as a model for expressing his suffering, whereas, in Barthes's last seminar on 'Proust et la photographie', the novelist's work is used to demonstrate an ecstatic 'intoxication' via photography (PR, 397). For a detailed discussion of this seminar, see Peter Geimer, '"Ich werde bei dieser Präsentation weitgehend abwesend sein." Roland Barthes am Nullpunkt der Fotografie', *Fotogeschichte*, 29 (2009), 21–30 and my 'Reading Through Photography'.

and metaphorical resources provided therein, and an in-built distance between author and narrator, whereas Barthes's is intricately embedded in an exploration of photography that is simultaneously a directly personal narrative. From this perspective, Barthes's failure to distinguish between Proust and his hero or narrator here, as Beryl Schlossman and others have pointed out,[31] is an indirect reflection of the autobiographical nature of his own photographic narrative. Some creative distortion of Barthes's actual experience (as evidenced by his diary) aside, in order to fulfil its apparent purpose, the narrative voice in *La Chambre claire* must be identified with the author's. In conceptual terms, the existential-phenomenological framework of Barthes's book, as centred on the concrete, conscious experience and perception of the 'I', provides a more abstract theoretical and methodological support for this strong identification.

Aside from the indirect link between the photograph of the grandmother in *À la recherche*, in which she appears condemned to a subsequently occurring death, and the portrait in *La Chambre claire* of Lewis Payne, who is literally sentenced to death,[32] it is remarkable that Barthes fails to mention the grandmother's portrait, and the hero's engagement with it, when referring to and actually quoting from the 'Intermittences du cœur' episode in a book on photography. Upon closer inspection of the associative and metaphorical significance of the central photograph in the novel, however, it perhaps becomes clear why Barthes refrains from drawing this parallel: the photograph in Proust's novel is essentially associated with sexual 'perversion'. As the last remark on the portrait of the grandmother in the penultimate volume of *À la recherche* reveals, the development of the photograph in the dark room served as a pretext for homosexual advances.[33] And although the dominant connotation of the photographic portrait in the 'Intermittences du cœur' scene is one of remorse and guilt on behalf of the hero – who learns only now that his grandmother had her picture taken not for reasons of vanity (as he believed at the time), but because she wanted her grandchild to have a picture of her once she is gone (as the hero finds out after her death)[34] – the

31 See Beryl Schlossman, 'The Descent of Orpheus. On Reading Barthes and Proust', in Jean-Michel Rabaté (ed.), *Writing the Image after Roland Barthes* (Philadelphia: University of Pennsylvania Press, 1997), 144–59: 154. See also Johnnie Gratton, 'Text, Image, Reference in Roland Barthes's *La Chambre claire*', *Modern Language Review*, 91 (1996), 355–64: 362.

32 For a more detailed analysis of this connection, see my 'Barthes et Proust: La *Recherche* comme aventure photographique', paragraphs 19–20.

33 See Proust, *À la recherche*, vol. 4, 259–60.

34 See ibid., vol. 3, 172–3.

image remains inseparably bound to the 'profanation' that accompanied its genesis. This leads Marty to suggest that 'tout le travail de Barthes va consister à protéger la Mère du risque de la perversion' ['Barthes's entire work will consist in protecting the Mother from the risk of perversion'].[35] Following Marty's implicit reasoning, Barthes's lack of reference to the grandmother's portrait is inescapably related to his homosexuality which, according to friends and acquaintances, Barthes wrestled with throughout his life. Reportedly of particular distress to Barthes was his feeling that he could never acknowledge it to his mother. Given what is known of Barthes's own views of his sexuality, and others' opinions as to how he presented it in his life and work, together with his relationship with his mother, this interpretation is not as speculative or excessively biographical as it might otherwise appear. And yet, it should also be acknowledged that there is a possible narrative and conceptual reason for this notable absence. Namely, as I have explicated, to the extent that Barthes wishes to associate the Winter Garden photograph with a truth about the loved one (just like that which Proust's hero identifies with the involuntary memory of the grandmother), citing the hero's belief that the photographic portrait is entirely antithetical to such a truth would certainly not have supported Barthes's account. This, then, is an alternative rationale, for the missing reference to the fictional photograph, quite apart from the desire to keep the memory of the mother 'unsullied' by sexual 'perversion', as Marty argues.

Setting this omission and the possible reasons for it aside, both the hero of *À la recherche* and the writer of *La Chambre claire*, through an involuntary memory and a photographic portrait, respectively, regain the lived reality of the past in the form of a 'vérité du visage' of the beloved yet irrevocably lost human being. Although Barthes's implicit recourse to the *mémoire involontaire* in this respect closely aligns the Winter Garden photograph to a story of positive redemption, as we shall see, the dominant theme in *La Chambre claire* and the episode in *À la recherche* is one of suffering. In fact, Compagnon has argued that the significance for Barthes of the 'Intermittences du cœur' episode is precisely the fact that it represents the pivotal scene of suffering within the novel.[36]

---

35 Marty, 'Proust dans "la chambre claire"', 132.

36 See Compagnon, 'Proust et moi', 72–3. The significance of 'Les intermittences du cœur' for Proust (he pondered whether this should be the title of his entire œuvre) differs, however, from Barthes's interpretation of it, as becomes clear in Compagnon's more detailed analysis of this passage in *Proust entre deux siècles* (Paris: Seuil, 1989), 143–52.

As Knight has suggested with reference to Barthes's 'creative explorations of maternal space', his description of the rediscovery of his mother through the photograph is linked to another, related scene of *À la recherche*,[37] which Proust at some stage planned to call 'Intermittences du cœur II'.[38] This is the scene at the end of the third volume in which the Proustian narrator 'resurrects' his dead grandmother by mistaking his mother for her in the early hours of dawn, when the lack of light in his bedroom in Balbec 'm'avait pendant une seconde empêché de la reconnaître et fait hésiter si je dormais ou si ma grand-mère était ressuscitée' ['had for a moment prevented me from recognizing her and had made me uncertain whether I was still asleep or my grandmother had come back to life'].[39] By way of this episode, the Proustian nature of the figurative resurrection of the mother via photography is further solidified.[40] But the metaphorical resurrection in Barthes's case is occasioned by a photograph's alchemical and magical presence rather than a perceptual illusion, a trick of light like a mirage, also associated with dreams, with which the grandmother's temporary return from the dead is associated. The more deliberate, wilful resurrection in *La Chambre claire* has as its enabling object a more solid, persistent reality in the photograph's perceptual facticity and a-temporal fixedness, again contrasting with the creative fluidity of memory, dream and, in this case, direct perceptual experience of the world.

Knight couples the Proustian scene not only with Barthes's remark on the luminosity of his mother's eyes, which ultimately guides him 'vers une identité essentielle, le génie du visage aimé' (CC, 105) ['toward an essential identity, the genius of the beloved face' (CL, 66)] – that is to the Winter Garden photograph – but also with the frontispiece of *La Chambre claire*. This originally blue-green colour photograph by Daniel Boudinet, a friend of Barthes who took some of the most accomplished portraits of him, is also the only colour photograph in the entire book and materializes, as Knight convincingly argues, the 'bleu-vert' of the mother's eyes (CC, 104).[41]

37 Knight, *Barthes and Utopia*, 259–69. Her thesis is that Barthes 'uses the Proustian grandmother as a symbolic mediator of his own creative explorations of maternal space' (259).

38 See Compagnon's editorial comments in Marcel Proust, *Sodome et Gomorrhe*, ed. Antoine Compagnon (Paris: Gallimard, 1989), 628.

39 Proust, *À la recherche*, vol. 3, 513; *In Search*, vol. 4, 613.

40 Cf. Lombardo's interpretation of the resurrection theme as opposed to Proustian memory, in *The Three Paradoxes of Roland Barthes*, 140.

41 See Knight, *Barthes and Utopia*, 266. Schlossman has similarly commented on this connection ('The Descent of Orpheus', 149).

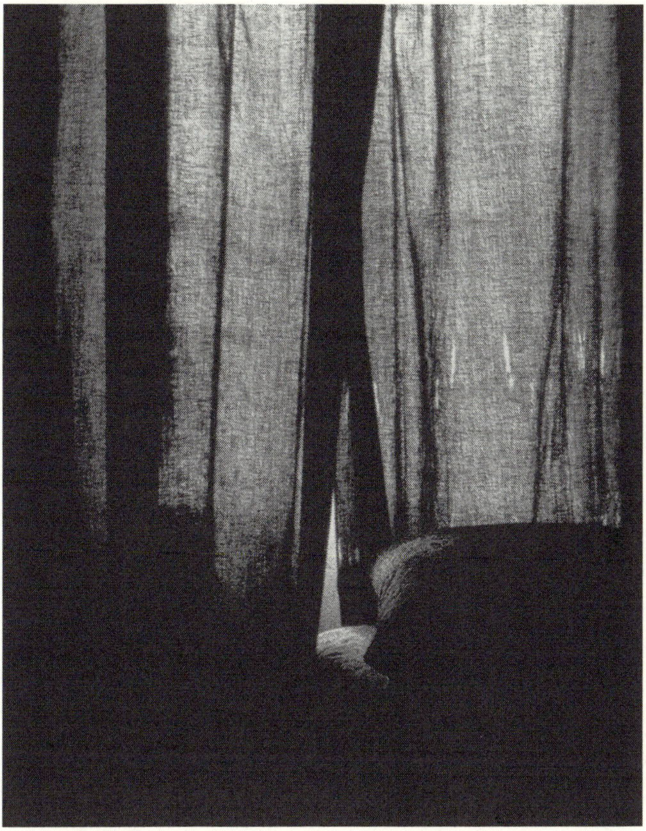

PLATE 15 Daniel Boudinet, *Polaroïd*, 1979 (original in colour).

The literary as well as photographic connection between the Proustian morning resurrection and the mother-as-child photograph, on the one hand, and the prominent position of Boudinet's *Polaroïd*, on the other, is significant. It suggests that Barthes's exploration of photography is placed under the transformative light of the resurrection scene in *Sodome et Gomorrhe*: 'la lumière du soleil qui allait se lever, en modifiant les choses' ['the light of approaching sunrise, modifying the appearance of things'].[42] But, the light that illuminates Barthes's encounter with his mother is in fact photographic, a trace of this light inscribed on sensitive paper. He thus places his own written search for his mother under the guiding star of photography. The Boudinet image can be seen as complexly related to the mother-as-child photograph in other ways. The latter's pivotal role as

42 Proust, *À la recherche*, vol. 3, 512; *In Search*, vol. 4, 612.

Barthes's Ariadne, his guide through the 'labyrinthe' created by 'toutes les photographies du monde' (CC, 114) ['all the world's photographs' (CL, 73)], is echoed in the title of the 1979 portfolio project by Boudinet, to which the *Polaroïd* is an addendum, *Fragments d'un labyrinth*.[43] Comprising a series of photographs of different shadowy views of the same interior of an apartment, this work is an exploration of the particular de-materializing quality of light as filtered through windows and curtains, in this context recalling the light-determined hallucination of the grandmother in *À la recherche* and the light-dependent, i.e. photographic, discovery and resurrection of the mother in Barthes's case.

In sum, for Barthes, as well as in the mirror of Proust, it is literally and metaphorically in the light of photography, endowed with magical powers, that the mother is resurrected, in a medium that arrests, preserves or transcends time: 'la Photographie a quelque chose à voir avec la résurrection' (CC, 129) ['the Photograph has something to do with resurrection' (CL, 82)], analogous to the time- and death-defying potential of the Proustian *mémoire involontaire*.[44] In reality, this resurrection is a saving of the mother's photograph and her memory from time and forgetfulness. In other words, the discourse on metaphorical resurrection with respect to photography transforms, within Barthes's narrative recounting of the photographic experience of singularity, into one of literal redemption, of 'preservation' in Benjamin's sense – not just of keeping, but of 'saving' in the midst of loss. Whereas for Benjamin this is both a personal and collective loss associated with the historically forgotten, which in turn resonates with Agamben's previously discussed thesis on the redemptive aspect of photography in the context of the apocalyptic end of history, for Barthes it is adamantly personal.[45]

43 See Christian Caujolle, Emmanuelle Decroux and Claude Vittiglio (eds.), *Daniel Boudinet* (exhibition catalogue) (Paris: Éditions La Manufacture, 1993), 108–15.

44 In *Le Temps retrouvé*, in particular, involuntary memory is associated with happiness, intellectual development, and an indifference towards time and death (as I argued earlier in relation to Benjamin). For instance, the narrator comments on an occurrence of an accidental memory: 'Comme au moment où je goûtais la madeleine, toute inquiétude sur l'avenir, tout doute intellectuel étaient dissipés' ['Just as, at the moment when I tasted the madeleine, all anxiety about the future, all intellectual doubts had disappeared'] (Proust, *À la recherche*, vol. 4, 445; *In Search*, vol. 6, 217).

45 See Agamben, *Profanations*, 27. Cf. Stiegler's account of 'resurrection' as a photographic metaphor (*Bilder der Photographie*, 27–31).

Delayed Recognition: *Punctum*, Memory and Redemption

As we have seen, the dialectical relation between a general theory of photography and the autobiographical engagement with selected photographs in the works of Benjamin and Barthes is linked to the problems and paradoxes of Proust's two types of memory. The overall function of Barthes's alignment of the Winter Garden photograph with *mémoire involontaire* is to provide a photographic afterlife for his mother through a Proustian narrative of singularity and redemption. With respect to photography more generally, however, involuntary memory is also structurally akin to Barthes's definition of the *punctum* in the first half of *La Chambre claire*. On this latter point, two aspects of the *punctum* as detail are of paramount importance: first, its metonymic power and second, its relation to latency. Barthes writes of the *punctum's* power of expansion with reference to metonymy: 'Si fulgurant qu'il soit, le *punctum* a, plus ou moins virtuellement, une force d'expansion. Cette force est souvent métonymique' (CC, 74) ['However lightning-like it may be, the *punctum* has, more-or-less potentially, a power of expansion. This power is often metonymic' (CL, 45)]. Indirectly, yet unambiguously, Barthes defines this power as Proustian. He illustrates his point with regard to another photograph by Kertész of a young boy leading a blind violinist across a gravelled road.

Barthes remarks somewhat enigmatically that the image calls on him to add something to it, and the *punctum* of the image identified with the gravel of the road is coupled with an evocation of his travels in Eastern Europe long before. With his 'whole body' he remembers 'les bourgades que j'ai traversées lors d'anciens voyages en Hongrie et en Roumanie' (CC, 77) ['the straggling villages I passed through on my long-ago travels in Hungary and Rumania' (CL, 45)]. Barthes clearly constructs the *punctum* here in dialogue with Proust's literary depictions of involuntary memory as the chance encounter with a seemingly insignificant object (such as the madeleine), whose properties trigger a remembrance of a past moment that, in turn, renders the coincidental discovery of the object highly significant and places it in the context of a life-narrative. The fact that Barthes stresses that his memorial experience is sensual and somatic, rather than intellectual, also resonates with Proust. The metonymic 'power of expansion' Barthes refers to is a matter of how a perceptual sensation of a small part of a larger whole can call to mind that whole in a way in which, in its affective power and spatio-temporal depth, the mental reality evoked far surpasses the initial, seemingly insignificant perceptual trigger. Proust, in fact, explaining the *mémoire involontaire* for the first time in

Du Côté de chez Swann [*Swann's Way*], uses exactly the same expression, namely 'la force d'expansion' that Barthes describes in *La Chambre claire* with regard to the *punctum* (without explicitly citing Proust).[46]

Barthes's description of his experience of the *punctum* of the Kertész photograph exemplifies what he describes as an anti-analytical attitude towards photography, with analysis pitted against memory in its truest and richest – i.e. involuntary – form: 'Pour percevoir le *punctum*, aucune analyse ne me serait donc utile (mais peut-être, on le verra, parfois, le souvenir)' (CC, 72) ['In order to perceive the *punctum*, no analysis would be of any use to me (but perhaps memory sometimes would, as we shall see)' (CL, 42–3)]. Analogous to Proust's conception of voluntary recollection of an event as diminishing its past experiential depth and vividness, as a consequence of the intellectual mediation that always accompanies wilful remembrance (thus leading to a shallow memory-image), the intellectual scrutiny of the photograph, which gives due consideration to each surface detail of the image, is seen to block access to its personal and subjective truth for the beholder. For Barthes, the knowledge arrived at through such active and instrumental analysis, guided by a rationally circumscribed purpose, is antithetical to the non-rational *punctum* and to its latency as associated with an unconscious and necessarily passive process. Just like the Proustian trigger for *mémoire involontaire*, as distinct from the subsequent contemplative and immersive experience it stimulates (which has a much more extended duration),[47] the *punctum*, as a momentary impression of a perceptual detail is neither conceptually mediated nor wilful.

As we have seen, in Benjamin's reading of Proust, latency is bound to the Freudian notion of memory-trace and the temporal delay

46 Proust, *À la recherche*, vol. 1, 46. Similarly, in *La Préparation du roman*, Barthes couples the Proustian madeleine with the 'extension' of a 'fleur japonaise dans l'eau' (PR, 74) ['Japanese flower in water' (PN, 39)]. For an interpretation that emphasizes the differences between Proust and Barthes in this respect, see Haustein, '"La Vie comme œuvre": Barthes with Proust', 185–6.

47 In *Du Côté de chez Swann*, the latency of involuntary memory is unequivocally expressed inasmuch as the tasting of the madeleine results in an unspecified sensation: 'Un plaisir délicieux m'avait envahi, isolé, sans la notion de sa cause' ['An exquisite pleasure had invaded my senses, something isolated, detached, with no suggestion of its origin'] followed, some paragraphs later, by a sudden realization: 'et tout d'un coup le souvenir m'est apparu' ['and suddenly the memory revealed itself'] (Proust, *À la recherche*, vol. 1, 44; 46; *In Search*, vol. 1, 51; 53).

inherent in trauma.[48] Unlike Freud, however, who draws an analogy between psychic latency and the gap between picture taking and the later development[49] – and also diverging from aspects of Benjamin's argument, rooted in the same analogy – Barthes clearly links latency to the act of photographic viewing and regards it as relating to the gap or delay between the initial stimulation of the *punctum*-detail and the more reflective, imagistic and affective recollection that may follow from it. In *La Chambre claire*, one specific photograph, a group portrait of an African-American family from 1926, taken by James van der Zee in his Harlem studio, serves Barthes as an example for this process at work.

Barthes notes that, for him, the *punctum* of this photograph is the belt and strapped shoes of the third person represented in the image (apart from the husband and wife), whom he refers to as either the daughter of the couple or a sister (see CC, 73). Despite the specificity of this attribution, Barthes writes that he does not know why either the belt or the shoes have such an effect upon him.

In a manifestation of the phenomenological double bind between the direct perceptual encounter with the photograph and the temporally/conceptually mediated and belated writing about it (that Marty has characterized as the Proustian double temporality of *La Chambre claire*),[50] some pages later Barthes suddenly returns to the same image and modifies his first association. He suggests that the photograph has subsequently 'travaillé en moi' (CC, 87) ['worked within me' (CL, 53)] and that he only now realizes that 'le vrai *punctum* était le collier qu'elle portrait au ras du cou' (CC, 87) ['the real *punctum* was the necklace she was wearing' (CL, 53)]. The 'work' in question, as triggered by the photograph, is the work of memory, which has belatedly found its true object in Barthes's recollection of his father's sister. He enthusiastically confirms that the necklace in the Van der Zee portrait reminds him of his aunt: '(sans doute) c'était ce même collier (mince cordon d'or

48 While trauma echoes Barthes's discussion of traumatic images in 'Le Message photographique', it is reasonable to assume that Lacan rather than Freud is the decisive influence on Barthes in relation to *La Chambre claire*. Cf. Iversen's psychoanalytic reading in relation to shock 'What Is a Photograph?', 453-6. There is, however, another reference point, namely Derrida's definition of 'supplément', which he, in turn, derives partly from Freud's notion of 'Nachträglichkeit' or delay ('Freud et la scène de l'écriture', in *L'Écriture et la différence* (Paris: Seuil, 1967), 293–340: 314).

49 See Freud, *Fragen der Gesellschaft*, 571.

50 See Marty, 'L'Assomption du phénomène', 745.

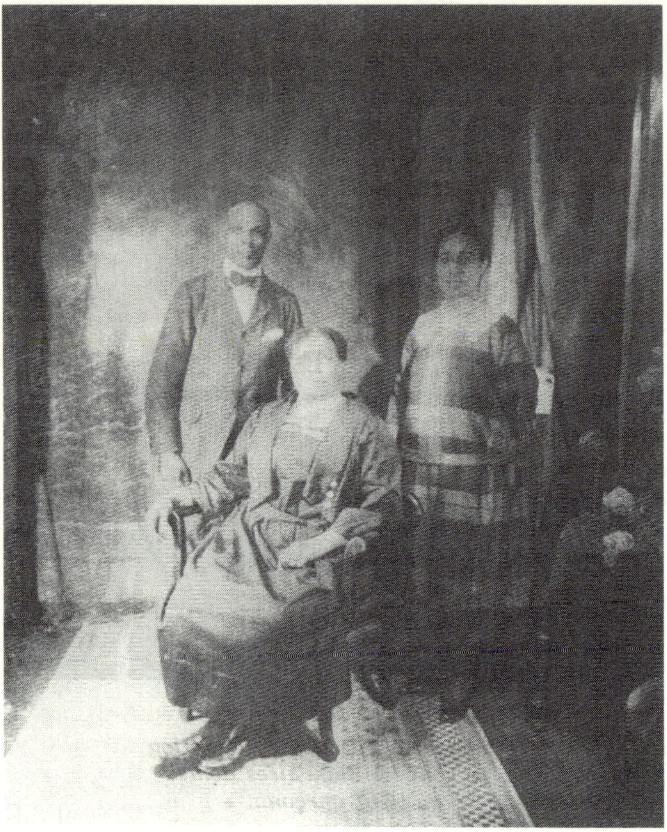

PLATE 16 James van der Zee, Family portrait, 1926.

tressé) que j'avais toujours vu porté par une personne de ma famille, et qui, elle une fois disparue, est resté enfermé dans une boîte familiale d'anciens bijoux' (CC, 87–8) ['(no doubt) it was this same necklace (a slender ribbon of braided gold) which I had always seen worn by someone in my own family, and which, once she died, remained shut up in a family box of old jewellery' (CL, 53)]. Olin has astutely observed that the Van der Zee photograph depicts a pearl necklace rather than a slender gold ribbon.[51] This 'mistaken detail', as Olin calls it,[52] leads her to consideration of another photograph, reproduced in *Roland Barthes par Roland Barthes*, where Barthes's grandparents and his aunt Alice

51 See Olin, 'Touching Photographs', 101–8.
52 Ibid., 106.

are posed in a manner strikingly reminiscent of the sitters in the Van der Zee photograph.

Although in this portrait the aunt is prominently wearing a necklace, it indeed is not the particular one that Barthes remembers as a consequence of seeing the Van der Zee portrait. He does not refer to the photograph of his aunt in *La Chambre claire*, perhaps with some notion that the very careful reader would make the relevant associative connection to this family portrait reproduced in his earlier autobiography.[53]

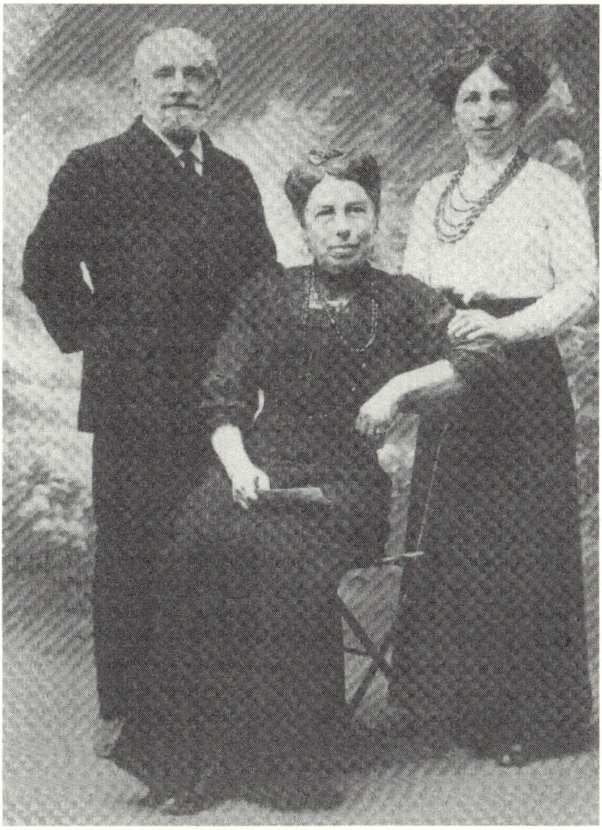

Plate 17 Léon and Berthe Barthes with their daughter Alice.

53 In relation to these two images, Olin has suggested that the most significant power of photography's indexicality in *La Chambre claire* is rooted in a 'performative index' that pertains to the identification between the viewer and the photograph, rather than between the image and the sitter (ibid., 114–15).

The photograph by Van der Zee is thus superimposed over Barthes's memory of his aunt, possibly by way of another photograph, recalling Benjamin's superimposition of the Kafka image with one or more self-portraits. The necklace is presented as the poignant detail of the photograph that possesses a latent metonymic power to the extent that it is capable of triggering an accidental memory in the perceiver that 'develops' into the entire life of his dead aunt, as emerging from this piece of jewellery: 'cette sœur de mon père ne s'était jamais mariée, avait vécu en vieille fille près de sa mère, et j'en avais toujours eu de la peine, pensant à la tristesse de sa vie provinciale' (CC, 88) ['this sister of my father never married, lived with her mother as an old maid, and I had always been saddened whenever I thought of her dreary life' (CL, 53)]. (This description of his aunt Alice also evokes Proust's aunt Léonie with whom this life story matches mutatis mutandis.)[54] As noted, both the *punctum* and the trigger of the *mémoire involontaire* provide the occasion for a spontaneous memory that is as unpredictable, unique and non-chronological as an individual's mental life and psychology.

All in all, then, Barthes's inter-textual referencing of Proust in *La Chambre claire* is two-fold in a way that is highly reminiscent of Benjamin's use of *À la recherche* in relation to photography. For both, most photographs, and even the medium as such, are seen as antithetical to 'Proustian', that is, involuntary, memory, with Benjamin and Barthes each citing 'anti-photographic' passages from *À la recherche* in support of this contention. At the same time, however, some privileged portrait photographs, owing to the nature of the experience they engender for the viewer (in relation to the sitter/referent) are directly and indirectly conjoined with the experience of a profound, involuntary memory as it is described in Proust's novel. Benjamin's view of photography as 'anti-Proustian' (expressed in his 'Über einige Motive bei Baudelaire'), however, evolves with time and is inescapably tied to a general, historical and cultural thesis concerning the nature of modernity and photography's role in the decline of *Erfahrung*. The latter is associated with a more authentic and profound type of experience, which modern urban, technical/instrumental life challenges, to the extent to which it severs one of the self's most powerful mental links to the past. This is a departure from the previous suggestion of a strong affinity between some portrait photographs and involuntary memory in Benjamin's earlier texts, and most notably with reference to his own mnemonic experience of the Kafka-as-child portrait

54 In a different context, Calvet has similarly compared Barthes's aunt Alice with Proust's (*Roland Barthes*, 30).

in the 1932 *Berliner Kindheit* (as well as the speech on Proust from the same year). In *La Chambre claire*, by contrast, Barthes's comments on the 'anti-Proustian' nature of the photograph exist alongside a clear alignment of *mémoire involontaire* with some selected photographs (those with a *punctum*) and, especially, with the Winter Garden portrait.

Yet, despite their similarity in this respect as in others, the distinction between the *punctum* and the experience of singularity focused on the viewer's relation to the represented other must be retained. For the rediscovery of the Winter Garden photograph and the recognition of the truth of the mother which it allows are not passive, non-mediated and unconscious *punctum*-responses, but instead the products of a deliberate search for the true memory and being of the loved one. Both involve the expansion of an authentic personal memory and are a matter of the unique relation between the viewer and the image – but photographic singularity needs to be searched for in order to be found. Although Barthes suggests that he did not expect to find the mother's essence in a photograph, the actual encounter is nonetheless hoped for, that is, mediated by the wilful empathy of his mourning for her. Singularity, in the terms that I have described it, is never accidental in the way the *punctum* is because it has only one potential object: the face of the loved one who is lost or dead, but is still powerfully present in the subject's consciousness. Whereas the *punctum*, by definition, (a) can be *any* detail of a photographic image; (b) is not always associated with loss and mortality; and (c) may be conjoined with the memory of otherwise long forgotten, seemingly trivial realities that only it calls to mind. While centred on the photographic image as a visual reality in-itself, the experience of singularity via the photograph (that is, of the singularity of the other) is dependent on its situational context in the conscious life of the viewer to a much greater extent, and in a much more profound way, than the *punctum* even at its most affecting.

The Winter Garden portrait is distinct from all other photographs, including all those *punctum*-images reproduced in *La Chambre claire* by virtue of their emotional effect on Barthes, because of its unequalled ability to elicit an emotive and existential certainty about the mother's absolute singularity in the context of her death and absence. In other words, it is not mainly the function of involuntary memory as described by Proust that differentiates the Winter Garden photograph from all others, since this is shared by the *punctum*-images. Rather, its Proustian source is the larger narrative context in which the hero of *À la recherche* has such experiences, namely, of loss, death and the hope for resurrection and redemption, which Barthes, in turn, equates with Proust's life-project as a writer, one with which Barthes so powerfully identified. More specifically (and as previously noted), the experience of singularity – the singularity of the other through photography – is for both Benjamin and Barthes necessarily connected to its narrative recounting within a larger historical-theoretical and autobiographical context. Given that the value of the unique winter-garden photographs is personal, in the strongest possible sense (and potentially emblematic of any individual's experience of uniquely meaningful photographs), it is crucially unstable and insecure by nature of the sort of event it constitutes. For singularity is occasioned only when the beholder of a given photograph experiences it; like Orpheus's glance at Eurydice that causes her to disappear into the shades of Hades, once the critic puts his or her finger on it, it escapes. In the case of Benjamin and Barthes, however, the ephemerality of the event of their experience of singularity occasioned by the encounter with the other in the winter-garden set photographs is bestowed with a lasting permanence through their writing on these images; in fact, the radical subjectivity and ephemerality of the experience requires this translation – if always only partial and incomplete – into a more objective and fixed form of language.

Thus, the redemptive and implicitly ethical dimension of Barthes's discourse on photography is foregrounded through the exceptional emotional effect of the Winter Garden photograph. For the singularity *he* experiences when viewing the portrait of the mother as a child transcends the mortifying characteristic that all other photographs have for him. And yet, implicitly, there is for every viewer and reader potentially one special portrait photograph of a loved one that is capable of initiating the same redemptive process. And this is, in turn, the most profound reason for the Winter Garden portrait's visual absence from *La Chambre claire*: Barthes knows and acknowledges that for anyone but himself (i.e. any reader and viewer), this portrait is necessarily but one more photograph, and not the absolute, privileged exception. Just as the Proustian hero is able to embark on his literary project by virtue of the time-defying nature of the *mémoire involontaire*, for Barthes, the Winter Garden photograph's alchemical preservation of his mother's essence allows for the Proustian narrative that communicates the most affectively and existentially profound potentials of photography.[55] While this photographic

55 See, by contrast, Schlossman's comparative analysis of Barthes and Proust, which aligns Orpheus's loss of Eurydice with Barthes's loss of his mother ('The Descent of Orpheus', 156-8).

resurrection is 'fugitive' (CC, 101), as Barthes acknowledges, the writing on the photograph that is *La Chambre claire* bestows it with a more permanent afterlife, saving what it represents against the 'écrasement du Temps' (CC, 150), despite the fact that this 'crushing of Time' is inherent in the nature of the photograph's temporality. In writing in this way, Barthes also gives voice and expression, testifies to, all other experiences of singularity on the part of other subjects in relation to their respective privileged and self-defining images, including Benjamin's encounter with the photographic other in the Kafka-as-child portrait that evokes his own Berlin childhood. In this way, the present study's attempt not only to read Barthes's theory of photography by way of Benjamin's, as its predecessor, but also to view Benjamin's engagement with photographic images from the perspective of Barthes's phenomenology comes full circle.

Postscript: Singularity and Photography in the Age of Digitization

Neither Benjamin's nor Barthes's writings contain a single, systematic theory of photography and, in many ways, they problematize the value and possibility of such a theory. Yet, due to the remarkable range of different aspects of the medium and its experience that each writer addresses in his work, and the often profound significance of what is revealed – as we have now traced – their explorations remain ubiquitous and vital reference points for any critical and theoretical consideration of photography in our contemporary digital-image environment: be it focused on the technical and cultural evolution of the medium, the photographic referent, indexicality, magic and photography, photography and memory or, above all else, the affective and existential dimensions of the experience of photographic images. These specific topics and themes represent key points of commonality and correspondence between Benjamin and Barthes. This is in addition to the critical, methodological and philosophical orientations (Marxist-informed social and cultural criticism and a general phenomenology) and inter-texts (most notably Proust's *À la recherche du temps perdu*) that they also share. Although numerous scholars have attempted to draw a clear line between (or even equate) each thinker's best known photographic concepts – aura, *air*, *punctum* and the optical unconscious – and although there are indeed numerous important affinities between them (recognition of which leads to a better understanding of each of them), as I have shown, these concepts nonetheless resist any direct, one-to-one analogy or equivalence. This is largely owing to the complex, sometimes ambiguous, embeddedness of these concepts in Benjamin's and Barthes's different intellectual projects, together with the divergent historical, cultural and intellectual climates within which each author lived and worked.

For these reasons, only a historically, textually and contextually informed 'close reading', offering a more holistic understanding of these key concepts and texts, of the sort I have attempted, allows the most significant points of similarities and differences between Benjamin and Barthes to fully emerge. Most notable among the similarities is the theme or concept of singularity, as related to the other represented in the portrait photograph. This has been shown to interpenetrate, often dialectically, all other aspects of Benjamin's and Barthes's engagement with photography, including the relation between the photographic image and processes of memory, perception and imagination; the relation between the past and present as embodied in, and conveyed by, the image; the loss of personal and collective experience and history to time and forgetting; and, finally, the recapturing and redemption of this experience. Moreover, those existential and ethical aspects of the photographic image and its potentials – which I have discussed and analysed under the paradoxically general heading of 'photographic singularity' – provide the matrix by which aspects of Benjamin's and Barthes's texts and ideas may be connected or reconnected in new and illuminating ways, some fairly direct, others circuitous, allusive and elusive.

Above all, it is in relation to the two childhood winter-garden portraits that, by virtue of a historical coincidence (or a series of many), are at the emotional and associative centre of both Benjamin's and Barthes's most personal – and arguably most enlightening – conceptions of photography, that the many facets and meanings of the theme of singularity are most visible. Each of these photographs, the portrait of Barthes's mother as a child and the portrait of Kafka as a child, appears and disappears and is merged with other photographic images, memories and anecdotes, while at the same time remaining dissociated from others and from photography in general. They are the Proustian core of Benjamin's and Barthes's photographic searches for a lost personal and collective past and for the essence of photography, a search that is not always manifest in the practical, artistic and political-ideological uses of the medium but remains a latent potential within them and within any consciously intended function of the photograph.

Furthermore, it is through their writing on these images that we can recognize the oft-overlooked subjective and personal dimensions to Benjamin's treatment of photography, on the one hand, and the objective and more collective implications of Barthes's, on the other. Benjamin's concerns with the broad sweep of historical and technological change and its effects on the human psyche (inevitably seen in relation to the coming storm of fascism and the Second World War, in which Benjamin was tragically caught up) are revealed to coexist with a poignant nostalgia for a lost Berlin childhood and a keen sensitivity to the small details of nineteenth-century images that convey the true identity and life-world of the sitter. By contrast, Barthes's in-mourning search for his lost mother in *La Chambre claire* is revealed to transcend the merely personal, selfish (in the sense in which grief and mourning is always selfish) and even 'solipsistic'[1] and expands to encompass not only the maternal other but

1 Elkins, *What Photography Is*, 7.

also other lives and times – those of Civil-War era America, Victorian England, the Harlem of the 1920s and late-twentieth-century war-torn Nicaragua – far removed from his own cloistered Parisian milieu. Photography alone brought him into contact with these worlds, to which he felt an emotional connection through images that spoke to him of more universal suffering, loss, hope and the desire to create. The winter-garden portraits, then, are the routes of exchange between the autobiographical, existential and cultural-historical strands of Benjamin's and Barthes's observations, all of which, ultimately, are tied to a recognition of the absolute singularity of the other, to evoke Derrida's expression, and the necessity to be true to, to respect and safeguard that singularity.

There is another important similarity, which I have noted but not discussed in depth: both Benjamin and Barthes de-emphasize the aesthetic with respect to photography, that is, the medium as a means of distinctly formal expression. This is surely not because either denies that photographs can possess great aesthetic value and significance, as, for instance, Benjamin's celebration of the artistry of certain mid-nineteenth-century portraits demonstrates. Rather it reflects just how central the singularity of the photographic encounter is to their analyses, as this is tied to the natural and emotional expressivity of the human face and body in the portrait, which inevitably transcends any created, artistic expression (portraiture being the traditionally least aesthetic or formalized genre of photography). The recognition and subsequent acknowledgement of the other is ultimately a matter of representation, rather than form – the presence of the signified rather than the self-consciously creative mediation of the signifier. Aesthetic or artistic contemplation, traditionally defined as always disinterested in important respects, tends to abstract the other – not to completely deny the ethical, but to suspend it via the mediation of style and form and the consciousness of the artist.[2] The so-called 'aesthetic attitude' with respect to the photograph is thus emphatically out of keeping with the profoundly direct relation between the viewer and the person depicted in the photograph that Benjamin and Barthes posit,

2 In these respects, the singularity of photography here discussed is fundamentally different from Attridge's notion of singularity, in spite of the fact that it shares some of its properties. The latter is first and foremost aesthetic and closely related to invention and alterity, which are viewed as 'lying at the heart of Western art as a practice and an institution' (*The Singularity of Literature*, 2). In fact, Attridge's important contribution to literary scholarship consists in the fertile introduction of such neglected concepts into its discourse.

albeit in different ways, a relation that precisely closes down, and makes impossible, the maintenance of an intellectual and aesthetic distance.

Just as the aesthetic in photography can never usurp the ethical and the existential for Benjamin and Barthes, so too, despite the fact that it is rooted in the photograph's material basis and genesis, the ontology of the photographic image is always secondary to the psychological and phenomenological effects of the photograph. These effects/affects are thus never reducible to the material, factual and objective.

Beyond Analogue Photography

Inherent reproducibility and indexicality are generally held to be the two defining features of photography as a form of visual representation. We have seen that the experience of photographic singularity is by and large uneffected by the image's multiplication through reproduction. This is owing to the fact that the referent inheres in the image no matter how many times it is reproduced, or which individual 'version' of it is experienced. What is more, in experiential terms, unlike a painting, there is no original artefact that is *the* photograph (with the exception, of course, of the daguerreotype and, later, the Polaroid). Any analogue photograph one encounters, including those that Benjamin and Barthes describe, is never a first-generation, originally registered image, as one does not (normally) view and frame the negative, but a positive print, a version. In the terminology of analytic philosophy, the photograph, like the text making up a novel, is a 'type' capable of being reproduced and yet remaining itself, whereas the painting or sculpture is instead a 'token' and one-of-a-kind as a physical object.

With respect to indexicality, the physical fact of the photograph's (past) causal relation to the person it pictures, is an essential aspect of its singularity as an encounter with the other, and it distinguishes this encounter from that occasioned by a portrait painting or drawing. From a contemporary, twenty-first-century perspective, this raises the question as to whether or not the advance of new photographic technologies and the emergence of digital photographic image production and manipulation in any way negate or historicize the notion of singularity that I have extrapolated from Benjamin's and Barthes's writings. On this subject, and by way of conclusion, I wish to argue that with respect to existential and ethical singularity, as in other ways, although firmly rooted in the practices, assumptions and axioms of analogue photography (the only form of photography that either Benjamin or Barthes was ever aware of), their views are not only still relevant but provide important guidance for any rounded consideration of digital photography. This is so by virtue of their generally phenomenological, viewer-based approach to the medium, which inherently counters any reductive technological determinism that seeks to equate the concrete experience of the photographic image with the actual or presumed facts of its creation in any simplistic, non-dialectical fashion.

With the digitization of visual representation from the late 1980s onwards, photography theorists began to conceptualize digital imaging in a predominantly production-oriented fashion that strongly emphasized the differences, rather than the similarities, between analogue and digital. Among these accounts, Mitchell's study *The Reconfigured Eye: Visual Truth in the Post-Photographic Era*, published in 1992, has become a major reference point. Mitchell heralds the advent of digital imaging as an opportunity to powerfully re-state anti-realist arguments, and to retrospectively 'expose' and 'deconstruct' the 'very ideas of photographic objectivity and closure' that had become orthodox in relation to analogue photography.[3] Playing on Barthes's idea of the adherence of the photographic referent, he contends that 'the referent has come unstuck'.[4] For Mitchell, the (apparently) stable relation between the photograph and its referent in analogue photography has become unstable, raising the question as to the truthfulness of the photographic image.

Continuing this line of argument, *if* digital photography, which at the present moment is photography in so many ways and for so many people, had no indexical, directly casual relation to the real (or one not-at-all comparable to analogue photography), and/or creates a situation where the viewer's belief in or sense of this relation is totally undermined, the singularity marking the experienced presence of the other in the image, and the demands the image is felt to make on the beholder – as epitomized in Benjamin's and Barthes's respective relationships with the winter-garden portrait – would truly be an 'experience of the past' (in more than one sense).

However, this is clearly not the case. From a technical and ontological standpoint, a photograph taken with a digital camera is still a registration of light, even if it is transformed into a digital code that does not rely on photo-chemical development in order for the image to be captured on the screen or paper and viewed. In the digital photograph, there is still always an indexical relation between the image and the depicted reality.

3 Mitchell, *The Reconfigured Eye*, 8.

4 Ibid., 31.

Whether it originates in a photo-chemical or in a photo-digital process, the *photo-graph*, in the etymological root of the word, is a photograph *only* if there is this inscribed trace of the object in the image, however much its appearance may be altered through pre- or post-picture taking manipulation. If this is lacking, the image is not a photograph at all, but some other form of representation – artistic or virtual (i.e. wholly computer-generated), for instance – which can only borrow a photographic style or language. The term 'photo-realism' applied to a painting or a computer image only has meaning in this stylistic context, and the use of the term acknowledges the actual photograph as the standard of visual realism.[5] Mitchell himself implicitly acknowledges this in often referring to the fundamental differences between photography and 'digital imaging', rather than between analogue and digital 'photography', as well as writing (as in his subtitle) of the 'post-photographic' era. But, while Mitchell's study has been prophetic in some ways, there is no sign that photography, as defined above, is in any sense over. [6]

As we have seen, for Barthes as well as for Benjamin – to an admittedly lesser degree, given his more substantial considerations of the stylistic features of mid-nineteenth-century portraiture and turn-of-the-century as well as early twentieth-century photography – issues of style, and form more generally, have only limited bearing on the deeper experiential dimensions of photographic portraits, as occurring in the imaginative and affective space between image and beholder. Rather than its indexicality per se, the digital capturing and manipulation of images changes, problematizes or produces greater awareness of the photograph's variable iconicity or verisimilitude, i.e. how features of the image do or do not correspond to the visual perception of what is represented (or of other photographs), with reference back to the situation in which the photograph was taken. What digital photography provides for in bypassing the chemical (and alchemical), but retaining the optical and (some) mechanical features of analogue photography, and transforming light into digital information

5 Computer-generated images, for instance, are being perfected in order to look more and more 'realistic', which means, as Lev Manovich points out, 'photo realistic' ('The Paradoxes of Digital Photography', in Liz Wells (ed.), *The Photography Reader* (New York and London: Routledge, 2003), 240–9: 246).

6 Manovich points out that even if we accept Mitchell's contention about the physical differences between analogue and digital photography, the concrete cultural uses of digital technologies problematize the (presumed) dichotomy. Focused on the question of realism, he suggests that the logic of the digital photograph is 'paradoxical', hinging simultaneously on continuities and discontinuities with the analogue photograph and its uses (ibid., 241–2).

rather than visual impressions, is a near-instantaneous relation between picture taking and viewing and an exponentially increased ability to manipulate the image in a variety of new ways. Undoubtedly, this leads to a much more fluid relation between photographer, represented object, image and viewer. While the psychological and ethical dimensions of these capacities and their uses in particular cases are highly significant, they are not necessarily determinative of the concrete experience of digital (or, indeed, pre-digital) photographic images in the non-realist ways that are often suggested and may, in fact, even work in the opposite direction.

And here we can remind ourselves that, certainly for Barthes, visual resemblance, while of course playing an important role in the revelatory, affective experiences of photographs of people that he describes, is not the essence of this experience, and may in fact diminish or challenge it. In relation to the photographic other, both Benjamin and Barthes draw attention to the beholder's active role in establishing a truth *beyond* the mere appearance of a person before the camera in some emphatically past moment in time: namely, a recognition of both his or her true nature, or some aspect of it, and the presence and value of that person for the beholder in the perpetual now of the photograph's concrete apprehension. This is first and foremost a truth for the self, an experiential rather than an objective relation, visual or otherwise, and as such the search for this truth proceeds through subjective acts of memory, identification and imagination to which the image is related, rather than an objective relation of perceptual likeness between the photographic image and the world.

Thus, turning from technical and ontological considerations to experiential ones, and to the role of knowledge, beliefs and the cultural and historical mediation in the viewing of photographs, Sarah Kember's discussion of the viewer's '*investments* in the photographic real' is illuminating.[7] Drawing on psychoanalytical thought, she rejects the technological determinism characteristic of Mitchell's approach and instead emphasizes epistemological issues raised by the advent of the digital manipulation of photographs and computer-generated images, as well as foregrounding the social and cultural embeddedness of photography and its necessary relation to human agency. Starting from the premise that a loss of the real has always been characteristic of the photographic image, or indeed of any mode of representation, Kember suggests that the shift

7 Sarah Kember, '"The Shadow of the Object": Photography and Realism', in Liz Wells (ed.), *The Photography Reader* (New York and London: Routledge, 2003), 202–17: 203.

from analogue to digital photography, triggering the viewer's 'increased awareness' of 'the constructedness of the real', actually results in what she calls a 're-fetishization of the photographic image-object as evidence'.[8] Kember turns to *La Chambre claire* in order to highlight the 'affective capacity of the photograph', and argues that 'we can *know* the impossibility of the real in representation (as Barthes clearly does), but we can nevertheless *feel* its presence'.[9] This acknowledgement of the discrepancy between knowing and feeling, which are both potentially at play in our experience of photographs – analogue or digital – testifies to a significant continuity rather than a break between the experience of analogue and digital photography, even if this continuation is neither straightforward nor teleological, and is perhaps even paradoxical, as theorists such as Lev Manovich and Martin Lister have repeatedly noted.[10]

These issues are undoubtedly too complex and far-reaching in their implications to be adequately discussed here.[11] However, given Hans Belting's view that theories or histories of photography have always primarily addressed image-production, that is, the optical-chemical or electronic process of the photograph's creation, at the expense of concrete viewing,[12] Benjamin's and Barthes's accounts of specific photographs, as well as the more general perceptual and imaginative dynamics that the apprehension of photographic images entails, allow us to rediscover the importance of photographic reception as a complex, variable and dialectical process that tends to resist any overtly homogenizing or reductive systematization.[13] This puts emphasis on the relativity and multivalence of the experiences of photographic representation as rooted

8 Ibid., 210.

9 Ibid., 212.

10 See Manovich, 'The Paradoxes of Digital Photography', and Martin Lister, 'Photography in the Age of Electronic Imaging', in Liz Wells (ed.), *Photography. A Critical Introduction* (New York and London: Routledge, 2004), 295–336.

11 For an account of the complex issues involved in relation to art photography alone, see the various articles in Hubertus von Amelunxen, et al. (eds.), *Photography after Photography. Memory and Representation in the Digital Age* (Munich: G + B Arts, 1996).

12 See Belting, *Bild-Anthropologie*, 41.

13 With respect to Barthes, Douglas R. Nickel argues that the 'emphasis on reception' challenges traditional assumptions of photographic criticism, from which he concludes that in the wake of *La Chambre claire*, 'a history of photography . . . might well be radically reoriented towards the vernacular' ('Roland Barthes and the Snapshot', *History of Photography*, 24 (2000), 232–5: 235).

not only in cultural and historical mediation and construction but also in the singular, lived subjectivity of the beholder. There are, undoubtedly, unconscious psychological mechanisms at work in this experience, including, perhaps, a fetishization of the photo-object, as Kember points out with respect to Barthes. Yet the phenomenological thrust of both Benjamin's and Barthes's writings on photography (even when countered or complemented by other methodologies and aims) foreground the existential and ethical dimension of their own, and others', fundamentally conscious and self-reflexive photographic experiences. Barthes's contention that a better understanding of the role of the photograph in the intellectual and emotional life of the individual subject requires moving beyond the realist versus constructivist debate with respect to the photographic image seems even more apt and powerful in a digital context. This would necessarily involve an acceptance of a high degree of subjective as well as cultural and historical relativity without, however, denying all of the ways in which the photographic medium is 'objectively' unique, powerful and affecting by its very nature.[14]

The singularity of photography in Benjamin's and Barthes's writings emerges in an experientially concrete, phenomenological context, which underscores and justifies the power of a certain belief, namely that when one engages with the image there is some necessary relation between the referent or photographed person, living in the moment when the picture was taken, and the image. And this image may, beyond this fact, prove to be a more or less authentic and 'true' reflection of this life. Ultimately, for Barthes, and also Benjamin, what secures this belief is not some abstract calculation, but the personal knowledge and experience of and with the photographic referent or sitter (Barthes's relationship with his mother), or a profound empathy with the person as a result of a shared culture or historical experience (Benjamin's relation to Kafka via a cultural, religious and artistic lineage). Both manifestations are a part of the relationship between viewer and sitter, as mediated by the photograph, rather than solely caused or determined by it.

The acknowledgement of the singularity of the other in the photograph hinges on the fact that the represented person is identifiable as the person that one knew at some past time, in a profound rather than superficial way,

14 Since the 1990s, there have been a number of historical studies on photography and related media that take vision and viewing as opposed to objective technological developments as their starting point. See, for example, Jonathan Crary, *Techniques of the Observer: On Vision and Modernity in the Nineteenth Century* (Cambridge, MA and London: MIT Press, 1990).

that is to say, not that this portrait is of the mother or Kafka, but that this portrait captures something of her or his being as the viewer remembers or imagines it. And this is, paradoxically, true even if the person does not physically resemble the one known to the beholder (both winter-garden photographs show children that neither Benjamin nor Barthes knew nor could have known). Moreover, as I have stressed, the truth for the self via the truth of the other, that Benjamin and Barthes experience in relation to the respective childhood photograph can only be expressed and communicated through writing, which makes these images and what they represent endure, redeeming them from time and forgetting, as a consequence of each author's fulfilment of the ethical obligation towards the other that the portrait photograph demands. The existential experience of singularity, then, is cast as a holistic and contextual one that is perhaps challenged in some respects by the perceptual ambiguity augured by digital photography, but certainly not overthrown, just as it is not a matter of the literally visual and imagistic alone but of narrative and description in language.

Finally, I have suggested how Benjamin's and Barthes's discussion of specific photographs, and the existential dynamics at work in the process of viewing them, also render the notion of any one, comprehensive theory of photography inherently problematic. Despite this, the two thinker's works provide a rich, endlessly surprising and provocative source of material for later theoretical accounts of photography, which take many different conceptual routes and arrive at many different conclusions. Indeed, their writings, and the inherent theme of singularity that runs through them, suggest that it is more appropriate to speak of theorie*s* or historie*s* of photography, whereby the necessary plural indicates the diversity of experiences that particular photographic images may trigger in different circumstances. From this perspective, the singularity of photography serves to highlight the potential ethical dimension of *any* engagement with photography, as the ethical is always a matter of coming to terms with the reality of relativity, plurality and difference in a way that not only tolerates but celebrates it.

Bibliography

Adams, Timothy Dow, *Light Writing and Life Writing: Photography in Autobiography* (Chapel Hill and London: University of North Carolina Press, 2000).

Adorno, Gretel and Walter Benjamin, *Briefwechsel 1930–1940*, eds. Christoph Gödde and Henri Lonitz (Frankfurt a.M.: Suhrkamp, 2005).

Adorno, Theodor W., *Über Walter Benjamin* (Frankfurt a.M.: Suhrkamp, 1970).

Agamben, Giorgio, *Profanations*, trans. Jeff Fort (New York: Zone Books, 2007).

Albers, Irene, 'Proust und die Kunst der Photographie', in Wolfram Nitsch and Rainer Zaiser (eds.), *Marcel Proust und die Künste* (Frankfurt a.M. and Leipzig: Insel-Verlag, 2004), 205–39.

Alphant, Marianne and Nathalie Léger (eds.), *R/B Roland Barthes* (exhibition catalogue) (Paris: Seuil/Centre Pompidou/IMEC, 2002).

Amelunxen, Hubertus von, 'D'un état mélancolique en photographie. Walter Benjamin et la conception de l'allégorie', *Revue des Sciences Humaines*, 81 (1988), 9–23.

——, 'Skiagraphia – Silberchlorid und schwarze Galle. Zur allegorischen Bestimmung des photographischen Bildes', in Willem van Reijn (ed.), *Allegorie und Melancholie* (Frankfurt a.M.: Suhrkamp, 1992), 90–108.

Amelunxen, Hubertus von et al. (eds.), *Photography after Photography. Memory and Representation in the Digital Age* (Munich: G + B Arts, 1996).

Andrew, Dudley, 'The Neglected Tradition of Phenomenology in Film Theory', in Bill Nichols (ed.), *Movies and Methods. An Anthology*, 2 vols. (Berkeley: University of California Press, 1985), vol. 2, 625–32.

Arnaud, Alain, *Pierre Klossowski* (Paris: Seuil, 1990).

Atget, une rétrospective (exhibition catalogue) (Paris: Bibliothèque Nationale de France, 2007).

Attridge, Derek, 'Innovation, Literature, Ethics: Relating to the Other', *PMLA*, 114 (1999), 20–31.

——, 'Roland Barthes's Obtuse, Sharp Meaning and the Responsibilities of Commentary', in Jean-Michel Rabaté (ed.), *Writing the Image after Roland Barthes* (Philadelphia: University of Pennsylvania Press, 1997), 77–89.

——, *The Singularity of Literature* (New York and London: Routledge, 2004).

Barthes, Roland, *Camera Lucida. Reflections on Photography*, trans. Richard Howard (London: Vintage, 2000).

——, *La Chambre claire. Note sur la photographie* (Paris: Cahiers du cinéma/ Gallimard/Seuil, 1980).

——, *The Eiffel Tower and Other Mythologies*, trans. Richard Howard (Berkeley and Los Angeles: University of California Press, 1997).

——, *Empire of Signs*, trans. Richard Howard (London: Jonathan Cape, 1983).

——, *The Grain of the Voice. Interviews 1962–1980*, trans. Linda Coverdale (London: Jonathan Cape, 1985).

——, *Le Grain de la voix. Entretiens 1962–1980* (Paris: Seuil, 1981).

——, *Image, Music, Text*, selected and trans. Stephen Heath (London: Fontana Press, 1977).

——, *Journal de deuil* (Paris: Seuil/IMEC, 2009).

——, *Le Lexique de l'auteur. Séminaire à l'École pratique des hautes études 1973–1974, suivi de fragments inédits du Roland Barthes par Roland Barthes*, ed. Anne Herschberg Pierrot (Paris: Seuil, 2010).

——, *Mythologies*, ed. Jacqueline Guittard (Paris: Seuil, 2010).

——, *Mythologies*, selected and trans. Annette Lavers (New York: Hill and Wang, 1994).

——, *Mourning Diary*, trans. Richard Howard (New York: Hill and Wang, 2010).

——, *Le Neutre. Cours au Collège de France (1977–1978)*, ed. Thomas Clerc (Paris: Seuil/IMEC, 2002).

——, *Œuvres complètes*, 5 vols., ed. Éric Marty (Paris: Seuil, 2002).

——, *La Préparation du roman I et II. Cours et séminaires au Collège de France (1978–1979 et 1979–1980)*, ed. Nathalie Léger (Paris: Seuil/IMEC, 2003).

——, *The Preparation of the Novel. Lecture Courses and Seminars at the Collège de France (1978–1979 and 1979–1980)*, trans. Kate Briggs (New York: Columbia University Press, 2011).

——, *Roland Barthes by Roland Barthes*, trans. Richard Howard (Basingstoke: Macmillan, 1977).

——, *Roland Barthes par Roland Barthes* (Paris: Seuil, 1975).

Batchen, Geoffrey, '*Camera Lucida*: Another Little History of Photography', in Robin Kelsey and Blake Stimson (eds.), *The Meaning of Photography* (Williamstown, MA: Sterling and Francine Clark Art Institute, 2008), 76–91.

——, 'Dreams of Ordinary Life. Cartes-de-visite and the Bourgeois Imagination', in Martha Langford (ed.), *Image and Imagination* (Québec: McGill-Queen's University Press, 2005), 63–74.

——, 'Palinode. An Introduction to *Photography Degree Zero*', in Geoffrey Batchen (ed.), *Photography Degree Zero. Reflections on Roland Barthes's Camera Lucida* (Cambridge, MA: MIT Press, 2009), 3–30.

Baudelaire, Charles, *Écrits sur l'art*, ed. Francis Moulinat (Paris: Le Livre de poche, 1992).

——, *Les Fleurs du mal*, ed. Jaques Dupont (Paris: Flammarion, 1991).

Baudrillard, Jean, *L'Échange symbolique et la mort* (Paris: Gallimard, 1976).

Bazin, André, 'Ontologie de l'image photographique', in *Qu'est-ce que le cinéma?* (Paris: Éditions du Cerf, 1999), 9–17.

Belting, Hans, *Bild-Anthropologie. Entwürfe für eine Bildwissenschaft* (Munich: Fink, 2001).

Benjamin, Walter, 'Les Analphabètes de l'avenir', trans. Maurice de Gandillac, *Le Nouvel Observateur, Spécial Photo*, 2 (1977), 7–20.

——, *The Arcades Project*, trans. Howard Eiland and Kevin McLaughlin (Cambridge, MA and London: Belknap/Harvard University Press, 1999).

——, *Aussichten. Illustrierte Aufsätze*, (Frankfurt a.M.: Insel-Verlag/Suhrkamp, 1977).

——, *Gesammelte Briefe*, 6 vols., eds. Christoph Gödde and Henri Lonitz (Frankfurt a.M.: Suhrkamp, 1997).

——, *Gesammelte Schriften*, 7 vols., eds. Rolf Tiedemann and Hermann Schweppenhäuser, with the collaboration of Theodor W. Adorno and Gershom Scholem (Frankfurt a.M.: Suhrkamp, 1972–1989).

——, *Gesammelte Schriften. Supplemente*, 3 vols., eds. Rolf Tiedemann and Hella Tiedemann-Bartels (Frankfurt a.M.: Suhrkamp, 1999).

——, *Das Kunstwerk im Zeitalter seiner technischen Reproduzierbarkeit und weitere Dokumente*, ed. Detlev Schöttker (Frankfurt a.M.: Suhrkamp, 2007).

——, *Œuvres*, 2 vols., trans. Maurice de Gandillac et al. (Paris: Denoël, 1971).

——, *Œuvres choisies*, trans. Maurice de Gandillac (Paris: Julliard, 1959).

——, *Origin of German Tragic Drama*, trans. John Osborne (London: Verso, 2003).

——, 'Petite histoire de la photographie', trans. André Gunthert, *Études photographiques*, 1 (1996), 7–38.

——, *Selected Writings*, 4 vols., eds. Michael Jennings et al. (Cambridge, MA and London: Belknap/Harvard University Press, 1996–2003).

Berg, Ronald, *Die Ikone des Realen. Zur Bestimmung der Photographie im Werk von Talbot, Benjamin und Barthes* (Munich: Fink, 2001).

Bittel, Johannes, *Proust–Benjamin, Benjamin–Proust: Traum, Rausch, Erwachen* (Frankfurt a.M.: Verlag Neue Wissenschaft, 2001).

Blanchot, Maurice, *L'Espace littéraire* (Paris: Gallimard, 1955).

Bloom, Harold, *The Anxiety of Influence. A Theory of Poetry* (New York and Oxford: Oxford University Press, 1997).

Boehm, Gottfried, *Wie Bilder Sinn erzeugen. Die Macht des Zeigens* (Berlin: Berlin University Press, 2007).

Bolz, Norbert, 'Der Fotoapparat der Erkenntins', *Fotogeschichte*, 32 (1989), 21–7.

Bossert, Helmuth and Heinrich Guttmann, *Aus der Frühzeit der Photographie, 1840–70. Ein Bildbuch nach 200 Originalen* (Frankfurt a.M.: Societäts-Verlag, 1930).

Bourdieu, Pierre (ed.), *Un Art moyen. Essai sur les usages sociaux de la photographie* (Paris: Éditions de Minuit, 1965).

Bowie, Malcolm, 'Barthes on Proust', *Yale Journal of Criticism*, 14 (2001), 513–18.

Brassaï, *Marcel Proust sous l'emprise de la photographie* (Paris: Gallimard, 1997).

Brodersen, Momme, *Spinne im eigenen Netz. Walter Benjamin: Leben und Werk* (Bühl-Moos: Elster Verlag, 1990).

Brown, Andrew, *Roland Barthes. The Figures of Writing* (Oxford: Oxford University Press, 1992).

Buck-Morss, Susan, *The Origin of Negative Dialectics. Theodor W. Adorno, Walter Benjamin, and the Frankfurt Institute* (New York: Free Press, 1977).

Burgin, Victor (ed.), *Thinking Photography* (London: Macmillan, 1982).

Busch, Bernd, *Belichtete Welt. Eine Wahrnehmungsgeschichte der Fotografie* (Munich and Vienna: Carl Hanser, 1989).

Cadava, Eduardo, *Words of Light: Theses on the Photography of History* (Princeton: Princeton University Press, 1997).

Cadava, Eduardo and Paola Cortés-Rocca, 'Notes on Love and Photography', in Geoffrey Batchen (ed.), *Photography Degree Zero. Reflections on Roland Barthes's Camera Lucida* (Cambridge, MA: MIT Press, 2009), 105–39.

Calvet, Louis-Jean, *Roland Barthes. 1915–1980* (Paris: Flammarion, 1990).

Caujolle, Christian, Emmanuelle Decroux and Claude Vittiglio (eds.), *Daniel Boudinet* (exhibition catalogue) (Paris: Éditions La Manufacture, 1993).

Chevrier, Jean-François, *Proust et la photographie. Avec des photographies de Pierre de Fenoyl et Holger Trülzsch* (Paris: Éditions de l'Étoile, 1982).

Chevrier, Jean-François and Jean Thibaudeau, 'Une inquiétante étrangeté', *Le Nouvel Observateur, Spécial Photo*, 3 (1978), 5–14.

Collier, Peter, 'Roland Barthes: The Critical Subject (an Idea for Research)', *Paragraph*, 11 (1988), 175–80.

Compagnon, Antoine, *Les Antimodernes. De Joseph de Maistre à Roland Barthes* (Paris: Gallimard, 2005).

——, 'L'Objectif déconcerté', *La Recherche photographique*, 'Roland Barthes, une aventure avec la photographie', 12 (1992), 73–7.

——, *Proust entre deux siècles* (Paris: Seuil, 1989).

——, 'Proust et moi', in Mary Donaldson-Evans et al. (eds.), *Autobiography, Historiography, Rhetoric: Essays in Honour of Frank Paul Bowman* (Amsterdam: Rodopi, 1994), 59–73.

Compagnon, Antoine (ed.), *Prétexte Roland Barthes* (Paris: Union Générale d'Éditions, 1978).

Coquio, Catherine, 'Roland Barthes et Walter Benjamin: image, tautologie, dialectique', in Catherine Coquio and Régis Salado (eds.), *Barthes après Barthes. Une Actualité en questions* (Pau: Publications de l'Université de Pau, 1993), 195–208.

——, 'Walter Benjamin et Roland Barthes', in Klaus Garber and Ludger Rehm (eds.), *Global Benjamin*, 3 vols. (Munich: Fink, 1999), vol. 2, 1147–66.

Costello, Diarmuid, 'Aura, Face, Photography: Re-Reading Benjamin Today', in Andrew Benjamin (ed.), *Walter Benjamin and Art* (London and New York: Continuum, 2005), 164–84.

Cozea, Angela, 'Proustian Aesthetics: Photography, Engraving, Historiography', *Comparative Literature*, 45 (1993), 209–29.

Crary, Jonathan, *Techniques of the Observer: On Vision and Modernity in the Nineteenth Century* (Cambridge, MA and London: MIT Press, 1990).

Critique, 25 (1969).

Damisch, Hubert, 'Five Notes for a Phenomenology of the Photographic Image', in Alan Trachtenberg (ed.), *Classic Essays on Photography* (New Haven: Leete's Island Books, 1980), 287–90.

——, 'L'Intraitable', *Critique*, 38 (1982), 681–7.

——, 'La "Prise de langue" et le "faire signe"', in Antoine Compagnon (ed.), *Prétexte Roland Barthes* (Paris: Union Générale d'Éditions, 1978), 394–406.

Dant, Tim and Graeme Gilloch, 'Pictures of the Past: Benjamin and Barthes on Photography and History', *European Journal of Cultural Studies*, 5 (2002), 5–23.

Dauthendey, Max, *Der Geist meines Vaters. Aufzeichnungen aus einem begrabenen Jahrhundert* (Munich: Albert Langen, 1912).

Delord, Jean, *Roland Barthes et la photographie* (Paris: Créatis, 1981).

Derrida, Jacques, *Chaque fois unique, la fin du monde*, eds. Pascale-Anne Brault and Michael Naas (Paris: Galilée, 2003).

——, *Copy, Archive, Signature. A Conversation on Photography*, trans. Jeff Ford, ed. Gerhard Richter (Stanford: Stanford University Press, 2010).

——, 'The Deaths of Roland Barthes', in *The Work of Mourning*, ed. Pascale-Anne Brault and Michael Naas (Chicago: University of Chicago Press, 2001), 34–67.

——, 'La Double séance', in *La Dissémination* (Paris: Seuil, 1972), 199–317.

——, 'Freud et la scène de l'écriture', in *L'Écriture et la différence* (Paris: Seuil, 1967), 293–340.

——, 'Les Morts de Roland Barthes', *Poétique*, 47 (1981), 269–92.

Didi-Huberman, Georges, *Ce que nous voyons, ce qui nous regarde* (Paris: Éditions de Minuit, 1992).

——, *Images malgré tout* (Paris: Éditions de Minuit, 2003).

——, *Invention de l'hysterie. Charcot et l'iconographie photographique de la Salpêtrière* (Paris: Macula, 1982).

——, *Phasmes. Essais sur l'apparition* (Paris: Éditions de Minuit, 1998).

Downing, Eric, *After Images. Photography, Archaeology, and Psychoanalysis and the Tradition of Bildung* (Detroit: Wayne State University Press, 2006).

Draaisma, Douwe, *Metaphors of Memory. A History of Ideas about the Mind*, trans. Paul Vincent (Cambridge: Cambridge University Press, 2000).

Dubois, Philippe, *L'Acte photographique* (Paris: Nathan, 1983).

Duttlinger, Carolin, 'Imaginary Encounters: Walter Benjamin and the Aura of Photography', *Poetics Today*, 29 (2008), 79–101.

——, *Kafka and Photography* (Oxford: Oxford University Press, 2007).

Duve, Thierry de, 'Time Exposure and Snapshot. The Photograph as Paradox', in James Elkins (ed.), *Photography Theory* (New York and London: Routledge, 2007), 109–23.

Eco, Umberto, 'Critique of the Image', in Victor Burgin (ed.), *Thinking Photography* (London: Macmillan, 1982), 32–8.

Eisenstein, Sergei M., 'The Montage of Film Attractions', in *Selected Works*, 4 vols., trans. and ed. Richard Taylor (London: BFI Publishing, 1988), vol. 1, 39–58.

Elkins, James, *The Object Stares Back. On the Nature of Seeing* (San Diego: Harcourt, 1996).

——, 'What do We Want Photography to Be? A Response to Michael Fried', in Geoffrey Batchen (ed.), *Photography Degree Zero. Reflections on Roland Barthes's Camera Lucida* (Cambridge, MA: MIT Press, 2009), 171–85.

——, *What Photography Is* (New York and London: Routledge, 2011).

Elkins, James (ed.), *Photography Theory* (New York and London: Routledge, 2007).

Ette, Ottmar, *Roland Barthes. Eine intellektuelle Biographie* (Frankfurt a.M.: Suhrkamp, 1998).

Europe, 35 (1957).

The Family of Man (exhibition catalogue) (New York: The Museum of Modern Art, 1955).

Farge, Arlette, 'Le Temps logé en la photographie. À partir de Barthes et de Kracauer', *Intermédialités/Intermedialities*, 7 (2006), 205–13.

Ferguson, Jeanine, *Developing Clichés: Walter Benjamin and Roland Barthes at the Limits of Photographic Theory*, PhD University of Minnesota, 1997.

Ffrench, Patrick, *The Time of Theory. A History of Tel Quel (1969–1983)* (Oxford: Clarendon Press, 1995).
Finkelde, Dominik, *Benjamin liest Proust: Mimesislehre, Sprachtheorie, Poetologie* (Munich: Fink, 2003).
Flusser, Vilém, *Towards a Philosophy of Photography*, trans. Anthony Mathews (London: Reaktion, 2000).
Fotogeschichte, 'Barthes' Bilder: Roland Barthes und die Fotografie', 29 (2009).
Foucault, Michel, 'La Peinture photogénique', in *Dits et écrits 1954–1988* (Paris: Gallimard, 1994), vol. 2, 707–15.
Freud, Sigmund, 'Beyond the Pleasure Principle', in *On Metapsychology and the Theory of Psychoanalysis* (The Pelican Freud Library, vol. 11) trans. and ed. James Strachey (Harmondsworth: Penguin, 1982), 269–338.
——, 'Entwurf einer Psychologie', in *Aus den Anfängen der Psychoanalyse. Briefe an Wilhelm Fliess, Abhandlungen und Notizen aus den Jahren 1887–1902*, eds. Marie Bonaparte, Anna Freud and Ernst Kris (London: Imago Publishing, 1950), 371–466.
——, *Fragen der Gesellschaft/Ursprünge der Religion* (Studienausgabe, vol. 9) (Frankfurt a.M.: Fischer, 1975).
——, *Psychologie des Unbewußten* (Studienausgabe, vol. 3) (Frankfurt a.M.: Fischer, 1975).
Freund, Gisèle, *Photographie et société* (Paris: Seuil, 1974).
Fried, Michael, *Why Photography Matters as Art as Never Before* (New York and London: Yale University Press, 2008).
Fuld, Werner, 'Die Aura. Zur Geschichte eines Begriffs bei Benjamin', *Akzente*, 3 (1979), 352–70.
Garnier, Marie-D. (ed.), *Jardins d'hiver. Littérature et photographie* (Paris: Presses de l'École Normale Supérieure, 1997).
Geimer, Peter, '"Ich werde bei dieser Präsentation weitgehend abwesend sein." Roland Barthes am Nullpunkt der Fotografie', *Fotogeschichte*, 29 (2009), 21–30.
——, *Theorien der Fotografie. Zur Einführung* (Hamburg: Junius, 2009).
Gerber, Margarethe, 'Die Kinderbuchsammlung Walter Benjamins', in *Bucklicht Männlein und Engel der Geschichte. Walter Benjamin, Theoretiker der Moderne* (exhibition catalogue) (Giessen: Anabas-Verlag, 1990), 84–91.
Gratton, Johnnie, 'The Subject of Enunciation in Roland Barthes's *Camera Lucida*', in Diana Knight (ed.), *Critical Essays on Roland Barthes* (New York: G.K. Hall, 2000), 266–78.
——, 'Text, Image, Reference in Roland Barthes's *La Chambre claire*', *Modern Language Review*, 91 (1996), 355–64.
Greffrath, Krista R., 'Proust et Benjamin', in Heinz Wismann (ed.), *Walter Benjamin et Paris* (Paris: Cerf, 1986), 113–31.
Grojnowski, Daniel, 'Walter Benjamin, les auras de l'aura', *Critique*, 659 (2002), 287–302.
Guittard, Jacqueline, 'Impressions photographiques: les *Mythologies* de Roland Barthes', *Littérature*, 143 (2006), 114–34.
——, 'Jardin d'hiver: formation d'une relique', *Revue des Sciences Humaines*, 278 (2005), 147–61.
Gumbrecht, Hans Ulrich and Michael Marrinan (eds.), *Mapping Benjamin: The Work of Art in the Digital Age* (Stanford: Stanford University Press, 2003).

Gunthert, André, 'Archéologie de la "Petite histoire de la photographie"', *Images re-vues*, 2 (2010) <http://www.imagesrevues.org/292> (accessed 25 May 2011).

——, 'Le Complexe de Gradiva. Théorie de la photographie, deuil et résurrection', *Études photographiques*, 2 (1997), 115–28.

——, 'Le Temps retrouvé. Walter Benjamin et la photographie', in Marie-D. Garnier (ed.), *Jardins d'hiver. Littérature et photographie* (Paris: Presses de l'École Normale Supérieure, 1997), 43–54.

Habermas, Jürgen, 'Bewußtmachende oder rettende Kritik – die Aktualität Walter Benjamins', in Siegfried Unseld (ed.), *Zur Aktualität Walter Benjamins. Aus Anlaß des 80. Geburtstags von Walter Benjamin* (Frankfurt a.M.: Suhrkamp, 1972), 173–223.

Hamacher, Werner, 'The Word *Wolke* – If It Is One', in Rainer Nägele (ed.), *Benjamin's Ground. New Readings of Walter Benjamin* (Detroit: Wayne State University Press, 1988), 147–76.

Hamilton, Peter and Roger Hargreaves, *The Beautiful and the Damned. The Creation of Identity in Nineteenth Century Photography* (exhibition catalogue) (Aldershot: Lund Humphries, 2001).

Hanney, Roxanne, 'Proust and Negative Plates: Photography and the Photographic Process in *A la Recherche du Temps Perdu*', *Romanic Review*, 74 (1983), 342–54.

Hansen, Miriam, 'Benjamin, Cinema and Experience: The Blue Flower in the Land of Technology', *New German Critique*, 40 (1987), 179–224.

Haustein, Katja, '"La Vie comme œuvre": Barthes with Proust', in Peter Collier, Anna Magdalena Elsner and Olga Smith (eds.), *Anamnesia. Private and Public Memory in Modern French Culture* (Oxford: Peter Lang, 2009), 175–91.

Haverkamp, Anselm, 'The Memory of Pictures: Roland Barthes and Augustine on Photography', *Comparative Literature*, 45 (1993), 258–79.

Hirsch, Marianne, *Family Frames: Photography, Narrative, and Postmemory* (Cambridge, MA and London: Harvard University Press, 1997).

Hollier, Denis (ed.), *Le Collège de Sociologie (1937–1939)* (Paris: Gallimard, 1979).

Hollington, Michael, 'Benjamin, Fourier, Barthes', *Journal of the Australasian Universities Language and Literature Association*, 81 (1994), 33–53.

Ivernel, Philippe, 'Paris capital du Front populaire ou la vie posthume du XIXe siècle', in Heinz Wismann (ed.), *Walter Benjamin et Paris* (Paris: Cerf, 1986), 249–72.

Iversen, Margaret, 'What Is a Photograph?', *Art History*, 17 (1994), 450–63.

Jay, Martin, *Downcast Eyes: The Denigration of Vision in Twentieth-Century French Thought* (Berkeley: University of California Press, 1993).

Jefferson, Ann, 'Roland Barthes: Photography and the Other of Writing', *Journal of the Institute of Romance Studies*, 1 (1992), 293–307.

Kahn, Robert, *Images, Passages: Marcel Proust et Walter Benjamin* (Paris: Éditions Kimé, 1998).

Kember, Sarah, '"The Shadow of the Object": Photography and Realism', in Liz Wells (ed.), *The Photography Reader* (New York and London: Routledge, 2003), 202–17.

Kemp, Wolfgang (ed.), *Theorie der Fotografie*, 3 vols. (Munich: Schirmer/Mosel, 1979–1983).

Kim, Young-Ok, *Selbstporträt im Text des Anderen. Walter Benjamins Kafka-Lektüre* (Frankfurt a.M.: Peter Lang, 1995).

Klossowski, Pierre, 'Lettre sur Walter Benjamin', *Mercure de France*, 1067 (1952), 456–7.

Knight, Diana, *Barthes and Utopia. Space, Travel, Writing* (Oxford: Clarendon Press, 1997).

——, 'Roland Barthes in Harmony: The Writing of Utopia', *Paragraph*, 11 (1988), 127–42.

——, 'Roland Barthes, or The Woman Without a Shadow', in Jean-Michel Rabaté (ed.), *Writing the Image after Roland Barthes* (Philadelphia: University of Pennsylvania Press, 1997), 132–43.

——, 'Vaines pensées: la *Vita Nova* de Barthes', *Revue des Sciences Humaines*, 268 (2002), 93–107.

Kofman, Sarah, *Camera obscura, de l'idéologie* (Paris: Éditions Galilée, 1973).

Kracauer, Siegfried, *Das Ornament der Masse. Essays* (Frankfurt a.M.: Suhrkamp, 1963).

——, *Theory of Film. The Redemption of Physical Reality* (Princeton: Princeton University Press, 1997).

Krauss, Rolf H., *Walter Benjamin und der neue Blick auf die Photographie* (Ostfildern: Cantz, 1998).

Krauss, Rosalind, E., *The Optical Unconscious* (Cambridge, MA and London: MIT Press, 1993).

Kriebel, Sabine T., 'Theories of Photography. A Short History', in James Elkins (ed.), *Photography Theory* (New York and London: Routledge, 2007), 3–49.

Kritzman, Lawrence D., 'Barthes's Way: *Un Amour de Proust*', *Yale Journal of Criticism*, 14 (2001), 535–43.

Kuhn, Annette, *Family Secrets. Acts of Memory and Imagination* (London and New York: Verso, 1995).

Landy, Joshua, 'Proust, The Narrator and the Importance of the Distinction', *Poetics Today*, 25 (2004), 91–135.

Lang, Tilman, *Mimetisches oder semiologisches Vermögen? Studien zu Walter Benjamins Begriff der Mimesis* (Göttingen: Vandenhoeck & Ruprecht, 1998).

Langer, Daniela, *Wie man wird, was man schreibt. Sprache, Subjekt und Autobiographie bei Nietzsche und Barthes* (Munich: Fink, 2005).

Laouyen, Mounir, 'L'Imago maternelle dans *Roland Barthes par Roland Barthes*', *Revue des Sciences Humaines*, 268 (2002), 129–41.

Lebrave, Jean-Louis, 'La Genèse de *La Chambre claire*', Genesis, 19, 'Roland Barthes' (2002), 79–107.

Lenman, Robin (ed.), *The Oxford Companion to the Photograph* (Oxford: Oxford University Press, 2005).

Les Lettres nouvelles, 11 (1954).

Levinas, Emmanuel, *Dieu, la mort et le temps*, ed. Jacques Rolland (Paris: Grasset, 1993).

Lier, Henri Van, *Philosophie de la Photographie* (Paris and Bruxelles: Les Impressions Nouvelles, 1983).

Lindner, Burkhardt, 'Benjamins Aurakonzeption: Anthropologie und Technik, Bild und Text', in Uwe Steiner (ed.), *Walter Benjamin (1892–1940) zum 100. Geburtstag* (Frankfurt a.M.: Peter Lang, 1992), 217–48.

Lindner, Burkhardt (ed.), *Benjamin-Handbuch. Leben, Werk, Wirkung* (Stuttgart and Weimar: Metzler, 2006).

Link, Jürgen and Ursula Link-Heer, 'Synchronische Diachronie. Von Benjamins "Kleiner Rede über Proust" zu den Aphorismen "Über den Begriff der Geschichte"', in Harald Hillgärtner and Thomas Küpper (eds.), *Medien und Ästhetik. Festschrift für Burkhardt Lindner* (Bielefeld: Transcript Verlag, 2003), 16–33.

Link-Heer, Ursula, 'Aura hysterica oder das Blick-Aufschlagen des Objekts', *Kaleidoskopien*, 1 (1996), 78–87.

——, *Benjamin liest Proust*, (Cologne: Private Print of the German Proust Society, 1997).

Lister, Martin, 'Photography in the Age of Electronic Imaging', in Liz Wells (ed.), *Photography. A Critical Introduction* (New York and London: Routledge, 2004), 295–336.

Lombardo, Patrizia, 'Le Leurre d'une recherche', *La Recherche photographique*, 'Roland Barthes, une aventure avec la photographie', 12 (1992), 53–7.

——, *The Three Paradoxes of Roland Barthes* (Athens and London: University of Georgia Press, 1989).

MacCabe, Colin, 'Barthes and Bazin: The Ontology of the Image', in Jean-Michel Rabaté (ed.), *Writing the Image after Roland Barthes* (Philadelphia: University of Pennsylvania Press, 1997), 71–6.

Macé, Marielle, 'Barthes Romanesque', in Alexandre Gefen and Marielle Macé (eds.), *Barthes, au lieu du roman* (Paris: Desjonquères – Nota Bene, 2002), 173–94.

——, '"C'est ça!" Expérience esthétique et pensée de l'effet, à propos de Barthes' (2008) <http://www.fabula.org/atelier.php?C%27est_%26ccedil%3Ba> (accessed 25 May 2011).

Mallarmé, Stéphane, *Œuvres complètes*, 2 vols., ed. Bertrand Marchal (Paris: Gallimard/Bibliothèque de la Pléiade, 2003).

Malraux, André, *Le Musée imaginaire* (Paris: Gallimard, 1965).

Manovich, Lev, 'The Paradoxes of Digital Photography', in Liz Wells (ed.), *The Photography Reader* (New York and London: Routledge, 2003), 240–9.

Marder, Elissa, 'Flat Death: Snapshots of History', *Diacritics*, 22 (1992), 128–44.

——, 'Nothing to Say: Fragments on the Mother in the Age of Mechanical Reproduction', *L'Ésprit Créateur*, 40 (2000), 25–35.

Marty, Éric, 'L'Assomption du phénomène', *Critique*, 38 (1982), 744–52.

——, 'Marcel Proust dans "la chambre claire"', *L'Esprit Créateur*, 46 (2006), 125–33.

——, *Roland Barthes, la littérature et le droit à la mort* (Paris: Seuil, 2010).

Megay, Joyce, *Bergson et Proust. Essai de mise au point de la question de l'influence de Bergson sur Proust* (Paris: Vrin, 1976).

Menke, Bettine, *Sprachfiguren: Name, Allegorie, Bild nach Walter Benjamin* (Munich: Fink, 1991).

Menninghaus, Winfried, *Walter Benjamins Theorie der Sprachmagie* (Frankfurt a.M.: Suhrkamp, 1995).

Mèredieu, Florence de, 'La Photographie et la critique photographique: Benjamin, Barthes et la question du référent', in Jean-Marc Lachaud (ed.), *Présence(s) de Walter Benjamin* (Bordeaux: Université Michel de Montaigne, 1994), 11–24.

Merleau-Ponty, Maurice, 'What Is Phenomenology?', in *The Essential Writings of Merleau-Ponty*, ed. Alden L. Fisher (New York: Harcourt, Brace and World, 1969), 27–43.

Milner, Jean-Claude, *Le Pas philosophique de Roland Barthes* (Lagrasse: Verdier, 2003).

Mitchell, Erin, 'Writing Photography: The Grandmother in *Remembrance of Things Past*, the Mother in *Camera Lucida*, and Especially, the Mother in *The Lover*', *Studies in Twentieth-Century Literature*, 24 (2000), 325–39.

Mitchell, William J. T., *Picture Theory: Essays on Verbal and Visual Representation* (Chicago and London: University of Chicago Press, 1994).

——, *The Reconfigured Eye: Visual Truth in the Post-Photographic Era* (Cambridge, MA and London: MIT Press, 1992).

Moholy-Nagy, László, 'A New Instrument of Vision', in Liz Wells (ed.), *The Photography Reader* (London and New York: Routledge, 2003), 92–5.

——, *Painting, Photography, Film*, trans. Janet Seligman (London: Lund Humphries, 1969).

Molderings, Herbert, *Die Moderne der Fotografie* (Hamburg: Philo Fine Arts, 2008).

Monnoyer, Jean-Maurice, *Le Peintre et son démon. Entretiens avec Pierre Klossowski* (Paris: Flammarion, 1985).

Moriarty, Michael, *Roland Barthes* (Stanford: Stanford University Press, 1991).

Münster, Arno, '"Eingedenken" – "mémoire pure" und "mémoire involontaire". Walter Benjamin im philosophisch-literarischen Spannungsfeld zwischen Henri Bergson und Marcel Proust', in Klaus Garber and Ludger Rehm (eds.), *Global Benjamin*, 3 vols. (Munich: Fink, 1999), vol. 2, 1135–46.

Nadar, *Quand j'étais photographe* (Paris: L'École des Lettres/Seuil, 1994).

Nancy, Jean-Luc, *Le Regard du portrait* (Paris: Éditions Galilée, 2000).

Newhall, Beaumont, *The History of Photography* (New York: The Museum of Modern Art, 1982).

Nickel, Douglas R., 'Roland Barthes and the Snapshot', *History of Photography*, 24 (2000), 232–5.

Nitsche, Jessica, *Walter Benjamins Gebrauch der Fotografie* (Berlin: Kulturverlag Kadmos, 2010).

Le Nouvel Observateur, *Spécial Photo*, 2 (1977).

Olin, Margaret, 'Touching Photographs: Roland Barthes's "Mistaken' Identification"', *Representations*, 80 (2002), 99–118.

Opitz, Michael and Erdmut Wizisla (eds.), *Benjamins Begriffe*, 2 vols. (Frankfurt a.M.: Suhrkamp, 2000).

Orlik, Emil, 'Über Photographie', in *Kleine Aufsätze* (Berlin: Propyläen-Verlag, 1924), 32–42.

Ortel, Philippe, '*La Chambre claire* ou le refus de l'art', *Les Cahiers de la photographie*, 'Roland Barthes et la photo: le pire des signes' (Paris: Contrejour, 1990), 32–9.

Pauleit, Winfried, *Filmstandbilder. Passagen zwischen Kunst und Kino* (Frankfurt a.M. and Basel: Stroemfeld Verlag, 2004).

Phillips, Christopher, 'The Judgment Seat of Photography', in Annette Michelson et al. (eds.), *October. The First Decade, 1976–1986* (Cambridge, MA: MIT Press, 1987), 257–93.

Poster, Mark, *Existential Marxism in Postwar France. From Sartre to Althusser* (Princeton: Princeton University Press, 1975).

Price, Mary, *The Photograph. A Strange Confined Space* (Stanford: Stanford University Press, 1994).

Prosser, Jay, *Light in the Dark Room. Photography and Loss* (Minneapolis: University of Minnesota Press, 2005).

Proust, Marcel, *À la recherche du temps perdu*, 4 vols., ed. Jean-Yves Tadié (Paris: Gallimard/Bibliothèque de la Pléiade, 1987–1989).

——, *Jean Santeuil*, ed. Pierre Clarac (Paris: Gallimard/Bibliothèque de la Pléiade, 1971).

——, *In Search of Lost Time*, 6 vols., trans. Scott Moncrieff and Terence Kilmartin, revis. D. J. Enright (London: Vintage, 1996).

——, *Sodome et Gomorrhe*, ed. Antoine Compagnon (Paris: Gallimard, 1989).

Raoux, Nathalie, 'Walter Benjamin, Gisèle Freund, Germaine Krull et Hélène Léger. Deutschland–Frankreich; Mann–Weib. Eine Folge von Briefen', *Revue Germanique Internationale*, 5 (1996), 223–53.

Recht, Camille, *Die Alte Photographie* (Paris and Leipzig: Henri Jonquières, 1931).

Recki, Birgit, *Aura und Autonomie. Zur Subjektivität der Kunst bei Walter Benjamin und Theodor W. Adorno* (Würzburg: Königshausen & Neumann, 1988).

Richter, Gerhard, 'Acts of Self-Portraiture: Benjamin's Confessional and Literary Writings', in David S. Ferris (ed.), *The Cambridge Companion to Walter Benjamin* (Cambridge: Cambridge University Press, 2004), 221–37.

——, *Walter Benjamin and the Corpus of Autobiography* (Detroit: Wayne State University Press, 2000).

Ritchin, Fred, *In Our Own Image. The Coming Revolution in Photography: How Computer Technology is Changing Our View of the World* (New York: Aperture, 1990).

Roger, Philippe, *Roland Barthes, roman* (Paris: Bernard Grasset, 1986).

Röttger-Denker, Gabriele, *Roland Barthes zur Einführung* (Hamburg: Junius, 1989).

Rugg, Linda Haverty, *Picturing Ourselves: Photography and Autobiography* (Chicago and London: University of Chicago Press, 1997).

Rupp, Gerhard, 'Benjamin und Bataille. Deutsch-französische Kreuzungen auf der Suche nach einem anderen Diskurs', in Klaus Garber and Ludger Rehm (eds.), *Global Benjamin*, 3 vols. (Munich: Fink, 1999), vol. 2, 827–38.

Saint Marc, Stéphanie de, *Nadar* (Paris: Gallimard, 2010).

Sander, August, *Sehen, Beobachten und Denken* (Munich: Schirmer/Mosel, 2009).

Sartre, Jean-Paul, *L'Imaginaire. Psychologie phénoménologique de l'imagination* (Paris: Gallimard, 2005).

——, *The Imaginary. A Phenomenological Psychology of the Imagination*, trans. Jonathan Webber (London and New York: Routlegde, 2006).

Schaeffer, Jean-Marie, *L'Image précaire. Du dispositif photographique* (Paris: Seuil, 1987).

Scharf, Aaron, *Art and Photography* (Harmondsworth: Penguin, 1974).

Schlossman, Beryl, 'The Descent of Orpheus. On Reading Barthes and Proust', in Jean-Michel Rabaté (ed.), *Writing the Image after Roland Barthes* (Philadelphia: University of Pennsylvania Press, 1997), 144–59.

——, 'Looking Back: Luminous Shadows and the Auras of History', *Nottingham French Studies*, 36 (1997), 76–87.

Scholem, Gershom, *Walter Benjamin und sein Engel. Vierzehn Aufsätze und kleine Beiträge*, ed. Rolf Tiedemann (Frankfurt a.M.: Suhrkamp, 1983).

Schöttker, Detlev, 'Benjamin liest Wittgenstein. Zur sprachphilosophischen Vorgeschichte des Positivismusstreits', in Daniel Weidner and Sigrid Weigel (eds.), *Benjamin-Studien 1* (Munich: Fink, 2008), 91–105.

——, 'Benjamins Bilderwelten. Objekte, Theorien, Wirkungen', in Detlev Schöttker (ed.), *Schrift Bilder Denken. Walter Benjamin und die Künste* (Frankfurt a.M.: Suhrkamp, 2004), 10–29.

——, 'Dolf Sternberger und Walter Benjamin. Ein Photographie-Aufsatz und seine Folgen', *Sinn und Form*, 62 (2010), 437–53.

——, *Konstruktiver Fragmentarismus: Form und Rezeption der Schriften Walter Benjamins* (Frankfurt a.M.: Suhrkamp, 1999).

Schöttker, Detlev (ed.), *Schrift Bilder Denken. Walter Benjamin und die Künste* (Frankfurt a.M.: Suhrkamp, 2004).

Schwarz, Heinrich, *David Octavius Hill. Der Meister der Photographie* (Leipzig: Insel-Verlag, 1931).

Sekula, Allan, 'On the Invention of Photographic Meaning', in Victor Burgin (ed.), *Thinking Photography* (London: Macmillan, 1982), 84–109.

——, 'The Traffic in Photographs', *Art Journal*, 41 (1981), 15–25.

Shawcross, Nancy, 'The Filter of Culture and the Culture of Death. How Barthes and Boltanski Play the Mythologies of the Photograph', in Jean-Michel Rabaté (ed.), *Writing the Image after Roland Barthes* (Philadelphia: University of Pennsylvania Press, 1997), 59–70.

——, *Roland Barthes on Photography. A Critical Tradition in Perspective* (Gainsville: University Press of Florida, 1997).

Simmel, Georg, 'Die Großstädte und das Geistesleben', in *Aufsätze und Abhandlungen 1901–1908*, 2 vols. (Frankfurt a.M.: Suhrkamp, 1995), vol. 1, 116–31.

Snyder, Joel, 'Picturing Vision', *Critical Inquiry*, 6 (1980), 499–526.

Sontag, Susan, *On Photography* (New York: Dell Publishing, 1977).

——, *Regarding the Pain of Others* (London: Penguin, 2003).

——, 'Remembering Barthes', in *Under the Sign of Saturn* (New York: Picador, 2002), 167–77.

Stamelman, Richard, *Lost Beyond Telling. Representations of Death and Absence in Modern French Poetry* (Ithaca: Cornell University Press, 1990).

Stevenson, Sara, *Hill and Adamson's The Fishermen and Women of the Firth of Forth* (Edinburgh: National Galleries of Scotland, 1991).

Stiegler, Bernd, *Bilder der Photographie. Ein Album photographischer Metaphern* (Frankfurt a.M.: Suhrkamp, 2006).

——, 'Medienphilosophie der Photographie', in Mike Sandbothe and Ludwig Nagl (eds.), *Systematische Medienphilosophie* (Berlin: Akademie Verlag, 2005), 253–71.

——, *Theoriegeschichte der Photographie* (Munich: Fink, 2006).

Stoessel, Marleen, *Aura. Das vergessene Menschliche. Zu Sprache und Erfahrung bei Walter Benjamin* (Munich: Carl Hanser, 1983).

Stoichita, Victor I., *The Pygmalion Effect. From Ovid to Hitchcock*, trans. Alison Anderson (Chicago: University of Chicago Press, 2008).

Stüssi, Anna, *Erinnerung an die Zukunft. Walter Benjamins 'Berliner Kindheit um Neunzehnhundert'* (Göttingen: Vandenhoeck & Ruprecht, 1977).

Surya, Michel, *Georges Bataille, la mort à l'œuvre* (Paris: Gallimard, 1992).

Szondi, Peter, 'Hoffnung im Vergangenen. Über Walter Benjamin', in *Schriften II* (Frankfurt a.M.: Suhrkamp, 1978), 275–94.

Talbot, William Henry Fox, *The Pencil of Nature* (New York: Da Capo Press, 1969).

Tagg, John, *The Burden of Representation. Essays on Photographies and Histories* (Basingstoke and London: Macmillan Education, 1988).

——, *The Disciplinary Frame: Photographic Truths and the Capture of Meaning* (Minneapolis: University of Minnesota Press, 2009).

——, 'Evidence, Truth and Order. Photographic Records and the Growth of the State', in Liz Wells (ed.), *The Photography Reader* (London and New York: Routledge, 2003), 257–60.

Taminiaux, Pierre, *The Paradox of Photography* (Amsterdam and New York: Rodopi, 2009).

Teschke, Henning, *Proust und Benjamin. Unwillkürliche Erinnerung und dialektisches Bild* (Würzburg: Königshausen & Neumann, 2000).

Thobo-Carlsen, John, 'Barthes Meets Benjamin? A Relating of their Views on the Conjunction between Language and Literature', *Orbis Litterarum*, 53 (1998), 1–41.

Thomas, Chantal, 'La Photo du jardin d'hiver', *Critique*, 38 (1982), 797–804.

Tiedemann, Rolf, Christoph Gödde and Henri Lonitz (eds.), *Walter Benjamin 1892–1940* (exhibition catalogue) (Marbach: Deutsche Schillergesellschaft, 1990).

Tisseron, Serge, *Le Mystère de la chambre claire. Photographie et inconscient* (Paris: Champs arts, 1996).

Trachtenberg, Alan (ed.), *Classic Essays on Photography* (New Haven: Leete's Island Books, 1980).

Weber, Samuel, 'Das Erwachen bei Benjamin und Proust oder Wie Verrenkung erfahren wurde', in Thomas Amos et al. (eds.), *Les Mots de la Tribu: Für Gerhard Goebel* (Tübingen: Stauffenburg, 2000), 387–94.

——, 'Mass Mediauras; or Art, Aura and Media in the Work of Walter Benjamin', in David S. Ferris (ed.), *Walter Benjamin: Theoretical Questions* (Stanford: Stanford University Press, 1996), 27–49.

Weigel, Sigrid, 'Das Detail in Benjamins Theorie photo- und kinematographischer Bilder. Zur Verschränkung von Kultur- und Mediengeschichte', in *Literatur als Voraussetzung der Kulturgeschichte: Schauplätze von Shakespeare bis Benjamin* (Munich: Fink, 2004), 39–62.

——, *Entstellte Ähnlichkeit. Walter Benjamins theoretische Schreibweise* (Frankfurt a.M.: Fischer, 1997).

——, *Walter Benjamin: Die Kreatur, das Heilige, die Bilder* (Frankfurt a.M.: Fischer, 2008).

Weingrad, Michael, 'The College of Sociology and the Institute for Social Research', *New German Critique*, 84 (2001), 129–61.

Weissberg, Liliane, 'Bilderwechsel: Barthes, Benjamin, Freud und der Exkurs der Photographie', in Ortrud Gutjahr (ed.), *Kulturtheorie* (Würzburg: Königshausen & Neumann, 2005), 217–40.

Wells, Liz (ed.), *Photography. A Critical Introduction* (London and New York: Routledge, 2004).

—— (ed.), *The Photography Reader* (London and New York: Routledge, 2003).

Werneburg, Brigitte, 'Ernst Jünger, Walter Benjamin und die Photographie. Zur Entwicklung einer Medienästhetik in der Weimarer Republik', in Hans-Harald Müller and Harro Segeberg (eds.), *Ernst Jünger im 20. Jahrhundert* (Munich: Fink, 1995), 39–57.

Wetzel, Michael, 'Il y aura. Über die Kunst, die Herzen schneller schlagen zu lassen', *Fotogeschichte*, 9 (1982), 11–20.

Wiggershaus, Rolf, *The Frankfurt School. Its History, Theories and Political Significance*, trans. Michael Robertson (Cambridge: Polity Press, 1994).

Wismann, Heinz (ed.), *Walter Benjamin et Paris* (Paris: Cerf, 1986).

Wohlfarth, Irving, 'Walter Benjamin's Image of Interpretation', *New German Critique*, 17 (1979), 70–89.

Wolf, Herta, 'Das, was ich sehe, ist gewesen. Zu Roland Barthes' *Die helle Kammer*', in Herta Wolf (ed.), *Paradigma Fotografie. Fotokritik am Ende des fotografischen Zeitalters* (Frankfurt a.M.: Suhrkamp, 2002), 89–107.

Wolf, Herta (ed.), *Diskurse der Fotografie, Fotokritik am Ende des fotografischen Zeitalters* (Frankfurt a.M.: Suhrkamp, 2003).

—— (ed.), *Paradigma Fotografie. Fotokritik am Ende des fotografischen Zeitalters* (Frankfurt a.M.: Suhrkamp, 2002).

Yacavone, Kathrin, 'Barthes et Proust: La *Recherche* comme aventure photographique', *Fabula LHT (Littérature, histoire, théorie)*, 4 (2008) <http://www.fabula.org/lht/4/Yacavone.html> (accessed 25 May 2011).

——, 'Die Photographien "zu ihrem Rechte kommen lassen". Zu Roland Barthes' Rezeption von Benjamins "Kleiner Geschichte der Photographie"', in Daniel Weidner and Sigrid Weigel (eds.), *Benjamin-Studien 2* (Munich: Fink, 2011), 15–32.

——, 'Reading Through Photography: Roland Barthes's Last Seminar "Proust et la photographie"', *French Forum*, 32 (2009), 97–112.

Index

Page numbers in italics refer to illustrations.

Adams, Timothy Dow 87n. 39
Adamson, Robert 31, 47–50, *48*, 52, 54, 59–60, 70, 72, 74, 108, 171
Adorno, Gretel (Karplus) 77, 78n. 14
Adorno, Theodor W. 4, 7, 15, 17n. 18, 70n. 1, 114n. 43
Agamben, Giorgio 9–10, 17n. 16, 51–2, 93–4, 117–18, 184, 206
air 172–4, 217
  in relation to aura 174–5
Albers, Irene 107n. 28
alchemy 124, 175–6, 179, 181, 198, 214, 222, *see also* magic
Alphant, Marianne 167n. 15
alter ego 32, 90–2, 116, *see also* other
Amelunxen, Hubertus von 80–1, 86n. 35, 223n. 11
Andrew, Dudley 148n. 49
Arago, François 1
Aragon, Louis 17
Arguments (group and journal) 15
Arnaud, Alain 17n. 20
Atget, Eugène 23, 31, 36, 41–2, 44–5, 47, 56, 62n. 63, 68, 96, 135
Attridge, Derek 9–10, 92n. 49, 110–11, 117n. 53, 118, 143n. 39, 185, 218n. 2
aura 31–2, 57–8, 67, 69, 96, 104–5, 110, 159, 178
  as experiential phenomenon 45, 55–7, 61, 67–9, 107–8, 110
  in relation to *air* 174–5
  in relation to artworks 66–7
  decline of 61–2, 107–8
  in relation to the gaze 107–10
  in relation to involuntary memory 107–10
  in relation to nineteenth-century photographs 45, 56–61
  in relation to *punctum* 155, 159–60
  in relation to singularity 69, 110–11, 182n. 45
avant-garde 2, 13, 31, 33–4, 38, 45
Avedon, Richard 22, 145n. 42, 174

Bachofen, Johann Jakob 16n. 15
Balzac, Honoré de 108, 178
Baraduc, Hippolyte 178
Barthes, Henriette (Binger) (Barthes's mother) 7, 168, *168*, 196, *196*
Barthes, Roland *165*, *166*
  La Chambre claire (*Camera Lucida*) 7, 19–20, *23*, 71, 91n. 48, 121, 128, 131 n.13, 139, 140n. 36, 142, 144–60, 161–86, 187–215, 224
  Journal de deuil (*Mourning Diary*) 161, 163–4, 194–5
  'Le Message photographique' ('The Photographic Message') 14, 132–6, 141, 153, 209n. 48
  Mythologies 16, 43, 126–33, 141
  La Préparation du roman (*The Preparation of the Novel*), 18, 145, 150, 156n. 69, 169n. 18, 193, 195, 201n. 30, 208n. 46
  reception of Benjamin 11–27, 159, 172
  'Rhétorique de l'image' ('Rhetoric of the Image') 14, 132, 135–9, 148, 156, 176
  Roland Barthes par Roland Barthes 151n. 57, 165n. 13, 195–7, 210–11
  'Le Troisième sens' ('The Third Meaning') 123, 139–43
Bataille, Georges 15–17
Batchen, Geoffrey 20n. 30, 64n. 65, 72n. 5, 74, 105n. 22, 131n. 13, 154n. 65
Baudelaire, Charles 12–13, 33, 41, 45–6, 58, 97–8, 104–5, 163n. 10
Baudrillard, Jean 179
Bayard, Hippolyte 59
Bazin, André 12, 54, 87n. 38, 91, 121, 127, 176n. 33, 198

Belting, Hans 138n. 30, 161n. 3, 224
Benjamin, Walter *63*, *65*
'Aus einer kleinen Rede über Proust' ('From a Litte Speech on Proust') 112–15, 200, 213
'Der Autor als Produzent' ('The Author as Producer') 43–4
Berliner Chronik (*Berlin Chronicle*) 62, 75, 79n. 17, 84–5
Berliner Kindheit um Neunzehnhundert (*Berlin Childhood Around 1900*) 31, 70, 75–80, 82–91, 115–16, 166, 172, 212–13
'Das Kunstwerk' ('The Artwork') 8, 15, 17, 39n. 8, 44–5, 65–9
Das Passagen-Werk (*The Arcades Project*) 12, 26, 41n. 15, 46n. 27, 47, 62n. 62, 113n. 42
influence on Barthes 11–27, 159, 172
'Kleine Geschichte der Photographie' ('Little History of Photography') 6, 19–20, *21*, 23, 29–30, 36–65, 68–9, 70–5, 108, 114–16, 131n. 13, 144, 157, 159, 167, 169, 171–2, 175
'Über einige Motive bei Baudelaire' ('On Some Motifs in Baudelaire') 96–112, 155, 178, 212
Ursprung des deutschen Trauerspiels (*Origin of German Tragic Drama*) 80–2
Berg, Ronald 2n. 1, 13n. 1, 36n. 3, 47n. 28, 62n. 61, 79n. 19, 134, 142, 153n. 62, 174
Bergson, Henri 98–9
Bittel, Johannes 97n. 7
Blanchot, Maurice 17, 51n. 36, 161n. 2, 189n. 10
Bloom, Harold 12n. 15, 159
Bloßfeldt, Karl 35–6, 38–40, 62n. 63
Boehm, Gottfried 136n. 21
Bolz, Norbert 104n. 20
Bossert, Helmuth 22n. 34, 36, 38, 47, 53–4, 59n. 51
Boudinet, Daniel 145, 204–6, *205*
Bourdieu, Pierre 25n. 41, 125n. 1, 135, 144, 146
Bowie, Malcolm 188n. 5
Brassaï 106n. 27
Brecht, Bertolt 13–14, 131, 143
Breton, André 17, 41n. 16
Bröcker, Michael 83n. 27
Brodersen, Momme 36n. 4
Brown, Andrew 134n. 19, 152n. 60
Buck-Morss, Susan 96n. 3
Burgin, Victor 137nn. 24, 26–7
Busch, Bernd 72nn. 5–6, 80n. 21, 82n. 26, 95n. 1, 102n. 16, 114, 154n. 64, 176n. 32

ça-a-été 149, 155–8, 174
Cadava, Eduardo 87n. 37, 92n. 48, 103n. 18, 113n. 42, 184n. 53, 194n. 17
Caillois, Roger 15
calotype 1, *48*, 59, 60n. 56
Calvet, Louis-Jean 161n. 2, 212n. 54
Cameron, Julia Margaret 47n. 29
captioning (of photographs) 42–4, 54n. 41, 118–19, 136, 158, 162n. 8, 170
carte-de-visite photograph 46, 61–2, *63*, 64, *65*, 72n. 5, 105
Caujolle, Christian 206n. 43
Chevrier, Jean-François 23–4, 106n. 27, 187n. 2
Clarke, Arthur C. 175
Cohn, Alfred and Grete 35
Collier, Peter 19n. 25
Communications (journal) 14–15, 135
Compagnon, Antoine 18n. 23, 19n. 24, 155n. 67, 188n. 5, 201, 203, 204n. 38
Constructivism 33, 40n. 13, 40
Coquio, Catherine 13nn. 1–2
Cortés-Rocca, Paola 184n. 53
Costello, Diarmuid 45n. 24, 57n. 48, 111n. 38
Cozea, Angela 187n. 2
Crary, Jonathan 225n. 14

Daguerre, Louis 1, 59n. 51
daguerreotype 1, 20, *21*, 59, 85, 95, 107–8, 179, 220
Damisch, Hubert 18–19, 147
Dant, Tim 13n. 1

Dauthendey, Karl 31, 52–4, *53*, 57, 67, 70, 85, 155, 158, 162, 171
Dauthendey, Max 54, 63, 175, 176n. 31
death 32, 51, 54, 67, 81, 116, 156–8, 161–3, 179–80, 184, 186, 195n. 19, 206, *see also* mourning
 of Barthes's mother 161, 179, 189, 197–9, 201–2, 213
Decroux, Emmanuelle 206n. 4
Delord, Jean 148n. 50
Derrida, Jacques 9–10, 55, 81, 91, 150, 154–5, 163, 182–6, 209n. 48, 219
Didi-Huberman, Georges 45, 109nn. 32, 34, 174n. 30, 177, 178
digitization 8n. 8, 20, 119n. 57, 220–5
Disdéri, André 46, 61, 105
Döblin, Alfred 36
Downing, Eric 103n. 19
Draaisma, Douwe 104n. 19
Dubois, Philippe 137–8, 148
Duttlinger, Carolin 55n. 44, 68, 76n. 10, 79n. 18, 82n. 24, 110n. 36
duty (towards the other), *see* responsibility
Duve, Thierry de 61, 134n. 19, 138, 158n. 73, 162

Eco, Umberto 137
Eisenstein, Sergei M. 123, 140–1, 143
ekphrasis 64, 71–2, 74–6, 78–9, 88, 91, 166–71, *see also* superimposition
Elkins, James 50n. 33, 61n. 58, 109n. 33, 145n. 41, 154n. 63, 159n. 75, 172n. 25, 218n. 1
ethics of photography 9–10, 42, 45, 51–2, 93–4, 110–11, 115–16, 118–19, 185n. 54, 186, 218–20, 226, *see also* responsibility
Ette, Ottmar 15n. 6, 165n. 13

The Family of Man (exhibition) 125, 128–31
Farge, Arlette 117n. 52
Faunières, Daniel 164–6, *165*
Ferguson, Jeanine 2n. 1, 174n. 28
Ffrench, Patrick 14n. 5, 15n. 9, 16n. 14, 132n. 14
film 38n. 8, 123, 125, 139–41, 143
Finkelde, Dominik 97n. 7
Flusser, Vilém 52n. 39, 96n. 4
Foucault, Michel 62, 137
Fourier, Charles 13
Freud, Sigmund 39, 95, 96–7, 99–101, 102–4, 114n. 43, 115, 208–9
Freund, Gisèle 24, 41–2, 46n. 26, 47, 58, 144
Fried, Michael 149n. 53, 154n. 63
Friedmann, Georges 14
Fuld, Werner 68n. 73
Fürnkäs, Josef 56n. 45, 159n. 75

Gadamer, Hans-Georg 10n. 10, 55
Gandillac, Maurice de 19, 169n. 20
Gardner, Alexander 21–2, *22*, *23*, 156–7, *157*, 171
Garnier, Marie-D. 169n. 19
Geimer, Peter 137n. 27, 201n. 30
Gerber, Margarethe 85n. 32
Gilloch, Graeme 13n. 1
Godard, Jean-Luc 174
Gödde, Christoph 65n. 66,
Gratton, Johnnie 195n. 20, 202n. 31
Greffrath, Krista R. 110n. 12
Greimas, A. J. 138n. 28
Grojnowski, Daniel 19n. 27
Guittard, Jacqueline 25n. 42, 126n. 2, 129, 176n. 32
Gumbrecht, Hans Ulrich 67n. 70
Gunthert, André 20n. 32, 36nn. 3, 5, 54, 79n. 19, 161n. 2
Guttmann, Heinrich 22n. 34, 36, 38, 47, 53–4, 59n. 51

Haas, Willy 71n. 3
Habermas, Jürgen 9n. 9, 93n. 50
Hamacher, Werner 84nn. 29–30
Hamilton, Peter 62n. 62, 161n. 4
Hanney, Roxanne 187n. 2

Hansen, Miriam 93nn. 50, 52
Hargreaves, Roger 62n. 62, 161n. 4
Haustein, Katja 194n. 18, 208n. 46
Haverkamp, Anselm 200
Heartfield, John 43, 131
Heidegger, Martin 10
Hill, David Octavius 31, 47–50, *48*, 52, 54, 59–60, 70, 72, 74, 108, 171
Hine, Lewis 22, 42n. 18
Hirsch, Marianne 40n. 12, 92n. 48, 130n. 11
Hjelmslev, Louis 138n. 28
Hollander, John 78
Hollier, Denis 16n. 12, 17nn. 17, 19
Hollington, Michael 13n. 2
Holmes, Oliver Wendell 95, 178
Horkheimer, Max 14–15, 16n. 11, 17
Hugo, Charles 47n. 29
Husserl, Edmund 151, 156n. 96

icon/iconicity 49–50, 87, 92, 138n. 30, 172, 200, 222
index/indexicality 8, 49–50, 90, 105, 122, 132–4, 138, 147, 149n. 53, 172, 176, 191–2, 200, 211n. 53, 220–2
Ivernel, Philippe 26n. 45
Iversen, Margaret 112n. 40, 209n. 48

Jay, Martin 140n. 36
Jefferson, Ann 143n. 39
Jünger, Ernst 44n. 22

Kafka, Franz *73*
  childhood portrait of 32, 68–80, 82–3, 85, 88–94, 110, 115–19, 162
  in relation to the Winter Garden photograph 7, 8, 71, 159–60, 169–72, 186, 212–15, 218–19
Kahn, Robert 97n. 7
Kaulen, Heinrich 53n. 40, 93n. 51
Kember, Sarah 223–5
Kemp, Wolfgang 6n. 5, 122
Kertéz, André 145n. 42, 155, 192, 207, 208
Kim, Young-Ok 79n. 19
Klee, Paul 51
Klein, William 155
Klossowski, Pierre 15, 17
Knight, Diana 148n. 52, 164n. 11, 167, 170, 195n. 21, 204
Kofman, Sarah 104n. 19
Kracauer, Siegfried 4, 6, 9n. 9, 34–5, 58, 68, 83, 89, 93n. 50, 106, 117, 162, 191–2
Krauss, Rolf H. 1n. 1, 13n. 1, 36n. 3, 54n. 41, 172n. 25
Krauss, Rosalind E. 39–40, 149n. 53
Kriebel, Sabine T. 136, 149n. 53
Kristeva, Julia 142
Kritzman, Lawrence D. 189n. 9
Kuhn, Annette 171n. 24, 187n. 22

Lacan, Jacques 10n. 13, 92n. 48, 112n. 40, 134n. 19, 209n. 48
Lacoue-Labarthe, Philippe 92n. 48
Lagarde, François 166, *166*
Landy, Joshua 188n. 4
Lang, Tilman 86n. 36
Langer, Daniela 151n. 56, 58
Laouyen, Mounir 187n. 22
Lebrave, Jean-Louis 188–9
Léger, Nathalie 167n. 15
Leibniz, Gottfried Wilhelm 4
Leiris, Michel 15
Lemke, Anja 75n. 8
Les Lettres nouvelles (journal) 16, 126
Levinas, Emmanuel 10nn. 10, 13, 185n. 54, 186n. 56
Lier, Henri Van 137n. 28
Lindekens, René 138n. 28
Lindner, Burkhardt 56n. 45, 75n. 8, 80n. 20
Link, Jürgen 114n. 45
Link-Heer, Ursula 97n. 7, 109n. 32, 114n. 45
Lister, Martin 224
Lombardo, Patrizia 169n. 19, 204n. 40
Lonitz, Henri 65n. 66

MacCabe, Colin 176n. 33
Macé, Marielle 140n. 33, 173n. 26, 188n. 6

magic 32, 54–5, 83–6, 88, 124, 139, 175–6, 179–81, 198, 206, *see also* alchemy
Mandery, Guy 154
Mann, Thomas 36
Mallarmé, Stéphane 81
Malraux, André 66
Man Ray 34
Manovich, Lev 222nn. 5–6, 224
Mapplethorpe, Robert 145n. 42
Marder, Elissa 163n. 10, 177n. 37
Marrinan, Michael 67n. 70
Marty, Éric 142n. 37, 161n. 1, 164, 168, 187, 188n. 6, 189nn. 9, 11, 199, 203, 209
Mayer, Hans 16n. 12
McLuhan, Marshall 132
Megay, Joyce 98n. 8
melancholy 32, 72–3, 80–2, 124, 161–2, 194–5
memory 32, 54, 79, 83–5, 89–90, 95–103, 113–14, 123, 186–7, 190–3, 195, 199, 204, 208–9, 212–3, 217
  involuntary (*mémoire involontaire*) 98–100, 102–4, 107, 112–16, 124, 190, 193–4, 198–201, 206–8, 212–13
  voluntary (*mémoire volontaire*) 98–100, 105–6, 193, 208
Menke, Bettine 80n. 20, 111n. 39
Menninghaus, Winfried 83–4
Mèredieu, Florence de 19n. 27
Merleau-Ponty, Maurice 7, 121, 146n. 44, 148n. 49, 151n. 59
Metz, Christian 14, 125
Milner, Jean-Claude 182
Mitchell, Erin 171n. 23
Mitchell, William J.T. 78, 119n. 57, 170n. 22, 221–3
Moholy-Nagy, László 6, 20n. 28, 34, 40
Molderings, Herbert 34n. 1, 36, 40n. 13, 62n. 62
Monnier, Adrienne 16n. 15
Monnoyer, Jean-Maurice 17n. 18
Moriarty, Michael 133n. 16, 151n. 57
Morin, Edgar 14–15, 179
mourning 9, 124, 141–2, 156, 161–2, 188–9, 195n. 19, 213, 218, *see also* death
Münster, Arno 98n. 8
Musil, Robert 36
Muybridge, Eadweard 38–9

Nadar, (Félix) 22, 47n. 29, 59, 108nn. 29–30, 128n. 4, 170, 178
Nadar, Paul 169n. 18
Nadeau, Maurice 16–17
Nancy, Jean-Luc 49, 173, 174n. 27
Newhall, Beaumont 72n. 4, 105n. 22, 144, 170n. 22
New Objectivity 33–5
Nickel, Douglas R. 224n. 13
Niépce, Nicéphore 1
Nitsche, Jessica 2n. 1, 29n. 1, 77n. 12, 79n. 16, 112n. 39
Nietzsche, Friedrich 17, 150, 151n. 56
Le Nouvel Observateur (magazine) 19–25, *21–2*, 126, 144, 157–8, 169

Olin, Margaret 19n. 27, 164n. 11, 169, 195n. 20, 210, 211n. 53
Opitz, Michael 52n. 40, 56n. 45, 83n. 27, 90n. 43, 93n. 51, 159n. 75
optical unconscious, the 29, 38–40, 131, 153n. 62, 217
Orlik, Emil 38–9
Ortel, Philippe 154n. 36
other, the 9–10, 32, 88, 91–2, 94, 110–11, 118, 181–6, 214–15, 219–20, 223, 225–6, *see also* referent

painting 7n. 6, 33, 46, 49, 54, 61–2, 66, 92, 105, 110, 116n. 48, 133, 145–7, 173, 176, 220
Pauleit, Winfried 140n. 32
Peirce, Charles Sanders 50, 137, 138n. 28

phenomenology 7, 47, 70, 74n. 7, 89, 114, 121, 123, 146n. 44, 147–8, 151, 163, 189–90, 209, 221, 225
Phillips, Christopher 66n. 67
photomontage 43, 131
Pic, Roger 131
Pictorialism 33, 40–1, 62
Pierson, Pierre-Louis 59
Poe, Edgar Allan 85
Poster, Mark 15n. 9
Price, Mary 158n. 72
Prosser, Jay 161n. 2, 195n. 19
Proust, Marcel 7, 83, 89n. 42, 90n. 44, 95, 97–100, 105–9, 116–17, 124, 187–95, 198–208, 212–14, *see also* memory
punctum 142–3, 152–5, 182–6
as detail 153–5, 209–10
in relation to aura 155, 159–60
in relation to involuntary memory 124, 207–8, 212–13
in relation to singularity 182–6, 213
as time 155–6

Raoux, Nathalie 24n. 37
Recht, Camille 20, 36, 38, 48n. 31, 68n. 73, 157
Recki, Birgit 56n. 46, 108n. 31, 109n. 35
redemption 9, 51–2, 91–4, 115–18, 186, 206, 214–15, 218, *see also* responsibility
referent, the photographic 10, 67, 91–2, 146–50, 156, 175–8, 180, 182–5, 220–1, 225, *see also* other
Renger-Patzsch, Albert 44n. 22
reproducibility 8, 66–7, 92, 104–5, 148, 150, 182–3, 185, 220
responsibility (for the other) 9, 94, 117–18, 186, *see also* ethics of photography
Richter, Gerhard 55n. 43, 70n. 1, 84n. 29, 88n. 40, 91n. 47
Richter, Hans 34
Riis, Jacob 42n. 18
Ritchin, Fred 119n. 57
Roger, Philippe 187n. 1
Röttger-Denker, Gabriele 1n. 1, 185n. 54
Rugg, Linda Haverty 77nn. 11–12, 84n. 29, 91
Rupp, Gerhard 16n. 12
Ruskin, John 106n. 25

Saint Marc, Stéphanie de 170n. 22
Sander, August 36, 129, 131n. 13
Sartre, Jean-Paul 7, 15, 74n. 7, 114, 121, 189–90
Saussure, Ferdinand de 6, 86n. 36, 126, 138n. 28
Schaeffer, Jean-Marie 42n. 19, 137n. 28, 147n. 48, 177n. 37
Scharf, Aaron 58n. 50, 59n. 53, 106n. 25
Schlossman, Beryl 24n. 38, 202, 204n. 41, 214n. 55
Scholem, Gershom 52n. 38, 71n. 2, 82n. 25
Schöttker, Detlev 15n. 8, 26n. 44, 29n. 1, 68n. 72, 71nn. 2–3, 77, 112n. 41, 174
Schwarz, Angelo 144
Schwarz, Heinrich 36, 38, 47, 48n. 31, 50, 59n. 52, 61
Scott, Walter 50n. 34
Sekula, Allan 129n. 6, 130n. 10, 137
Selz, Jean 16n. 15
semiology (semiotics) 2, 3, 6, 14, 16, 43, 50, 121–3, 125–6, 129n. 8, 132–9, 146–7, 152–3, 180
Shawcross, Nancy 46n. 25, 142n. 37, 144n. 40, 162n. 8, 176
Simmel, Georg 96–7, 101
singularity 8–11, 30, 69, 75, 91–4, 118, 123–4, 148, 163–4, 181–6, 206, 214–15, 217–21, 225–6
in relation to aura 69, 110–11, 182n. 45
in relation to *punctum* 182–5, 213–14
in relation to uniqueness 8, 92
Snyder, Joel 50n. 33, 60n. 54, 147n. 48, 149n. 53, 170n. 22

Sontag, Susan 12, 22, 24–5, 45, 118–19, 144, 146–7, 162n. 5, 177
Stamelman, Richard 171n. 23
Steichen, Edward 128–30
Stelzner, Ferdinand 59
Stevenson, Sara 50n. 34, 60n. 56
Stiegler, Bernd 29n. 1, 52n. 39, 62n. 60, 79n. 16, 95n. 1, 96n. 4, 129n. 9, 132n. 15, 148n. 51, 176n. 32, 178, 206n. 45
Stoessel, Marleen 60n. 55, 159n. 75
Stoichita, Victor I. 180
studium 142, 152–4, 157, 172
studium-punctum dichotomy 121, 124, 150–4, 159, 163, 191
Stüssi, Anna 75–6
Suhrkamp, Peter 29n. 1
superimposition 32, 54, 70, 78–9, 168–70, 212
Surrealism 33–4, 41
Surya, Michel 15n. 10, 17n. 19
Szondi, Peter 83n. 28

tableau vivant 81
Talbot, William Henry Fox 1, 177
Tagg, John 42–3, 159n. 74, 179n. 41
Taminiaux, Pierre 46
Teschke, Henning 97n. 7
theatre 14, 81, 131
Thibaudeau, Jean 23–4
Thobo-Carlsen, John 13n. 2
Thomas, Chantal 164n. 12
Tiedemann, Rolf 65n. 66
Tisseron, Serge 153n. 61
Trachtenberg, Alan 42n. 18, 85n. 33, 95n. 2, 178n. 40
Tzara, Tristan 34–5, 155

Valéry, Paul 101–2, 109
Van der Zee, James 22, 155, 209–12, *210*
Vittiglio, Claude 206n. 43

Weber, Samuel 110n. 37, 113n. 42
Weigel, Sigrid 7n. 6, 39, 52n. 38, 57n. 47, 93n. 50, 104n. 20, 115–16
Weingrad, Michael 16n. 12
Weissberg, Liliane 167n. 15
Werneburg, Brigitte 43n. 21, 44n. 22
Wetzel, Michael 56n. 45, 57n. 48
Wiertz, Antoine 33
Wiggershaus, Rolf 14n. 4
Wilson, George Washington 22, *22*
Winckelmann, Johann Joachim 38
Winter Garden photograph, the 124, 163–86, 193–4, 197n. 22, 198–204, 207, 213–15
  in relation to the Kafka childhood photograph 7–8, 71, 159–60, 169–72, 186, 212–15, 218–19
Wismann, Heinz 26n. 43
Wizisla, Erdmut 52n. 40, 56n. 45, 83n. 27, 90n. 43, 93n. 51, 159n. 75
Wohlfarth, Irving 86n. 36
Wolf, Herta 197n. 22